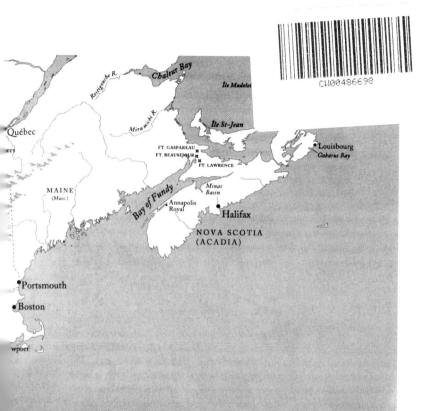

Québec

rcs

Restigouche R.

Chaleur Bay

Île Madelei

Miramichi R.

Île St-Jean

FT. GASPAREAU
FT. BEAUSEJOUR
FT. LAWRENCE

Louisbourg
Gabarus Bay

MAINE
(Mass.)

Bay of Fundy

Minas
Basin

Annapolis
Royal

Halifax

NOVA SCOTIA
(ACADIA)

Portsmouth

Boston

wport

ATLANTIC OCEAN

PUBLICATIONS
OF THE
ARMY RECORDS SOCIETY
VOL. 20

AMHERST AND THE
CONQUEST OF CANADA

The Army Records Society was founded in 1984 in order to publish original records describing the development, organisation, administration and activities of the British Army from early times.

Any person wishing to become a member of the Society is requested to apply to the Hon. Secretary, c/o the National Army Museum, Royal Hospital Road, London, SW3 4HT. The annual subscription entitles the member to receive a copy of each volume issued by the Society in that year, and to purchase back volumes at reduced prices. Current subscription details, whether for individuals living within the British Isles, for individuals living overseas, or for institutions, will be furnished on request.

The Council of the Army Records Society wish it to be clearly understood that they are not answerable for opinions or observations that may appear in the Society's publications. For these the responsibility rests entirely with the Editors of the several works.

An East View of Montreal in Canada. Drawn on the spot by Thomas Patten. Engraved by P. Canot. (From *Crucible of War* by Fred Anderson, Faber and Faber, 2000. With permission.)

Amherst and the Conquest of Canada

Selected Papers from the Correspondence of
Major-General Jeffery Amherst while
Commander-in-Chief in North America from
September 1758 to December 1760

Edited by
Richard Middleton

Published by
SUTTON PUBLISHING LIMITED
for the
ARMY RECORDS SOCIETY
2003

First published in the United Kingdom in 2003 by
Sutton Publishing Limited · Phoenix Mill · Thrupp · Stroud
Gloucestershire · GL5 2BU

British Library Cataloguing in Publication Data
A catalogue record for this book is available from the British Library.

ISBN 0-7509-3142-6

Endpapers: New France and the British Mainland Colonies in the
Seven Years' War, 1754–63

Typeset in Ehrhardt.
Typesetting and origination by
Sutton Publishing Limited.
Printed in England by
J.H. Haynes & Co. Ltd, Sparkford.

Contents

Preface and Acknowledgements

Jeffery Amherst was one of most distinguished figures in eighteenth-century British military history. Surprisingly little has been written on him. The last major biography was that by John C. Long, which appeared in 1933. Other more general histories still mention his part in the capture of Louisbourg and the final conquest of Canada, but the nature and extent of his contribution are usually blurred.

The reasons for this neglect are various. Amherst's military reputation was later tainted by the loss of the American colonies, when, as Commander-in-Chief of the forces in Britain after 1778, he seemingly helped preside over the dismembering of the first British Empire. Secondly he was not a heroic figure in the mould of James Wolfe or Lord George Augustus Howe. As the following documents show Amherst was more akin to a chief executive than a warrior leader. In part this was the inevitable consequence of the nature of his mission. Wolfe was able to sail to the heart of his enemy's terrain and fight a set-piece battle. Amherst in contrast had to force his way through a hostile wilderness simply to get near his enemy. Logistical organisation, not heroic gestures, was the key to success for him.

It is to correct some of these omissions and misunderstandings that the present volume is offered. The volume is divided into two sections. Part I begins with Amherst's appointment as Commander-in-Chief in North America and covers the triple offensive of 1759 against Canada. But though officially in overall charge, Amherst's authority was effectively restricted to the overland offensives against Montreal and Niagara, since Wolfe enjoyed an independent command against Quebec. Moreover reduced responsibilities did not mean fewer difficulties as Amherst struggled to co-ordinate the military effort over a huge area involving many disparate elements. The result was less progress than at first expected. Though the gateways to Canada, Niagara, Ticonderoga and Crown Point, were captured, Montreal survived to fight another campaign.

Part II sees the conquest completed, this time under Amherst's overall direction, with a three-pronged offensive against the French at Montreal via the St Lawrence River, Lake Champlain and Lake Ontario, the last and largest of the armies being commanded by Amherst himself. Remarkably all three converged on Montreal within a day of each other. However there was little time for celebration, as Amherst had to provide for the governance and security of Canada and the rest of North America. The volume concludes with his return to New York in time for Christmas 1760.

This project has only been possible with the help of a number of individuals and institutions. I am particularly indebted to the Public Record Office, London, and the Centre for Kentish Studies, Maidstone, for allowing publication of the documents contained in this edition, in the preparation of which I have been greatly aided by a grant from the British Academy for the purchase of the PRO collection on microfilm.

I should also like to thank Professor Ian Beckett, the editor of the series, for his friendly and helpful advice, and the Army Records Society for agreeing to sponsor the publication of the volume. I am also indebted to Tim Bowman for help at various times.

Finally I should like to thank the Queen's University of Belfast for granting me study leave, without which the completion of this project would have been much delayed.

Richard Middleton
November 2002

Principles of Documentary Selection and Editorial Methods

Principles of documentary selection

Although this volume comprises the first publication of documents devoted to Amherst as Commander-in-Chief, this does not mean that none of his correspondence has been published before. There are in fact a number of printed sources containing Amherst correspondence, most notably Gertrude S. Kimball, *The Correspondence of William Pitt when Secretary of State with the Colonial Governors and Military and Naval Commissioners in America*, two vols (London, 1906). However, in line with the policy of the Army Records Society, no attempt has been made to duplicate such materials (with one or two exceptions for the sake of chronological sequence). For those readers wanting further guidance, a full list of previously published materials containing Amherst documents is appended in the bibliography.

Despite the existence of already printed materials, it has not proved possible to included more than a small selection of Amherst's unpublished correspondence in this volume. The main collection of Amherst papers in the Public Record Office, London, contains over 200 volumes of official papers, comprising 40,000 documents, almost half of which relate to the period of Amherst's command in America. A second substantial collection of official and family papers, perhaps equivalent to twenty volumes, is to be found in the Kent County Archives at Maidstone. In addition there are a further eight volumes of correspondence in the William L. Clements Library at the University of Michigan, Ann Arbor, while numerous individual letters can be found in other depositories in Great Britain, the United States and Canada. However, since Amherst kept copies of his own correspondence and filed almost all the letters sent to him, I have for convenience largely based my selection on the Public Record Office papers (WO/34), with some additional items from the family archives in Kent (U1350). Where the Clements Library has duplicates of the documents selected, this has been noted.

Some types of document of necessity have had to be either excluded or limited to a few examples. Among the former are military accounts, in the second category promotions and patronage, of which there are a great many in both the major collections. Furthermore, to keep the selection within manageable limits, I have had to concentrate on letters to and from Amherst, not those between third parties. In addition it has proved necessary to focus on Amherst's conduct of the war against Canada, which has meant omitting many important documents concerning other aspects of his position as Commander-in-Chief.

Despite the above constraints, the volume contains much correspondence which is included here for the first time. Among the more important exchanges are those between Amherst and a number of leading military and civil figures, notably Major-General James Wolfe, Field Marshal Viscount John Ligonier, Brigadier-General Thomas Gage, Brigadier General James Murray, Brigadier-General Robert Monckton, Colonel John Bradstreet, Major Robert Rogers, Lieutenant Governor James De Lancey, Governor Thomas Pownall, and the Secretary at War, William Viscount Barrington.

Editorial methods

The source of each document is given at end of the extract. All letters are in strict chronological order. However, because of the time lag between the dispatch and receipt of many letters, I have, wherever possible, supplied the date on which a particular letter arrived, so that the sequence of events can be more clearly established. Fortunately Amherst made a point of recording the arrival of most incoming dispatches.

The extensive nature of the collections means that many letters have not been reproduced in full. Where material has been excised this is indicated by an ellipsis [. . .]. Opening and closing familiarities are not included.

All the letters and documents are reproduced with original spellings and grammar. Occasionally I have inserted a word to make sense of a passage, but such additions are always in square brackets. Insertions by the author, in contrast, are indicated either by superscript for material above the line, or round brackets where the addition is in the margin. Where the meaning of a passage remains unclear or anachronistic, [sic] is added to indicate this.

All individuals are identified by their rank at the time of writing, later titles being indicated in the notes or biographical notes at the end.

Introduction

Early career, 1717–58

Jeffery Amherst was born at Riverhead near Sevenoaks in Kent on 29 January 1717. The family was of minor gentry rank, his father being a barrister, and had no military connections. However, the Duke of Dorset was a near neighbour, and it was his patronage which seemingly provided Amherst's entry into the army, though the exact circumstances are not clear. The usual account is that Dorset took Amherst into his household as a page before securing him an ensign's commission in the First Foot Guards in 1731.[1] The evidence however is circumstantial, and his appointment to such a distinguished regiment seems unlikely, given his obscure family and tender age. A more likely scenario, for which there is some documentary evidence, is that after making Amherst a member of his household, Dorset used his position as Lord Lieutenant of Ireland in 1735 to secure Amherst a cornet's commission in the Eighth Horse. This regiment was on the Irish establishment, over which Dorset had some influence. Its commander was Sir John Ligonier, who later wrote to Dorset in July 1740 recommending that Amherst be promoted a lieutenant in that same regiment.[2]

Whatever Amherst's initial route into the army, the connection with Ligonier was to prove most felicitous, since he was one of the most respected officers in the British army. By 1742 Ligonier, now a major-general, was sufficiently impressed by Amherst to make him one of his aides-de-camp when he was appointed commander of a division of the army sent to the continent to fight the French at the beginning of the War of Austrian Succession. This attachment to the divisional staff not only enabled Amherst to get his first taste of action at Dettingen in 1743 and Fontenoy in 1745, but also accelerated his promotion that same year to captain in the First Foot Guards with the rank of lieutenant-colonel in the army at large. Nor did Amherst's career suffer when his patron was subsequently captured in the battle of Laffeldt in 1747, since by this time he had been appointed an aide-de-camp to William Augustus, Duke of Cumberland, George II's younger son and Captain General of the Army.

With such connections as these it was no surprise that by 1756 Amherst was colonel of the relatively prestigious 15th Foot regiment.

By this time the Seven Years' War had broken out, a conflict which was to have momentous consequences for Amherst. This had begun as a struggle to define the boundaries between the French and British possessions in eastern North America. Since the peace of Aix-la-Chapelle, the French had been attempting to link Canada and Louisiana by a series of forts which, if successful, would restrict the British to a narrow coastal strip behind the Allegheny mountains. Such an outcome was totally unacceptable to the ministry of the Duke of Newcastle. It accordingly ordered the dispatch of two regular regiments under General Braddock and the raising of other local units in America itself, to assert British rights to the Ohio valley, the Great Lakes, and the borders of northern New York and Nova Scotia.

These moves did not go unnoticed by the French, and they responded early in 1755 by sending reinforcements of their own. However they recognised that in any colonial and maritime war they would be at a disadvantage, given the strength of Britain's navy. One way of countering this was to threaten the Electorate of Hanover, which the British were bound to protect because of George II's dynastic connection. Initially Hanover appeared an Achilles heel in the British position as Newcastle's ministry sought the assistance of Russia and a number of German princes in its defence. But early in 1756 the ministry seemingly pulled off a diplomatic coup by announcing an understanding with Frederick II of Prussia, the foremost military power in Central Europe. With Hanover under the protective wing of Frederick II, the Newcastle ministry could now confidently prosecute the naval and colonial war.

What the ministry failed to realise was that this agreement began a fundamental realignment of the powers of Europe. When the French found that Prussia had become the protector of Hanover, they looked in turn to the enemies of Frederick II, notably Russia and Austria. The result was the Diplomatic Revolution of 1756 which aligned France, Austria and Russia against Britain, Prussia and Hanover.

This reversal of alliances had ominous implications for the British plan to secure Hanover, for although Prussia was still ostensibly committed to its defence, it was clear by the end of 1756 that Frederick II would have his hands full dealing with the Austrians and Russians. Hence much of that defence would have to be provided by the British and Hanoverians themselves. Since the dispatch of British troops to Germany was politically unacceptable in England, the ministry had no alternative but to continue its previous policy of hiring the forces of neighbouring German princes, notably Brunswick and Hesse, in the hope that these, when added to the Electoral army, would constitute an effective defence.

The result was the formation of what was euphemistically called the Army of Observation to observe and resist the French armies if they crossed the lower Rhine to attack Hanover. To command this force George II appointed his younger son, the Duke of Cumberland, a veteran of numerous continental campaigns. But though no British troops were involved, the public remained fearful about the potential expense and British commissaries were accordingly appointed to control the issue of supplies. In view of their previous close ties it was no surprise that Cumberland should nominate Amherst to be one of these, with responsibility for the Hessian contingent of the army. The assignment was to prove an education for Amherst, revealing the potential for fraud and profiteering, and it made him determined that no such practices would disfigure any future campaign for which he might be responsible.

In June 1757 a much superior French army under the Duc de Richelieu began to advance on Hanover. Cumberland attempted to resist but was badly beaten at the battle of Hastenbeck. Thereafter he steadily retreated until effectively forced to surrender by the signing of the Convention of Klosterseven. This debacle might have ended Amherst's military career, since Cumberland was recalled to England and stripped of his position as Captain General. Fortunately Amherst's associations with Ligonier came to his rescue. Initially George II intended to be his own commander-in-chief. William Pitt however insisted that the ministers must have someone to consult on military matters during Cabinet discussions The King accordingly suggested they talk to Ligonier and a few days later his position was regularised by a commission as Commander-in-Chief of the army in Great Britain.[3]

While these dramatic events were taking place in Europe, the war in North America had also been going from bad to worse for the British. First in 1755 there had been General Braddock's defeat near the Forks of the Ohio. The following year had witnessed the loss of Oswego. Then in 1757 there was the even more catastrophic loss of Fort William Henry. British efforts in part had been stymied by political weaknesses at home. However, from the summer of 1757 a much stronger government had been formed under Pitt and Newcastle. Pitt in particular wanted a more effective effort in North America. This meant replacing the current commanding officer, the Earl of Loudoun, for the 1758 campaign. However, service in North America was not attractive to most officers, who saw Europe as the place where real military reputations were made. This created an opportunity for less senior officers, but it was undoubtedly Ligonier who recommended Amherst to the King. The eventual plan was for Loudoun's most senior colleague, James Abercromby, to take command of the overland operations, while Amherst led an amphibious expedition against the French naval base and fortress of Louisbourg, at the eastern tip of Cape Breton Island.[4]

Accordingly early in January Amherst was summoned back from Germany to London to receive his instructions.[5] Having crossed the Atlantic he went first to Halifax, Nova Scotia, to assemble his army after which he set sail with Admiral Boscawen, landing at Gaberouse Bay a few miles from Louisbourg on 7 June. After this it was a matter of hauling up supplies, digging trenches and bringing the artillery to bear, while the navy blockaded the approaches by sea. Slowly the stranglehold of the besiegers tightened, though James Wolfe was privately inclined to criticise Amherst for his pedestrian approach.[6] Nevertheless Amherst's patience and care finally bore fruit when the French surrendered on 26 July 1758.

Pitt's original orders were that Amherst and Boscawen should next proceed up the St Lawrence River to attack Quebec, as part of a three-pronged offensive against France's North American territories. But by the time the Louisbourg garrison had been put on board ship for France, Boscawen declared it was too late for any such venture. Amherst accordingly decided to go to the help of Abercromby, who had met a serious setback on 12 July at Ticonderoga during his advance on Montreal. Amherst's route took him by ship to Boston, followed by a march of 200 miles to Albany. He finally arrived at his destination early in October, by which time it was far too late to undertake any further operations against the French by way of Lake George. Amherst accordingly rejoined his army at Halifax, where he received the news that he had been appointed commander-in-chief in place of Abercromby.

The campaign of 1759: the British offensive resumed

The decision by the ministry in London to relieve James Abercromby was taken after the news of his setback at Ticonderoga and was unofficially communicated by Ligonier to Amherst on 15 September 1758 [1]. A more formal notification of Amherst's appointment, together with instructions and a commission under the great seal, were sent by Pitt three days later [2]. News of this promotion reached Amherst on

9 November 1758, but it was not until early December that he got to New York, whereupon Abercromby immediately turned over all his official papers and documents.

Since precise operational orders for the 1759 campaign were still many weeks away, Amherst was initially restricted to issuing a plea on 13 December to the provincial governors to prepare their assemblies to vote the same number of men as in 1758. However, he knew from Abercromby that a major impediment to the 1758 campaign had been the late arrival of the provincials. One way of avoiding this, Amherst suggested, was for the governors to retain over the winter some of the men from the campaign just ended [3]. It was the same desire for an early start that induced Amherst to write to Sir William Johnson, the superintendent for the Northern Department of Indian Affairs, urging him to raise in due course as many Native Americans as possible for the forthcoming campaign [4]. The perceived wisdom was that Indians were needed as scouts and rangers, in which department the British had been greatly deficient since the start of the war, though Amherst himself had not been impressed by their prowess during the siege of Louisbourg.[7]

It was not long before Amherst's plans for an early start received their first setback when the Governor of New York, James De Lancey, informed him that all the men raised for the 1758 campaign had been disbanded. Moreover it was unlikely the Assembly would be able to raise as many men again because of the losses suffered in the campaign just finished [5]. This was Amherst's first taste of having to deal with the civil authorities in North America which, as all British commanders since Braddock had found, made campaigning very problematical. The military could not simply issue orders and expect them to be obeyed, especially in the case of the provincial assemblies, which were extremely sensitive of their prerogatives.[8]

Fortunately not everyone was so backward in responding to Amherst's call for early preparations. Lieutenant-Colonel John Bradstreet, the Deputy Quartermaster General, had been in America since the beginning of the war, and knew the importance of logistics in the conduct of military operations on the North American continent [6].[9] Amherst accordingly ordered him to ensure that the army's transport service, especially its bateaux,[10] were in the best state possible for an early opening to the campaign, though he was to avoid any unnecessary expense [8].

Meanwhile important decisions were being made in London, as Brigadier-General James Wolfe informed Amherst on 29 December

1758. The ministry was determined to proceed with the conquest of Canada, for which two armies were to be formed: one proceeding by sea up the St Lawrence River, the other marching overland by way of Lake George, Crown Point and the Isle aux Noix. The majority of the regular army in America, supported by a formidable fleet, was to be allocated to the St Lawrence operation, the command of which, as Wolfe tried to explain, had been given to himself by the ministry against his real inclinations, which were to serve once more with Amherst. Wolfe was undoubtedly aware that his decision to return home at the end of 1758 might be seen as an opportune move to ensure that he got the best command [9].[11] However, as a paper by Ligonier made clear, Amherst, as commander in chief, was needed to direct operations on the continent as a whole [10].

Until firm orders arrived from London Amherst could do little beyond making sure that the frontier beyond Albany was secure under the command of Brigadier-General Gage, while the rest of the army was properly sheltered and ready to act when conditions permitted [11]. With respect to the general well-being of the army, two matters were of some concern: quartering and the recovery of deserters. The right to quarters for both officers and men under the Mutiny Act had been a matter of dispute since the first arrival of British troops and was something that Amherst, like Loudoun and Abercromby, could not afford to make concession on, as he told Governor Bernard of New Jersey [12].[12] Desertion too was a constant problem, given the attractions of a new life on high wages that existed in most colonies for able-bodied men. Amherst, though a strict disciplinarian, was naturally inclined to leniency. He was aware that successive commanders had found it difficult to recruit the ranks of their regiments because of the army's reputation for harsh discipline. Accordingly he issued a proclamation on 12 January 1759 pardoning all deserters who returned to their units [13]. But securing men was not merely a problem for the army, as the application of Admiral Durell, the commanding naval officer at Halifax, made clear. Durell had orders to sail early in the spring to blockade the St Lawrence River and was 500 men short of his proper complement. But however important the service, Amherst could only promise to write to the civil authorities in Massachusetts to see if men could be secured as part of that province's military contribution; for experience had shown there was little prospect of pressing men for the navy, as was done in England [14].[13]

Apart from recruiting the ranks and ensuring proper quarters, Amherst knew that the army must be ready in other respects for the coming campaign. The nature of the terrain and scope for irregular warfare meant that rangers and light infantry were at a premium. However, Amherst knew from his experience at Louisbourg that it was not only the Indians who left much to be desired in such matters. The colonial forces too, despite proud boasts about their fleet-footed backwoodsmen, had shown themselves woefully inadequate in this department. This led Amherst to seek an increase in the number of light infantry in the regular battalions, which had fully proved their worth. However, this did not mean that the rest of the regulars could rest on their laurels, for it was essential that all the units continued to practise marksmanship for campaigning in a wooded terrain, where traditional European tactics of massed ranks were often not appropriate [15]. As January came to a close Amherst confided to Ligonier that he believed he had done everything possible to ensure an early start to the campaign [16].

As Bradstreet had made good progress repairing the bateaux, Amherst judged it was time to consider hiring personnel to man these craft. He had already been warned by Gage that using provincial corps for this service was neither practical nor popular, since most of their men had volunteered for soldierly duties, not heavy manual work [17]. Consequently on 29 January Amherst ordered the insertion of an advertisement in the provincial newspapers for 'young, strong, active Men accustom'd to hardship and the use of a gun', for which they would receive three shillings a day. This was a substantial premium and not inconsiderable cost, which was something that Amherst was always anxious to minimise [18]. In addition, with one eye on the possibility of an operation up the St Lawrence, he told Captain Joshua Loring, the naval liaison officer, to place orders for the construction of whaleboats [19]. Finally Amherst gave preliminary orders to the provision contractors to start moving supplies up to the frontier so that the army could commence operations as soon as the snow melted. Since March 1756 this had been the responsibility of two contractors, Sir William Baker, an eminent merchant of the City of London, and his American partner, Christopher Kilby, both of whom were now well versed in the business [20].[14]

During this period Amherst had been in correspondence with Brigadier John Forbes, who had just returned from his expedition against the strategic French post of Fort du Quesne at the Forks of the Ohio. One question still to be decided as a result of Forbes's success was what to do with the post, though Amherst was in no doubt it should be held with a substantial garrison [7]. Another was the treatment of the

Indians. Forbes emphasised the need to keep the native peoples in the British interest by honouring the various treaties of friendship recently negotiated, and suggested a visit by Amherst to Philadelphia to address the Ohio chiefs.[15] Amherst acknowledged the good sense of Forbes's advice, but preferred to leave any negotiations to Forbes himself. It was a subject to which Amherst might well have paid more attention. In the meantime he was pleased to hear that Pittsburgh was well secured [21].

Although it was now mid-February, Amherst still awaited the ministry's final decisions about the forthcoming campaign, for although Pitt's letters of 9 December had arrived from England confirming the ministry's intention to continue the war in North America, they said little more than what Amherst had communicated to the Governors on 13 December, that the provinces should aim to raise as many men as previously for 'invading Canada by way of Crown Point, and carrying War into the Heart of the Enemy's Possessions'. The only new information was that the ministry wanted the campaign to open on 1 May 1759. Despite this lack of specific instructions, Amherst determined to order Bradstreet to begin the construction of bateaux for operations on Lake Ontario, making 10 April as the starting date for his operations. Even at this point Amherst clearly intended a third operation, namely the capture of Niagara and an approach to Montreal from the west [25]. However, as Bradstreet was quick to point out, such action would require a considerable injection of funds into the Quartermaster's budget [27].

Amherst's dislike of the locally raised rangers, European or Indian, was reciprocated by Gage, who the previous year had tried to solve the deficiency by forming a specialised unit under regular discipline, the 80th Light Infantry. In his experience the rangers rarely caught up with their quarry, while the native peoples had shown zeal only for alcohol [22]. However, a proposal had been made by Robert Rogers, the ranger commander, to form two companies from the Stockbridge Indians[16] and despite his contempt for the native prowess, Amherst ultimately found it politic to engage their services. To some extent Amherst was circumscribed in that he had been ordered to secure a substantial number of rangers by Pitt, while Rogers had too much of a reputation as an exponent of ranger warfare to be totally ignored [39]. Gage however remained unconvinced, especially about Rogers, describing him as 'a good man in his way but his schemes are very wild' [40].

In his letter of 18 February 1759 Gage also highlighted another problem concerning the supply services. The non-payment for goods and services the previous year was threatening the supply of wagons and horses for the current campaign, without which the army would not be able to move. Amherst in reply affected to be unconcerned, believing that the complaints about non-payment were being manufactured by 'People naturally litigatious' [23]. However he was shortly to learn that it was not only at Albany that such problems existed. Colonel Bouquet, one of Forbes's senior officers, was reporting similar difficulties in Pennsylvania, where the provincial Assembly was threatening to vote no further supplies until the issue was addressed. Bouquet also confirmed that the Indians wanted to speak with Amherst, especially since Forbes himself was on the verge of dying [24].

By this time James Wolfe was sailing back to America to take up the command of the Quebec expedition. During the eight-week voyage he had time to pen his thoughts to Amherst on the forthcoming campaign. Away from the heady air of London, where everything seemed possible, doubts were beginning to rise. Wolfe's principal concern was the under-strength establishment of his regiments, which would now have to depend on recruits from the units sent to the Caribbean the previous autumn for the capture of Martinique.[17] The effects of even a short campaign in such a diseased environment were too well known to give any chance of a meaningful reinforcement. Thus a force which on paper was estimated to comprise 12,000 troops, actually had fewer than 9,000 men. With forces such as these Wolfe believed he might be reduced to playing a subordinate role in the grand design to conquer Canada. Much would depend on the assistance that Amherst could render [26].

At last the period of shadow preparation ended with the arrival on 15 March 1759 of Pitt's dispatches of 29 December 1758 confirming the ministry's intention of launching an expedition by way of the St Lawrence under Wolfe, while Amherst, with the remainder of the army, invaded Canada, either by way of Ticonderoga or via Lake Ontario, though, if he judged it practicable, he could take both routes. However, Pitt's letter left little doubt that the St Lawrence operation was to have the priority. The first five pages dealt with the requirements of Wolfe's expedition, which Amherst was to attend to before turning to his own operations on the rest of the continent.[18]

Whatever his private thoughts, Amherst vigorously set about implementing Pitt's instructions. Almost his first letter was to Governor Pownall of Massachusetts. That province, the most populous in New England, would have a key role to play, providing not only most of the provincial troops for garrisoning Nova Scotia and Cape Breton while the regulars were away, but also supplying much of the shipping and other supplies required by Wolfe, which could best be found at Boston, the provincial capital and second largest city in North America [28]. It was for this reason that Boston was made the place of embarkation for the artillery train, which Amherst ordered Colonel Williamson to prepare [29]. To help with the shipping arrangements Amherst also ordered Loring to Boston to hire 3,000 tons of transports together with forty schooners and sloops [30].

Concern with getting Wolfe's expedition ready did not preclude Amherst from making preparations for his own operations and those elsewhere. The death of Forbes[19] meant that a successor was necessary for the southern command, an area comprising Pennsylvania and the colonies to the south. Although no major operations were anticipated there this time, the tenuous hold on Fort Pitt needed to be strengthened. In addition, Amherst knew that Pittsburgh could be a useful base, either for proceeding down the Ohio to attack the French on the Mississippi, or for opening a communication to Lake Erie, which would be especially important if Amherst was to attack Niagara by way of the Mohawk river and Lake Ontario. A force on Lake Erie at Presqu'Isle would help seal the fate of Niagara. The man Amherst chose for this important theatre was the experienced Brigadier-General John Stanwix, who had been in America since 1756 [31].

However, no campaign, whether by sea or land, could be successful without an adequate supply of food. Accordingly Amherst now informed Kilby that he and his partner must prepare to supply 13,000 men by way of the St Lawrence River, another 30,000 by way of Albany, plus an as yet undetermined number operating to the south [33, 34].

These early weeks were not without problems for the Commander-in-Chief. One setback was the failure of the Massachusetts Assembly to vote as many men as the previous year [32]. The shortfall of 2,000 was serious, because it meant fewer men, either to relieve the garrisons in Nova Scotia and Cape Breton Island, or to support Amherst's own attack via Crown Point. But the consequences might not stop there, Amherst told Pownall. Massachusetts was the most influential of the northern provinces, and its example was sure to influence the other colonies. Accordingly Pownall must do his best to reverse the decision of his Assembly [35].

The problems in Boston meant that Amherst had to delay his intended visit to Philadelphia, which he had planned for early March [36]. Since the Pennsylvania Assembly was still threatening to withhold supplies until the army's existing debts had been settled, Amherst agreed to the appointment of a special commission to look into such claims [37]. However the shortage of money for the supply services was not limited to that particular area. Even more critical was the situation facing Bradstreet at Albany. Not only were horses and carriages difficult to secure, but the want of money meant that Bradstreet was unable to hire men to run the bateau service. His position was compounded by the inability of the crown to compete with the bounties being offered by the provincial authorities for enlistment in their own forces. If the supply service was to proceed it would have to be undertaken by the regulars [38].

Nevertheless, in the second week of April Amherst was finally able to depart for Philadelphia, where he felt his presence was required to persuade the Assembly to be more constructive in its support for the war. Pennsylvania was the second most populous colony and capable of making a vital contribution. Going to Philadelphia was a path previously tried by Loudoun, though the results of Amherst's visit were to prove remarkably barren. To some extent Amherst, like all previous British commanders, was being dragged into an internal dispute between the governor, representing the proprietary family, and an Assembly anxious to undermine that link. Hence the Assembly would only pass a supply bill if it included a tax on the estates of the Penn family, which the governor had been ordered to veto.[20] In the end Amherst could only follow Loudoun's example of requesting the governor to put aside his instructions in the larger interests of the war effort [41].[21]

Fortunately there was slightly better news from Boston, where Pownall reported on 13 April that he had successfully persuaded the Assembly to raise a further 1,500 men, though he was doubtful how far the vote of the Assembly would produce actual recruits. As he explained to Amherst, there was no chance of the house agreeing to impressment from the militia, since this might lead to the sons of the Assemblymen themselves being levied into the provincial army. He was also sorry to report a serious affray between the local population and the soldiers waiting to embark from the town [42].

Meanwhile progress assembling Amherst's own army near Albany was continuing, albeit slowly, as Gage reported on 15 April. Apart from a lack of bateau men Gage also had to contend with poor weather [43]. Few provincials had yet arrived and any hopes of early assistance even from these were dashed by the refusal of the New York contingent to participate until they received their bounty from the provincial government [45]. However, as Amherst informed Ligonier on 16 April 1759, he was still optimistic that the present campaign would suffice [44].

But clearly if the ministry's timetable was to be met, it was time to start sending the regulars to Albany and beyond. While issuing marching orders, Amherst took the opportunity of giving instructions about the equipment which he thought would be appropriate for the regiments to take, given the likely nature of the forthcoming campaign [46].

Before leaving New York, Amherst took the opportunity of catching up with his correspondence. Most important was the need to reply to Wolfe's letter of 6 March. In his response of 27 April he informed Wolfe of the various steps he had taken and expressed the hope that everything was progressing smoothly. He acknowledged that the plans to recruit Wolfe's army were far from adequate and wished that he could secure the 500 pioneers that Wolfe had requested in his letter of 6 March 1759. Unfortunately the high cost of labour seemed to preclude this [47].

Shortly after arriving in Albany Amherst determined to proceed with his plan for an attack on Niagara by an army under Brigadier-General John Prideaux advancing via the Mohawk River and Oswego. This meant it was now essential that Stanwix push forward as quickly as possible to occupy the posts of Venango, Le Boeuf and Presqu'Isle between Fort Pitt and Lake Erie. Such action would not only prevent those posts sending reinforcements to Niagara but also allow Stanwix to garrison the place once it was captured. This would then allow Amherst to recall Prideaux's army 'to act offensively to the Eastward of Lake Ontario', shutting off the French escape west of Montreal [48]. The result he told Wolfe in a further short note, would be that the French, confronted by so many assaults, would not know which way to turn, thus assuring success to one or all of the advancing British forces [49].

To ensure the earliest possible start to the Niagara campaign, Amherst requested Kilby to have a sufficient supply at Fort Stanwix for that service [51]. The contractors, however, were only responsible for delivering basic rations. Hence, to supply his own men with additional comforts, Amherst issued a call on 9 May for sutlers to open a market near the main camp [50]. The only article not allowed was hard liquor, in lieu of which Amherst arranged for the brewing of spruce beer, which he believed was a valuable anti-scorbutic and far more healthy for the troops.

With the provincials finally arriving in numbers by the middle of May, Amherst was now able to give Prideaux his formal orders. He was to command an army of three battalions of regulars and 2,680 New York provincials. First he was to advance on Oswego, where he was to leave half his force to construct a fort to cover his line of supply. With the other half Prideaux was immediately to proceed along the south shore of Lake Ontario to Niagara. Once in possession of Niagara he was leave Stanwix's relief force in garrison so that he could return with this whole force to take post at La Galette, half way between Lake Ontario and Montreal. Amherst was confident that the French would be able to offer only token resistance, given their preoccupation elsewhere at Quebec and Ticonderoga [53].

Like any good commander Amherst was constantly trying to anticipate possible difficulties. One concern was the need to ensure naval superiority on Lake Champlain, where the French had several schooners. He accordingly ordered Captain Joshua Loring to prepare the construction of two snows,[22] for use once a foothold had been secured on that lake [54]. Otherwise the main problems were those relating to the supply services, especially the lack of manpower. So pressing was the shortage of bateau men and wagon drivers, that Amherst had to accept employing 'Negroes' and other persons rejected by the recruiting service [55]. A shortage of horse-drawn wagons was also causing problems, which led Amherst to issue a proclamation banning the sutlers from using such vehicles. In future they must limit themselves to ox carts [56]. In addition the progress of the army continued to be delayed by the late arrival of many of the provincial troops. Nevertheless, despite these difficulties, Amherst was still quietly optimistic about the eventual outcome, telling Whitmore that 'by baffling the Enemy in different quarters, I hope to reap the benefit of their surprise and confusion', for he was certain of finding his 'operations not so difficult to be executed as may be imagined'.[23]

In contrast Wolfe was increasingly less optimistic. In his penultimate letter to Amherst before setting out from Louisbourg, dated 29 May 1759, he found much to displease him. He acknowledged that Amherst had done everything in his power to assist him, but the same could not be said for others. Such was his disillusionment that he was 'determined never to take another command in the Army'. His spirits were not helped by the severity of the weather. Although the end of May, Louisbourg harbour was still full of ice [57].

Another commander suffering from pessimism was Stanwix. On first receiving Amherst's orders of 6 May he had doubted their feasibility. He pointed out in reply that his own advance would be almost entirely on foot through difficult terrain over even longer distances, whereas Prideaux for the most part would be travelling by water along a more direct route [52]. In response, Amherst wrote on 30 May reminding

Stanwix that the Indians were now almost entirely in the British interest and that the French would have few men to oppose him. Amherst was convinced that once he got to Fort du Quesne (now renamed Fort Pitt) the problems of getting to Niagara would seem less insurmountable [58].

As the month of June arrived, Amherst was able to move up to Fort Edward, his plan being to advance one stage at a time. His mood was still one of confidence despite a shortfall in the number of the provincials. 'Everything pleases me but the Rangers', he told Gage on 6 June [59]. Nevertheless another serious crisis was brewing in the commissariat, this time over the lack of money. Cash was essential for small purchases, since individual farmers and traders were no longer prepared to accept the army's promises of future payment. Supplies of specie were the responsibility of contractors in England,[24] but no delivery had been made since the beginning of the year. Bradstreet and Robert Leake, one of the civilian commissaries, had increasingly warned that they would not be able to carry on the service much longer. By 8 June the position was such that Amherst decided he would have to appeal to the provincial government of New York for an issue of paper money, even though this contradicted government policy [60].[25] Fortunately, Lieutenant Governor James De Lancey was ready to expedite the matter, though getting his Assembly together to vote on the issue would necessarily take time [62].

Despite these distractions, the preparations for Amherst's northern offensive continued, though the delay of many provincials to join the army was an increasing cause for concern [61]. Another persistent irritant was the problem of desertion. Though usually given to leniency, Amherst decided that severity was the only remedy now, even though the culprit was on this occasion a provincial. Otherwise it would be impossible to predict 'where desertion would end'. Acknowledging it to be a most disagreeable business, he ordered the execution to be carried out in front of the condemned man's regiment as a deterrent to future misconduct [63].

At last, having spent a few days repairing the army's wagon train and patching the roads to Fort Edward, Amherst ordered the main part of his army to Lake George. Since they were now approaching territory infested by enemy raiding parties, the march on 21 June was carried out in battle formation. Amherst was never a commander to take unnecessary chances [65].

The main concerns, however, remained those of supply. Complaints were received, the first of many as it proved, that the magistrates of

Albany were obstructing the work of the Quartermaster's department [64]. Then on 30 June Leake reported difficulties in the supply of provisions to Prideaux because of leaking bateaux and casks He also reminded Amherst that a lack of money must necessarily mean that he would be unable to supply the army with fresh meat [66]. Amherst in response could only urge him to do his best, until the New York Assembly agreed to the loan [67]. However, it was not simply a matter of the immediate needs of the army that Amherst had to consider. As he reminded Kilby on 7 July, the army would need feeding once the fighting was over [68]. It would be pointless taking enemy positions if they subsequently had to be surrendered through a lack of winter provision.

Even so, Amherst was now ready for the next critical stage of his campaign. This was to advance down Lake George to attack the strategic fort of Ticonderoga, which guarded the portage between Lake George and Lake Champlain, the main gateway to Canada. But before ordering the troops to embark in the bateaux which Bradstreet had been preparing since the start of the year, he penned a letter to Major Browning, the senior officer on the Mohawk river, to ensure the safety of the communication to Oswego and Prideaux's force at Niagara. It was typical of Amherst's attention to detail that he instructed Browning to take particular care of some ordnance that was being forwarded to Oswego for the vessels being built there, which were essential for naval superiority on Lake Ontario [69]. Then satisfied that all was in order on that front, on 20 July he issued instructions to Colonel William Haviland, who was to command the advanced guard, to proceed to the other end of Lake George [70, 71].

In the event the passage down Lake George, the landing near the sawmill, and capture of the enemy lines before Ticonderoga proved uneventful. The enemy at no stage offered any significant resistance. Bourlamaque, the French commander, had only three weak battalions of regulars, and of necessity could do no more than retire from Montcalm's old defence lines in front of the fort to the walls of the fortress itself [72].[26] Hence Amherst felt sufficiently secure to order one of the provincial battalions to Oswego to reinforce Prideaux [73]. At this point Amherst knew only that Prideaux had arrived at his destination. The reality was that Niagara was on the point of falling, which duly happened, as Sir William Johnson reported, on 26 July. The only serious mishap in the campaign was that Prideaux himself had been killed on 20 July along with his next senior officer. Nevertheless, under Johnson's command, a relieving force of French and Indians from the French western posts had been routed and its officers taken prisoner, which induced the defenders in Niagara to surrender [74].

Although Amherst did not learn of the fall of Niagara until a few days later, the prospects for a successful conclusion to the western campaign seemed excellent, and he was quick to appoint one of his most senior and experienced colleagues, Thomas Gage, to take over from Johnson [75]. It also induced him to write to Stanwix, pointing out that the southern army should now experience little difficulty in its advance on Presqu'Isle. To put him fully in the picture Amherst added a portion of his journal covering the army's departure from Fort William Henry to the capture of Ticonderoga [76].

The day after writing to Stanwix, Amherst heard that the enemy had abandoned the neighbouring post of Crown Point. This seemed to make an assault on La Galette even more imperative, as he informed Gage on 1 August, since 'now is the time' for pressing the French from all sides to secure an end to hostilities [77]. His only concerns for either army, as so often, were those relating to the supply. Sickness was beginning to threaten the army through the drinking of contaminated water and Amherst in response ordered Bradstreet to hurry up the equipment for brewing spruce beer [78]. Even more serious, perhaps, were the reports from Bradstreet that there was 'so little a Quantity of Provisions at Albany, that to prevent the army to the Westward failing', he had been obliged to send for provisions from one of Amherst's own depots to the northward. Kilby was accordingly urged to use the utmost dispatch, for as Amherst observed 'if any thing prevents all Canada being taken this Campaign it will be the want of Provisions' [79]. However, Kilby replied on 5 August that he was confident that supplies would not fail. The one exception was flour, where he was hampered by its illicit exportation to the West Indies. But he repeated: 'Provisions are not, nor cannot be wanted during the present Campaign, and I therefore depend upon the Total Reduction of Canada' [83].

One explanation for the lack of supplies was inadequate transportation. Accordingly when Bradstreet suggested on 9 August that more bateaux might be needed to keep the supplies moving up the Mohawk River [85], Amherst readily agreed to a fifty per cent increase in the number of craft [87].

Apart from provisions, the most critical factor determining Amherst's own advance on Montreal was the attaining of naval superiority on Lake Champlain. Without this Amherst would not be able to stir from his present position, given the French armament on the lake. Hence even before leaving for Crown Point he sent a reminder on 3 August to Loring to ensure that he was doing everything possible to forward that department [80]. But as he contemplated the success so far, Amherst did not allow himself to become obsessed merely with pushing ever deeper into enemy territory. It was equally important to hold what had already been taken. Hence orders were issued to Colonel Phineas Lyman, one of the senior provincial officers, to take command of two battalions to repair and strengthen the strategic fort of Ticonderoga [81]. Finally the occupation of Crown Point in August allowed Amherst to write to the Lieutenant Governor of New York, assuring him that the province's borders were now secure and open to settlement. The peopling of this area would affirm British claims to these territories, which had been a principal objective of the war since 1755 [82].

To further the British grip on this part of the continent, Amherst also ordered a detachment to explore the Otter River with a view to establishing suitable blockhouses. Many thought the river might provide an alternative route to Lake Champlain [86]. In the event it was found that the river was obstructed by eight waterfalls, not three as previously reported, underlining the relative lack of knowledge on the British side of the terrain beyond the line of settlement [95].

So far nothing had been heard from Quebec other than that Wolfe had arrived at the Isle of Orleans. Wolfe had promised to correspond regularly but had not done so.[27] Amherst now decided to take the initiative, chosing as his emissary Captain Quinton Kennedy of the 80th Light Infantry. However Kennedy was not simply to carry dispatches to Wolfe. He was also to take a message to the Indian peoples between Crown Point and Quebec, principally the Abenaki, who were still opposing the British advance. Amherst wanted to assure them that they had nothing to fear from the British and suggested that they become neutral. The consequences for them otherwise would be dire [84].

Amherst affected to be unconcerned at the lack of news from Wolfe, which he believed was inevitable, given the distances and difficult terrain separating them [88]. He might have been less optimistic had he known that all Wolfe's attempts to engage the French army and seize Quebec had been unsuccessful. Nor were appearances more propitious elsewhere, though Amherst had yet to realise it. To the westward Gage was experiencing increasing difficulties, resulting from the inability of the supply services to meet the requirements of the troops now operating up the Mohawk River [93]. Stanwix, too, was finding that a lack of provisions was hampering his attempts to advance by way of Fort Pitt to

Presqu'Isle. One reason was the large number of Indians he had to feed. However he was able to report the good news that the French had abandoned their posts at Venango, Le Boeuf and Presqu'Isle [90].

For the moment Amherst was oblivious to these difficulties, as was evident in his next letter to Gage, in which he detailed his own preparations for the next stage of his advance, the passage down Lake Champlain to St Johns and Montreal [89]. He was similarly upbeat about Wolfe's likely progress at Quebec. Ironically this was in part because he had now had news from an unlikely source. On 15 August a French emissary had arrived at his camp with a letter from Montcalm suggesting an exchange of prisoners. Amherst feared the emissary's real purpose was to spy, but he learnt from Montcalm's letter dated 30 July 1759 that Wolfe had been bombarding Quebec for eighteen days running, causing the French much distress [99].

Nevertheless, all was not well on a number of fronts. The commissariat at Albany was experiencing a lack of co-operation from the civil authorities over the impressment of wagons and men for the bateau service [92]. There was also conflict in Amherst's own camp between those working on the forts and those building the naval vessels [94].[28] Another problem looming on the horizon was that the service period of many provincials would shortly expire. Amherst had already been warned by Pownall on 18 August that any attempt to keep the men beyond this would produce serious unrest [91]. To meet this problem Amherst decided to issue a circular letter on 30 August asking the northern governors to extend the period of service by one month, which would hopefully give sufficient time to complete the objectives of the campaign while avoiding any constitutional objections on the part of the provincials [97].

While waiting for the completion of the naval armament [96], Amherst decided to facilitate matters by ordering a small detachment to burn one of the enemy vessels, which was believed to be fitting out at the Isle aux Noix [99]. The need for some kind of action seemed all the more necessary, since Amherst learnt from Governor De Lancey that his Assembly was unlikely to extend the period of service for its forces [104]. Nevertheless, as Amherst told Governor Pownall, he was confident that Wolfe would persevere in his operation, with every chance of success, given the emaciated and scattered state of the French regular forces [103]. It was for this reason that Amherst rejected the suggestion of Bradstreet for keeping a large number of draft animals over the coming winter [102]. As he informed the Quartermaster General on 14

September, another campaign in all probability would not be necessary, in which case Bradstreet's suggestion would simply mean an unnecessary expense [109].

Amherst's optimism at this point was reinforced by the supply situation which seemed good, though one possible threat, according to Kilby, was the continued illicit exportation of flour [100]. In passing on Kilby's complaints to De Lancey, Amherst took the opportunity of adding his own concern about the excessive freedom of the New York newspapers in publishing intelligence concerning the army [101]. In response, De Lancey promised to make further enquiries into the clandestine flour trade, but on the freedom of the press there was nothing that he could do. The only consolation was that the newspaper reports were usually so false as to be of little use to the enemy [104].

Meanwhile progress on the naval vessels was proving painfully slow. One reason was the numerous conflicting demands on the sawmill near Ticonderoga [107]. Though Amherst was clear that Loring's naval vessels were to have the priority it was difficult to ignore the demands of the engineers rebuilding Ticonderoga and Crown Point [108]. The need to focus on Loring's naval armament was emphasised by the failure to burn the enemy's sloop at the Isle aux Noix [110]. Hence anything that would speed the supply of timber from the mill received Amherst's prompt attention [111]. It was all the more distressing therefore when Amherst learnt on 19 September that the mill's crankshaft had broken, so that timber could only be sawn for the moment by hand [112]. His dismay turned to anger when he found that a contributing factor had been the readiness of one of the operators to experiment how fast the mill could turn [113].

Nevertheless Amherst still retained his optimism, as he told Gage on 11 September. A recent French envoy from Montreal had been suspiciously silent about the situation at Quebec, suggesting the receipt of bad news on their side. Elsewhere the enemy had given up Venango so that Stanwix must now get his reinforcements to Niagara [105]. But the very day he was writing this, Amherst was about to learn of Gage's abandonment of the plan to seize La Galette, principally because he had been unable to secure sufficient provision for the different posts under his command [106, 118]. The news of this was a heavy blow for Amherst, since it meant that his plan to surround Canada and force its surrender was greatly weakened. It was one of the few occasions when he let his disappointment show to a senior commander, making it clear that he believed a golden opportunity had been lost [114].

Amherst's sense of disappointment might have been increased had he known of the capture of Quebec on 18 September. The consequence of Gage's timidity was that another campaign might now be necessary to complete the conquest of Canada, adversely reflecting on Amherst's own generalship. However, as John Calcraft, the agent for his regiment, informed him from England, his efforts were warmly applauded there and the King in recognition had appointed him to the prestigious and lucrative post of Governor of Virginia. Fortunately it was also a sinecure, much to Amherst's relief, since he had no wish to remain in America once the fighting was over. Equally pleasing was the news that he had been promoted from a brevet to a full Major-General [117].

It was at this point that Amherst learnt of the capture of Captain Kennedy by the St Francis Indians. Finding that his attempt to neutralise the Abenaki had not succeeded, Amherst now ordered Rogers to attack the Indian settlement with his rangers. The march there would be difficult, the retreat more so in such a wilderness. To help execute the latter, Amherst ordered a detachment to take provisions to the Wells River to await Rogers on his return [119].[29]

At length, in the second week of October, the naval armament for Lake Champlain was finally ready. Before setting off Amherst penned a further letter to Stanwix urging him yet again to attempt the relief of the garrison at Niagara. Amherst admitted that his own ambitions were now limited to the destruction of the enemy vessels on Lake Champlain, in conjunction with an exploratory probe 'with what Troops can be spared . . . to see what may be further attempted' [121]. As before, Amherst issued meticulous instructions on how the armada was to conduct itself while on Lake Champlain, to minimise the risks from the enemy vessels and other possible misadventures [122]. In the event, Loring succeeded in trapping three of the four enemy vessels, forcing their crews to run them aground, but bad weather prevented the troops from proceeding to the St Lawrence, as he informed Ligonier on 22 October [125]. The final conquest of Canada would have to await another campaign. So too would the relief of the garrison at Niagara, which Stanwix had decided not to attempt following a council of war [123].

It was while Amherst was on Lake Champlain that news finally arrived of the fall of Quebec from some French deserters though official notification from Brigadier-General Robert Monckton only arrived on 15 November because of the interception of the original dispatches by a privateer [115]. Among the accounts of the campaign was that by Colonel Williamson, giving the artillery's perspective on events from the time of landing to the death of Wolfe and the surrender of Quebec [116]. At this point it seemed that the conduct of the Quebec expedition had been perfectly harmonious. It was not until early December that Amherst received a further letter from Brigadier-General George Townshend alerting him to the serious disagreements that had occurred between Wolfe and his brigadiers about the conduct of the campaign [120]. Amherst, of course, was in no position to judge the truth of these allegations and was in any case inclined to avoid getting involved in such disputes.

Meanwhile there was still much to be done if the full benefits of what had already been accomplished were to be secured. Although British naval superiority on Lake Champlain seemed assured, it was desirable to complete it by seeing if the sunken French vessels with their guns could be retrieved [126]. Possession of Crown Point and Ticonderoga would also be more secure if the communication between those posts and New England could be improved. A start had already been made in marking out a new road to Number Four on the Connecticut River, but Amherst now determined to allocate a much larger force of provincials to work on it [127]. Instructions were also sent to Colonel William Eyre at Niagara about the desirability of opening a road to Fort Pitt, since Amherst believed the latter post might be supplied more economically via Lake Erie [128].

There were limits however to what could be achieved in the time remaining. With the weather fast deteriorating and the expiry time of many provincials fast approaching, trouble was to be expected and duly occurred on 1 November when Colonel Putnam of the Massachusetts forces reported that many of his men were refusing to work. In the event Putnam was able to suppress the discontent without recourse to the regulars [129]. Since the mutineers were near the end of their service and appeared contrite, Amherst readily pardoned them [130]. However when Amherst received news from Lieutenant-Colonel Montresor of desertions at Fort George, he merely commented that those who deserted would forfeit all their pay, which would be a considerable saving to the public [133].

The ending of hostilities around Quebec meant that the army there came under Amherst's command. However the lateness of the season and difficulty of communication meant that there was little he could do to take effective control. Fortunately the garrison was well situated and the countryside under firm control, as Brigadier-General James Murray reported on 1 November. Most reassuring was the happiness of the inhabitants at receiving such lenient treatment, which was very different from what they had been led to expect by their former French masters [131].[30]

One late minor success, as Amherst reported to Governor De Lancey on 13 November, was the return of Rogers from his expedition against the St Francis Indians. The march to and assault on the village had been highly successful in terms of surprise and the number killed. The fact that many of those slaughtered at St Francis were women and children and that many perished in the flames of their own dwellings did not worry Amherst unduly. Brutality was a fact of eighteenth-century warfare, especially when Europeans made war against the native peoples. However the operation was not without cost since many of Rogers's party got lost in the woods after beating off an Indian counter-attack [134].

With the army about to go into winter quarters, the old problem of quarters for the troops began to resurface, especially at Albany and along the Hudson valley [135]. Arrangements were also needed for the reception of the sick [136]. After this it was time to start sending the units down to Fort Edward before Lake George froze [137]. Amherst's last act was to give orders to Haviland to take command at Crown Point where he was to keep a special guard on the naval vessels. These would be the key to the invasion of Canada the following year and the French were bound to try and destroy them [138].

Amherst himself finally quitted Crown Point on 25 November. If he had any regrets about not fulfilling all his objectives, he did not say so. Certainly his conduct did not raise any criticism in England, where Calcraft painted a glowing picture of his reputation [139]. He arrived in New York city on 11 December.[31]

Though meriting a well-earned break, Amherst was already thinking about the next campaign. He was aware of the need for an early start, and accordingly began writing to the northern provincial governors in mid-December, as in the previous year, urging them either to keep their existing forces in being, or to make early preparations for raising new forces even before the official orders arrived from England [140].

Earlier Amherst had received a letter from Governor Lyttelton that a war had broken out with the Cherokee [124]. Amherst, in response, took the precaution of bringing two regiments with him to New York in case the South Carolinians needed help. However, as he informed Lyttelton on 21 December, it was much better if the authorities in South Carolina could handle the situation themselves [141]. As to the present crisis on the southern frontier, Amherst firmly believed that the only way to treat the Indians was 'to reward or punish them according to their Deserts'.[32]

The campaign of 1760: the conquest completed

The new year opened quietly for Amherst. The bitter cold and deep snow meant that all military operations had ceased, other than the occasional scouting or raiding party. The lack of activity was reflected in his letter to Ligonier on 9 January [142]. However, on 22 January he received the gratifying news that Massachusetts, unlike the other colonies, had agreed not only to keep 2,500 of its troops in service during the winter 'beyond the time of their enlistment', but also had voted to raise 5,000 more for the service of the new campaign [143]. This was especially important for the garrisoning of Cape Breton and Nova Scotia, which must otherwise have been dangerously insecure, given the need to keep a large force at Quebec.

Fortunately the position there remained satisfactory, as Murray reported on 25 January, despite reports from Montreal that the French were going to attack him in the spring. Like many, Murray exuded a new confidence bordering on arrogance about the ability of the British to defeat their old adversary. Accordingly his only concern was that the French might get a fleet into the St Lawrence before Lord Colville [144]. Amherst also received the good news from Stanwix that the Ohio Indians were ready to give up their prisoners according to the newly signed treaties. The only disturbing thing was the refusal of many of these captives to be repatriated with their families. Choosing to live with 'savages' was inexplicable in the minds of the British military [145].

Otherwise it was a matter of dealing with the now familiar problems of the civil versus military authority that had confronted British commanders since Braddock. One concerned the improper enlistment of recruits for the regulars which led to a complaint from the New Jersey authorities. But as Amherst pointed out to Governor Bernard, any abuses by the recruiting party did not justify the inhabitants attacking them. Disputed enlistments must be handled by the lawful authorities, the magistrates, to whom the local population should take their grievances. Recruitment for the regular army was hard enough without it having to suffer this kind of abuse [149]. For, as Captain Legge reported from Boston, once the provinces started recruiting their own forces, the regulars would be unable to compete against the high bounties being offered for enlisting in the provincial units [153].

Meanwhile, as January gave way to February, the ever-active Bradstreet reminded Amherst that 15 February had been the date set for the commencement of preparations for the last campaign [147]. Amherst responded that it was not necessary to prepare so early this year, since many things were already in place from the previous campaign [150]. Nevertheless he did order Loring to ensure that the rigging and other supplies for the vessels necessary for securing naval superiority on Lake Ontario and Lake Champlain, were ready by the end of March [151]. It proved a propitious moment since the next day, 16 February, Amherst received Pitt's preliminary orders of 11 December 'to make all necessary preparations for pushing the war with the utmost vigour, as early as the season shall permit'.[33] Amherst accordingly ordered Bradstreet to draw up a list of 'what additional boats will be wanted for Lakes Ontario and Champlain' [152]. Even at this stage he had resolved to launch two offensives, in addition to any operations by the garrison at Quebec, with one army going by way of Lake Champlain and the other crossing Lake Ontario to approach Montreal from the west, as he had planned in the previous year. Bradstreet duly obliged within forty-eight hours with his thoughts on the army's likely transport requirements. He believed the principal difficulty would be securing sufficient bateau men and wagon drivers [154].

Three days later Pitt's dispatches of 7 January 1760 arrived with the ministry's definitive plans for the ensuing campaign. As expected the objective was the total conquest of Canada, as it had been since 1757. The difference this time was that Amherst would not only control all parts of the operation, but have considerable latitude as to how it should be done 'either in one body, or by different operations, at one and the same time'.[34] This was a degree of latitude that had not been accorded to any commander in North America before.[35] In his letters to the provincial governors Pitt urged them to have their men ready to take the field by 1 May. However, Amherst, mindful of the distances to be covered, suggested 10 April rather than 1 May as the start date [155].

Next day Amherst began writing to the various heads of the army's departments. Gage was once more to take charge of the advanced guard at Albany. Bradstreet was to be responsible for the army's transport, in particular the building of bateaux at Oswego [156]. Johnson was to enlist as many Indians again in the British cause, doing his best to win over those still hostile [158]. However, one imponderable factor for the supply services was the Treasury's appointment of new contractors to replace Baker and Kilby [156]. Since Amherst had not received a copy of the new provision contract, he judged it advisable to inform the new contractors' American agents about the army's likely requirements during the forthcoming campaign, including those of the men about to depart for South Carolina to fight the Cherokee [161].

Until recently the Cherokee had been friends of the British. Now they were thoroughly alienated, as Amherst learnt from Governor Lyttelton, following the collapse of a recently negotiated peace treaty [146]. The consequence was that Amherst, in the middle of his other preparations, had to order Colonel Archibald Montgomery with two battalions to help the beleaguered province [159]. Amherst never doubted that the Indians were to blame for this breakdown in relations and he accordingly told Lyttelton that Montgomery's orders were to chastise 'that perfidious race of savages', reducing 'them so low that they may never more be able to be guilty of the like again'. However, Montgomery's campaign was to be a short spring one, since his troops would be needed soon for the offensive in the north [160].

By this time Amherst was facing the usual difficulties which preceded the opening of any campaign. Bradstreet was disputing Amherst's decision to build the bateaux for the western army at Oswego rather than Schenectady, arguing that it would be impossible to get sufficient carpenters and materials there [162]. Loring was pessimistic about finding seamen for the naval armaments on Lake Champlain and Ontario because of the high wages offered by provincial merchants [164]. Bradstreet too believed that the high cost of labour meant that the bateaux, even if built, could not be manned. Only the early arrival of the provincial units could remedy the situation. And that was an unlikely prospect [165].

The provincial assemblies were also promising Amherst their customary difficulties, especially Pennsylvania, where Governor Hamilton reported continuing attempts by the lower house to undermine the proprietary family. As before, the Assembly had drafted a supply bill with the aim of provoking Hamilton into rejecting it [166]. Unfortunately the Pennsylvania Assembly was not alone in its prevarication. Even Massachusetts was languishing in its endeavours, as Pownall reported on 30 March, despite his earlier optimism. The principal problem was the reluctance of the Assembly to authorise an immediate impressment from the militia. But Pownall believed it would greatly help recruitment if Amherst could give firm assurances that the period of provincial service would not be extended beyond that agreed on their initial enlistment [167]. This was a point on which Pownall felt so strongly that he returned to it in a second letter on 25 April 1760 [171]. Amherst in response could only assert that he must retain some flexibility, especially regarding the men serving in the eastern seaboard posts, otherwise the campaign might collapse before it started [168].

Fortunately there was better news from Bradstreet about the state of the transport service. Communication both to Oswego and Crown Point was open, though a lack of money was again cause for concern [169]. The prospect of being able to start moving men and supplies encouraged Amherst to issue campaign orders to Murray. He was to assemble all the forces he could spare from garrison duty at Quebec and proceed in due course up river towards Montreal where Amherst was hopeful that all three armies could converge should the French attempt one final stand [170].

One potential threat to Amherst's preparations was the restless state of the Ohio Indians, despite the signing of several recent peace treaties. Frederick Post, a Moravian missionary, who was planning a diplomatic mission for the Pennsylvanian authorities, had earlier suggested that the native peoples would appreciate an address from Amherst reassuring them about his intentions [163]. With another campaign about to begin, Amherst accepted the desirability of calming the western Indians and accordingly issued a formal declaration assuring them that 'his Majesty has not sent Me to deprive any of you of your Lands and Property'. On the contrary he was there to protect them, while those who joined against the French would be rewarded [172]. However, when the Indian deputy superintendent, George Croghan, suggested employing the western Indians against the Cherokee, Amherst demurred, believing they could not be trusted to accomplish their mission at such a distance [176].

Since Brigadier Stanwix had requested leave to return home, Amherst appointed Monckton to replace him in the southern command. His orders were similar to those of Stanwix in 1759. Monckton was to relieve the garrison at Niagara, secure the communication between it and Pittsburgh, and strengthen all the forts through western Pennsylvania [173]. Then Amherst set out for Albany where he arrived on 8 May. Here he found that few of the provincial forces had yet arrived. To speed their progress he issued a circular letter on 11 May, urging the northern governors that since 'the season is so far advanced, and so proper to begin the operations of the Campaign' they should do everything possible to hasten their forces. Without a substantial number of provincials it would be difficult sustaining offensive operations over such an extensive countryside [175].

Late arrival was not the only cause for disquiet concerning the provincials, for Pownall's warning the previous August, that there would be trouble if they were kept beyond their agreed time of service, had been realised with several mutinies in the posts on the Bay of Fundy. Fortunately the French were in no position to take advantage of the situation, as Amherst confessed to Whitemore on 18 May. Indeed, despite these difficulties, Amherst did not think the late arrival of the provincials 'will be of any bad consequence, as I hope we shall have time enough to Execute everything that is yet to be done in this part of the World' [177].

It was, therefore, all the more shocking to learn next day that Murray had been defeated on 28 April by the Chevalier de Levis in a second battle on the Heights of Abraham. Murray was not certain that he would be able to retain Quebec [174].

Amherst's immediate response was to send all the reinforcements he could to Murray. But his options were limited, especially if he were to continue with his own plans. Accordingly the best he could do, as he informed Murray on 19 May, was the dispatch of two battalions from Louisbourg, that were currently earmarked for carrying out the demolition of that fortress [178].[36] They would need replacing, which meant finding additional provincial forces, as Amherst informed Whitemore that same day [179]. However, to relieve the pressure on Murray, Amherst instructed Rogers a few days later to lead a large raiding party of 300 men against the enemy at St Johns, near Montreal. This time there was to be no killing of women and children, nor plundering either. Amherst clearly believed that looting had hampered Rogers's previous expedition against the St Francis Indians during its retreat [184].[37]

Although affairs had reached a crisis, Amherst still felt obliged that same night to address patronage and promotion matters, since he had just received a letter from Lord Barrington requesting that something be done for Captain McNeil, a protégé of the Duke of Argyle [148]. The combination of the Secretary at War and the most powerful member of the Whig party in Scotland was something that Amherst could only respond to deferentially by promising to promote McNeil as soon as a position became vacant [180].

Ironically, the day that Amherst heard of the army's plight at Quebec, Murray was writing that the enemy had retired in disorder, following the arrival of several British warships [181]. This was just as well, since finding transports for the dispatch of Murray's reinforcement was not proving easy, due to the merchants demanding a substantial premium for their services [183].

But whatever the problems in the St Lawrence and at Boston, Amherst pressed on methodically with his own preparations. First he confirmed to the contractors his provision requirements for 25,000 men from 1 June 1760 [182]. Then he began ordering the regulars and provincials to start moving towards their respective base camps at Oswego and Crown Point, even though the latter were still far from complete [185, 186]. This reluctance of the provincials to engage was explained to Amherst by Captain Wheelock, together with the reasons why a vote in the Assembly bore so little correlation to the number of men actually appearing in the field [187].

Nevertheless, a sufficient number had arrived by mid-June for Amherst to give his final instructions for the conduct of the campaign. He was certainly encouraged to do so by Indian intelligence that the French had been forced to raise the siege of Quebec [188]. As he explained to Haviland, his intention was to advance on the French 'by their three Avenues; namely from Quebec up the River St Lawrence; from Lake Ontario down the River St Lawrence; and from Crown Point by the Isle aux Noix'. Haviland was to command the advance from Crown Point, Murray that from Quebec, while Amherst sealed the enemy's escape by approaching from the west via Lake Ontario down the St Lawrence River. Since it would be some time before all the troops were ready, Haviland was in the meantime to continue strengthening the works at Crown Point and Ticonderoga [189].

By now Rogers had completed his raid on Lake Champlain, as he reported to Amherst on 21 June. The fort at St Johns had proved too strong, so he had attacked the settlement of St Etherese before returning unscathed to Crown Point. The male inhabitants had been brought back captive, while the women and children this time had been allowed to go to Montreal [190]. The difference in treatment of St Etherese and St Francis was in large part because the former was a French village, the latter an Indian settlement. Rogers's achievement, of course, fell below what Amherst had originally intended. Fortunately, it no longer mattered, for the same day that Rogers penned his report, Amherst received formal confirmation of the welcome news that the French had raised the siege of Quebec. The final conquest of Canada was now virtually assured [191].

At the end of June there was good news too from Niagara, where Loring was building several vessels to ensure command of Lake Ontario and the upper St Lawrence [192]. On 6 July Loring confirmed his two snows were almost ready and requested orders how he should proceed, though he still wanted men to crew his vessels properly [194]. Amherst quickly ordered this defect to be remedied by the provision of 100 seamen on his arrival at Oswego on 9 July. Three days previously the French sloops had boldly appeared before the British camp, making it clear that until they were destroyed, no advance on Montreal could be contemplated [195]. To assist in their destruction, Amherst ordered some troops to set off in bateaux towards Niagara to act as a decoy so that Loring could get between them and the entrance to the St Lawrence [196]. In addition Amherst ordered a detachment to Grand Island at the entrance of the St Lawrence to help map the navigation of that crucial channel [197]. Sadly the stratagem to lure the French boats towards Niagara failed, as did Loring's subsequent attempts to engage them. All three vessels escaped into the St Lawrence, still able to dispute Amherst's advance on Montreal [198].

So far the supply services had given Amherst little cause for concern. However at the end of July he received information of renewed tension between the civil and military authorities at Albany. The dispute initially was trifling enough, involving some of the King's oxen which had strayed onto the fields of Mr Vroman, a brother of one of the local ministers. Vroman then instituted a suit for damages which resulted in the arrest of Captain Brown, a key figure in the supply service. The consequences promised to be serious for, as Amherst pointed out in some exasperation to Governor De Lancey, the detention of Brown 'must put a great stop to that essential Service in the Transportation of Provisions to the Army'.[38] But despite an appeal from both Amherst and the Lieutenant Governor, the sheriff remained unrepentant. Any subject could bring a writ which he was legally bound to serve. Brown could have been bailed, had Coventry, the Assistant Deputy Quartermaster General, agreed to stand surety for him [200].

Despite Loring's setback and the shenanigans in Albany, progress continued not only at Oswego but by the army at Crown Point [193]. Amherst accordingly informed Haviland on 29 July that he would begin his advance on 10 August. Haviland should do the same, taking care to keep up a regular communication so that they could co-ordinate their operations on approaching Montreal. This should be possible now that a path had been discovered leading from Lake Champlain to Oswegatchie on the St Lawrence River [199].[39] Amherst's own army numbered 10,961, a figure which including 706 warriors of the Six Nations. But any satisfaction Amherst might have had at the support of the Indians was diminished by the presence of an equal number of women and children who were being fed at Oswego at huge expense to the Crown. Amherst could only console himself that these non-combatants would have to return home once the army began to advance, as he informed Monckton on 2 August [201].

Before beginning his advance, Amherst ordered Colonel Haldimand on 6 August to take a detachment to Grand Isle, near the mouth of the St Lawrence. This would provide a forward base from which Loring could be supported as he searched for the passage into the St Lawrence River [202]. Then, having repeated his orders to Loring to sail for the river, Amherst prepared to embark [203]. Haviland too was ready, even though some of his provincials were only just arriving. In the event Amherst embarked on 10 August, with Haviland starting the following day [204].[40]

After crossing the Lake, Amherst's flotilla entered the St Lawrence, though only after a passage of several days, as Amherst informed Bradstreet on 15 August. Bradstreet had been hoping to join the army for the final assault but, as Amherst emphasised, his presence was more important behind the lines to ensure the smooth forwarding of supplies [205]. Not that Amherst intended making any premature rush to reach Montreal. In the methodical manner that had been the hallmark of his generalship, he first gave orders to one of the senior provincial officers for the establishing of a base at Swegatchie, opposite La Galette, where spruce beer could be brewed, bread baked, and a hospital organised [206]. Only on 19 August did Amherst order the rest of the army to continue slowly down the north bank to the Isle Royale, where the French had a fort protecting the approaches to the rapids [207]. Although the French post was only five miles from Swegatchie it took another three days to implement the initial orders for investing the fort. Fortunately, Loring was now able to bring his own vessels up in support, following the destruction of the enemy naval craft [208]. The main assault itself was to be under the direction of Colonel Haldimand [209]. However certain aspects of his plan did not please Amherst, as he reported to Ligonier on 26 August. Instead he continued his artillery bombardment and it was this that finally persuaded the enemy to seek terms, leaving the way open for a final advance on Montreal [210]. After reorganising his forces, Amherst resumed his advance on 31 August. Now the only obstacle was the rapids in the St Lawrence River and it was at this point that his army suffered its most serious casualties, with some eighty-four men being lost on 4 September through the overturning of several bateaux. Nevertheless by Saturday 6 September Amherst was before Montreal with 7,000 troops. Murray was just to the east with another 4,000 men, while Haviland arrived on the Monday with a further 3,600 men.

Vaudreuil and Levis had just 3,700 dispirited regulars and troops *de la marine* and were in no position to fight or escape.[41] They had therefore no option but to seek terms. The French initially sought the honours of war, allowing them to depart with their personal weapons, regimental colours, and the right to fight again. But Amherst would have none of it, insisting on the surrender of all weapons and colours and the condition that they should not serve again in the present war [213]. Amherst did this, he explained to Ligonier, believing their 'Corps should be disgraced for having Carried on a Cruel and barbarous war', meaning their readiness to employ Indian methods of warfare [212]. Levis and the French regulars considered these terms so dishonourable that they wanted to fight one last battle, but Vaudreuil, to spare the Canadian people further suffering, overruled them and signed Amherst's formal articles of surrender.[42] The whole of Canada including the maritime provinces and the region of the Great Lakes (though not Illinois) was to become British territory and its inhabitants subjects of George II.

Because Amherst had taken a moral stance on the conduct of the war, he was determined that nothing should disfigure the British occupation of Montreal. He had already done his best, while advancing on the city, to persuade the inhabitants that they should return to their properties. Now his first action on taking possession was the posting of an elite force of Grenadiers and Light Infantry inside Montreal under Colonel Haldimand to control access into and out of the town [211].

In the privacy of his journal, Amherst wrote: 'I believe never three Armys, setting out from different & very distant Parts from each other, joyned in the Center, as was intended, better than we did, and it could not fail of having the effect of which I have just now seen the consequence'.[43] But whatever the euphoria Amherst might have felt on the capitulation of the French, there was no time to waste if the British hold on Canada was to be consolidated. Accordingly, three days after the surrender, Amherst began ordering the provincial units to start returning the way they had come so that they could continue working on the various fortifications between Canada and New York, many of which were still incomplete [214]. Arrangements also had to be made to ensure an adequate supply of provisions before winter arrived [215]. Another consideration was the taking possession of the more distant outposts. Many were garrisoned by only a few men though, as Amherst explained to Monckton, it was right that they should be occupied since French Canadians were living beside them and it was important that 'the inhabitants should give up their arms and take the oath of Allegiance' [216]. Rogers was therefore ordered westwards with two companies of rangers. Most important was the need to secure Detroit and its dependencies, notably Michilimackinac [217].

Meanwhile the process of disarming the inhabitants and taking the oath of allegiance had begun, though not as smoothly as Amherst might have wished. One excuse from the inhabitants for not surrendering their weapons was that the Indians had stolen them. Others pleaded that they were physically prevented by the Indians from taking the oaths [218]. However, Amherst was not to be deterred and to make the population's compliance more effective, he instructed his officers to work through the captains of the militia, making them responsible for summoning all the male inhabitants with their weaponry [220].

Amherst had no specific instructions from the ministry in London on how to administer the conquered territories, and there were few precedents for such situations other than by the use of *ad hoc* military courts, since Britain had no formal system of martial law for the control of the civil population.[44] Another consideration was that any arrangements could only be provisional until a final peace settlement had been concluded with France.

Amherst therefore had to proceed cautiously. The peace terms stated that the inhabitants were to be treated as equal subjects of the King, entitled to the protection of their property and practice of their religion. The French had administered the settled parts of Canada as three districts, an arrangement which he decided to keep, with Murray as Governor of Quebec, Gage in command at Montreal, and Ralph Burton in charge of Trois Rivières, the smallest of the three. In keeping with his desire for conciliation, Amherst decided that wherever possible the inhabitants should settle differences among themselves according to their own laws and customs, since such arrangements would be less onerous for the military and help make British rule more acceptable [221]. But in an addendum on 23 September, Amherst decided he had been too lenient in his initial edict and ordered Burton and the other two governors that serious crimes like murder and theft must remain the prerogative of the military courts [226].

Regarding the security of Canada, Murray was given the pre-eminent responsibility, reflecting the strategic location of Quebec. He was to command nine battalions, Gage six, and Burton just one. However, in an emergency Gage and Burton were to be ready to reinforce Murray. And whatever transpired all three were to 'Correspond, and Co-operate together, and reciprocally give each other all the Information & Intelligence you may receive' [227].

One responsibility arising out of the capitulation was the need to arrange for the departure of the French garrison and repatriation of their prisoners. In a mood of magnanimity Amherst was inclined to indulge those Canadians who wished to stay in the British colonies, unless they had served with the French regular forces, all of whom were to be repatriated to France [223]. But the issue of enemy prisoners raised serious difficulties, as Captain Wheelock reported from New York, where many of those captured earlier were interned on Long Island. Not least was the fact that a number of the French regulars had formed family ties while living in Canada and wanted to remain. Fearing that they would not be allowed to do so, they were already beginning to abscond [228].

Although Amherst had tried to protect the inhabitants and their property, he was not completely successful in this, since on 14 September he had to order Murray to put detachments on board the transports to search for stolen property and request that similar searches be carried out on the warships too [219]. Even more regrettable was the experience of Les Cedres, the most westerly village from Montreal, as Captain Moncrieffe reported on 18 September. This was on the return route of many of the provincials, who proceeded to strip the inhabitants of their possessions despite Moncrieffe's efforts to stop them with a party of regulars [224]. Fortunately few of the Native Americans were present, otherwise the inhabitants might have lost their lives as well, since the Indian code of warfare demanded scalps or captives as revenge or recompense for previous loss. All but 200 of Johnson's Indians had deserted on the army's arrival at Oswegatchie because Amherst had refused to allow them to plunder Fort Levis and scalp the garrison. Amherst was so disgusted by their desertion that he resolved to have a special campaign medal struck for the few who had remained faithful. They alone were to be welcomed at the army's posts in future [222].

Sadly, the Indians were not the only ones neglecting their duty, as the same was true of many regimental chaplains. Amherst had for this reason dismissed one chaplain and demanded that another now attend to his duty. Such absenteeism was especially embarrassing, given the need to show the Canadians that their new masters were no less dedicated Christians [225].

Having completed his arrangements for the safety of the occupying army, Amherst made a quick tour of the St Lawrence settlements before setting out on 5 October to return to Albany by the more direct route of Lake Champlain.[45]

Meanwhile news of Amherst's success had reached London. Amherst had sent Captain Prescott with dispatches following the capture of Fort Levis, but he was overtaken by Major Isaac Barré, one of Amherst's other aides, with the news that Canada itself had fallen. Nevertheless Prescott dutifully delivered his dispatches to Pitt, before visiting Mrs Amherst. While with the Secretary of State, Prescott tactfully enquired about the possibility of Amherst returning home. Pitt's response was not encouraging. Amherst's presence in America was 'absolutely necessary, and would remain so till a Peace was concluded' [230].

Barré's purpose in rushing to England, as for many others shortly, was to secure promotion. He knew it was customary to reward those who brought news of victory, but in this he was initially disappointed. He ascribed his setback in part to divisions within the service, and partly because American victories were maligned when compared to success in Europe [232]. However Ligonier commented that Barré had already been favourably treated, having risen recently from a humble lieutenant to brevet major in America [231]. Hence, despite another interview with Pitt, Barré for the moment remained disappointed. He did however learn something of the ministry's plans for the American army. Among the likely objectives were Mobile and Martinique [233].

Back in Albany, Amherst was having to deal with the usual run of military business, ranging from suggestions on how to deal with the Indians [234]; petitions for compensation for losses caused by the abuse of property by the military [235]; and requests for permission to go to England to settle family affairs [238].

After this he continued on his way to New York, where he arrived on 26 November 1760. Here he received an address of thanks from the City Council [240] to which he replied with as few words as possible [241]. Amherst was not a natural speaker. For this reason he had earlier told Calcraft in London to ensure that he was not adopted for any constituency in the forthcoming parliamentary elections, which he feared might happen following his success in Canada [237].[46]

Awaiting him in New York was a letter from Governor Bull of South Carolina. Hostilities had once more broken out with the Cherokee, culminating in a massacre of the garrison of Fort Loudoun [229]. Clearly Montgomery's expedition had been insufficient to bring the Cherokee to submission. Equally clear was that the provincial authorities were still incapable of handling the situation and that the regulars would have to do the job. However, this time Amherst insisted to Colonel James Grant, who was to lead the expedition, that the province must co-operate in the provision of carriages and other things that had previously been denied Montgomery. Otherwise Grant was to return and leave the people of South Carolina to their own devices [243].

The year ended with the usual disputes between the supply services and local population, although the memorial of one Albany farmer, Hans Feeling, about his treatment and that of his wagon, explains much why there was often an undercurrent of feeling against the army [239]. It was because of incidents like this that the New York Assembly passed an act holding those persons impressing wagons and drivers responsible for any damage. However, according to Bradstreet, this had opened the gates to numerous lawsuits by a people who had reaped the benefit from the mother country's exertions and were now ungratefully refusing to acknowledge any obligation [242].

Chief among those with an 'insatiable Avarice and thirst for Oppression', was the Sheriff of Albany, Jacob Van Schaick. Hence it was no surprise that, shortly after Bradstreet's complaint about the New York Act, another fracas occurred, this time involving the Sheriff and Lieutenant Coventry, the Assistant Deputy Quartermaster General. Van Schaick asserted that his life had been endangered by Coventry with a loaded pistol and when he insisted in issuing his warrant found that several soldiers with their wives and children had been quartered on him [244]. It was disputes like this that made Amherst wish to be back in England.

Traditional accounts of the war in North America have emphasised its heroic aspects, notably Wolfe's ascent of and death on the Heights of Abraham. In reality that incident was the exception, for warfare in North America was largely a matter of logistics, with just the occasional confrontation with the enemy. In addition, many of the things that the commanding officer was required to deal with were only indirectly related to events on the battlefield. As a result Amherst spent infinitely more time at his desk writing letters than facing the muskets of the enemy, for whether in New York, Crown Point or Montreal, his first and most onerous task each day was the writing of orders and requests to officers and officials throughout eastern North America. Since these were often hundreds if not thousands of miles away, Amherst had to convey his intentions and receive their replies in writing. The consequence was a huge and varied selection of documents, some of which are reproduced in the following collection.

Section I
The Campaign of 1759:
the British Offensive Resumed

1

Field Marshal Viscount John Ligonier to Major-General Jeffery Amherst

London

15 September 1758

[Secretary's hand,[1] signed by Ligonier]   [Received 19 November 1758]

Since my last Letter to You of the 3^d Ins^t – His Majesty has been pleas'd to appoint you Commander in Chief of his Forces in North America. I most sincerely congratulate You on this extraordinary mark of His Majesty's Favour, which your Conduct, I am persuaded, will improve.

General Abercrombie is recall'd from this Command, and a Government is intended for him – In consequence of your succeeding to it, the Royal North American Regiment is of your particular appointment . . .[2]

I need not repeat to You my sincere wishes for your Welfare and Success, as I am persuaded you believe my Friendship for You is real and unfeign'd.

Your Brother will give you this Letter who is order'd to join you as soon as the Winds and Waves will permit him.[3]

U1350/O/35/4

1

2

William Pitt to Major-General Jeffery Amherst

18 September 1758
Whitehall

[Duplicate copy, signed by Pitt]   [Received 9 November 1758[4]]

The King having judged proper that Major-General Abercromby should return to England, I have the Pleasure to acquaint You, that His Majesty having the firmest reliance on the Continuance of the Zeal & Abilities which you have already shewed for His Service, is most graciously pleased to appoint You to be Commander-in-Chief of the King's forces in North America, and you will accordingly receive herewith the proper Commissions & Instructions for this Purpose, which have been prepared, in every respect, the same, as was done for Major-General Abercromby,[5] and the inclosed Copy of a Circular Letter, which I have wrote to all the Governors will shew You, that they are ordered to correspond with, and obey You in the same manner as they were directed to do, with regard to His Majesty's former Commanders in Chief.[6]

The King hopes, agreably to what You mention in Your Letter of the 10th past, that this Dispatch will find You with the Army on the Continent of America, so that You will be able to enter immediately on the Command thereof.

I have nothing in Command from the King, in <u>addition</u> to the ample Instructions and Orders given to Major-General Abercromby, Copies of which You will see, by the inclosed Copy of my Letter to him, he is directed to put into Your Hands, and which by the 7th Article of your Instructions, You are ordered, <u>to consider, where necessary, as Instructions to Yourself</u>. And it is His Majesty's further Pleasure, that You do take all other vigorous Measures, which you shall judge practicable, & most conducive to annoy and distress the Enemy, and at the same time to secure and defend the King's Possessions from all Attacks & Inroads; And I am particularly to recommend to You the Recruiting and Compleating, as far as possible, in America, the Forces under Your Command.

I am to acquaint You, that His Majesty will wait, with Impatience, for the Event of the Expedition against Fort Du Quesne, under the Command of Brigadier General Forbes,[7] as well as of the very important Enterprize against Cadaraqui, on which Service General Abercromby mentions having detached Col° Bradstreet, an Officer, who from his great Activity & Knowledge of the Country, is so well qualified for an Attempt of such Difficulty.[8]

I most sincerely congratulate You on this very high & distinguishing Mark of His Majesty's Favor and Confidence, and beg Leave to assure You of my warmest Wishes for Success in all your Undertakings, in the Execution of the most important Command, with which the King has been pleased to honor You.

U1350/O/20/4

3
Major-General Jeffery Amherst to the Provincial Governors of New Hampshire, Massachusetts, Rhode Island. Connecticut, New York, New Jersey, Pennsylvania, Maryland and Virginia[9]

New York

[Copy in Secretary's hand]   13 December 1758

The King having been pleased to appoint me Commander in Chief of all His Majesty's Forces in North America, and having at the same time Signified to me His Royal pleasure that I should Correspond with and apply to all His Majesty's Governors on the Continent for their Aid and Assistance in carrying /ᵒⁿ the Service pointed out to me, I am in obedience to those Commands to acquaint you that although I have not as yet any particular Orders relative to the Operations of the ensuing Campaign, I imagine they will require the same number of Provincial Troops that were Voted by the respective Provinces & Colonies this year. And it will likewise be necessary in order to carry those Operations the more effectually into Execution that those Troops Should be at the place of rendezvous as early in the Spring as possible. I would therefore recommend it to you, if the Troops raised by your Province (or Colony) for the Services of last Campaign are not already disbanded that you would move your Assembly to continue them in their pay during the Winter, which will not only be a great saving in point of time, but by what I can understand a great saving of expence to the Province (or Colony), wherefore I hope you will the more easily succeed in your Application. But if it should happen that before the receipt of this Letter, those Troops had already been disbanded in that case I most desire that You will lose no time in using your influence with your Assembly to move them to order new Levies and to cause these to be provided with the usual necessaries, and to be ready by the time the Season will admitt their taking the Field.

Having also received H.M.ˢ Orders to recruit and Compleat the Regiments now serving on the Continent, I am likewise to beg Your Countenance and Protection to the Officers, I shall have Occasion to send, as well as to those that have already been sent by my Predecessor on that Service, and that you will be Aiding and Assisting unto them in the Execution thereof.

WO/34/36 fol. 157¹⁰

4
Major-General Jeffery Amherst to Sir William Johnson¹¹

	New York
[Copy in Secretary's hand]	13 December 1758

The King having been Pleased to honor me with the Chief Command of all His Forces in North America and having directed me, to keep up a Correspondance with You, <u>as sole Agent and Superintendant of the Northern Indians</u>, and to assist You in Endeavouring to engage the said Indians to take Part and Act with the Kings Forces in all such Operations as I should judge most Expedient; I am in Obedience to those Commands to Acquaint You with my Arrival here, and to signify to You that as It is my intentions to begin the Operations of the Ensuing Campaign, as early in the next Spring as the Season will admitt of; and that as it will be greatly for His Majesty's Service to engage as many as you can of the Indians within your Department to take part in those Operations and Act with His Majesty's Forces, I am to recommend to you to use all Your Weight and Influence, to engage as many of them, as possible, for those Purposes; and to desire that You will report to me so soon as Conveniently you can, the Number you think You shall be able to engage adding thereto such further Informations & Intelligences as you shall think requisite and Necessary to enable me to give you the Assistance I am Directed.

WO/34/38 fol. 52[12]

5
Governor James De Lancey to Major-General Jeffery Amherst

New York,
23 December 1758
[Holograph]   [Receipt not dated]

I received your letter of the 13th instant last Saturday and as I had conferred with your Excellency on the principal matters in it I did not think an immediate answer necessary, it is however of such a nature as to require one tho' late. In the first place Your Excellency may be assured, that I shall from inclination as well as duty give you all the aid and assistance I can in carrying on the Services what are or shall be pointed out to you.

As to raising the same number of men as was done this year, I may tell your Excellency, my apprehension that I am afraid it will not be practicable, this Province having lost many men at Tienderoga and by sickness afterwards, however I shall use my utmost efforts for that end, and I make no doubt, that whatever number I can obtain, will be ready at the Rendezvous at the time appointed and as soon as the season will admit, as they were before.

Before your Excellency wrote your letter to me, the troops of this Province were disbanded, and being raised on the publick faith that they should not be obliged to serve beyond the first of December they could not be kept up longer without a breach of it . . .[13]

WO/34/29 fol. 24

6
Colonel John Bradstreet to Major-General Jeffery Amherst

Albany
23 December 1758
[Holograph]   [Received 26 December 1758]

I . . . beg leave to acquaint you I conceive the necessary preparations to be made and provided for the next campaign this way to be so extensive, expensive & will take up so much time & workmen that it becomes absolutely necessary the whole should be laid before your Excellency soon for your approbation or such alterations as you may judge proper and that I am ready to attend you whenever you may think proper and as I would have this letter get to your hands as soon as possible I send it by express and in the mean time I shall begin building some battoes in lieu of those distroy'd & lost.

WO/34/57 fol. 15

7
Major-General Jeffery Amherst to Brigadier-General John Forbes

New York
[Copy in Secretary's hand]   25 December 1758

On my arrival here the 12th Instant, I met with the most welcome and pleasing Reception I cou'd have wished, on the Receipt of Your Letter of the 26th & 30th of November, which wanted nothing added to it to have compleated my Wishes, but a better Account of your own Health.

I most sincerely give you Joy of this Signal Success of his Majesty's Arms, in taking this very important Post of Fort du

Quesne by the Troops under your Command; This certainly will reconcile and fix the various Tribes of Indians to Our Interest, and will be of the utmost Consequence in the future Operations of the War; as well as insuring a quiet Settlement to many of his Majesty's Subjects at present.

I find by your Letter that you have applied to M.G. Abercromby for his Orders & Instructions in case you took the Place, which you now desire to have Directions about. I have shew'd your Letter to Gen. Abercromby, who says, that you on the spot cou'd judge much better than he cou'd of what was best to be done for H.M's. Service, and as his Majesty has been most graciously pleased, on M.G. Abercomby's desiring to go to England, to confer on me the very great Honor of the Command of the Troops in North America, I must now join in Opinion with Gen. Abercromby that from the Events that have happen'd under your Eyes, and being Master of Fort de Quesne, no one can better judge of the Advantages to be taken for the Protection of the Country, and for the Good of his Majesty's Service, and I must desire that you will make the Disposition for the Quarters of the Troops under your Command, in the manner, that you shall think the most conducive thereto. At this Distance it appears to me absolutely necessary to leave a sufficient Force at Pittbourg[14] to keep Post there, for which a Blockhouse is soon built, if the Fort is so ruin'd as not to be made Use of. The Garrison is in no Danger of being attacked by the Enemy, the only Difficulties are to cover them from the Weather, and supply them with Provisions, and I think we shou'd at any Rate rather struggle through these Difficulties than abandon the Post . . .[15]

WO/34/44 fols 236–7

8
Major-General Jeffery Amherst to Colonel John Bradstreet

New York

[Holograph copy]   26 December 1758

Your letter of the 23[d] Inst. was deliverd to me this morning, the necessary preparations for the Campaign will undoubtedly take up a great deal of time, & I had already spoke to B^r G^l Gage, who will see you soon at Albany, of my present intentions, which are, to get every thing in such readiness, as that we may be sure of no failure, in whatever will be wanted for acting offensively at the earliest time, & I should be glad to know the present state of the Battoes, & you will be so good to provide every thing for compleating the number. I should be glad to have every thing so forward, as that nothing may fail of being ready at a proper time, & I would not, yet do more than that, for fear it should prove to be an unnecessary expence.[16]

I hope soon to be much more explicit on this subject for I am now in confidence to tell you I have not as yet any orders as to the operations of the Campaign, but I expect them every day, if I should not receive any my inclinations will be to act offensively, as much as possible. I shall talk fully to B^r G^l Gage on this subject, & I must desire you will forward everything so far with him, of what can be prepared at Albany, that nothing may be wanted, & I shall then desire that you will be so good to come here, when I hope to settle everything for the Campaign.

WO/34/58 fol. 13

9
Major-General James Wolfe to Major-General Jeffery Amherst

[Bath?]

29 December 1758

[Holograph]   [Received 14 March]

Upon my arriving in England, I learnt that the command in America had devolved upon you, & that an order was gone to keep me there; I went immediately to the Mareschal[17] and told him, that I had no objection to serving in that Country, & was ready to return upon the first order. We had some discussion concerning the navigation of the River St Lawrence, & the project of besieging Quebec, and I found it was a settled Plan to carry on two separate attacks, one on the side of Lake George and one up the River; this much passed at our first conversation with this addition, that I express'd my desire to go up the River, but to be excused from taking the chief direction of such a weighty enterprize. I came immediately to this place, but in about a week was called back to Town, to be present at a meeting of some of the principal Officers of State, who were to examine into and give Sanction to the intended operation. The Mareschal questioned me upon the disposition of the Troops and how they lay most conveniently for the different attempts, I named the following Corps as a part of the Army to act in the River; Forbes, Braggs, Otways, Amhersts, Kennedy, Anstruther & 2^n Batt^n of Americans, & the three Companies of Grenadiers in Louisburg under Major Murray[18] . . . This body was thought much too small for the undertaking and I was desired to name some Regiments upon the Continent to reinforce it; accordingly Webb's, Lascelle's & Frasers highlanders /were mentioned, under this limitation, that if the Government thought fit to send the 8 companies of Grenad^{rs} compleat from Gibraltar, to be commanded by Persons That I should chuse, or, if they wou'd send a good Batt^n from Ireland, one of the three last mention'd Regiments might remain with you upon the Continent. What resolution has been taken in consequence of these deliberations you are no doubt informed of. This one important Point, I must beg to lay the greatest stress upon, that to second your operations with the vigour you have a right to expect, great Plenty of provisions must be furnished as we have no resource in case of Accidents, & must depend wholly upon the /first supplies from the Continent . . . We shou'd Sail /from the Rendezvous with six month's Provision, & have two month's more in reserve at Louisburg. Mollasses, are as necessary to preserve the health, as Bread is to the life of a Soldier feeding upon salt meat; and to men accustom'd to Drink, a little rum well applied (notwithstanding all that can be said upon the Subject) is not only wholesome & beneficial in the proper, & moderate use of it, but absolutely necessary in such operations, as our's are like to be.[19]

I can't promise you that we shall take Quebec, because I neither know the Place, nor the People appointed to defend it – but this I will venture to promise, that let the Fleet carry us up, and we will find employment for a good part of the Force of Canada, and make your progress towards Montreal, less difficult and dangerous; and unless the Enemy can contrive to throw early & Powerfull succours, I should imagine that the two Armies might meet and unite for their destruction. I should have told you, that during my absence from London, Mr Pitt had named me to the King for the command in the River, upon which I told the Mareschal, that unless he could give me the assistance of such Officers, as I shou'd name to him, he wou'd do me a great kindness to appoint some other Person to the chief direction and permit me to serve under him; this I fear was not understood, as it deserved to be, & People think it civil to doubt our sincerity, sometimes in matters where it is most our true Interest to deal plainly. In short, they have put this heavy task upon my Shoulders, and I find nothing encouraging in the undertaking, but the warmest & most earnest desire to discharge so great a trust to your satisfaction as my General, and to his Majesty and the Publick I shall spare no pains, and shou'd be happy if the sacrifice of my own health & constitution, or even my Life, cou'd any how contribute to bring this bloody war, to an honourable & speedy conclusion . . .

WO/34/46B fols 286–9

10
Proposals for the Expedition to Quebec

29 December 1758

[Unsigned memorandum][20]   [Received 7 April 1759]

As it is thought absolutely necessary for the King's Service, that Genl Amherst remain upon the Continent as Commander in Chief to direct all Operations, it is proposed that, for the Reduction of Quebec.

A Detachment, hereafter named, shall be made, out of the Army commanded by Major-General Amherst.

That Colonel Wolfe shall have the Command of the said Detachment, with the Rank of Major-General, for, and during the

Expedition to Quebec only, after which he will return to his Rank of Brigadier, to act in Consequence of such Orders as he shall receive from the said General Amherst.[21]

Brigadiers to act under the same Restrictions: Monckton, Murray, Burton . . .[22]

U1350/O/20/29

11
Major-General Jeffery Amherst to Brigadier-General Thomas Gage

[Holograph copy]

New York
31 December 1758

Brigadier General Stanwix, having made application to come to New York & it being absolutely necessary that the important post of Albany should not be left without an Officer of Rank & Experience, I must desire you will please to repair there on the receipt of this, & take on you the command of the Troops in Albany, the advanced posts on the Hudson River to Fort Edward, & those on the Mohawk River to Fort Stanwix the troops at Schenectady, & the late Ld Howe's Reg^t /$^{\&\ your\ own}$ in Cantonment below Albany.

On your arrival at Albany you will please to inform Colonel Haldimand or the Officer commanding in Fort Edward, as likewise the Officers commanding the different posts between Albany & Fort Edward, of my having appointed you to this command, & you will demand a return of the state & condition of the troops, in Fort Edward, from which return, if you judge it necessary to increase their numbers, you will advance whatever you may think proper, as an additional force for the defence of that place, & though I think it hardly possible for the enemy to come in any force, against it, it will be right that the Commanding officers of each post have proper signals ordered to be made on the approach of an enemy, so that it may be immediately known in all the different posts, & the troops to advance, as you shall judge necessary, my intentions being, not only to put it out of the power

11

of the enemy, to attack any of our advanced posts, but to march out, & attack them whenever they will give an opportunity by their venturing near our posts.

WO/34/46A fols 136–7

WLC/AP/4

12

Major-General Jeffery Amherst to Governor Francis Bernard

New York

[Copy in Secretary's hand]   4 January 1759

The Representation of the Officers of the Inniskilling Regiment Quartered at Trenton and Burlington in His Majestys Province of New Jersey setting forth the difficulties they labour under at those places with respect to Billets, compells me to apply to you, not doubting but upon the receipt hereof, You will issue the proper & Necessary Orders, to remove all Complaints of that kind in the Province, where you preside, more particularly as you are so well versed in the Laws & Customs of the Mother Country, which in times of Actual War, not only allott Quarters to every Officer, from an Ensign to a field Marshall, but Subjects every Householder where there are not a sufficiency of publick houses, or those are not fitt for the reception of Officers, to receive and admit so many of them, as the Exigency and Circumstances of times and places may require; Agreeable to that custom which undoubtedly must take place over /all His Majestys Dominions and particularly those where the seat of War lies. I shall expect that where there are not a Sufficient Number of publick houses, or those not properly accommodated for the reception of Officers, you will direct the Magistrates of the respective places within Your Government, where this may happen, to grant such Officers billets on private houses, or in default thereof a proper a proper allowance to pay for them as is the Custom of this City.

From the time the war has Continued on this Continent, I had hoped all those matters had been well understood and that every Province & Colony were Informed of every necessary they are, agreeable to the Act of Quartering, Obliged to furnish His Majesties Troops with;[23] and indeed I must own I have met with no difficulty on that head, but from the Colony of Connecticut, who from what Mistaken notion I cannot say, have likewise taken it for granted, that they are not Obliged to Quarter any Officers above the rank of a subaltern and accordingly refused such to all others, which having also been represented to me, I forthwith wrote to the Governor of that Colony, to the same purpose I now do to you, and enclosed to him a Copy of the within agreement between the Province of the Massachusetts Bay and the deputy Quarter Master General, which I desired might be Complied with: as the Contents of it are entirely agreeable to the Exigencies of the present times, and Conformable to the Customs of the Mother Country during the War . . .[24]

WO/34/31 fol. 160

13
By order of the Commander-in-Chief, Major-General Jeffery Amherst

New York
[Draft copy]   12 January 1759

His Excellency Major-General Amherst is pleased to pardon any Soldiers who have deserted from the Regiments in America & have inlisted and are now serving in other Corps in America, in which Corps they are to remain, & likewise to pardon any deserter from a Regiment in America who shall voluntarily join his Colours on or before the first day of March next, which deserter on application to the Commanding Officer of any Regiment, or the Officers Commanding in any of the Quarters of the Regiments Serving in America, shall receive a passport to join the Regiment to which he belongs, and in joining his Corps, Shall receive pay from the date of the said passport.

PS This to be printed in the New York papers, Philadelphia,

Boston &ca., and Colonel Townshend to send a Copy of it to the Governors of Nova Scotia & Cape Breton.

WO/34/79 fol. 5

14
Major-General Jeffery Amherst to Rear Admiral Philip Durell

New York

[Unsigned holograph copy]   14 January 1759

. . . I mentioned to You when I was at Halifax that I would Join with You in demanding, and use my best endeavors to procure from the different Governors any number of Seamen that might be wanted for manning the Fleet under Your Command early in the Spring. I find the difficulty of getting Seafaring people so very great, that Men cannot be got here for two Transports bound to England, and I am told the only Chance of pressing any is by Cruizing off this Port, Rhode Island and Boston, and how far that may be feasible You are the best Judge. But as I am very Sensible that nothing can distress the Enemy more than hindering any Succours getting up the River St Lawrence, if You are in want of Men I will write to Governor Pownall to desire him to furnish from the Massachusetts Government the number You may desire, which shall be allowed in the Quota to be furnished to the Army. I know there are some Towns on the Eastern Coast of the Massachusetts Government, particularly Gloucester who would furnish Men to the Fleet, provided they are insured of their being released so Soon as that Service is over and their Wages to be paid, sent home, & not to be forced from this Country, and those Towns to be allowed that Number, in the Men they furnish for the Provincial Troops.

I have so great reason to be satisfied of Governor Pownalls Zeal and Alacrity in forwarding every thing for the good of His Majestys Service, and am so convinced of the great advantages that must ensue from the early Cruizing of the Fleet, that I doubt not but Governor Pownall will readily comply with it upon

Application, and I shall most willingly lessen the numbers to be furnished to the Army, if absolutely wanted in the Fleet to forward that very essential Service.

WO/34/42 fol. 201

15
Major-General Jeffery Amherst to Governor Brigadier-General Whitmore[25]

New York

[Holograph copy] 16 January 1759

I intend to encrease the number of light Infantry of each Batt: for the next Campaign, to be appointed on the same manner as the last, and as I imagine, it will very probably happen that not more than two Batt[s] will be left in Louisbourg, & that those which remain I think will be the better for having their light Infantry fixed, I beg you will please to order the Commanding Officers of the Battalions to chuse out the properest men for that service . . .[26]

The sooner the Officers are appointed & the men chose for the light Infantry the better, & pray be so good to order that they practice firing ball that they may be good marks men, the Reg[ts] should likewise fire ball, as much as may be necessary to accustom the men to it.

The officers will find out a great conveniency in having small Horsemen's Tents, I would recommend it to the whole, for if we come to any marching in this country, the great Tents will certainly be left behind.

You will please to order that the Officers are to receive their Portions of Provisions in the same manner as has been allowed to the different ranks in America, & that they be paid four pence p[r] portion in lieu of Provisions that they do not draw this allowance to begin on the first of Novem[r].

B[r] G. Forbes, writes to me on the 6th ins[t] from Shippensbourg, that he was better in his health & hoped soon to reach Philadelphia, but by all I hear of him, he is in a very bad way, & 'tis not thought he can recover.

Gen¹ Abercromby is very well, is to sail in the Kennington on Thursday next if the winds will permit him.

As soon as the operations of the campaign are fixed, I shall rob you of some of the light french arms for the light Infantry, everything seems to promise well & I hope next Campaign will set all matters right.

WO/34/17 fols 161–2

16
Major-General Jeffery Amherst to Field Marshal Viscount John Ligonier

New York

[Holograph copy]   18 January 1759

As M.G. Abercromby is setting out for England, I can't omit seizing the occasion to write, though you will be better, & more particularly informed of the state & condition of every thing in this country, than by all I can write.

I have done every thing that I imagine, can conduce for being prepared for as early a campaign, as the weather in this country will allow, appearances look well, & if we can hinder the french from throwing in great succours by the River Sᵗ Lawrence, *il me semble nous avons beau Jeu.*

I have wrote to Mʳ Pitt which your Lordship will see, & I have taken the liberty to write my thoughts from the present view of things in this country; I was very near sending some troops to joyn what Provincials could have been collected on the occasion, to have tryed at the Mississippi & Mobile, for, from the informations, & all the intelligence I can pick up since I came here I think the enemy might be drove from thence in winter better than in summer, & I would have tryed it, but as I must have taken only half Battalions, & left the rest in their quarters for recruiting, & preparing all necessaries for the campaign, I thought it might exceed the time, that these Regᵗˢ might be wanted for other services before that Could have been effected, & that I should be lopping off a branch, when it would be time that I should try at the Stem & the Root.

16

Nothing has happened here, since I last did myself the honour of writing to your Lordship, when I acquainted you that I intended to increase the light Infantry of each Reg^t, which I have now ordered shall consist of 1 Capt. 2 Lieut^s. 1 Ensign 4 Serg^{ts}. 1 Drummer & 100 Rank & File in the Battalions of a thousand men; and of 1 Capt. 1 Lieut. 1 Ensign, 3 Serg^{ts}. 1 Drummer & 70 Rank & File in the Reg^{ts} of seven hundred; my Reg^t being of different numbers furnishes 88 for the light Infantry, this will make a fine light alert Corps for this country, & I intend they shall all be good marksmen, & that all the Reg^{ts} likewise shall be well practised in firing ball.

Capt Ord has represented to me, that the Guns which they are obliged to make use of in the Forts, are extremely bad, five out of eight which were sent from hence, & ought to have been proved before they sent them burst, he thinks 20, 18 pounders & as many more 12 pounders on Garrison carriages are greatly wanted here, with some travelling carriages of both kinds, to make use of occasionally.

I have order'd Colonel Williamson here to settle everything, that nothing may be neglected which can be prepared, he has made some demands of men, Artillery, Ammunition, & Stores which I hope your Lordship will think reasonable should be sent, he does it from a conviction of their being wanted for carrying on His Majesty's Service, for which his Zeal & *bonne Volonté* cannot be too much commended.

I have sent B^r G^l Gage (who has taken unto himself a wife) to command at Albany, with orders *de donner dessus à la première occasion*, that may offer by the Enemy's venturing near any of our posts . . .

Recruiting goes on very well & I hope with the Drafts that are coming, everything will be compleat.[27] Brig^r Gage's light infantry who wanted a great many men are compleated, the Yankees love dearly a brown coat . . .

U1350/O/35/5

WLC/AP/SLIPCASE

17
Brigadier-General Thomas Gage to Major-General Jeffery Amherst

Albany

[Holograph]   21 January 1759

. . . I have told Genl Stanwix, what you mentioned to me in Regards to Colonel Bradstreet; we are to meet on that Business tomorrow, & I believe it will be found necessary, that he should set out for York in a very few Days, & fix matters finally with you; for if he executes what he proposes should be done, no Time is to be lost. He proposes besides building Batteaux, to make a Number of ox Carts & purchase oxen, as a better, & Cheaper Method, than hiring Them, as heretofore, also to make a Number of Waggons, that you may have less occasion for the Country Carriages, which are always sent with a very ill will; & the worst staff the Country People can collect. These are his Reasons, and was it the Beginning of a War, or might we expect many Campains on this side, I believe him in the Right. I think it's highly Necessary that materials for Building Batteaux should be immediately provided, & the work-men engaged that every Thing may be in Readiness whenever you think proper to order that work to go forward; & this I hope we shall fix tomorrow, & tho' it will be an Expence, it is an unavoidable one, for you will not else have Them ready so soon as you may have occasion for Them. Colonel Bradstreet will fix with you how the other Carriages shall be provided, as also the Inlisting Batteaux-men, which He should begin early, at least before the Provincials are raised, or we shall fail in that Respect, in the same manner as last year. And I am informed, the Provincials are so disgusted at being employed in that Kind of Service last year, That they will now make it a Condition of their Enlistment, That they shall neither serve as Batteaux-men or waggoners.

WO/34/46A fols 4–5

18

By his Excellency General Amherst, Commander-in-Chief of his Majesty's Forces in North America

New York

[Copy in Secretary's hand]   29 January 1759

Whereas a number of Battoe Men will be wanted for his Majesty's Service [in] the ensuing Campaign I have thought fit to publish the following proposals for the encouragement of such persons as are inclin'd to enter into that service, Viz., That they be form'd into Companys of 50 men each with a Captain & one Lieutenant, the Captain ten shillings per day the Lieut six shillings per day and each private man three shilling per day New York currency with 20 days advance pay to be paid the 10th day of March next at Boston, Rhoad Island, Harford, New York, Elizabeth Town and Philadelphia and to be found in provisions agreable to the practice of the Army. Every fit man for a Captain that raises 30 Men shall have the Commission, likewise every fit man for a Lieutenant that raises 20 men shall have the Commission, and every man is to be well Cloth'd and be furnish'd with a good Firelock, powder Horn, Shot Bagg a cover for the lock of his Gun with 3 Pounds of Ball fit for his gun and a good Blanket; the whole to be at Albany the 20th March next without fail there to be reviewd by proper Officers and no Man shall be accepted in that Service but young, strong, active Men accustom'd to hardship and the use of a Gun, and to remain in the Service during the Campaign and no longer. All who intend to engage in the above Service as Captain are to send their Names & places of abode to Col Bradstreet at Albany as soon as possible.

WO/34/79 fol. 12

19

Major-General Jeffery Amherst to Captain Joshua Loring

New York

[Copy in Secretary's hand]   1 February 1759

In Confidence that the operations of the ensuing Campaign may be carried up the River St Lawrence, and will require a number of whaleboats, I take this early Opportunity of Acquainting you with their number and dimensions, that no time may be lost in procuring the same; you will therefore, upon receipt hereof, Apply to & Contract with such builders as you shall think capable of undertaking, and compleating on or before the latter End of April – Fifty Whaleboats, 28 feet in the Keel; 5 feet 2 Inches broad; 25 Inches deep; 34 feet from Stern to Stern . . .

But if in your knowledge in these matters You are certain the before mentioned number of Boats, every /^{Way} compleated as above, can be got ready, (altho not order'd till three weeks after the receipt of these orders) within the time prescribed, You may delay giving directions about them till then, by which time I shall be more certain of their real necessity and if not wanted, be able to save the Expence of them to the Publick . . .

WO/34/64 fol. 182

20
Major-General Jeffery Amherst to Christopher Kilby
New York
[Copy in Secretary's hand] 3 February 1759

I am to acquaint you, that I have order'd all the provisions at Albany that can be spared to be forwarded to Fort Edward, Saratoga, Stillwater, and as near the Fort as possible, and that I have likewise directed some of them to be sent /^{to} Schenectady . . .

And I must further, particularly recommend it to You, to cause a thousand half Barrels of good pork (which may be wanted on many occasions) to be prepared for Transportation.

I should likewise be glad, that a Number of Oxen could be drove up to the Lake, and be there at the time of the arrival of the Troops on that spot which I design shall be the very first day after the season permitts: If therefore, a Sufficient number of Barrels and a proper quantity of salt was provided for that purpose, it would forward things greatly. Upon the whole, I shall depend on your utmost Zeal & care, in having such quantities of provisions ready, that, whatever our Motions may be, either from the successes which I hope will attend His Majestys Arms during the Campaign, or from the Movement that we may be forced to, we shall always be in a Situation with regard to provisions to follow & Execute the Operations that will tend to the good of His Majestys Service and to distress the Enemy.

WO/34/69 fol. 130

WLC/AP/4

21
Major-General Jeffery Amherst to Brigadier-General John Forbes

New York

[Holograph draft]   4 February 1759

S^r Jn St Clair delivered to me your letter of the 28th of Janry[28] with the Indian Conference at Pittsbourg, which like most other conferences with those Scoundrels, ends with their asking for Rum, however it is necessary for us to try to make them our friends, which they will be if they think we are superior to the French.

I rejoice at your having found the Cannon that the Enemy had thrown into the River, all the force the french can /^now bring against Pittsbourg, cannot possibly hurt us, if the garrison does its duty.

I wait with impatience for news from England, as I hope, that so soon as a Packet comes I may immediately set out for Philadelphia.

S^r Jn St Clair acquaints me that there have been some few difficulties /^with the ~~in furnishing~~ with the necessaries furnished for the troops in their quarters; I have therefore given him a Copy of what the Massachusetts government agreed to, & ~~which~~ I hope that will remedy all ~~difficulties~~ Disputes.

As to the Embassy of the head warriors of the Alliganey & Ohio Indians whatever their Business may be, you may be assured that what you shall judge right to do in it, cannot but meet with my approbation . . .

WO/34/44 fols 243–4

22

Brigadier-General Thomas Gage to Major-General Jeffery Amherst

Albany

18 February 1759

[Holograph]   [Received 24 February 1759]

. . . I hope the Enemy's Indians will not go off unpunished, should They make a Second Attempt near our Posts . . . But I despair of this being done by Rangers only, Judging from the many Pursuits of those People after Indians during my service in this Country, in which, They have never once come up with Them. The light Inf^{ty} of the Reg^t headed by a brisk off^r, with some of the boldest Rangers mixed with Them, to prevent their being lost in the woods will be the most likely People to effect This Service. – No Rangers are yet arrived nor do I expect to see many till towards the middle of next month, notwithstanding your Letters and Advertisements; when you are better acquainted with Them, you will find Them not very alert in obeying orders, especially when at a Distance & at Home. They have never been on a proper Footing, & want to be new modelled.

I understand by letters from Col^o Haldimand, that Major Rogers has made you Proposals, concerning the Stockbridge Indians, That they may be again employed next Campain; Rogers has sent me four Letters, two, for each of the Jacobs, (who were Captains of those Indians) . . . These Indians were last Campaign a great Nuisance to the Army, & did no manner of service: some People say they were not properly managed, I own myself ignorant of the management that is proper for those gentry, can only say, that neither Orders or Entreatys could prevail on them to do Service, always lying drunk in their Hutts, or Firing round the camp . . .

There are Complaints throughout the Country, That many People have not been payed for work done for the Publick, this has happened either from People's Ignorance where to make Application, or Neglect of officers who Employed their sloops or Carriages and from various other Causes: There has been also great Change of hands, & nobody will pay what did not happen in

22

his own Time. From whatever Cause this Neglect of Payment has happened, The Publick Credit is hurt by it, & the Publick service will of Course suffer. If Notice was given by Advertisements for all Persons that have any Demands, to give Them in by such a Time to any person appointed to receive Them, to examine the same & Pay such as are found just; it might be of great use, and induce The Country-People to bring in their Carriages &c². more chearfully & without being forced.

WO/34/46A fols 11–12

23
Major-General Jeffery Amherst to Brigadier-General Thomas Gage

New York

[Copy in Secretary's hand]   26 February 1759

Cap¹ Jacobs of the Stockbridge Indians was with me some time since; I sent him with a Letter to Major Rogers, to give in his Proposals to him, & directed Major Rogers to report to me his Opinion of their Services. I know what a vile Crew they are, and I have as bad an Opinion of those lazy Rum drinking Scoundrels as any One can have; I shall however take him into His Majesty's Service, for this next Campaign, to keep them from doing mischief elsewhere, and as I am in hopes We shall be able to act offensively and successfully, they may be of more Service, than what they have hitherto been. The French are afraid of them, and tho' they have but very little reason for it, it will be right not only to keep up their terror, but to increase it as much as we can, which the name of Numbers [sic] will do, and I shall for that reason Engage as many of them as I can for the Ensuing Campaign . . .

I am sorry to hear by your Letter, as well as by One I have received from Major Claphane of yᵉ Scurvy making its appearance at Fort Stanwix; I approve entirely of your design of sending up fresh men, and Quarters of refreshment will soon recover the relieved, and this may easily be Executed without a formal relief of the Garrison.

23

Mr Appy just now tells me that the great Warriour Capt Jacobs marched off to Fort Edward without taking the Letter to Major Rogers, as he was directed to do; I therefore send it you, to forward to Major Rogers, and pray acquaint Major Rogers, that time may not be lost; I shall leave it to him to fix finally with Capt Jacobs for bringing his Company into the Field as soon as possible.

I Fear there are many Complaints in the Country of Non Payments, and from various Causes; the People naturally Litigious are glad to wait a change of hands to encrease their demands, or to make such as they know would not be allowed at all, by those who are thoroughly acquainted with them. I have seen instances of this kind already; nothing should be left unsettled and I will of-[offer?] an Advertisement to that Purpose . . .

WO/34/46A fols 144A–B

WLC/AP/4

24
Colonel Henry Bouquet to Major-General Jeffery Amherst
Philadelphia
1 March 1759
[Holograph]   [Received 3 March 1759]

Having been left on the frontier to dispose the Troops in the different Forts upon the Communication with the Ohio, and forward a Sufficient Supply of Provisions to these Posts: I received ten days ago orders from Brigadier General Forbes to come to this Town; But found him So far gone that I could not See him, nor do any business.

Expecting daily to See your Excellency here, I differred to give you an Account of the Situation of affairs in this department: But the last Intelligences I received last night from Pittsburgh, appears to be of too much consequence to loose any time in transmitting them to you.

All the accounts of the Campaign remains unsetled. The Wagons and Pack Horse requires chiefly to be paid as soon as possible, and any further delay would be attended with a general dissatisfaction in the People, and be of bad Consequence for the Service of the next Campaign.

I Should not even be Surprised if the assembly of this Province Should represent the Case to you by their Governor, and postpone their Proceeding on the King's Service, till you are pleased to give your orders for the paiment of Said Carriages.[29]

The Provincial Troops of Pensilv[a] are not 900 Effective men, and no orders are given yet, or money raised to recruit them.

The 100 men left at Cumberland of the Maryland Troops are reduced by desertion to 25, and in a Short time I expect that Fort will be abandoned; The men having neither Pay nor certainty of receiving any.[30]

Several Sums are due for the Provisions Sent to Pittsburgh, which can not be paid without your orders.

I must also inform your Excellency that there are Some Indians of Consequence in this Town: They are Deputies of the Six Nations Settled on the Ohio, and they insist upon an answer to their message; The Contents of which I suppose Brigadier Forbes has communicated to you.

I shall not trouble you with any more Particulars, Intending only to inform you of the necessity of Sending your orders to prevent the Confusion in which we are ready to fall, by the unhappy Sickness and approaching loss of Brigad[r] Forbes; The Doctors not expecting that he can live two days.

WO/34/40 fol. 73

25
Major-General Jeffery Amherst to Colonel John Bradstreet

New York

[Holograph copy]   5 March 1759

. . . Cap[t] Loring is at present employed in building Whale Boats intended for the service of troops in the Transport Ships. I would be prepared for every thing that the situation of the enemy, and the number of His Majesty's troops which are to act this campaign, may put in my power to attempt. I have named the 10th of April, to press things forward as much as I can, and I would begin to act from the first moment that the Season will permit, at the same time I am to tell you in confidence that the time prescribed to me from England is the first of May, and as that will give you time for building battoes at Albany, for any service that may be hereafter thought proper to execute by the Lake Ontario I shall be very glad that you will be prepared for it, as you will have the workmen with you. This will take off a very great expence that would be incurred in building them at Boston. Capt Loring may finish what he is about there & then I think the sooner he come to Albany the better.

I have given a warrant to you on Mr Mortier for £3000, that he may give you the necessary credit for paying the advance pay to the Battoe men &^{c}. & as Mr Normandy acquaints me he waited for your orders I send him to you with this which will be quicker than the Post, & give you time for sending proper people to the towns where the Battoe men &^{c}. are to repair.

The Purchases of Oxen & Horses must yet remain some little time, for no money is come; you will however be prepared & at a certainty where to have them, when called for . . .

WO/34/58 fols 15–16

26
Major-General James Wolfe to Major-General Jeffery Amherst

HMS *Neptune* at sea
6 March 1759
[Received 13 April]

[Holograph]

The Admiral dispatches the Lizard with letters to you and to the Governors of the Province, and this opportunity offers very conveniently to pay my respects to you, and to mentions some particulars relative to our undertaking.

We have undoubted intelligence . . . and are well assured that there are 30 to 40 store Ships, at Rochefort & Rochelle intended for the River St Lawrence; these Ships are to risk the Ice, & venture as early as possible into the River.

The Government has fitted out a vast Fleet, and put itself to an immence expence for this Quebec expedition, knowing well that a blow there is Death to the Colony, and yet, they have fail'd in the most material article, which is <u>The Number of Troops</u> with submission to their judgement, it wou'd have been wiser to have secured it, by putting you at the head of 15 or 16 Battalions for this enterprize, and let the rest of your Army with the Militia, create what diversion they cou'd on the Tyconderoga side. The Fleet wou'd set you and your Army down within five miles of Quebec, and in a Month you are master of all Canada.

My Lord Ligonier has calculated that the Troops for the expedition amount to 12000 men, concluding that Recruits will arrive from Martinico, sufficient to compleat the Regiments, whereas, there is the greatest probability, that these People are scorched long since; you know what the remains of a west India Campaign must be;[31] besides this uncertain refreshment there are 500 more it seems to be deducted from the two American Battalions for Halifax, and the Bay of Fundy.

By last year's experience of the Navigation of the Bay of Fundy, and by the dilatory proceedings of Colonies, I am apprehensive, that the Militias will not get to their posts in that Bay, so soon as we cou'd wish, and consequently, the two Battalions will be late at the rendezvous – as our success depends in a great measure upon an early beginning, I trust you will do your utmost to get us together as soon as possible, and in as great force as possible. It is mightily to be wish'd that we had 4 or 500 Pioneers from the Colonies to make our Fascines & Gabions, and to work at the entrenchments; an Army of 9000 men (for that I take to be the utmost) which is to invest and besiege an Army equal in number (I am fully persuaded, they will have as many) can spare but few hands to work at any distance from the Camp.

If, by accidents in the River, by the Enemy's resistance, by sickness, or slaughter in the army, or, from any other cause, we find, that Quebec is not likely to fall into our hands (persevering however to the last moment), I propose to set the Town on fire, with shells, to destroy the Harvest, Houses, & Cattle, both above & below, to send off as many Canadians as possible to Europe, & to leave famine and desolation behind me; belle resolution, & tres chretienne! [?], but we must teach these Scoundrels to make war in a more gentleman like manner.

If the french Fleet gets into the River before us, they will either post themselves at some narrow passage to obstruct our proceedings, or they will anchor above Quebec; in the first case it becomes a trial of naval skill, and in the last, I guess what is most likely to happen, they /<u>will be burnt</u>. But if Mr Durell is earlier than the Enemy, we have a fair prospect, and may then be in our power to assist your operations, by running up with Sloops & Schooners as high as the Fort de Chambly, to facilitate your debaeché [sic] into the River St Lawrence, and favour an attack upon Montreal, or your junction with the Troops under my orders; and here we shall find the very great use of a naval Force of this kind in the river St Lawrence, cruising between Quebec & Montreal, and I have no doubt but these small Vessels, will easily get by Quebec in the night.

It occurs to me that the French will endeavour to dispute the lake Champlain with you – because as they have Sloops & Schooners ready built upon that Lake, and you have none, they must be superior for a time, unless Mr Bradstreet constructs some Vessels at Tyconderoga or crown Point (with wonderful Expedition) able to encounter those of the Enemy, or unless he can place your Artillery upon floating Platforms or rafts of such a navigating nature, as can protect your Boats going down that Lake. The Marquis de Vaudreuil knows the importance of Quebec, & therefore I believe he will more than divide his Force, which make me judge & hope that Tyconderoga /^{& Crown Point} will soon fall into your hands.

Would it be possible to find an Indian of the Mohawk Tribe, cunning enough to bring me advice of your proceedings; we shall have a post at La Chaudiere, which might help him; The Messenger will not be under the necessity of crossing the River St Lawrence.

The moment we are landed at Quebec, I shall dispatch a Sloop to Boston, with intelligence of it, & with such other information, as I can pick up; and if afterwards I can corrupt a Huron (a thing not altogether impossible)[32] you may learn it, by a shorter Route . . .

WO/34/46B fols 292–5

27
Colonel John Bradstreet to Major-General Jeffery Amherst

Albany

10 March 1759

[Holograph]   [Receipt not dated]

I am honor'd with your Excellencys letter of the 5th instant and was in hopes of hearing from Mr Mortier but have not concerning the Credit you gave me with him – should it only be 3000£ York money it will not go far should we raise 2000 Battoe Men & 500 Drivers as their advance pay will be between seven & eight thousand pounds.

I have done the best I could to have them properly examin'd & paid their advance pay in the Several Towns directed by your Excellency and now write to Mr Mortier to establish what Credit he can give at Boston, New York & Pensilvania.

The Carpenters are all here and at work and every thing goes on very well as yet and I shall endeavour to keep it up.

I shall not fail of providing every thing necessary for an Attempt by Lake Ontario in time.

I beg leave to observe to your Excellency that there are large sums due to the People of this Country ever since Genl Shirleys time . . .

WO/34/57 fol. 22

28
Major-General Jeffery Amherst to Governor Thomas Pownall

New York

[Copy in Secretary's hand]   15 March 1759

Late last Night arrived the Mail by the General Wall Packet, who left Falmouth the 20th of January,[33] & early this morning I sent to the Post Office for your Letters which are only three in number, and which will be delivered to you together with this by Maj^r Scott.

By those Letters you will doubtless be informed that an Expedition up the River St Lawrence is intended & as this Expedition must take away a ~~great~~ Part of the Garrison of Louisbourg, I have, in Order to provide for the Security of that most important Place, received His Majesty's Orders to replace the Part of the Garrison that will be sent up the River by a Battalion of Provincials of not less than 1000 Men, to remain there in Garrison only so long as may be absolutely necessary and on a Certainty of Being relieved at the End of the Campaign by His Majesty's Regular Troops.

The greatest Part of the Troops in Nova Scotia and the Bay of Fundy, will likewise be ordered on the same Expedition, wherefore it will also be absolutely necessary to have a Body of Provincials to join what may remain of the King's Regular Troops, for the Protection of Halifax, the Province of Nova Scotia and the Bay of Fundy, who will be relieved in like Manner as those in the Garrison of Louisbourg; and that it may be entirely out of the Power of the Enemy to make any Attack on all or either of those Places I have received his Majesty's Commands to send 1500 Provincials for that Service.

Transports shall be provided at Boston or sent there to take the 2500 Men to their Destination, so early, that the troops from Halifax and Nova Scotia may be assembled at Louisbourg, to join the Part of that Garrison and other Regiments intended for the expedition, that the whole may be ready to sail from Louisbourg on or about the 7th May.

Altho' His Majesty has not particularly directed that the Troops of the Massachusetts Bay should be employ'd on this Expedition; yet from their Proximity to Nova Scotia; The Shortness of the Passage from Boston to it; The Saving it will be to the Publick in Transporting them by Sea rather than march them by Land from the different Parts of the Province to Albany; and the great Inclination I know the People of New England, particularly those of your Government, have always shewn to be employ'd up the River St Lawrence, have made me think it for the Good of the Service, and has determined me to give them the Preference upon this Occasion; for altho' I mention they are to

Garrison these Places only, yet I make no doubt but some of them may accompany the Regular Troops.

WO/34/27 fol. 132

29
Major-General Jeffery Amherst to Colonel George Williamson

New York

[Holograph draft]   15 March 1759

I have rec'd His Majesty's Orders that the battering Train & the Stores of every kind thereunto belonging shall forthwith be put in most perfect repair and order for immediate service (this is in obedience to orders, for I know every thing of that sort that you could possibly do, is done) that the same may be in readiness to be employed on the expedition against Quebec in the beginning of May, and I am informed that the necessary additions to the said Train and Stores were preparing in England to be sent from thence.

His Majesty's intentions are that the battering Train & Stores together with /^{three} Companies of the Royal Reg^t of Artillery should be embarked in such manner as to be at Louisbourg by the 20th of April.

You will obey any orders you may receive from the Lieutenant General and board of Ordnance with regard to detaching part of the Royal Reg^t of Artillery, and as the battering train with three Companies are ordered for the Expedition, you as the first Officer must of course take that command, which nothing but the very great importance of the expedition you are going on, and where I am sensible your presence will be of the greatest help towards the success, could induce me to permit you to quit that part of the service where I must be, and where your assistance would be a great benefit to me.

You will please to order the Officer next in command to you for the service on the continent, and make such disposition of the train & Stores &c. as will answer the service intended up the River, as well as that on the Continent.

31

There are Transports ordered from England, but to prevent any delays, or disappointments happening in their arriving too late, I have ordered immediately Transports to be taken up at Boston, for the above essential service, and I shall order a Reg^t to Boston to assist you in embarking the Artillery.[34]

You will please to send the necessary orders that every thing may be prepared for the embarkation so as to be at Louisbourg by the time directed, and on your arrival there, you will put yourself under the command of Maj^r Genl Wolfe, or the Officer Commandg the expedition to Quebec.

WO/34/79 fols 37–8

30
Major-General Jeffery Amherst to Captain Joshua Loring

New York

[Copy in Secretary's hand]   15 March 1759

Immediately upon Receipt hereof You will Cause the Number of Fifty Whale Boats, which I directed You by my Letter of the 1st of February to have built, to be Augmented to the Number of Seventy, all to be ready by the first of April next, and You will also lose no time in taking up at Boston, 3000 Tons of Transport Ships, to be ready by the first of April: vizt Double Deck'd Vessels at 13^s Sterling a Ton; Single at Nine, or Ten at most; the whole upon the same Conditions as last Year, with this difference only, that they are, if ordered, to Sail without Convoy; and the option of discharging them at the Port of Boston, or giving them a month's pay, if discharged at any other Port in America, to be in the Crown.

The Enclosed Rule for Measuring them to be strictly conformed to.

We shall likewise want by the time above mentioned Forty Schooners or Sloops, that will draw but little Water; And as they are intended for the Service of the Troops on the Expedition up the River St Lawrence, You are the best Judge what Sorts are the fittest for that purpose and You will provide them accordingly.

You will also, privately, Enquire at what Rate Rum and Molasses can be purchased at Boston, and to send me notice of the Prices, and the Quantitys that can be got . . .[35]

WO/34/64 fol. 186

31

Major-General Jeffery Amherst to Brigadier-General John Stanwix

New York
[Copy in Secretary's hand]   16 March 1759

As it is become absolutely necessary, on the Death of Brig[r] Gen Forbes, that an Officer of Rank and Experience shou'd without Loss of Time proceed to Pensylvania to take on him the Command of His Majesty's Forces in Conjunction with the Forces directed to be raised in the Southern Provinces as by M[r] Sec[ry] Pitts /[Letter] of the 9th of December, in Consequence of which I wrote to the several Governors, and I herewith enclose you Copys of the above Letters.

I must for the above Reasons, desire that you will please to repair to Philadelphia and to take on you the Command of the Troops, and that you will immediately make such Dispositions as will remove all Dangers which seem to threaten the important Post of Pittsburg, to which Intelligence I can indeed give no Credit, but nevertheless all Measures must be taken to secure that Pos[t] & to ensure a Communication to it; and I imagine that will easily be effected by encamping a proper Corps at Fort Ligonier.

The situation of Pitt'sburg appear to me to be such as not to admit of carrying on any offensive Operations with great Numbers from the Distance and very great Expence that must attend the taking up Provisions, When the Enemy is otherwise employ'd and can't send Reinforcements that Way, which I hope will soon be the Case, a small number might act and clear every thing to the Lake, there is nothing but <u>Presqu' Isle</u>, & I don't see that a larger Force can do more, as nothing can be done to the Right or the Left, but

33

what can be much more easily executed from the Mohocks river or from Carolina or the Mississippi, Niagara is every thing on the Right and I know of nothing between Fort du Quesne and Fort Assamption and Prud homme[36] which are at an immense Distance from Pittsburg.

I shall be glad that you will on the Spot inform yourself of the thorough State of the present Appearance of Things, from whence you will better judge how far it may be expedient for carrying on any offensive Operations which may most annoy the Enemy from Pittsburgh or from the Frontiers of any of the Southern Colonies on the Continent.

I enclose you a Warrant for holding of General Courts Martial as likewise one for the Payment of the Subsistence and such Contingencies as may be wanted . . .

WO/34/45 fols 203–4

32
Governor Thomas Pownall to Major-General Jeffery Amherst

Boston
16 March 1759
[Secretarial hand, signed by Pownall]   [Received 20 March 1759]

I have the pleasure to acquaint you that this Province which hath on every Occasion of the Kings Service exerted it self hath this Year notwithstanding the Exhausted state it is in as to Men and the great difficulties it Labours under in its Treasury ~~hath~~ made Provision for the Raising 5,000 Men for the General Service of this Year and have by an Act enabled me to Draught the same out of the Militia on the sixth day of April if not rais'd by enlistment by that time.

Having reciev'd his Majestys Commands to urge the General Court to raise the same number of Men as they did last Year[37] or as many more as the number of Inhabitants wou'd allow – As I knew it wou'd be impracticable to get them to Vote more Men at this Levy I did not urge it in that Light But recieving what they already had done <u>in part</u> as the best means to raise such men as were <u>immediately</u> wanted for the most early operations of the Campaign I by the inclosed Message urg'd them to make such Augmentations as shou'd be necessary for the future operations of the Campaign. In answer to which I have reciev'd the message inclos'd, in which altho' they do not expressly promise me to make an Augmentation, yet I am assur'd that it is their intention shou'd any Event or operation of the Campaign render more men absolutely necessary, to make an Augmentation in such Emergency . . .

WO/34/25 fols 212–13

33
Provisions for 1759

New York

[Copy in Secretary's hand]   21 March 1759

The first Care will be to put Provisions on board the Transports that are now order'd at this Place & Boston, sufficient for Thirteen Thousand men for Eight Months commencing the first of May, besides what Provisions must be put on board for the Service of the Troops in their Passage to Louisburg, Halifax &ca.

The Provision for the Thirteen Thousand is for the Troops intended for an Expedition up the River St Lawrence.

The next is to supply Provisions for thirty Thousand men at least for the Army which is to assemble at Albany, and that provision be forwarded for that Service as fast as possible.

The Numbers to the Southward remain yet uncertain; Mr Kilby is desired only to take such measures there that in Case an Army shoud assemble there Provisions may not be wanted and he shall have the first Intelligence when any Operations on that side are fixed.

WO/34/69 fol. 131

WLC/AP/4

34
Major-General Jeffery Amherst to Christopher Kilby

New York

[Copy in Secretary's hand]   22 March 1759

In the Instructions I gave You Yesterday for the providing of
Provisions for the two Armys that are to be Employed up the
River St Lawrence and above Albany, I did not, altho' I mentioned
it in Conversation, Specify, that as among the Transports I have
Ordered to be taken up here, there is one fitting for an Hospital
Ship, and that it would be necessary to cause her to be provided
with fresh provisions and with four Cows for the use of the Sick,
Wherefore lest it should have Escaped Your Memory, I must now
repeat to You, to take particular Care that the same be provided
and furnished; And I must also recommend to You, to procure as
much fresh Provisions for the above Two Armys, as will afford the
Issuing of it to the Troops, at least twice a Week which You will
direct Your Commissaries strictly to Observe.

WO/34/69 fol. 132

WLC/AP/4

35
Major-General Jeffery Amherst to Governor Thomas Pownall

New York

[Copy in Secretary's hand]   23 March 1759

I have now before me Your two Letters of the 11th and 16th Instant;
the first of which I have already Acknowledged,[38] and shall make
Answer to so soon as I have taken into Consideration the Subject
Matter of the Latter, which I am Sorry to say, by no means
Answers my Expectations, which from Mr Secretary Pitt's Letter,
were very Sanguine, that the Province of the Massachusett's Bay,
upon this urgent and important Occasion, would not have Exerted
themselves less this Year than they did the last, Especially as in all
human probability, this Campaign must put an End to the War in

this Country, if the respective Provinces did furnish the Aid and Assistance recommended to and expected from them; and how the other Provinces will act, when they see that of the Massachusetts, who generally gives the Lead, has Voted 2000 men less than they did the Year before is to me a matter of Doubt, and I must own I cannot but think it must be productive of the worst of Consequences, and perhaps subvert the wise Measures planned at home for the entire Reduction of Canada, and the giving a lasting peace to this Country, which I again Repeat, under the divine providence, could not fail of Success, if the Colonies were to Exert themselves upon this Occasion, as is recommended to, and behoves them both for the honor of their Country, and the quiet and peaceable possession of their Liberties and Properties; and as nothing can more effectually answer those great and wished for Ends, than by making the most vigorous and early Efforts, on which all depends, and which I am resolved to pursue, You will be sensible that an Augmentation after that cannot avail the present intended Operations; I must therefore request of You, to lose no time in Obtaining as great an Augmentation as possible, in order that they may be at the Place of Rendezvous, by the same time with the Others of Your Province, that are destined to Serve with me . . .

WO/34/27 fols 134–5

36
Major-General Jeffery Amherst to Brigadier-General Thomas Gage

New York

[Copy in Secretary's hand]   28 March 1759

My Letters are of the 10th of Feby. Admiral Boscawen writes me word Mr Wolfe goes out on his Expedition on his own terms, better equipped and better officer'd than any expedition he ever knew . . .[39]

I wanted to go to Philadelphia but can't get an Answer from Boston, and I fancy I shall not have time enough, I shall look towards Albany as soon as we can attempt anything for which I desire you will be so good to keep a look out.

The Provincials fall short in their Numbers, I am pressing all I can to augment and quicken their motions, when Major Rogers has the Rangers compleat I would raise another Company or two with all my heart if it can be done before 'twill be too late.

Not a shilling of money yet come but I cannot defer any longer the Oxen and Horses, pray tell Colonel Bradstreet the situation we are in, but the Service must not be retarded and he shall have all the Credit that Messrs Apthorpe & Bayard can give and I should be glad he would provide the Oxen & Horses as fast as he can in the cheapest and best way for his Majesty's Service.

Col^o Bradstreet made Complaints of a Waggon Master, Barrack Master & Storekeeper if they are good for nothing we must get rid of them.

WO/34/46A fols 152–3

WLC/AP/4

37
Major-General Jeffery Amherst to Lieutenant Governor William Denny

New York

[Copy in Secretary's hand]   30 March 1759

Agreeable to my Letter of the 7th ^{4o} I then wrote to Sr John St Clair to call in all the out Standing accounts of Expenses incurred last Year in the Expedition against Fort du Quesne, which I find ——— has been done; but that they are of so intricate and Complicated a Nature, as to require a very Narrow inspection to Set them in Such a light as will warrant the payment of them with Justice to the Crown and the persons concerned therein; for which purpose I am come to a Resolution to follow the Measure pursued in a similar Case after the demise of General Braddock, by Appointing Commissioners to inspect and Settle the Same; and to prevent all partiality on either Side these Commissioners Shall be two on the part of the Inhabitants & two in behalf of the Crown who are to meet as often as possible, and with the utmost dispatch proceed to the Examination of all Such accounts as Shall be brought before them, and that no time may be lost nor no pains Spaired in the Carefull Inspection of those Accounts each two Commissioners Shall be allowed a Clerk, to transcribe and take down what-ever Shall be /^{necessary} to be Committed to writing, during such their Examination, after which they will digest the whole, and report likewise in writing their Sentiments thereupon, Setting forth the Validity or invalidity of the respective Claims, what part thereof may have been paid, and finally to determine what may be still Justly due in which they will have a Strict regard to the Rules of Justice and Equity; Then agreeable to such report, what part thereof I think myself authorized to Discharge, I Shall do it without delay; the remainder, if there Should be any that I have reason to believe I cannot take upon me to acquit, I will readily transmit to the Kings ministers for their decision: and this I apprehend, You will own with me, is all I can do in a transaction that has happened before I was honoured with the Command, and to which from the distance I have been at, I am an utter stranger.

The two Gentlemen I have named in behalf of the Crown are Sr John St Clair, the Dep Q^r Master General, who from his Station in the Army and his having been an Eye Witness to the whole, must be thoroughly informed of every thing and be a Competent Judge of what may be Justly due, unless Brigad^r Stanwix Should think Sr John can be more usefull in giving those lights by way of Information to the Commissioners, in which case he will appoint another in his Stead; the other is Mr Barrow, the Dep: pay Mr General who being an accomptant must give great care to all matters of Calculation . . .

WO/34/32 fol. 38

38
Colonel John Bradstreet to Major-General Jeffery Amherst
Albany
1 April 1759
[Holograph]   [Received 4 April 1759]

Your Excellency sees the immense Bounty & other encourage-ments given by the several Governments for raising their Men together with their taking every method in their power to prevent the raising Battoe Men has in a great measure stopt it and will lay you under the necessity of carrying on the Service in like manner as it was done last year; which was, for want of a Sufficient number of Battoe Men the troops were oblig'd to do the principal part of that work.

As to the working oxen and Horses we shall want [since] few of the owners will deliver them without the Cash which is a melancholy consideration considering the uncertainty of its arrival soon, the season advancing fast and the time it will take to collect them together with Mr Apthorp's proposal for paying for them which will by no means do and upon which I now write him to see if it cannot be put upon a better footing and I beg leave to say it will be necessary that your Excellency lets me know the time I should collect the whole here that it may be kept of as long the Service will admit to save the Forage which is difficult to be had & expensive.

I have wrote for Corn, Hay & many other things necessary for the Service to York and must beg the favor of your Excellency not to let any person meddle or stop any Vessells taken up for that Service . . .

It is become a Rule with the Inhabitants upon the Continent to impose upon Government more & more every year and without we may empress grass lands and have them properly valued the Service will suffer much – be pleas'd to direct me upon this head . . .

WO/34/57 fols 23–4

39
Major-General Jeffery Amherst to Major Robert Rogers

New York

[Copy in Secretary's hand]   1 April 1759

Your letter of the 28th Ultimo is come to my hands, and as you seem Confident that two Companys of the Stockbridge Indians Commanded by the Jacobbs will be very useful to us the ensuing Campaign & amply repay the expense to the Government, I am very well Satisfied with your having directed them to be raised, provided they keep to their Engagement of being Compleat and at Albany by 28th of April, you will therefore particularly direct them not to Exceed that time, and Neglect nothing to see those orders put in Execution.

I shall always chearfully receive your opinion in relation to the Service You are Engaged in and Shall take an opportunity of writing to Sr William Johnson in regard to what You mention about Capt Lotteridge & a Company of Indians from the five Nations, who I am very glad to find you have reason to think so well of . . .

WO/34/79 fol. 62

40
Brigadier-General Thomas Gage to Major-General Jeffery Amherst

Albany
9 April 1759

[Holograph]   [Received 14 April 1759]

I have forwarded your Letter to Major Rogers, who left this Place a few Days ago, with orders to put his Companys in some order, but, as I know him to be a true Ranger, & not much addicted to Regularity, I had before sent Directions on this head to Col^o Haldimand, and which I have likewise repeated to Lt Col^o Eyre, who marched with four Companys to relieve Fort Edward . . .

Your Opinion of Major Roger's Proposals for the taking the Mohawks into Pay, is very just, nor is it possible to bring those Indians to be useful in that way; was it practicable, they would certainly be preferable to all the Rangers on the continent. Rogers is a good man in his way but his schemes are very wild, & he has a new one every Day . . .[41]

The Season is very fine, & the Waters fall very fast, & I think you may take the Field as soon as ever your Preparations necessary for the Campain are finished. I have given Directions to Lt Col^o Eyre to lay the Bridge, & prepare materials to erect covering for the Provisions &cᵃ. & have ordered the A.D.Q.M. Genˡ to send up proper Persons to repair the Batteaux. I hope in about six Days we may be able to forward Provisions, unless there are some heavy Rains . . .

WO/34/46A fols 27–8

<h1 style="text-align:center">41</h1>

Major-General Jeffery Amherst to Lieutenant Governor William Denny

Philadelphia

[Copy in Secretary's hand]   11 April 1759

Finding upon my arrival here that the Assembly of this Province still continued to refuse passing the Supply Bill unless You made such Concessions as You do not think You can, without deviating from Your propriatary Instructions & endangering Your Sureties for the due performance thereof; I accordingly took an opportunity of Conferring with the Speaker and Several of the leading Men of the Assembly to shew them the Necessity of their passing the Bill agreable to your proposal and Instructions which I did hope they would under the present pressing Circumstances have been Sensible of and have had Influence enough to have brought the House to assent to: but having faild in my Expectations & finding that they continued obstinate in their former resolutions,⁴² I sent them a Message of which the enclosed is a Copy, Setting forth as You will see the Absolute Necessity of their Complying with the measure proposed or that I Should be Obliged to give over all thoughts of carrying on the intended Offensive Operations & the Building a Fort, which I imagined would have had a great weight with them; notwithstanding which it seems they are still deaf to all kind of remonstrance & persist in their Obstinancy; but as this must by no means prevent His Majesty's Instructions being put in Execution, and that they cannot be Complyed with, unless the Supply bill does pass, I must for the good of the Common Cause, and in order to enable me to pursue His Majesty's Commands[,] beg of You, as I understand You did upon a Similar occasion at the request of the Earl of Loudoun, wave your propriatary Instructions & give Your assent to the bill as brought in by them and I shall take the very first Opportunity of Informing the Kings Ministers with the necessity for Your so doing that no inconvenience may arise to You from the same.

WO/34/32 fol. 40

42
Governor Thomas Pownall to Major-General Jeffery Amherst

Boston
13 April 1759
[Secretary's hand, signed by Pownall]   [Received 18 April]

On ye 11th I mett my Assembly after their short recess: I laid the Matter of raising more Men before them. They went into a large Comittee of both Houses & the Comittee have reported an Augmentation of 1500 Men to be rais'd by enlistment at a bounty of £10 p^r man. The House this afternoon have it under consideration: I have no confidence nor Trust in ye Effect of this Measure, For as already every Man that cou'd be gott to enlist is enlisted at a bounty of 16 & 18 £ p^r man (The Inhabitants of every town adding by private Subscription one man with another 10£ to ye Bounty given by ye Gov^t) I shall have little hopes of raising them by enlistment, be ye Bounty what it will: But whatever be ye Effect of this Measure, 'tis certain that ye Last Impress came so near the upper class of People amongst whom are ye Sons & Relations of ye Representatives & Magistrates that they will never come into a second impress which must extend to these . . .

As to ye Men of ye last Levies they are rais'd[,] some trifling deficiencies by Quakers[43] & People down of ye Meassles excepted. All those for ye Eastern Service I have orderd to ye Castle & they are there. The Thousand for ye Bay of Fundy shall be ready to embark on Monday if the Transports are ready. I imagine I shall gett 189 or 200 Sailors, if not more, I have already sent part down to Halifax the rest wait for Transports and Passages.

That I might be sure of 2500 Men for ye Eastern Buisness when I considerd that deficiencies might arise besides ye deductions for Seamen I order'd to ye Castle 3000 men, so that 1560 is all that will go West at present . . .

I find by Major Ross, sent to me by Col Burton, that there has been an Affray betwixt some of ye Inhabitants & some officers, Col Burton, than whom no One can act more prudently or with a more sincere attention to carrying on ye Service & conducting Ev'ry thing with Peace & Harmony, immediatly cleard the Streets of every Soaldier sending them to their Barracks & sent to Me to desire I w^d direct ye Magistrates to disperse the Inhabitants. Which they have had orders these 3 Daies to do on every occasions, & did do, & all is quiet. & notwithstanding the Ugly Disposition there seems to be in ye Common People & the privates on both sides, Yet I trust from ye good dispositions of ye Magistrates on one hand, & of ye officers on ye other, that ye means We have taken, I with ye Inhabitants & Col Burton with ye Soldiers that no matter of any consequence will happen . . .[44]

WO/34/25 fols 237–8

43
Brigadier-General Thomas Gage to Major-General Jeffery Amherst

Albany
15 April 1759
[Receipt not dated]

[Holograph]

The Waters are very much out, which has hurt the Roads & carried away many of the Bridges betwixt this, & Fort Edward. I told you in my last, that I hoped in a very few Days to be able to forward up Provisions, but I find the Roads & Waters are not the only obstructions; for proposing to Col° Bradstreet to furnish 100 Batteaux & as many waggons to carry half the Provision wanted for the Campain, computed at about 5000 Barrells, & lodge the same at Still-Water, without any Noise or Hurry, He told me He had no Batteaux-Men, & it could not be done till the Provincials arrived, who must furnish him with Batteaux-Men, & there are also Difficultys in procuring the Number of Waggons. His Scheme is to leave all till the Forces come up, & carry all away together, which I can by no means think a good one, as the Numbers will only confound & hinder one another. I saw too much of this sort of Work last Campain; the Troops were hurryed and harassed, prodigious Quantitys of Provisions spoiled, & the Horses destroyed; so that the Army was reduced, for want of Carriages at the End of the Campain, to harness their Men to drag the Batteaux & Artillery to Fort-Edward, besides Numbers of Batteaux & Whale-Boats, sunk in the Lake or hid in the Woods.

To bring more Batteaux to a carrying /Place one Day, than can be cleared off the next, or crowd a Carrying Place with more Carriages than it can conveniently contain, must be productive of much Hurry & Confusion, but is not Expedition.

You see nothing can be done without Batteau-Men, & They as well as the Waggoners must be taken from the Provincial Troops, in doing which you will meet with some opposition; and as the affair of forwarding the Provisions must be postponed, till Hands arrive to carry it away, you will have Time to consider this Business, & give such Directions as you judge convenient; I shall in the mean Time, as soon as the Waters subside, get the Bridges & Roads repaired, as well as I am enabled; Waggons may Work as soon as you please, but there will be scarcely Food sufficient for the Oxen till next month, nor do I expect to see them before.

WO/34/46A fols 29–30

44
Major-General Jeffery Amherst to Field Marshal Viscount John Ligonier

New York

[Holograph copy]   16 April 1759

I have been a little journey to Philadelphia where I staid two days, in hopes to settle every thing right in that province, as all was going on at Boston, & here to my wishes. The Diana Frigate came in here the day I set out, & I was honoured at night with your L^dships letter of the 23^d of January,[45] with the dispatches which overtook me at Brunswick . . .

In my way to, & from Philadelphia, I reviewed Ld Blakeney's & Lascelles's Reg^{ts}, & at Philadelphia I saw my late Friend Forbes's, Lascelles's being assembled to embark directly, & the other two Reg^{ts} are in motion to day to get in time up the Hudson's River, where I have likewise ordered Montgomery's Reg^t, as B^r G^l Stanwix has chose to have his own Battⁿ with him.

Nine companies of Fraser's are only yet arrived here, but I hope the rest will be very soon be down,[46] & they shall embark directly and though there are but two english transports come in, I shall get the Train, & Webbs from Boston, & the three Reg^{ts} from hence, the Provincials to Halifax, & Louisbourg, & the Reg^{ts} from the Bay of Fundy embarked, & I hope in good time at their rendezvous, tho' not so soon as I ordered.

I have wrote fully to Mr Pitt, which your Lordship will be informed of, & all I can say, will be but repeating to you, which trouble you will like as well to be rid of.[47]

I have now ordered all Officers to their Posts, it has been in obedience to orders that the Reg^{ts} at Halifax, & Louisbourg have sent to the continent to recruit, but I hope it will never be done again, so long as this country is in the situation it at present is in, for it is attended with vast expenses & not a man gained to the Army by it, for the Reg^{ts} quartered on the Continent would get the men.

I shall hurry every thing on as fast as I can, & get together as fast as possible, then I take leave of hurry, but I hope we shall go fast enough to finish matters this campaign. I think it must do, & I do assure your Lordship it shall do, if I can make it, by the next packet I shall hope to acquaint your Lordship of what the first operations may be.

U1350/O/35/9

45
Brigadier-General Thomas Gage to Major-General Jeffery Amherst

Albany
18 April 1759
[Holograph]   [Receipt not dated]

I said a great deal to you in my last about forwarding Provisions, since which Col° Corsa of the New York Reg^t is arrived in order to Muster some of the Companys: He never came near me, but I sent for Him, & desired He would as fast as possible collect his Companys & bring them into this Town; He answered, his Men had neither Clothing Money &c^a. & there would be great grumbling if they were put on any Duty before they got their Bounty, with many other Objections. I have however prevailed on him to say He would bring them in, & shall use all means to prevail on them to work in the Batteaux, for which they must be paid, & shall endeavor to forward up Provisions in the manner I proposed to you. I know I shall have great Difficulty in doing this Business, as the Officers as well as the Men are much averse to the Batteaux Service, & every excuse will be made use of. I shall however try,[48] & beg of you in the mean Time to apply to the Lt Governor, that Money be immediately sent up; & Clothing follow as soon as possible, that these Pretences may be got over, & that Col° Corsa & all the Companys this Way have immediate Orders to assemble here & follow such orders as they shall receive from me in every Thing that Regards the Publick Service without Distinction. I can provide them with Arms & Tents.

WO/34/46A fol. 35

46
Major-General Jeffery Amherst to Colonel Arthur Morris

New York
[Copy in Secretary's hand]   19 April 1759

I enclose this to Colonel Haviland to forward to you, as I send him an Order to Embark the Inniskilling Regiment of Foot which will make room for the Regiment under Your Command to take up their Quarters at Elizabeth Town.

I write to Col° Haviland to inform you of the Route he took, that you may take the good and avoid the bad of any part he may have found on the march, and I therefore transmit to you with this a discretionary march route, and I would have you march the Regiment under your Command immediately to Elizabeth Town, where I will send Sloops and Provisions to take the Regiment up to Albany without loss of time.

You will forward the Enclosed to Brig^r General Stanwix and acquaint him when you march out of your present Quarters that Montgomerys Regiment may move forward.

As I have cut the French Arms shorter which makes them much lighter and Handyer for the Light Infantry I shall Send you to Elizabeth Town Seventy five Firelocks which are for the three Sergeants inclusively,[49] and you will deliver into the Comptroller of the Ordinance Stores the French Firelocks you have that they may be Shortened as the Others, for I Shall want more Firelocks I believe than what I have.

I have acquainted You that I would leave the Swords of the Several Reg^{ts} behind as they will be an impediment to the Marching of the Men in this woody Country, the Grenadiers must take their Caps with them, I leave it to the Commanding Officers that the Grenadiers take their Swords or Not as the Commanding officers Judge Best, Bayonets must be well Secured I hear many were lost last Year. I Should have no objections to leave Sword belts behind.[50]

WO/34/79 fol. 81

47
Major-General Jeffery Amherst to Major-General James Wolfe

New York

[Copy in Secretary's hand]   27 April 1759

I hope Maj^r Barré will have deliver'd you a letter from me before this can reach you, as by him I intended you should be informed all the most minute particulars that you might like to know, in regard to the preparations here for supplying you with every thing I could for your expedition.

On the 7th ins^t I had the favour of receiving your letter of the 29th of Janry[51] by Capt Schomberg, & on the 13th one of the 6th of March which Captain Doake of the Lizard man of war deliver'd to me.

I hope all the Regiments allotted to serve under your command will be at their rendezvous, by the time the weather will permit you to proceed up the river, those from the bay of Fundy, I think will not be the last, some of Fraser's were unluckily situated,[52] but I was resolved if possible to make no change in the Corps's, but to send them as they were named in England, and Fraser's are all this day on board, & Lascelle's I hope will embark to morrow.

You will see I have named young Montresor to serve with you, as Lt Goddard is hors du Combat for the present, and as you by your letter desire to have Capt Green, I have ordered him accordingly, & he sails with the transports to morrow if the wind permits. Maj^r Barré shewed me your Letter informing him he was to be D. Adj^t. Genl, or I should have sent you my Brother, as I have two D. A. G^s here.

The french fleet is arrived at Martinique, & this coast alarmed at the intelligence of a 64 Gun Ship and Frigates detached from them to this coast, though it is extremely unlikely they should lessen their strength, by sending off a Ship of Force, yet the report amongst these people gains not the less credit for it, & they are all frighted about it.

I wish it was in my power to send the Reg^{ts} compleat to you, on my being appointed to the command of this army I foresaw the recruiting in this country could not fill up the Reg^{ts}, and resolved to get of the provincials as many as would have completed the Reg^{ts} for the service of the campaign, allowing the number on the quota they are to furnish, and returning the men to their provinces when the campaign was finished, this would have had difficulties, but not such, but might have been got the better of; on my arrival here I had an account of the drafts to be sent out, I notwithstand^g continued recruiting as much as possible, then the drafts were otherwise disposed of, and till I saw by your letter that you are to be recruited ~~by~~ /^{from} the troops at Martinique, I heard not a word how the army was to be compleated, or have I heard any thing about it, but by your letter.

I wish from my heart you had 4 or <u>500</u> pioneers with proper tools only, I am very sensible they would be of great advantage to you, but where to get them I know not, all the provinces furnish less numbers than they did last year, the first price here is fifteen pounds for a man & several instances of ~~their~~ paying sixty & seventy pounds a man, Carpenters, Masons & Labourers get such immense wages, that I wonder almost we ever ~~get~~ /^{recruit} a man, the two first will earn in a day as much as a Capt. of Horse is paid in England, & any Labourer makes as much as the pay of an Ensign.[53]

Col. Williamson, & my Brother have settled a Cypher that no one but themselves, if they themselves can, can find out, & by this means I intend to inform you by some Scoundrel of an Indian of what passes.

As to winter quarters for the troops, I hope we shall meet & talk about that, Quebec will require a good garrison, Louisburg requires four Battalions, those that have been there this winter are seasoned, & seasoning I think costs us more men than any thing else, three Batt^s are not too much for Halifax, two for the bay of Fundy, and Boston is a good winter quarter, though not yet taken as such, but I hope we shall find other places that will want garrisoning by english troops.

I send you extracts of my letters to B^r G^l Whitmore, which will inform you what I have done in regard to your Paymaster & Cash, but I am very sorry to say we have no money, I will beg, borrow, & steal & do all I can for you, you will see by that likewise what is promis'd as to fresh provisions, so that I'll say no more on those articles.

You will have received by M. Barré the proportion of stores for your hospital, sent from hence & judged sufficient by Mr Adair, who will give you likewise an account of them, he takes four milch cows, & several Sheep in the hospital Ship.

The rum and Molasses is all provided, & I hope will prove good, & sufficient.

I send you a draft of the river St Lawrence, & a journal which Lt Goddard gave to me.

I set out to morrow for Albany when I hope the two Reg^{ts} from hence will sail; I will forward every thing for you to the utmost of my power. I most heartily wish you health, & success.

WO/34/46B fols 308–9

48
Major-General Jeffery Amherst to Brigadier-General John Stanwix

Albany

[Copy in Secretary's hand]   6 May 1759

I send you this by Capt. D'Arcy to Acquaint you of my resolves of the Operations to be carried on this side, which I do not chuse to trust to the Post. I have before informed You of my intentions of an Enterprise against Niagara[54] which I have now determined to Execute as near as may be at the same time that I shall be Assembled at the Lake to distract the Enemy as much as possible and oblige them to abandon some posts, or to divide their Forces which will weaken them so much in every part as will almost ensure Success to Our undertakings.

I must now desire that you will prepare as fast as possible to be ready to push forward a Corps from Pittsburg to Venango, Le Beuf and Presqu' Isle at the same time that the Attack at Niagara will be Attempted; the reduction of those places I imagine will meet with little or no opposition, as the Indians in all appearance, will be wholly in our Interest,[55] so that most probably the Enemy will quit these Posts on the first Intelligence they receive of the Attack on Niagara.

Nobody here knows what I intend, my preparations have been making for sometime past for Acting by Oswego as well as Lake George, and no one but yourself will know it till I can Execute it: If I tell Sir Wm Johnson or the Indians the french would know it directly, therefore it is a Secret, and I know it is not the less so for informing You of it.

I shall give the Command of this Expedition to B^r Genl Prideaux and I shall send about 5000 Men with Batteaus and Whaleboats sufficient, the whole shall move at once and when they move I shall demand the Indians, my intentions are that about half the number shall proceed to <u>Niagara</u> while the other half will take post at <u>Oswego</u> a place I hope never more to be abandoned.

I am willing to think the Conquest of Niagara will be easy and I must keep it, and it will so effectually secure every thing on your side of Lake Erie from every thing but Indians who I hope now will at least not be against Us, that I must desire that You will Garrison it from the first Battalion of Royal Americans with what Provincials You may think proper to be Commanded by a regular Officer for it must not be trusted to any other: I mean this that I may recall the Troops to Act offensively to the Eastward of Lake Ontario or where His Majestys Service shall most require them.

This at first Sight may have some difficulties from the want of Batteaus and Whaleboats, for which You shall have all the information and Assistance Brig^r Genl Prideaux can give You, who will on the Spot be able to transmit to You sure and good Intelligence, and I design to supply them with Provisions from this side.

I imagine two or three hundred Men will be sufficient for the Garrison of Niagara, as I dont see any thing can hurt them when Oswego is secure and We are acting Offensively in every other part.

So soon as I have fixed the day for the departure of the Troops intended for this Expedition which waits only the arrival of the Provincials, and that I can give a near guess of the time they may arrive at <u>Niagara</u> I shall send to Acquaint You of it in the meanwhile I must beg You will be so good to forward every thing to be ready to clear Your road to <u>Lake Erie</u> and that You will make such dispositions that I may depend on your sending from the Troops under your Command, a sufficient Garrison for <u>Niagara</u>, which I hope will soon be Ours . . .

WO/34/45 fol. 221

49
Major-General Jeffery Amherst to Major-General James Wolfe

Albany
[Copy in Secretary's hand]   6 May 1759

. . . I am forwarding every thing to the Lake as fast as possible; I shall send a Corps to take post at Oswego and make an attack on Niagara which the Enemy I think cannot hinder our Success in, and I will keep them in hot Water at La Galette.

I will close in upon the Enemy to the utmost I can at the time You are up the River and till then I will Act so as to give them Jealousies in different Corners at a greater Distance and distract them and force them to abandon some posts or divide, to defend them that they shall weaken themselves every where, which I hope will ensure Success to Us . . .

WO/34/46B fol. 310

50
By His Excellency Major-General Jeffery Amherst

Albany
[Copy in Secretary's hand]   9 May 1759

Whereas the Army destined to Lake George and beyond it, cannot be /too well Supplied with all sorts of Refreshments, which must greatly Contribute toward the preservation of the health of the Troops; These are therefore to make known to the People of the Provinces, that such of them as shall be inclined, to Convey to the Lake, Live Cattle, Sheep, Fowles, Eggs, Butter and Cheese, or any other Refreshments, or Necessaries whatsoever (Rum and Spiritous Liquors Excepted) shall not, on any Account, have their Men taken from them or detained; and that for their further Encouragement, they shall not only meet with all Protection for themselves, their Servants, Carriages and Goods, but a Market shall be Established at the Lake to Expose said Refreshments, &ca, to Sale, and Strict Orders given out, that upon their behaving as becometh, any Soldier, or whosoever else, should molest or Wrong them, shall be severely punished, and make them due Reparation; Whosoever proposes to follow the Army upon the foregoing Conditions, will send in their Names to Head Quarters at Albany, or wherever the Army may be, that the necessary Pass ports may be Granted . . .

WO/34/79 fol. 108

51
Major-General Jeffery Amherst to Christopher Kilby

Albany

[Copy in Secretary's hand]   10 May 1759

As Fort Stanwix will be the Deposit for Provisions that may be necessary for the Service to the Westward, and that I do not know how soon I may have Occasion for a large Quantity there, and that I must Supply that Post with Five Thousand Barrels, and that I shall certainly want a larger Quantity hereafter (which Intelligence is for Yourself only) I must recommend it to You not to lose any time in giving Your Directions to Your Agents at New York or Elsewhere, to Send up as large a Quantity as possibly they can Collect, in order that We may be able to Send up to Fort Stanwix what farther Quantity of Provisions may be requisite there, independent of what is necessary here and at Lake George, or beyond it.

WO/34/69 fol. 134

52
Brigadier-General John Stanwix to Major-General Jeffery Amherst

Philadelphia

13 May 1759

[Holograph]   [Received 21 May 1759]

I am to own the favour of your letter I rec^d on fryday night last by your Aid de Camp Capt Darcy informing me of your resolves for an Enterprise against Niagara, in which you have my warmest wishes for that success you have so favourable a prospect of meeting with, and you may be assured of my utmost endeavours to prepare as fast as possible to be ready to push a body of Troops from Pittsbourg to <u>Venango</u>, <u>Lebeuf</u> & <u>Presquil</u> to enable me if possible to send a Detachment of the first Batt: R.A.R^t with some provincials to Garrison Niagara, and wish I could have any reasonable hopes to effect it at the same time with the attack of Niagara, but the difficulties of marching by land so as to keep pace with this enterprise by water is but too obvious, for all that I have been able to do hitherto has been just to support with provisions the small present Garrison in the posts to the Westward for want of Carriages, I have advertized the most advantageous terms for Waggons after having consulted wth the learn'd in their way in order to bring them in Voluntarily wch if effect'd tho dear will be a hundred per Cent cheaper than last year, what number this will produce a little time will shew, if it do's not answer must have recourse to the Assembly who meets the 21st for a bill to oblige the Waggons to come in under a Certain Fine as was done last year, few of them yet are paid for the last Campaigne for want of money which gives a general dissatisfaction, more than from the want of dispatch from the commiss^{rs}, On enquiry of Mr Barrow D.P.G. & Mr Nelson cashier am told by them that the cash do's not come in as expect'd by circulation, and that the necessitys of New York has taken from them upwards of £400,000, Ster: recourse must therefore be had to the Assembly to strike us £100,000 currency in paper money and lodge bills of exchange as security to the province for some month's 'till it can be sunk, again, [I] have mention'd this our great necessity to the speaker and to Govr Denny who give me some hopes that this in some shape may be done as it is to pay themselves, for as no money is sent from England to come this way the whole cash of this province is insufficient to buy the bills of exchange ever so low, even to pay the debts of last year, and it will be an immense sum that will be want'd to build a respectable fort at Pittsbourg and to carry on the Service of this year thro' so much land carriage, so dear & so difficult to be had for every thing we want . . .

The roads from Carlisle to Pittsbourg 200 miles the Winter has made impassable for Waggons till repair'd & the freshet has carried away almost all the Bridges these will retard the march of the troops and provision.

If part of the army is to march to Lake Erie and dispossess the Enemy of their three forts, Batteaus must be built at Pittsbourg for their provisions artillery and ammunition, roads must be also open'd and their march must be slow work, in that rough country where so many creeks are to Bridge.

The necessary preparations for that expedition, the opening the roads the <u>portage</u> at la Beuf and the taking of the forts cannot be supposed to take less time than six weeks, which would carry us to the middle of septemb^r or the beginning of October which will make it too late for any Garrison left at Niagara to be reliev'd and march back to joyn the Grand Army. We are buying Waggon Horses for 50, Waggons wch we propose to fix at fort Legonier for constant carriage of Provisions & Stores from thence to Pittbourg & if we can get money are in hopes of being able to contract for a number of Packhorses to go constantly between fort Bedford and Legonier if this can be effect'd it will give great encouragement to the Country Waggons to come in as they will have only to travel between Carlisle & Bedford which we are in hopes will procure a Succession of provisions thro' the Communication.

I know of no Enterprise that can be more interesting than that of taking Niagara and fixing once more a good post at Oswego, & I find my self very unhappy to be in such a Situation as not to be able to second your Expectations at so critical a moment in point of time, but the Obstackles are so apparrent & real, that was I not to mention them I should not only deceive you but my self, what is possible to be done I shall attempt and from time to time acquaint you with the advances I make, which you must foresee from the nature of the service this way will be very slow . . .

WO/34/45 fols 63–6

53
Major-General Jeffery Amherst to Brigadier-General Prideaux

17 May 1759

[Copy in Secretary's hand]   Albany

In Obedience to the Kings commands to me for making an Irruption into Canada and for pushing the Operations of the Campaign with the utmost vigour, and His Majestys pleasure having been signified to me at the same time, that I would give a due attention to Lake Ontario and the reestablishment of the important Post of Oswego, a place so highly essential to his Majestys Dominions in America in time of Peace as well as of War, and His Majestys Commands having also been sent to me that if I should find it practicable, I should push on the Operations as far as Niagara, the taking of which Fort would effectually cut off the Communication between Canada and the French settlements to the South. I have on a mature Consideration of what Operations will be the best towards the Success of this ensuring Campaign resolved to send a large Corps of Troops under Your Command consisting of Abercromby's, Lieu^t. Genl J. Murrays, 4th Batt^n of Royal Americans and the 2680 New York Provincials, with the necessary Engineers and Artificers and a proper proportion of Artillery, Stores and Provisions, as You will see by the enclosed Lists, that you may March with the said Corps to Oswego and Niagara, at the same time that I shall March with the remainder of the Army to the Lake to proceed to Tienderoga.

A Sufficient number of Batteaus are provided and are ready at Schenectady for the Transportation of Stores and Provisions.

You will therefore take on You the Command of the above Corps and proceed without loss of time to Fort Stanwix (where You will leave One Hundred and Fifty men of Your provincials to be added to the Garrison I have ordered for that post) and from thence to the East end of the Oneida Lake where I imagine it will be necessary to leave a post of Fifty Men; after crossing the Oneida Lake, it appears to me, another post should be established at the West End, and may be of One hundred and fifty men; and between that and Oswego, at the Falls, a post on the right of the Carrying Place, where there is a rising Ground, will be absolutely necessary, and, I think, should not be of a less number than One hundred Men; these three posts properly Stockaded, some Swivels mounted, the Garrisons will be in no danger, and they may keep up a Safe Communication from Fort Stanwix to Oswego; of which posts, You, when on the Spot, will be best able to determine on the proper numbers, and You will encrease or diminish them (except that of Fort Stanwix) as You shall judge best.

On your arrival at Oswego, You will leave near half your Corps with the next Officer in Command under You,[56] with Orders to him, to immediately set about and build a Fort according to the enclosed Plan, or with such Alterations, on a nearer view of the Ground, You may think necessary to make in the position of it, taking the advantages of the high Ground and Commanding the Harbour for the protection of Boats . . .

It will tend greatly to the Success of Your Enterprize, that you make the greatest dispatch, to proceed with the other half of Your Corps and the Indians, who will Join You under the Command of Sir William Johnson, with such number of Boats as You Judge necessary, from Oswego, along the South side of Lake Ontario, to Niagara, where you will Land Your Corps, and pursue all such measures as You shall think the most effectual for the Speedy reduction of Niagara; for your Assistance in which, You will see, by the enclosed paper from Sir William Johnson, that I have the greatest reason to Expect all the helps the Indians can give, who are extremely desirous this plan should be put in Execution, and think the Conquest will be easy.[57]

I have determined on this Enterprize as I think the Enemy cannot possibly parry the blow, it is of the utmost consequence to the future Operations of the Campaign that no time should be lost in making yourself Master of Niagara, for which place You will see by my Letter to Brig[r] Gen[l] Stanwix that I depend on him to Garrison it from the Troops under his Command, which You will accordingly apply for, but if from any difficulties that may arise he should not be able to send Troops forward by the time You are in possession of the place, I would have You leave a sufficient

THE CAMPAIGN OF 1759

Garrison for the defence of it, untill Brig^r Genl Stanwix can relieve it; which Garrison when reliev'd will follow You, and You will with the utmost dispatch return to Oswego and from thence proceed with such part of Your whole Corps, as will be over & above what is necessary for continuing the Fort and securing the Post of Oswego (which when You go towards the River St Lawrence cannot want the same numbers for its Defence), to the River St Lawrence and take post at La Galette which will greatly help towards the Conquest of Canada, by this time I hope the Enemy will find so much to do in other Corners, as not to make any opposition to You and that You may be able to post Yourself at La Gallette when I am willing to think the Army on this side may be at Crown Point . . .

WO/34/46B fols 137–8

54
Major-General Jeffery Amherst to Captain Joshua Loring

Albany

[Copy in Secretary's hand]   22 May 1759

Besides the two Briggs which I mentioned to You in Mine of the 13th I intended Building for the Navigation of Lake Champlain, I am come to a Resolution of building Two Snows,[58] capable of Mounting Eighteen Six Pounders for Other Uses; And as the Building of these several Vessels will Require a Number of Ship Carpenters more than are already Employed here; These are to direct You, immediately upon Receipt hereof, to Engage Seventy good Ones, which I propose to divide into Two Companies, wherefore it will also be necessary to have a good Overseer to Each of said Companies, which You will likewise Engage, the whole upon the Conditions, and at the Several Prices that was allowed to the same kind of Artificers last Year, unless they can be procured Cheaper, in which You will do Your Utmost for the good of the Service, and the Saving of the Public money, and these Carpenters are to go wheresoever His Majesty's Service may require them, without any Engagements with them to go to particular places.

You will also take Care to purchase at as Cheap a Rate as possible what Rigging and Other Materials You think necessary for Rigging out and Equipping both the said Snows, which Necessaries You will order to be forwarded to this place without loss of time, & Come up Yourself so soon as these Orders are Executed, which must not meet with any Delay.

WO/34/64 fol. 198

55
Major-General Jeffery Amherst to Captain Anthony Wheelock

[Copy in Secretary's hand]

Albany
25 May 1759

. . . The disappointment I have met with in my Numbers of Batteau Men, Waggoners & Ox Team Drivers, obliges me to make them up out of the provincials, and therefore I wrote to Lieut. Governor Hutchinson that I Should allow the rejected Men as well as the Negroes to pass, indeed it is what I am obliged to under these Necessitous Circumstances, you will therefore pass all the men that shall be brought before you and such as may be rejectable as soldiers shall be Employed as Batteau Men or Drivers.

WO/34/98 fol. 135

56
By His Excellency Major-General Jeffery Amherst

[Copy in Secretary's hand]

Albany
27 May 1759

Whereas His Majesty's Service will require as Large a Number of Waggons as can possibly be procured for Carrying on the Same with more Vigour and Dispatch; These are to Warn all Sutlers or Others that already have, or hereafter may Obtain my Pass to follow the Army, agreeable to my Proclamation of the 9th Instant, that in the Transportation of their Provisions, &ca, they must not, by any means, Employ Waggons or Carts drawn by Horses, As from the Orders, which the necessity of the Service has Obliged me to give to the several Officers of the respective Posts, they will be Stopped and not suffered to pass; Wherefore all such Sutlers or Others as are enclined to Benefit of the Encouragement I have offered /ᵗʰᵉᵐ must provide themselves with Ox Teams or Ox Carts, as none Others will be suffered to pass.

WO/34/79 fol. 144

57
Major-General Wolfe to Major-General Jeffery Amherst
Louisburg
27 May 1759
[Holograph]   [Received 18 June]

Tho' you left nothing undone that cou'd forward our affairs, yet unfavourable winds & thick weather have prevented your good designs; the Halifax Garrison and Otways Regᵗ from the Bay of Fundy are not yet arriv'd – but as a number of Ships are seen in the offing, I conclude they will soon be in . . .

I applied for Barré, not knowing that you had an Adjutant General to spare, your Brother would have been very acceptable to me, and I should have thought myself honoured by the distinction.

As you did not write to Mʳ Whitmore about the Compˢ of light Infantry, he has refus'd them, tho' both the Admiral & myself assured him, that Mʳ Pitt in his last conversation, made no kind of doubt, of Mr Whitmore's consent. Lawrence, whose situation is very different from this, was so sensible of the necessity of it, that he included the sick & recovering men in the number of 500 destin'd for the defence of Nova Scotia. Whether I succeed or not in this affair – I am fully determined never to take another command in the Army: There is no carrying on the Publick business; with People who will not judge according to circumstances, & act for the best, when it is obviously pointed out to them. I cou'd have been glad of 2 or 300 Pioneers, of the Boston

61

Militia, & their Colonel wou'd gladly go with us, but it would be to no manner of purpose to ask it.

Mr Durrell has been some time in the Gulph, but we have no account of his proceedings; Two Ships going to join him, took a vessel with Cloathing, & Ammunition, & have sent her in here; nothing can be gather'd from her but that the French are trying to throw in succours of all kinds, which we were pretty sure of before. Ships were seen upon the Coast six weeks ago, whilst our Squadron lay at Halifax, believing that the Ocean was Ice – the Rear Admiral did not sail till 4th May.[59]

If I find that Montcalm, & most of the Regulars are at Quebec, I shall proceed cautiously, giving you time to use y^r superiority – if their force is nearly divided we will push in vigorously.

If the French should collect their Naval Force at Gaspée, or in any of the Bays of Newfoundland, & shou'd attack Mr Saunders with a superiority, that might decide in their Favour, & afterwards come up to Quebec, we may be a little put to it for a Retreat, unless you secure the Lake Champlain, & the Fort of Chambly; then, if we are not able to do better, that is, to winter in Canada, Our Ships, Schooners & Boats, if they don't carry us to Montreal, may run us up the River Sorrel.

There is a great quantity of Ice still floating between Cape North & Newfoundland; it was a doubt not many days ago – if the passage was open for a Fleet so numerous as our's . . .

We now await now for Otway's Battalion & Dank's Company of Rangers – when they arrive, it will take perhaps two Days to make some changes in the Transports, & to regulate the Naval business – & then, with the first fair wind, we shall sail; I conclude it may be about the 2d or 3d of June.

The Harbour is now so full of Ice that a Boat can scarcely get ashore . . .

WO/34/46B fols 300–1

58
Major-General Jeffery Amherst to Brigadier-General John Stanwix

Albany

[Copy in Secretary's hand]   30 May 1759

I have delayed till now returning You my thanks for the favor of Your Letter of the 13th Instant which was Delivered to me by Capt D'Arcy on the 21st, as I had so fully Acquainted You of my intentions of an Enterprize against Niagara and that I therefore chose to tell You when I did write to You, of the time that the Troops order'd for this Expedition might probably arrive there.

The whole is now in motion and Brig^r Genl Prideaux will set out from Schenectady to morrow; I have taken the greatest care I could /^{so} to furnish every thing that can be wanted towards the Success of this Expedition that I am willing to believe it cannot fail.

As you know the Mohawk River, You will know as well as any one here what time it will take to reach Oswego, Brig^r General Prideaux will most undoubtedly make the greatest Expedition he can and I must repeat to You my most earnest desires that You may be able to benefit of the great advantages there must be in seizing the time for pushing forward a Corps to <u>Venango</u> <u>Le Boeuf</u> & <u>Presqu' Isle</u> when he will arrive at Niagara . . .

I have in my last Acquainted You of my Expectations of the Indian Interest towards this Enterprise and I sent You some papers relative thereto; I now have informed Sir William Johnson of the intended Operations[60] and I have the greatest reason to believe from every thing that Sir William tells me that the Indians will be unanimous in assisting Us, and as Sir William Johnson goes with them, I doubt not but they will keep up to the promises they have made him; for their Engagements to serve with him on this occasion are entirely in Consequence of their own desires.

I have nothing further to add on this most essential Service than my hopes that when You are at Fort du Quesne You will find the difficulties of advancing much less than what they appear to be from the representation of others; the Conviction I have of your doing every thing that can tend towards the Success of this Expedition and making the best use of this occasion of dislodging the Enemy entirely from every part between You and the Lake that the Communication may be open to Niagara from Fort du Quesne, as well as from Fort Stanwix, leaves me nothing further to recommend, I shall therefore conclude with my Assurances of regard and esteem.

WO/34/45 fol. 222

59
Major-General Jeffery Amherst to Brigadier-General Thomas Gage

Fort Edward

[Copy in Secretary's hand]   6 June 1759

I am Arrived here today, where I find the Artillery Arrived, the Massachusets Come, part of the Royal Highlanders with the Artillery; the Rhode Islanders were first here, and Every thing is going on well.

I Have sent out two parties, One to the Right, the Other to the left, that if the Enemy should think of sending any small Corps to fall on our Communication on the West Side, or on Scorticook on the East Side I may send You notice in time, though I think We are at every place provided for them . . .

Everything pleases me but the Rangers; I have taken some for Escorts; they are the most unknowing for every part of the Service that is to be Conceived; At their rate of going on they must always be beat; I have tryed to rub them up, and Shew them the way to March in Woods, for those I have had with me know nothing of the matter.[61]

WO/34/46A fol. 162

WLC/AP/4

60
Major-General Jeffery Amherst to Lieutenant Governor James De Lancey

Camp at Fort Edward

[Copy in Secretary's hand]   8 June 1759

Considerable Expenses having necessarily been incurred for the preparations of the Campaign, and the persons to whom the Same are due being very loud & pressing for their payments, without which indeed they may not be well able to fulfill their Engagements, the Consequences of which are but too Obvious; I immediately upon Mr Mortier's representing to me that the Military Chest was quite Exhausted, directed him by Letter; to lay these Matters before the Contractors' Agents at New York, and to Signify to them the Absolute necessity there was for their Exerting themselves to the Utmost in collecting as large a Supply of Money as they possibly Could, and that they should forthwith inform him how much they had in Cash; What they were certain they Could within a short time Collect; And whether they had any Visible prospect of Any; and what Supply shortly coming out from England. Mr Mortier accordingly Wrote to Mr Apthorp, and transmitted him a Copy of Mine, in Answer to which, just Received, I find that the Contractors' Agent has heard nothing further in relation to the Money he Expected would before this time have Arrived from England, and that it will not be in his power to Supply any Considerable Sum soon, unless some Expedient be found to procure it; That he now has no money by him, nor has any Dependance upon raising any great Matter, but from England; Wherefore, as he finds by my above mentioned Letter to Mr Mortier, that large Demands are daily and pressingly made, he is reduced to the necessity of laying his Situation before me, and of desiring that I would take such Measures as I may think best to procure the Necessary Supplies of Money for the Service.

In this Situation, that nothing may retard our Operations, nor the Success of His Majesty's Arms, I am Compelled to have recourse to You, and to request of You to move Your Council and

Assembly for a Loan of £150,000 New York Currency, in Bills of the Province, redeemable in Twelve Months after their date, by the moneys arising from the Bills of Exchange which I shall direct Mr Mortier, the Dep Paym^r Genl to draw upon the Lords Commissioners of His Majesty's Treasury for the like Sum, whom I shall Advise thereof, as well as of the Necessity of the Measure, which I make no doubt will appear such to them, and that of Course they will Order the payment of Mr Mortier's Bills, particularly as by One of the Articles of his Instructions, he is Authorized, (in Case the Contractors' Agents cannot furnish him with the Supplies necessary for Carrying on the Service) with the Consent and Approbation of the Commander in Chief for the Time being, to Draw upon the Treasury.

The Distress We are in as You may perceive by what I have already Observed, and the incapacity of the Contractors Agents to remove the Same, sufficiently Evinces and Warrants the Necessity I am under of having recourse to this Method; and as the greatest part of this money is due to the people of the Province of New York, which must greatly benefit by so large a Circulation, and that the Province can run no manner of Risque in granting this Loan, since they cannot have a better Security than that Offered, I am hopefull they will not hesitate in Complying with my Request; but on the Contrary that they will readily & Chearfully give this new proof of their Loyalty & Zeal for the Common Cause . . .

WO/34/30 fols 47–8

61
Major-General Jeffery Amherst to Governor Thomas Pownall

Camp at Fort Edward,

[Copy in Secretary's hand]   9 June 1759

On Saturday last Capt Abercromby delivered me Your favour of the 30th Ultimo, at half moon on my road hither, for whence I should have Set out long before, if it had not been, that I wanted to see the Provincial Troops arrived at Albany, wherein I have not succeeded, as by the returns of the 30th of May there were only 1038 of the Massachusetts Forces, including Officers arrived, and 457 Expected; and of the whole of the Provincial Troops including the Massachusetts no more than 3978 come & 2210 Expected to Join exclusive of Colonels Whiting & Worcesters Regiments of Connecticut, the Newhampshire Troops and the additional 1500 Massachusetts & 1000 Connecticutts, besides the New Yorkers who are destined to the Mohawk River. However the Season advancing and being desirous to prepare every thing up here, against what is wanting if the Said Troops do join me, I set out and left Brig^r General Gage at Albany to forward matters there and come up so Soon as they are come in, which I am willing to think will be Shortly, as I am in hopes they are now recover'd of the meazles which I dare say has been the Chief Occasion of their Staying so long behind.

In Your Absence, I Sent /^{Capt} Abercromby to Boston with a Letter to Lieut Govr Hutchinson, desiring he would Send three hundred of the New Levies to join Major Genl Wolfe & Serve under him as pioneers; the dispatch and Readiness with which the Lieut. Governor Comply'd with this request, merit my most Sincere thanks, which I beg You will make him.

WO/34/27 fol. 155

62
Lieutenant Governor James De Lancey to Major-General Jeffery Amherst

New York
15 June 1759
[Holograph]   [Receipt not dated]

I yesterday called a Council & by their advice sent Circular letters to call the Assembly together on Tuesday the 26th instant, which is as soon as the members can possibly be here, when they meet, I shall press them to come into your Excellency's proposal: in the Mean Time, it seems to me, it would be expedient for Mr Mortier to be here, to try what Bills he can dispose of. For I am informed, some may, upon the same footing of exchange, as has lately been done at Philadelphia, which is there at 50 pʳ Cent & would here be 60 . . .

My dear General, you tell me that both Mʳ Wolf and you want the Men expected,[62] as to Mʳ Wolfs wants I cannot say, but give me leave to say that I think, you pay too little regard to the department you are to act in, stripping yourself so liberally as you do.

WO/34/29 fol. 40

63
Major-General Jeffery Amherst to Colonel Archibald Montgomery

Camp at Fort Edward
[Copy in Secretary's hand] 15 June 1759

Enclosed are the proceedings and Sentence of a General Court Martial which I am very sorry to find myself obliged to approve of, or where desertion would end amongst the provincials I know not, but fear it is undoubtedly true that His Majestys Service would greatly suffer.[63]

I have ordered the picquets of the Line to be out at Six o'Clock tomorrow morning and Colᵒ Fitches Regiment to be under Arms. You will, as Colonel of the Day, take the Command of the whole, and order the proceedings of the General Court Martial to be read, and the Sentence to be put in Execution in the Front of Colonel Fitch's Regiment.

I hope in God this is the last Example of this kind that I shall be forced to make, & that I shall never send you again on so disagreable a service.

WO/34/80 fol. 24

64
Major-General Jeffery Amherst to The Mayor and Sheriff of Albany

Camp at Fort Edward

[Copy in Secretary's hand]   20 June 1759

Col° Bradstreet has just now laid before me a Letter he has received from his Assistant, Lieut. Coventry, a Copy of which I enclose; the accusation it contains, and that against Magistrates, who at all time ought to be aiding & assisting the Kings Officers in forwarding & Carrying on the publick Service with the utmost Chearfullness and alacrity but more particularly at this Juncture, that [sic] those very officers are Employed in the defence & protection of the Rights & properties of the Subject, has greatly astonished me, and is what I cannot by any means Countenance; I am therefore to Warn You, that if You do not immediately cause such irregularities to cease, and that You do not chearfully and to your utmost afford the Kings Officers all the aid and assistance which the service may require and which it is Your Duty, as Magistrate to lend, You will compell me tho greatly against my Inclinations to take such Measures, as Shall be most disagreable to You, and Meanwhile I shall not fail of representing the last unwarrantable behavior to the Lieut. Governor of New York.[64]

WO/34/80 fol. 37

65
Major-General Jeffery Amherst to Lieutenant Governor James De Lancey

Camp of Lake George

[Copy in Secretary's hand]   23 June 1759

On the 21st I Marched at Day break from Fort Edward, as I Wrote You word I intended to do, the Road being cut up between Fort Edward and Halfway brook with the Artillery Stores, and Batteaus etc etc, that I had forwarded to that post, though I had Employed most of my Camp two days in repairing it, I was forced to leave all my heavy Artillery behind me at Fort Edward, where I have left Montgomery's, the Newhampshire regim^t, the very few of Willards, and Colonel Montgomery to Command; I marched in Two Columns, the Rangers and Gages forming an Advanced Guard, the Right Column consisting of a Battalion of Grenadiers, Late Forbes's, Inniskilling Reg^t. – The Left Column of Whiting's Worcester's; Fitch's, Babcock, One Batt^n of Ruggles; Light Infantry Battalion form'd from the Regular Regiments (an Excellent Corps) made the Rear Guard; the Roy^l Highland Reg^t Joined me at Halfway brook; The Other Half of my Army is disposed of in different places at present where they are wanted, and from whence I can have them the first moment I can get forward; I Don't tell You where they are as nothing is impossible, this may fall into the Enemy's hands without reaching You & I would not have them know what a Corps I have to give them a Dose, which I shall do as soon as ever I can, now I find You are prepared for Securing the Prisoners.[65] – On my March I had a Ranger Report the Enemy was on this Side the Lake, the Officer of Rangers Saw their Advanced Guard, and Could not tell how many were behind; this made no Sort of Change, for I Set out to Come here, if the Enemy had been here or on the Road, (which indeed I thought quite impossible) and I am Sorry to Say I do not give the least Credit to any Ranger Reports, from all I have Seen of them, they are the most Careless, Negligent, Ignorant Corps I ever Saw, and if they are not beat on all Occasions I really cannot find out the reason why they are not – Mr Rogers a good man, but I must Rub his Corps up, or they are worse than Nothing.

I Don't mean that You should think I want Rangers, I think I have full Enough of them . . .

I thank You for Sending forward the Sixty New Levies, they will be very acceptable to Mr Prideaux, I am much more interested for Numbers for him than for myself, though I think We shall both have Enough. Every thing going on well here; my Rear Guard did not come into Camp the 21st till Nine at Night, and I halted but an hour & a half on the Road, except when I had taken possession of the Heights here, and halted to mark a Camp & Send in the Tents . . .

WO/34/30 fol. 52

66
Robert Leake to Major-General Jeffery Amherst

Albany

30 June 1759

[Secretary's hand, signed by Leake]   [Received 2 July 1759]

May it Please your Excellency To give me leave to lay before You, that the 28th Inst. I received a Letter from Brigad^r General Prideaux Aid de Camp, requiring a speedy supply of Provisions, as very near the whole of their Bread, was spoiled, by Leaky Battoes & Badness of the Casks, as to the last, I have remonstrated for these three years past, to have had them made stronger, tighter, & better Hooped, for in the State they now come in with the rough & careless treatment they received from Waggoners Battoemen and others, one hundred Coopers on the Crown's expense woud be insufficient if they could be got.

And as the greatest part of the Provisions lately come up is Bread & that but coarse and flinty it becomes necessary to send up Flour, for the Mohawk River, which has always been, since I knew it a grave to Provisions.

The Publick Cash, in my hands, for the supply of Fat Cattle, being very near expended, I need not lay before Your Excellency, the allmost impossibility of carrying it on, without Money . . .

WO/34/68 fol. 9

67
Major-General Jeffery Amherst to Robert Leake

Camp at Lake George

[Copy in Secretary's hand]   3 July 1759

In answer to Yours of the 30th Ultimo, receiv'd Yesterday, with the return of provisions in Store at Albany on the Day of its date, and Your memorial for a further Warrant of £8000 Sterling to enable You to continue to purchase fatt Cattle for the Use of the Troops, as the former Warrant I granted You on that account was near Expended. I can only Observe to You, that as the Military Chest will not at present allow of near so considerable a draft upon it, You must do the best You can for a little while without letting the service Suffer, as I have moved the Assembly of New York for a Loan of Money, which I am hopeful will ere long be granted,[66] I Shall then have it in my power to Comply with your request; meanwhile, notwithstanding all the Difficulties that arise in transporting provisions up the Mohawk River, and the Waste attending the Same thro' the Mismanagement of the Contractors and the badness of the Casks, that must not hinder You from forwarding up thither, the quantity Brig^r Genl Prideaux has or may ask, as that Service must by no Means Suffer; and when time & Circumstances permit, I will cause Enquiry to be made in the Carelessness You Complain of.

WO/34/67 fol. 103

68
Major-General Jeffery Amherst to Christopher Kilby

Camp at Lake George

[Copy in Secretary's hand]   7 July 1759

Altho' there may be at present at the different posts a Sufficient quantity of Provisions for Victualling the Troops during the Campaign, Yet as I am informed there is Scarce any left in Store at Albany, to keep up the Supply for the Ensuing Winter which cannot be done at a better time & with a greater saving to the publick than now, that the Teams and Waggons are in the pay of the Crown & must lay Idle if there are not provisions at Albany to keep them Constantly Employed; I must therefore beg to remind You of Your promise, (which I cannot too particularly recommend to You) of continuing to Send up to Albany Constant & frequent Supplies of all kinds of Provisions Sufficient for Victualling the Troops all the Winter.[67]

WO/34/69 fol. 135

69
Major-General Jeffery Amherst to Major William Browning

Camp at Lake George

[Copy in Secretary's hand]   17 July 1759

As the Enemy will doubtless Use all their Endeavors to thwart as much as possible the Operations Carrying on against them by the way of the Mohawk River, by Attempting to disturb Your Communication, & Intercept Your Convoys, You will in order to frustrate their designs, and the more Effectually to prevent any great Loss or Inconvenience to Us from any of their Attempts Succeeding, without Interrupting Your Convoys, keep constantly going, and make them so small and Composed of Such different kinds of Stores, that should We have the Misfortune to lose them they might be easily Replaced, or the Want of them not retard or delay Our Operations; This You will particularly Attend to in regard to the Eighteen Six pounders I have Ordered to Oswego for the Vessels building there, which You will Send by Three or Fours, which Number should they happen to be taken, We shall not miss much, whereas if they were all Eighteen to fall into the hands of the Enemy, We should be Considerable Sufferers, as before We Could get others in their Stead, & they got up to Oswego, the Season would be lost for Employing them to the purpose; However if it should so happen that they might all be immediately wanted, You will in that Case Send such a Strong Escort with them as may put it out of the Power of the Enemy to Succeed with any party they can be Supposed to Send that way whilst they are so much Employed every where Else.

WO/34/53 fol. 153

WLC/AP/4

70
Return of Troops as embarked on Lake George and Extract of Orders for Passing Lake George

[Holograph]
<u>Return of Troops as embarked on Lake George</u>
Regulars: 5743
Artillery: 111
Provincials: 5279
Total officers included, <u>11133</u>

Artillery on Lake George

24 Pounders	6	8 inch Hautwitzers	6
18 D^{to}	4	5 inch D^{to}	2
12 D^{to}	10	Royal Mortars	8
6 D^{to}	7	10 Inch Mortars	4
3 D^{to}	3	13 Inch D^{to}	1

Extract of orders for passing Lake George . . . Rangers, Light Infantry of Reg^{ts} & Grenadiers to be comanded by Col. Haviland, Lieut. Brehme to attend Col. Haviland. Willards R^{t} & 2^{d} Batt^{n} of Ruggles to be comanded by Col. Ruggles, Lt Gray to attend Col. Ruggles. The 2^{d} Column to be comanded by B^{r} Genl Gage. Col Schulyer will comand the two Reg^{ts} of the 3d Column, which will have each <u>100</u> Axes delivered to them, that they may be ready to clear the Roads the moment they are ordered to land, Lt Rose to attend Col Schulyer. The column on the left to be comanded by Col. Lyman & to be ready to land on the west side or where ordered. Signals to be made on b/°ard the invincible Radeau, or Halifax Sloop. A red flag is for sailing or Rowing, when struck is for halting, a small Union Flag for Majors of Brigade & Adjutants to come for orders. A blue flag is for the right Column to Land, when repeated for Gages, light Infantry & 2^{d} Column to Land, if repeated a second time for left Column to Land. The Artillery to Land after the second Column. Whiting's Reg^{t} to have the guard of the batteaus, Col Bradstreet will make such disposition for them as he thinks best: a 12 Pounder on the left of the Rangers, an 18 on the Right of Lymans. The men to land in their waistcoats, go as light as possible, carrying only their Blankets & Provisions. No Hurry or Huzzaing on any account whatever & no man to fire

74

without orders from his Officer. In whatever Situation the Regiments may be when landed, and Night comes on, no motions are to be made in the night; each Reg^t will secure their own ground, firing in the night must be avoided. The Enemy must be received with fixed Bayonets & the Reg^ts not to quit their Ground, even if the Enemy could break through. The Regiments are never to get up in heaps but keep their Ranks on all occasions. Silence among the men must be absolutely kept. No pass word to be regarded, no orders to be obeyed but such as are delivered or sent in writing by the D. Adjutants General, Aides de Camp, Majors of Brigade, D.Q. Masters General or Engineers. No man to go back when landed to fetch Provisions, Tent or any thing else, 'till there is a general order for it, they must expect to lay a night or two on their Arms, the Men must row in turns, there must not be any pressing forward, the whole will move gently that the men may not be fatigued, those that are not employed in rowing must go to sleep, that they may be alert & fit for Service when landed . . .

U1350/O/14, Personal Journal, pp. 51–4

71
Major-General Jeffery Amherst: Orders to Colonel William Haviland

Lake George
[Copy in Secretary's hand]   20 July 1759

Colonel Haviland to Land on the Right when Ordered to March, and try to Cut off any Advanced Parties of the Enemy from the Saw Mill, to follow any Parties over the Saw Mill, and to push over at the Saw Mill, and take Posts on the most Advantageous grounds bearing towards Lake Champlain, that the Saw Mill bridge may be Repaired if wanted, and that the Artillery may be brought forward, the Line will Sustain Colonel Haviland, who will take all the Advantages he can of Attacking the Enemy briskly, & when he takes his Post, will Secure them in the best manner he can.

WO/34/52 fol. 7

72
Major-General Jeffery Amherst to Colonel James Montresor

Camp before Ticonderoga
[Copy in Secretary's hand]   24 July 1759

Every thing going on well here, took possession of the Lines Yesterday, and my Camp, tho' not far from the Fort, well Covered from every thing but Shells & Ricochets, the last don't hurt, most of their Fuzees of their Shells bad. I send the Newhampshire Troops to Oswego. Forward them with all Dispatch – About Twenty Wounded Men which I am Sorry to Send You, must be put in the Hospital; Ensign Harrison of Forbes's killed. I hope Your Works go on well, keep all Artificers of Provincials that arrive with You.

WO/34/80 fol. 93

73
Major-General Jeffery Amherst to Brigadier John Prideaux

Camp before Ticonderoga
[Copy in Secretary's hand]   24 July 1759

As I hope to be Soon in possession of Tienderoga and to be able to Advance towards Montreal, I Send you a Battalion of Newhampshire Troops to help in Carrying on the Works at Oswego, that that Important Fort may be finished as soon as possible, and that You may take more men with You to proceed to La Galette after the Reduction of Niagara.

My numbers here are not equal to the Calls I have for them, but Colonel Haldimand Writing to me that he Could proceed much faster in his Works if he had more Men, I willingly part with them to forward the Service under Your Command . . .

WO/34/46B fol. 161

74
Sir William Johnson to Major-General Jeffery Amherst

Niagara

25 July 1759

[Holograph]   [Received 4 August 1759]

I Have the Honour to Acquaint You by Lieut. Moncrieff, Niagara Surrendered to His Majesty's Arms the Twenty fifth Instant; A Detachment of Twelve Hundred men with a Number of Indians, under the Command of Messrs Aubry and Delignery, collected from Detroit, Venango, & Presque Isle, made an Attempt to Reinforce the Garrison the 24th in the morning, but as I had Intelligence of them, I made a Disposition to Intercept them. The Evening before, I Ordered the Light Infantry & Picquets to take post on the Road upon our Left leading from Niagara Falls to the Fort; In the morning I reinforced these with two Companys of Grenadiers and part of the Forty Sixth Reg^t. The Action began about half after Nine; but they were so well received by the Troops in Front and the Indians on their Flank, that in an hours time the whole was Compleatly Ruined, and all their officers made Prisoners, among whom are Mons^{rs} Aubry, DeLignery, Marin, Repentini, to the Number of Seventeen. I cannot Ascertain the Number of the killed, they are so dispersed among the Woods, but their loss is great.

As this happened under the Eyes of the Garrison I thought proper to Send my Last Summons to the Commanding Officer for his Surrender, which he Listened to. – I enclose You the Capitulation; Mr Moncrieff will Inform You of the State of our Ammunition and Provisions; I hope Care will be taken to forward an Immediate Supply of both to Oswego. – As the Troops that were defeated Yesterday were drawn from those Posts which Lye in General Stanwix's Rout, I am in hopes it will be of the Utmost Consequence to the success of his Expedition.

The Publick Stores of the Garrison that can be Saved from the Indians, I Shall Order the Assistant Q^r Master General and the Clerk of Stores to take an Account of, as soon as possible.

As all my Attention at present is taken up with the Indians, that the Capitulation I have Agreed to may be Observed, Your Excellency will Excuse me for not being more particular.

Permit me to assure You, in the whole progress of the Siege, which was Severe and painfull, the Officers and Men, behaved with the utmost Chearfullness & Bravery; I have only to Regret the Loss of General Prideaux and Col° Johnson;[68] I Endeavoured to pursue the Late General's Vigorous measures, the good effects of which he deserved to Enjoy.

WO/34/39 fol. 96[69]

75
Major-General Jeffery Amherst to Brigadier-General Thomas Gage

[Copy in Secretary's hand]

Camp at Ticonderoga
28 July 1759

On this most unfortunate Accident of the death of Brigadier General Prideaux, of which I have this moment an Account, I am necessitated, very contrary to my Inclinations, to desire You will repair immediately to Oswego, where I am in hopes a great part of the Troops will be returned by the time You can arrive, and that Sir William Johnson will have left a sufficient Garrison for Niagara, (which I am willing to think he will have reduced) untill Brigadier General Stanwix can send Troops to Garrison in the place.

If the troops should not be returned to Oswego in the time of Your arrival, You will please to proceed to Niagara or remain at Oswego, as You shall Judge most conducive to the good of His Majestys Service from the Intelligence you will receive at Oswego.

You will please to take the Instructions I had given to Brigadier Gen¹ Prideaux, of which I have no Copy with me, but I find Sir Wᵐ Johnson has them, and You will look on those Instructions as Orders to Yourself.

I must recommend to You the forwarding [of] the intended Fort at Oswego, as likewise the Vessels to be built on the Lake, but no time must be lost after the return of the Troops from Niagara to Oswego in proceeding to La Galette with all the Expedition possible leaving a sufficient number for the Security & protection of the Post of Oswego and for carrying on the Works of the Fort, for which Service you will leave such Officer to Command there as You judge best.

It is of the utmost Consequence that you take post at La Galette, where a secure post should be erected & all measures taken for proceed^g to Montreal or at least to force the Enemy to keep a large body of Troops to hinder You, if the passage from La Galette to Montreal should be found impracticable.

If Success should have attended His Majestys Forces at Niagara & that the passage to Montreal should be found too difficult to Attempt, I would then have You take such a post at La Galette as may be kept during the Winter, as the Enemy by being Shut Out from Lake Ontario on that side must be greatly distressed, and I am in hopes to confine them on this side by taking post at least as far as Crown Point, which will cover all the country behind those two places, and put it out of the power of the Enemy to make any inroads.

If you should find the number of Indians which are with Sir William Johnson more than what is necessary, You will please to send to me, any that You may not want. I most heartily wish you Success.

PS My Intentions are to push on the Operations of the Campaign with the utmost Vigour, & my Opinion is, that We shall render Ourselves Masters of all Canada; You will therefore see, how very requisite it is that You should with the Corps under your Command, approach as near Montreal as possible, and if the Enemy is obliged to remain on the defensive against Mr Wolfe & me, at any distance from Montreal, Your taking that Place would be much easier than your getting at it.

If from the death of Brig^r Genl Prideaux, or from any unforeseen Accident, the reduction of Niagara may not have taken Place, I would in that case have you make Your dispositions, if possible, for returning to the Attack & taking the place, for which You shall have all the Assistance I can give You.

The reduction of all Canada is the Object of this Campaign, a Miscarriage at Quebec (nothing is more unlikely to happen) is the only thing that can frustrate the Attempt, but if it should happen, we may then be reduced to Confine the Operations, by taking the Posts as I have before mentioned of Crown Point and La Galette, which must not be given up, and must be made as respectable as time will permit.

WO/34/46A fols 169–70

WLC/AP/4

76
Major-General Jeffery Amherst to Brigadier-General John Stanwix

Camp at Ticonderoga

[Copy in Secretary's hand]   31 July 1759

I have now the Satisfaction to Acquaint You that on the morning of the 21ˢᵗ I Embarked with the Army on Lake George, and with a fair Wind proceeded so as to be at a distance to Land the next morning which I did, and marched to the Saw Mills, where the Opposition we met from the Enemy was not great; I took possession of the Commanding Grounds, on the Enemy's Side of the Saw Mills, which was all I intended or desired; I then made the Bridge and got some Cannon over by Night, which the Enemy Saw pass; I lay on my Arms the Night, Secured the Communication, and ordered the Army to March the next morning by the rising Grounds, intending to post myself in the Front of their Lines, the Right to the Saw Mill River, and Left to Lake Champlain; but as morning Cleared up the Officers Commanding Posts opposite the Fort reported the Enemy's Tents Struck, and that they were gone off in their Sloops, Batteaus &c, and this being Confirmed to me by other Reports, I marched and took possession of their Lines, a Cannonading and Bombarding Ensued, which was pretty well kept up; I Covered the Troops as much as the Ground would let me, and Opened the Trenches with all the Tools I had; The Army lay on their Arms.

24th The Enemy continued their Fire without doing us any great mischief; The Trenches advanced and the Batteries were fixed on; The Enemy burnt all Outhouses, Stript all the Shingles off of the Roofs in the Fort, and every thing looked like a Vigorous Defence, or an intended blowing up the Fort; I try'd all I could to get Boats across to Cutt off their Retreat.

25th The Enemy's fire increased, and they threw their Shells not badly; Our Trenches went on well; Some Artillery got up, and the Batteries traced out; Poor Townshend killed by a Cannon Ball.[70]

26th The Enemy's fire the Same, and our Batteries to be ready to night for to Open in the Morning, but about ten o'Clock a Deserter came in, told us they were going to blow the Fort up, and the whole Garrison was getting off; It proved true & Some Voluntiers went and brought the Colours when the Buildings were in Flames; One Bastion was blown up; But the Fort will be repaired at a small Expence; We have about 30 of the Enemy, Some prisoners, Some Deserters; The Indians have Scalped some few of Our Men.

I wait for nothing but my Boats & Batteaus (which are getting over the Carrying Place) to proceed to Crown Point, for which I am hopefull to Set out in two days.

On the 27th I had a Letter from Colonel Haldimand, Informing me that Brig[r] Prideaux was Set down before Niagara; that he had broke Ground on the 9th, was Erecting his Batteries, and that they were to Open the 15th, That 200 men of the Enemy intended as a Reinforcement against You, had been prevented from proceeding on their march, & had thrown themselves into the Garrison of Niagara; but unfortunately two days ago I received another Letter from him with the Melancholy News of Poor Brig[r] Prideaux being killed, when every thing was going on well, and his Batteries within a hundred & Forty Yards of the Place; On this distressfull Affair I immediately dispatched Brig[r] General Gage to take the Command of that Army, and to pursue the Ulterior Operations You are Acquainted with, as I make no doubt, by the time of his arrival at Oswego, Every thing will be over at Niagara, where, notwithstanding this unfortunate Event, I am still hopefull We shall Succeed, as Col[o] Haldimand is gone thither, & that Sir

William Johnson has with him a very Considerable Body of Indians, who are said to be extremely well Affected & hearty in the Cause; – I must therefore again Recommend it to You, to hasten up to Pittsburgh, that the Detachment of Your Army intended to Garrison Niagara, may be at hand to proceed thither upon the first Notice of the Reduction of that Fort.

We have not a Single Word from Adm^l Saunders nor Major-General Wolfe since they sailed from Louisbourg.

WO/34/45 fols 227–9

77
Major-General Jeffery Amherst to Brigadier-General Thomas Gage

Camp of Ticonderoga
[Copy in Secretary's hand]   1 August 1759

. . . I Hear this moment the Enemy have Abandoned Crown Point; my Batteaus won't let me Set out till tomorrow night; I shall pursue them to the utmost of my Power, & if Niagara is taken, as I greatly hope it is, or should it be taken without Your returning to the Attack, I then depend on Your pursuing Your Ulterior Operations with the utmost Expedition, and with leaving only a sufficient Number for Carrying on the Works of Oswego, You will so soon as possible take post at La Galette where You must likewise Secure the post, which a small Number will be sufficient to do, and You will proceed as near to Montreal as possible, which will so Confine the Enemy in every part that they must Submit, and You will try all You can to take the Place. – If Sir Wm Johnson can persuade the Indians to Join You in this last and Essential Stroke for the Reduction of Canada, it will Ensure Success to You, & I don't desire to have a Man with me that can be of Service to You.

On Your Arrival in Lake St Francis or the Cedar Falls it will be easy for You to Send me Intelligence, as I design to be at St Johns or Chamblay, if not farther by that time.

Now is the time, & We must make Use of it – Don't let people about You make Difficulties without a real Reason; We must all be Allert and Active day & Night, if necessary; If We all do our parts, the French must fall, and we shall Reap peace and Quiet for it hereafter.

WO/34/46A fol. 171

WLC/AP/4

78
Major-General Jeffery Amherst to Colonel John Bradstreet

Camp of Ticonderoga

[Copy in Secretary's hand]   1 August 1759

. . . Pray be so good to forward the Brewing Apparatus as fast as possible, the Army is beginning to grow Sickly, and I believe from no other reason but drinking Water wherever they find it, which Sickness will, I hope, be got the better of by Spruce Beer . . .

WO/34/58 fol. 26

79
Major-General Jeffery Amherst to Christopher Kilby

Camp at Ticonderoga

[Copy in Secretary's hand]   1 August 1759

Colonel Bradstreet has just now Shewn me a Letter from Lieut: Coventry, Setting forth that there were on the 30th Ultimo, so little a Quantity of Provisions at Albany, that to prevent the Army to the Westward failing, he was Obliged to Send for what Flour and Pork there was at Half Moon;[71] This obliges me once more to renew to You my most pressing Instances, that You will have a particular Attention in preventing any Inconveniences attending that Army thro' the want of that Article, and that You will pay a due Observance to my several Letters on that head desiring, that You would with the utmost Speed & dispatch, Collect & forward to Albany all the Provisions You possibly can gather, without prejudicing the Service up the River S[t] Lawrence; If any thing prevents All Canada being taken this Campaign it will be the Want of Provisions.

WO/34/69 fol. 141

80
Major-General Jeffery Amherst to Captain Joshua Loring
Camp of Ticonderoga
[Copy in Secretary's hand]   3 August 1759

I Proceed tomorrow to Crown Point, where You will please to Send me Reports of any thing Material that may happen; As the Success and Advantages that may be gained [in] this Campaign greatly depend on Your making the utmost Expedition in forwarding Everything in Your department, I must most earnestly recommend it to You, that You will make all the Dispatch possible in Building the Vessel and Boats for the guns according to the Intended Plan.[72]

WO/34/64 fol. 202

81
Major-General Jeffery Amherst to Colonel Phineas Lyman
Camp of Ticonderoga
[Copy in Secretary's hand]   3 August 1759

As His Majesty's Service requires that Two Battalions should remain here for the Repairs of the Fort, as well as for the defence and protection of the Place & Workmen, You will please to take on You the Command of the Troops Ordered to remain here, and to Use Your utmost Endeavors that the Repairs may be Carried on with all the Expedition possible.

I Have Ordered Lieut. Brehme, Assistant Engineer, to remain here to direct the Work, and I have left such Officers & Artificers as are Judged to be necessary from Schuyler's & Fitche's Reg[ts] to Assist in the Work with those You will furnish from the Two Battalions under Your Command.

It is of the utmost Consequence to the future Operations of this Campaign that the Repairs to the Fort are Compleated with the greatest dispatch, that I may then March on the Reg^ts & only be Obliged to leave a Small Garrison in the Place.

I have ordered a Captain & 130 of Montgomery's Reg^t to remain under Your Command to give Guards to the Fort, the Fort by Water, & the Garden, that the Battalions may not be taken from their Work by furnishing those Guards . . .

WO/34/43 fol. 230

82
Major-General Jeffery Amherst to Lieutenant Governor James De Lancey

Camp at Crown Point
[Copy in Secretary's hand]   5 August 1759

Your favor of the 29th Ultimo, requiring no Answer, I have only to thank You for it, and to Congratulate You on our possession of this Ground, which I took Yester Evening, the Enemy having Abandoned it, and blown up part of the Fort, three days before; Indeed I should have been here two days sooner, had not an Excessive heavy 24 hours Rain retarded our Batteaus, etc from getting over the Carrying Place, but now, no time shall be lost in building such a Fort as from its Situation & Strength will most effectually Cover the whole Country, & Ensure the peaceable and quiet possession of it on this Side; Wherefore You may, as soon as You please, advise & recommend it, to such of the Inhabitants of Your Province, as may have deserted their Settlements, to Come & Reoccupy the Same, and also to Encourage all those that You shall think proper, to Come and Settle such parts of it as You shall please to Grant and parcell out to them, as now they can have Nothing to fear from the Incursions of the Enemy, which they may from henceforth safely look upon to be at an End, not only on this side, but likewise along the Mohawk River, which Sir William Johnson's success (of which You will ere this have had the Accounts) has also Ensured . . .

WO/34/30 fol. 65^73

83
Christopher Kilby to Major-General Jeffery Amherst

Greenwich, New York
5 August 1759
[Holograph]   [Receipt not dated]

I have your Excellencys letter of the 1st instant which follow'd joyfull tidings from Ticonderoga and Crown Point and the Glorious news of Compleat success to His Majesty's Arms at Niagara.

That success and a very bountiful Supply sent from Albany gives me untroubled assurance of a full Stock of Provisions to the Western Army, for the remaining part of the Campaign and for any Garrison it may be found necessary to leave in that Quarter during the Winter or for a longer time. – I shall however in Obedience to your repeated letters accomodate the Arrival of Meat and Pease which I am advised of the Shipping of from Europe (and daily expect) together with so much Bread kind, as the Country affords, – towards a Supply at Albany to be removed from thence when and where the Publick Service may require it; – but am sorry to tell your Excellency that the Collusive and Illicit transportation of Flour has been so Excessive of late, that if any unexpected and Extraordinary Supply to the Army or rather for the Maintenance of Prisoners should become necessary in the Article of Bread kind, your letter to the Governor of this Province will become necessary to restrain such iniquitous Exportation and to Secure the Flour of the Country for the use of the Publick. – Be that as it will the Supply was compleat for all the Army before I left Albany, and you may in all Events depend upon every thing in my power for an Effectual Supply to the Troops in all their Dispositions, for the few months that may remain of my Connection with the Victualling Contract,[74] but I am not sure that I shall in the meantime be able to find employment for a useless Host of Waggons by an unnecessary transportation of Provisions between Albany or Halfmoon, and Schenectady only; which would not employ 20 a Week to feed that department a year.

Provisions are not, nor cannot be wanted during the present Campaign, and I therefore depend upon the Total Reduction of Canada, and shall be the most happy of all men to pay Your Excellency my Compliments upon the Event you are so absolutely sure of.

WO/34/69 fol. 95

84
Major-General Jeffery Amherst: Instructions to Captain Quinton Kennedy

Camp at Crown Point

[Copy under Amherst's hand seal]   8 August 1759

Upon Receipt hereof, You will, as I have before directed, Set out for and proceed to the Settlements of the Eastern Indians; And upon Your Arrival among them, You will Enquire for their Chiefs, whom You are to Acquaint from me, that I am got thus far with my Army, on my way to Canada, with a design of Reducing the Whole Country to His Majesty's Obedience, but that out of the good Will I bear those Indians, I do, before I proceed so far as their Settlements, Send You to them, to Offer them my Friendship, upon Condition that they do remain Neutral, and do not Join with any of His Majesty's Enemies in any Act of Hostilities against His Army, or any One of His subjects, in which Case, as I am not Come with an Intention of dispossessing or Annoying them, I will protect and defend their Persons & properties, and Secure unto them the peaceable and quiet possession thereof, and that without requiring any of their Aid or Assistance, which I have no manner or occasion for, as the Army under my Command is more than sufficiently Strong, not only to Reduce the French, but the Indians themselves, if they do not Accept of the Friendship I now Offer them; – You must therefore Insist upon their Immediate Answer, and I make no doubt they will Consult their own Interest, & gladly and sincerely Accept the friendly proposal I now make them thro' You; And with their Answer You will forthwith Repair to Major-General Wolfe at Quebec, and Inform him that it is my

Orders, that he do treat these Eastern Indians as Our Friends & Allies, and that he take Care to See my Engagements with them punctually fulfilled & Complied with; – After which You will without delay return to me and make a Report of Your Whole Proceedings in the Negotiation I do hereby Entrust You with.

WO/34/38 fol. 79

85
Colonel John Bradstreet to Major-General Jeffery Amherst
Landing

9 August 1759

[Holograph]   [Received 10 August 1759]

I beg leave to represent to your Excellency that I am apprehensive, from the augmentations of the Troops to the Westward, that the establishment of Battoes fix'd between Schenectady & Oswego will not be sufficient to carry, in time, a proper quantity of Provisions to maintain the Troops and leave enough for the Garrisons [in] the winter as you may, at least, allow Six Months that no supply can be sent to Oswego; wherefore I take the liberty to propose to your Excellency the adding Thirty Battoes to these between Schenectady & Fort Stanwix, and that those that now work between the north west end of the Onida Lake & Oswego be added to those who work upon the Onid[a] Lake & up Wood Creek and that Detachments from Oswego take up the two stations to the Falls & the Onida Lake upon the Onondaga River with Double the number of Boats now employed there.[75]

WO/34/57 fol. 36

86
Major-General Jeffery Amherst to Captain George Garth
Camp of Crown Point

[Copy in Secretary's hand]   10 August 1759

I Shall order a Detachment to proceed to morrow morning to the mouth of the Otter River, where I would have You go with the said

Detachment, and You will Reconnoitre the Ground on the South and North Sides of the Mouth of the Said River, to See where Posts may be Established to Command the River, & protect the Inhabitants that may now Settle between that and N°. 4, and to Obstruct any Scalping Parties from going up that River.[76]

WO/34/69 fol. 48

87
Major-General Jeffery Amherst to Brigadier-General Thomas Gage

[Copy in Secretary's hand]

Camp at Crown Point
10 August 1759

That the forwarding up of Provisions to Your Post, both for the daily Consumption of the Army under Your Command, and the Winter Garrisons to the Westward, may meet with all the Dispatch requisite, & in order to Secure the Certainty of its being laid in in time, I have Ordered an Encrease of Half the Number of Batteaus that were first Allotted for that Service, between Schenectady and Fort Stanwix; You will therefore See that You must on Your part Send some from Oswego to keep up the same proportion along the Chain of Posts, that there may be no Retardment any Where; I send You a Copy of my Letter to Bradstreet on that head.

WO/34/46A fol. 174

WLC/AP/4

88
Major-General Jeffery Amherst to Lieutenant Governor James De Lancey

[Copy in Secretary's hand]

Camp at Crown Point
13 August 1759

. . . I thank You for the Intelligence of Serg.t Syant, relative to our Operations up the River S.t Lawrence, concerning which I cannot help thinking We must yet remain greatly in the dark; All I can hitherto rely upon, with any probability of truth, is Mr Wolfe's having Landed on the Isle of Orleans upon the 5th of last Month Since when, from the distance We are at, I could not Expect any Letters from him, so that I am not at all Surprized at my being without, but I hope & trust that the first I shall receive will be agreable to all our Wishes, meanwhile it cannot be Expected that either he or I should fly . . .

WO/34/30 fol. 68

89
Major-General Jeffery Amherst to Brigadier-General Thomas Gage

Camp of Crown Point

[Copy in Secretary's hand]   14 August 1759

. . . I am at present building a very respectable Fortress here which I intend to finish before the Campaign is over, & at the same time I am Erecting this Post, at which all the Troops I have with me are at Work, I have five Batt^s at the Landing Place, Saw mills & Tienderoga, where I am making & repairing every thing wanting to Enable me to pass the Lake to St Johns and for putting the Fort of Tienderoga in as good, if not better State of Defence than when We Arrived there.

As I have sent Capt Kennedy and Lt Hamilton by land to try to Join Major-General Wolfe, & that I have likewise sent a Ranging Officer by the Kennebeck River for the said purpose, I doubt not but I shall by One Avenue or the Other Succeed in Acquainting Mr Wolfe of the Operations on this Side, & that I may Soon get information of his progress, from which my Motions here must be guided, & I hope the Brigantine I had ordered to be built will be ready in time, that I may proceed to St John's so soon as I find a proper Occasion, & I shall leave as great a Number of Men for Carrying on the Works here while I am advanced, as my Force will permit me . . .

I am glad to find Sir Wm Johnson can make immediate Use of the Vessels that were building at Niagara; they will help You greatly, & I hope will take You safe to La Galette, which is now indeed the Post of the utmost Consequence, by that We shall be entire Masters of Lake Ontario, & His Majesty's subjects on the Mohawk River will be thereby effectually freed from all Inroads & Scalping parties of the Enemy as I may say the whole Country from this to New York is by the Reduction of Tienderoga & this Important Post, which I'll take all the Care I can shall not fall again into the Enemy's hands.

In the present situation that the Enemy is in, it is impossible they can hinder You from taking Post at La Galette, & I must repeat to You my most Earnest desires for Your taking possession of that Post, & Erecting such a Fort as shall be tenable during the Winter in the most advantageous Ground you can find; I doubt not but We shall soon after find a practicable Road from thence to Fort Stanwix.

WO/34/46A fols 175–6

WLC/AP/4

90
Brigadier-General John Stanwix to Major-General Jeffery Amherst

Camp at Fort Bedford
16 August 1759
[Holograph]   [Receipt not dated]

. . . I have received the inclosed /extracts of letters from Colonel Mercer from Pittsburgh and intelligence from Captain Croghan Agent for Indian affairs, that the French on hearing of Niagaras being taken have retired from Venango Lebeouf & Presquile after burning all these posts.

Major Tullikens is at Pittsburg wth 400 Roy^l Americans destined for Niagara the 20 Batteaus ready, but the Ohio is so uncomonly low that it is not possible now to get up that river even with Canos, the French were obliged to burn all their Batteaus upon Beauf River for want of Water to carry them up to the Portage, this put a full stop to the march of the detachment as it will be absolutely necessary to go by water from Presquile to Niagara, knowing of no path leading by land which would be a vast circuit, but have some time ago wrote to Mr Croghan to get all the information that was possible, but have had no answer from which I conclude he has had no satisfactory acc^t . . .

The difficulty of forming even a small Magazeen at Pittsbourg is almost insurmountable, as we can form no calculation with so many Western Indians coming dayly to Pittsbourg and must be fed in spite of us, having had no assistance from the legislature, and not yet got one /^{half} of the Waggons want'd, for as their Law now stands the Penalty is only forty Shillings & that to go to the Parish which they with pleasure pay to get clear of the Service, last year the Penalty was twenty pounds which forced every Township to give their Quota, but absolutely refused this year after many many applications, I am not quite clear but it would be much cheaper and easy'r to be supply'd with flower at Pittsbourg from Niagara than to carry it this way attended with such an immense expense & Tedious land carriage, but this may be matter for future consideration.

My next letter to you I hope will be from Pittsbourg . . .

WO/34/45 fols 89–91

91
Governor Thomas Pownall to Major-General Jeffery Amherst

Boston
18 August 1759
[Received 26 August 1759]

[Holograph]

I was this day honor'd with your letters of the 5th & 8th Instant – by which I receiv'd the most agreable accounts of the Success of his Majesty's Arms under Your Command in restoring to the British Crown its Rights at Ticonderoga Niagara & Crown Point, so long Usurp'd from them. What You have already /^{done} is la[y]ing the Foundation of ye British Empire in America & You are going on to build it up an indissoluble edifice. And I will hope before You leave America to see a Statue erected to you as the Founder of yᵉ British Empire in America.

As You are now going into yᵉ Heart of Canada far remote from this place The opportunities & means of Communication must grow daily less & less. I therefore write this letter in hopes to catch You before it is too late for an answer to be back in time. I shall meet my Assembly the 19ᵗʰ of Sepʳ & I propose to continue the Sessions part of October. As I am desirous that every thing In my department shou'd be done which You desire to be done, or that can any way serve or promote the King's affairs in your hands I trouble you with this previously to concert such measures as You shall think necessary. If you think of sending any Troops here this next winter, tho' I can suppose from yᵉ nature of yᵉ events likely to be determined this Campaign that it is not very easy for you to say what Numbers You shall send But if you can form any Judgment I will do all in my power to prepare for their proper reception . . .

There is another Point of great delicacy & will require my attention. You know yᵉ method of yᵉ Assemblies in America (& what they can not be brought out of) is to make only temporary Provision for their Troops & to limitt the Levies to a Certain time. Our's are limited to yᵉ first of Novʳ. There will be no difficulty in getting the time revived & prolonged as to yᵉ Troops with you. But as there was once in Mʳ Shirly's time a most violent Flame in the country about Troops rais'd for the Reduction of Beausejour being kept in Nova Scotia beyond yᵉ time limitted so as to be detain all winter in Garrison when they were only rais'd for a summer campaign. As there was once a Flame & Disconcertion of Measures on this Account, one has great reason so farr to be apprehensive of the like again, as to guard against it. If any difficulty shoud arise in this Affair the point in which they will pinch will be here, namely, in their fears & jealousies that our people will be kept there all Winter. If I can be able to give such Assurances that That will not be yᵉ Case, as shall oversett yᵉ pretences of ill-designing Men working on yᵉ Peoples Jealousies I wou'd make no doubt but that I shou'd be able to obtain their Lengthening out yᵉ Levy & making further Provision to such time as shall be convenient to You to relieve them.

Tho' these matters shou'd be indeed previously concerted yet when You think proper to write to me on ye Subject there shou'd appear no such previous concert, and they /^shou'd seem to arise, as they do in fact, from ye Necessity of ye Service as ye Reason why you apply for & require them. Jealousy is one of ye grand counter springs of this Country, & by avoiding any appearances that shou'd give occasion to such, one gains a great point . . .

WO/34/25 fols 286–7

92
Colonel John Bradstreet to Lieutenant Governor James De Lancey[77]

Albany

19 August 1759

[Holograph copy]   [Received 20 August 1759]

No person can be more sensible than you are that one Evil minded person that has made himself popular, among the lower sort of people, by obstructing his Majestys Service upon all occasions is of infinite disservice to the publick measures; this has long been the Case of the present Sherriff of this City, a fresh instance of which I now inclose you.[78] This behavour is extremely hard upon the Service as well as upon the people in General whose natural inclination, now, lead them to do every thing in their power to serve their King & Country. – I hope, Sir, you will put an end to this Violent Man obstructing the Kings Service for the future, that we may thereby be enabled to discharge the trust repos'd in us which otherwise cannot be done and consequently I cannot be answerable for the Evil effects of the Armies, this way, wanting provisions &c^a. the transportation of which being in my hands.

WO/34/57 fol. 47

93
Brigadier-General Thomas Gage to Major-General Jeffery Amherst

Oswego
21 August 1759
[Holograph]   [Received 4 September 1759]

I arrive at this Place with Part of the Draught the 16th at Noon, the Remainder, as well as the New Hampshire Regt have joined since. I find Sr William Johnson & Col^o Haldimand have already mentioned to you the Situation the Troops on this Side are in, respecting Provisions. The number of Batteaux & Men calculated for this Service only, considering the further Services required of Artillery, Stores, Rigging &c^a will not answer. The Batteaux are too large to answer the waters at all Seasons, & the men very indifferent at the Business: I should not mention the unfitness of the Batteaux as they were made, & cant be helped, only as I imagine a further Supply must be built, it would be better that They were made smaller & stronger, after the Plan of those that have been used in these waters for so many years, by the Indian Traders, & I imagine also, men might be collected on the Mohawk and Hudsons Rivers that would engage, by the trip, a method they have been long accustomed to, & I believe would in the End prove more Expeditious & less Expensive than any other . . . The destruction of Boats here has been very great, no less than 172 Batteaux, & 72 whaleboats either stove, unfit for Service, or carried away by Indians, a few have been recovered from the Indians; After all the Repairs I can make, I shall be able probably to get 200 Batteaux, and near 30 Whaleboats in readiness for Service.

Of the two vessels taken at Niagara one is a small one, the other on the Stocks not quite finished; & I am told with some Additions, which were ordered to be made, would be a serviceable Vessel, & both these are daily expected here: The large sloop for the 18 /^{Six} Pounders is to be built at Niagara, where all the Carpenters now are. Every Body agreeing it is the best Place for building, there being the greatest Plenty of proper Timber. But from the

95

Complaints of the want of a sufficient N°. of hands, I despair of this last being built soon enough to have much service from her, this year. And how all these vessels are to be manned I can't learn, we may possibly make a shift whilst the Provincials remain, but when the Campain breaks up there will be a great want of sailors and I apprehend there will be occasion for the Vessels to make Trips betwixt this & Niagara during the Winter. I have wrote to Lieut Col° Farquhar to lose no Time in compleating the Vessels, & if the two above mentioned don't arrive here very shortly, I must send again to him to hasten Them. For I must get Them here in order to carry Them with me when I leave this, being the only assistance I find, that I can depend upon, to enter the River St Lawrence, at the Entrance of which River, I am told the Enemy have now three vessels, mounting two of them, Six Pounders & a few Twelves. The third vessel may be a false Report, but two have been seen . . .

In respect of my Proceeding agreeable to your Instructions, I shall proceed as soon as possible, tho 'tis not in my Power absolutely to fix the Time, as I wait Provisions, Sloops, Boats & Artillery. But I shall make the quickest Dispatch I am able with every Thing . . .

WO/34/46A fols 44–5

94
Major-General Jeffery Amherst to Captain Joshua Loring
Camp of Crown Point
[Copy in Secretary's hand]   27 August 1759

I Enclose You a Letter which Lt Col° Eyre has given me, at the same time has Acquainted me that You have Stopped some things that were sent for the use of the Works going on here.

I Have only to desire that You will be so good to Send immediately any thing You may have Stopped intended for the Works here, and if You have any Bellows, Anvil, Tools &ca, more than what You really want, that You will forward them here, as they will be of great Service.

I Can't Conceive that any Officers in their particular Departments will chuse to keep things that are Useless, when at the same time they must know they would be of great Service at Other Works, and None can be Ignorant that the Whole that is carrying on is for the King's Service, and that Every Body is to Assist as much as they can to every part of it, and yet I hear Complaints from Morning to Night, of Tools, Workmen &ca. being detained when not wanted . . .

I am glad to hear the Brigantine is in such forwardness; how could the Mistake happen of throwing away so much time to bring Guns here that were Sent for on Purpose for the Brig?[79]

I think it will be necessary to know the Soundings of the Lake from this as far as we can towards the Place where the Enemys Vessells lay, & not to bring the Brig here till You can Sail in force to Attack those Vessells, which appears to me should be done by getting by them in the Night, and not to give them an Opportunity of Seeing our Force, and Running off, before we can get there.

WO/34/64 fol. 206

95
Major-General Jeffery Amherst to Lieutenant Governor James De Lancey

Camp of Crown Point

[Copy in Secretary's hand]   28 August 1759

. . . The Otter River has been Explored from the first Falls to the Mouth on the Lake,[80] and there are Eight Falls instead of Three, and there would be more difficulties attending the Navigation of that River than perhaps of any known River in America; What an Ignorance many People have been in about this River?

The Saw Mill at Tienderoga has begun to Work, the Repairs of that Fort will be soon finished; All the Works at this Fortress are going on well; You may be Assured the Men are not Idle, for they know it is all to be finished before Winter Quarters, and I hope before that time we shall take another Frontier.

WO/34/30 fol. 74

AMHERST AND THE CONQUEST OF CANADA

96
Major-General Jeffery Amherst to Rear Admiral Charles Saunders

[Copy in Secretary's hand]

Camp of Crown Point
29 August 1759

. . . Capt Loring is at present building a Brigantine that will Mount Twenty guns, such as I can furnish for the present are not very Respectable, but I hope will Answer the purpose intended which is to be superior to four Sloops and Schooners, the Enemy has on this Lake carrying each ten guns mostly six Pounders, one of them has two twelve Pounders, and they are commanded by Monsieur de Le Bras, and another of their Sea Officers called Captain Rigal.

As I have only four Pounders with Some few sixes for the Brigantine I am fitting up boats for heavier mettle to ensure a superiority and I hope the Whole will Soon be ready . . .

WO/34/42 fol. 229

97
Major-General Jeffery Amherst to the Governors of New Hampshire, New York and New Jersey

[Copy in Secretary's hand]

Camp of Crown Point
30 August 1759

As the Assembly of Your Province has made provision for their Troops, only to the 1st of November, after which I am Sensible it is not very practicable to Carry on any operations in these Northern parts of America, Yet, as from the Events of the Campaign, it may happen those Troops can't be discharged soon enough to reach their respective Habitations by that time, I could therefore wish You would move Your Assembly to make a further provision for them for the whole of that Month, by the latter end of which, I should hope they may all get home, as I do not propose to keep any of the Provincial Troops after the Operations of the Campaign & the necessary works for Ensuring its

Conquests are Compleated; and that I do not intend to keep any part of them for Garrison Duty . . .

WO/34/36 fol. 171

98
Major-General Jeffery Amherst to Brigadier-General John Stanwix

Camp of Crown Point
[Copy in Secretary's hand] 31 August 1759

. . . I am glad to find by Your Letter[81] that Col° Mercer and Major Tullikens were to Advance to take Post at Venango, in which I am pretty Sure they can find almost but very little Opposition; they will meet with no more at Le Beuf and Presqu' Isle, all which Places must consequently fall by the Reduction of Niagara, and some of the French Officers said they had only One hundred & twenty Men at Venango, and Fifty at both the other places, & no more than three Weeks Provisions for them when Niagara was taken; by this & Your provisions getting up I don't doubt but all Obstructions to Your relieving the Garrison of Niagara will be removed; I am very Sensible You will Use Your utmost Endeavours to relieve it so soon as You can, & indeed it is of the greatest Consequence to the Ulterior Operations of the Campaign, that the Garrison left under the Command of Lt Col° Farquhar should return to Oswego, & Join the Army under the Command of Brig^r General Gage the first moment it can be Effected.

I Have taken such precautions as I think will most effectually Secure a proper Supply of Provisions being forwarded for the Garrison of Niagara in due time, and I have the Satisfaction to be Assured by Col° Bradstreet from Albany that the Supply can't fail.

I wrote to you on the 8th Instant, to Acquaint You of my Arrival here, since which Nothing very material has happened; I have had no News yet of Mr Wolfe, except by a Letter from Monsr de Montcalm of the 30th of July, which I received the 15th Inst. wherein he says Mr Wolfe seems resolved to burn the Town of Quebec, for Eighteen days past he has thrown in Shells, Carcasses,

&ca and that the two Armies were as near to Each Other as they could be without Coming to Action. – By that Mr Wolfe has gained his Point in Landing, and I doubt not but he has taken the Town before this . . .

WO/34/45 fol. 231

99
[Major-General Jeffery Amherst]: Orders to Sergeant Hopkins of the Rangers[82]

[Holograph draft copy]

Crown Point
4 Sept 1759

You are to take four men of the Rangers, one of Montgommerys, one of late Prideaux's, one of Whitings, one of Babcockes, and with an Officer of Ruggles's and one of Whitings, who have desired to go as Volunteers, You are to proceed with the whole (taking them under your Command and carrying Eighteen Days Provisions) down Lake Champlain.

As the Enemy is rigging and preparing a Sloop near the Isle aux Nois that I think may with proper precaution and resolution be set on fire and burnt, You have four men with You, who can swim well, and are to burn the Vessell.

Major Ord has proposed fire Darts to Screw into the ship and will likewise furnish You with small Carcasses and will Shew You the manner they are to be used. The worse the Night is, the better for the purpose, and the middle of the Night will probably be the best time. The Men must not be in a hurry in any thing they do and must fix two or three of the fire darts and two of the Carcasses either in the stern or the Bow of the Vessell where they find they can do it best not to be discovered, and if to the Wind ward it will be much better and securer for burning the Vessel for which You will have particular attention, for if there should be any Wind it will help greatly to encrease the Flames . . .

WO/34/81 fol. 2

100
Major-General Jeffery Amherst to Christopher Kilby
Camp at Crown Point
[Copy in Secretary's hand]   4 September 1759

On the 16th Ultimo, I acquainted You, that I had recommended it to L[t] Gov[r] De Lancey, to renew his Prohibitions against the Unwarrantable & pernicious practice of Illicit and Collusive Exportations of Flour: and I have now the Satisfaction to Communicate to You his Answer, Viz[t].

'I have already Spoke to M[r] Kennedy the Collector and informed him, that I had just cause to think that quantities of Flour were clandestinely Exported to foreign Marketts, particularly to Monto Christi,[83] thence to Supply the French, and told him that I insisted on his privately inquiring into it, and putting the Laws strictly in Execution against all such as should Offend.'

I Have likewise the pleasure to Inform You, that my Accounts from Albany in relation to Provisions, are most Satisfactory, Colonel Bradstreet telling me, that, from the Quantities lately arrived there, & the Calculations he had Sent You, of what more would be requisite for both Armies up the Hudsons and Mohawk Rivers, as well during the Winter as the Campaign, he had great reason to believe, they would be both provided for in time.

WO/34/69 fol. 144

101
Major-General Jeffery Amherst to Lieutenant Governor James De Lancey
Camp at Crown Point
[Copy in Secretary's hand]   4 September 1759

Your favor of the 24th & 27th Ultimo, both reached me on the 1st Instant; by the first, I See with pleasure that You have given Orders for strictly putting into Execution the Laws against all such as shall Offend in the Clandestine Exportation of Flour to foreign Markets, for which I return You my thanks.

101

... I Have nothing more from England than what You mention; – Nor have I yet, any further Accounts from Mr Wolfe, but I expect them daily, by the return of some of the Parties I have Sent out, provided they are not Intercepted, which would not at all be Surprizing, since the Public papers Avow so openly the Measures I have taken to obtain this Intelligence; I could wish these Liberties of the Press were discountenanced ...

WO/34/30 fol. 75

102
Colonel John Bradstreet to Major-General Jeffery Amherst
Albany
8 September 1759
[Holograph]   [Receipt not dated]

As the winter season advances fast I beg leave to remind your Excellency that the number of working Oxen & Horses belonging to the Crown is very considerable & that it appears to me the sooner it is determined how you would have them dispos'd off for the winter the better. – Should your Excellency determine to keep the oxen it appears to me were they distributed among the Inhabitants of the Country at so much a head it would save the Hay, we have, for the Spring and they be kept, for no great expence, fit for Service at any time you might think proper to call for them ...

WO/34/57 fol. 56

103
Major-General Jeffery Amherst to Governor Thomas Pownall
Camp at Crown Point
[Copy in Secretary's hand]   9 September 1759

Yesterday afternoon I was favored with Yours of the 3rd Instant, with the Intelligence enclosed, for which I am much obliged to

You; Part of it, I think, may be Credited; the remainder, I do not apprehend will turn out as may at first Sight be Imagined: General Wolfe I am sure will persevere, and I dare flatter myself, will still take Quebec, notwithstanding he may meet with many difficulties.[84] I have not as yet receiv'd any News from him; I have been in daily Expectations, when it comes in, I will send You what News I may get.

As to the numbers of the Enemy at Quebec, it is uncertain as there is no knowing what may have been raised in the Country for the defence of their Capital; It is certain they have but Eight regular Battalions in the whole, three of which were at Tienderoga and are at the Isle aux Nois, with five Picquetts of the Battalions which are at Quebec, three more Picquetts of those five Battalions were taken at Niagara, these will diminish five French Battalions; the number of the Marines at the Isle aux Nois, and on the Posts above Montreal, with what have been taken at Niagara, and deducting what were before taken at Louisburg, leaves but small remains of that Corps; So that, though the number the Enemy may have raised is uncertain, I am sure the Calculation, of their being between twenty and thirty thousand, must be greatly Exaggerated. . . .

WO/34/27 fol. 170

104
Lieutenant Governor James De Lancey to Major-General Jeffery Amherst

New York
9 September 1759
[Holograph]   [Received 15 September 1759]

I have made some inquiry as to the dispositions of the Assembly concerning making further Provision for the Regiment in the pay of this Province for one month longer, and by what I can find, an Application to them on that head, will have no Effect. For the very reason which induced them to make provision this year no farther than the first of November, (though the last year they had done it to the first of December), was, that great Numbers of the Men sickened and died by the severities they underwent in the Month of November; besides as the Troops of the Province are, some at Niagara, some at Oswego and in the Posts in that Quarter, if they do not leave them before the 1st of November, it will scarce be possible for them to reach Albany before the River is shut up, which will add to their hardships: upon these considerations I am advised, that it would be imprudent to call the Assembly upon this Point, as it would undoubtedly be refused.

[10 September 1759]

This morning I had your Excellency's favor of the 4th instant. I shall again repeat my directions to the Collector to prevent the clandestine exportation of provisions; and shall do it in writing to see what effect that may have on the officers of the Customs . . .

I wish I could withhold or regulate the liberties of the press, in communicating to the publick, Measures which ought to be concealed: however, as there is more of falsity than truth in what they /^{is} published, I do not suppose, if they should come into the Enemies hands, that great Stress will be laid on them. We have some important accounts of Mr Wolfe's being repulsed in an attack, but I shall not trouble you, with the Rumours here . . .[85]

WO/34/29 fols 97–8

105
Major-General Jeffery Amherst to Brigadier-General Thomas Gage

[Copy in Secretary's hand]

Camp of Crown Point
11 September 1759

. . . I Take it for granted Brig^r General Stanwix will immediately on the known Evasions [sic] of the Enemys Troops from the Posts between Pittsburg & Lake Erie, execute his Plan for the relief of the Garrison at Niagara, as I had desired him to be prepared for it, before I had made known my Intentions to any One of besieging the Place, what has passed since on that head You will have been

Informed of by the Copies of the Letters I have sent to You, and I can't but Say, that I think the relief of that Garrison /^{is} not only of great Consequence at present, if they can be back to Act in time, but that We may want them for the Garrisons during the Winter, and as part of the Troops under Brig^r General Stanwix's Command, cannot be better employed than in Garrisoning that Post, I would not on any Account that the Relief should not take place . . .

I am Carrying on my Works here apace: Monsr Bourlamaque with the Garrison of Tienderoga, the Little that was here, and some Canadians who were at Work on that Island, is Strengthening himself by retrenchments and Batterys on the Island as much as he can; he shan't Stir from thence, if I can help it, unless I force him away, and if I do, he cannot march away to put any Stop to Your Operations. I had a Flag of truce Yesterday from him, with Letters from Ms^r de Montcalm of no date, but by a Letter from Ms^r Bougainville to Abercromby I find the Enemy was yet in possession of Quebec the 30th past, and as the Flag of truce, a Captain of La Reine, knew or would know of nothing that had happen'd at Quebec since the 17th of August, on which day M. General Wolfe made an Attack that rather failed than Succeeded, and two Catts were burnt which had been hawled into Shore to Cover the Landing of some Troops, that is burnt by us, which the Enemy was ready enough to Speak of; I Conclude whatever has passed since the 17th to the 30th has been in favor of Mr Wolfe, and the Enemy is therefore silent . . .[86]

Capt Kennedy Lieut. Hamilton, &c^a. have been taken by some St Francis Indians who were a hunting; Monsr Montcalm writes me Word they are Prisoners; Lieut. Fletcher, on a scout at St Johns is taken likewise by a Number of Indians, and is Prisoner at Montreal; they seem to treat our Prisoners very Civilly; 'tis a very good proof of their Situation.[87] – I am sorry Kennedy was taken, it was of some Consequence he should not, but others I hope will Escape, which will near Answer the same End; It is impossible to pass the Enemys Posts with many Partys, some must be taken.

I am glad to find by Sir Wm Johnson's Letter of the 30th past, that he had then 200 Indians, & expected several more; they can but be of very /ᵍʳᵉᵃᵗ Use to You, and it gives me great pleasure to hear of any thing that can tend towards the Success of the Operations where You Command, in which I wish You all prosperity.

WO/34/46A fols 180–1

106
Brigadier-General Thomas Gage to Major-General Jeffery Amherst

Camp of Oswego
11 September 1759
[Holograph]   [Receipt not dated]

I judge by the Progress already made in the building Fort Ontario, in doing which the whole Army has been employed, that /ⁱᵗ will be as much as ever I shall be able to do with my whole Force to put it in a respectable condition before winter. The hands I have already given to the Batteau Service, & the Considerable Number I find I shall yet be obliged to give to that Necessary Service will be a great Diminution to our Numbers, & I shall have few boats unemployed. So that the erecting any other Post either at La Galette or elsewhere is utterly impossible; it would require three Times my Number of men & Artificers of all kinds to effect it, & after all, I could neither furnish it with Provisions or Artillery, without leaving this Post or Niagara destitute. I have scarcely had 30 days Pork & Flower in store, for the mouths there are to feed ever since my Arrival; The waters are now better & more Boats employed, & I hope soon to get a large Quantity, which I must with all Dispatch forward to Niagara, taking all the Precautions I am able, for if either of the Enemy's vessels fall in with our two small Schooners, she will take these both, unless they can out-sail her. All that can be done betwixt this & Schenectady must be finished by the end of October, nothing can be forwarded from thence after that Time or the Troops keep the Field any longer; unless its a very extraordinary season, the Frost will set in by that Time, and the waters be shut up.

106

I have told you that I expected little good from the Vessels of Force building at Niagara; it would have required two hundred Carpenters to finish two Vessels in proper Time, and by Col⁰ Farquhar's Return, they have not above Thirty Five & some of them sick.

Notwithstanding all your Care & Diligence I fear [for] the Article of Provisions, & have Thoughts of reducing the Garrison of Niagra, shall see more in a few Days, but shall by first opportunity desire Lt Col⁰ Farquhar to endeavor to get a letter to Brigʳ Stanwix, to desire, unless he is far advanced, to lay aside all thoughts of relieving Him, without declaring his Reasons. The largest of our Schooners will not contain as much as an Albany Sloop, I have no other way to bring off the Troops, & that you see will be attended with Risk, I dare not now attempt using Boats. The weather may be less boisterous next month, but I shall not venture Boats without urgent necessity, & fear I shall have few to spare from other Business.

It has been some Days before I could prevail on myself to write you this Letter, & was willing to believe I could send you more welcome News than telling you the Difficultys & impossibilitys; I have looked into every Thing, tryed every Thing, & I can now no longer deceive myself, or longer deferr letting you know the true Situation of this Army.[88]

WO/34/46A fol. 50

107
Lieutenant-Colonel Stephen Miller to Major-General Jeffery Amherst

Camp at the Sawmill, Ticonderoga
12 September 1759
[Holograph]   [Received 12 September 1759]

As I have not your Orders with Regard to the Sawmill, am at a loss whose Demands I am first to Comply with for boards &c from this mill, as Major Ord, Capᵗ. Loring and Mʳ Breme, all at once Call upon me, for boards plank &c; your instructions therein by . . . Mʳ

Crawford who is the Bearer of this, will greatly oblige your Excellencys Most Obedient Humble Servant.

WO/34/78 fol. 24

108
Major-General Amherst to Lieutenant-Colonel Stephen Miller

[Copy in Secretary's hand]

Camp at Crown Point
12 Sept 1759

Yours of this day is just Come to my hands; M. General Lyman had my directions in regard to repairing the Saw Mill, and to Supply the Boards at Tienderoga, where they are first and most Essentially necessary; and then to Crown Point; I would have You first Supply Capt. Loring, who is to be furnished with what Number are requisite to finish his Work, when that is Compleated, Lt Brehm must have all that he wants to finish the Repairs at Tienderoga; and after him the Mill must be kept going for what is wanted to Carry on & Compleat the works here; So that so soon as You have near finished with Capt. Loring & Lieut. Brehm, You will give me Notice, that I may then Inform You of what Quantity must be Cutt for this place.[89]

WO/34/81 fol. 21

109
Major-General Jeffery Amherst to Colonel John Bradstreet

[Copy in Secretary's' hand]

Camp at Crown Point
14 September 1759

Before I proceed to Answer Your Letter of the 8th I shall promise, that You cannot please me more, than in Communicating to me every thought that occurs to You tending to the good of the Service, as I shall always gladly receive them, and, as far as practicable, Improve all such Useful hints; That relative to the Working Oxen & Horses belonging to the Crown has already met with my most serious Consideration; the Expence of keeping them all the Winter, even in the manner You propose, will not only in the end amount to near half their Original Cost, but I am afraid when that is done, We shall not have the Service of them that You seem to Expect; for as the Inhabitants are Actuated by no other Motives than that of Gain and putting the Crown to all the Charge they possibly can devise, they will take very little if any Care at all of the Cattle, and let them be ever so unserviceable, they will Expect and Insist on their payment, by which means the Crown will be put to a double Expence, to prevent which, as well as to make all the Saving possible, I had proposed within Myself to kill as many of the Working Oxen as should be fit for Eating, and to distribute the Same among the Troops, reserving about a hundred for actual Service, which may be disposed of as You mention . . . [I] shall only add, that as from the present Circumstances, it is more than probable that this Campaign will be the last of the present War in these parts, it is not necessary to put the Public to the Expence of keeping so large a Number of Cattle as would be unavoidable at the beginning of One.

As to the Horses, from the Use they may be of, it would not be so well to dispose of them, they must therefore be kept in Stables, at as reasonable a Rate as possible . . .

WO/34/58 fol. 51

110
Major-General Jeffery Amherst to Captain Joshua Loring

Camp of Crown Point
[Copy in Secretary's hand]   15 September 1759

. . . I am Sorry You have had so many Carpenters Sick, if they are left to themselves they will Continue so, I dont mean that they would chuse to be Sick but their cure only Increases their disorder, for they will not Voluntarily Stir out of their Hutts, but live in dirt & nastiness which they are vastly careful never to Wash off from them, that & fryed Pork would kill the half of the Provincial Troops if they are not forced to be cleanly, pray order Your Sick to be Washed every day & walked about . . .

The burning /^{of} the Enemy's Vessell at the Isle au Noix has failed, which I am Sorry for if those employed had more punctually obeyed my orders I think it would have Succeeded they Attempted it at ten at night instead of two in the morning had Screwed in one dart when Discovered & the alarm taking in all the Camp & a number of Shots fired with Some Swivels from the Vessell & Some Guard appearing on board the Sloop they made off Unhurt leaving the Combustibles at her bow.

The Sergeant who Commanded the Party imagines the Enemy does not intend to rig her as She is laid across the Channell w^t Six Guns run out on one Side two Port holes shut up . . .

You will I Doubt not take care that a look out may be kept on Board the Duke of Cumberland that the Enemy may not Retort the Attempt on us, which indeed I do not Suspect them Capable of doing, I hope that Brig will very Soon be able and fit to Sail that we may Attack & beat the Enemy's Vessells & I hope so Effectually Destroy them that we may be the entire masters of this Lake which I think we may do with the Brig Radeau & boats without waiting for the Sloop which must nevertheless be likewise built as fast as possible.

WO/34/64 fols 212–13

III
Major-General Jeffery Amherst to Major-General Phineas Lyman

Camp of Crown Point

[Copy in Secretary's hand]   16 September 1759

Since my Letter to you of last night's date I have one from Lt Col^o Miller desiring Six Oxen to supply the Mill, Which otherwise will Stand Still. This is of so great Consequence to all our works that I Send the Six oxen directly tho' I can very ill Spare them & some Works here must be retarded by it.

WO/34/43 fol. 244

112
Captain Joshua Loring to Major-General Jeffery Amherst

Ticonderoga
19 September 1759
[Holograph]   [Received 19 September 1759]

. . . I am very sorry to acquaint your Excellency that They have broke another Crank at the Saw Mill, and I am affraid by bad management, I have never been able to get the Least Assistance from that Mill yet, sawing Twenty three plank which is not half a Days Worke, and am affraid shall be Oblidged to cut all the plank for the Sloop by hand, which will make Several Days difference in the Time of Building her, the other Saw is not going yet, nor will it be Ready for some Days. I see no way of your Excellency's getting any Service from this Mill, but by putting her into other hands . . .

P.S. I should think it would be very Right to send to New York for two Cranks as they may be made much Cheeper and better there than here, when you will allways have a Spare one to put in should any one brake.

WO/34/64 fol. 162

113
Major-General Jeffery Amherst to Captain Joshua Loring

Camp at Crown Point
[Copy in Secretary's hand]   20 September 1759

. . . From the Reports I had lately had of the Saw Mills, I must own I had flattered myself that all would have gone well, and little Expected to hear of another Crank being broke, but it is not at all Surprizing, if it has been occasioned as You Say, and if so, was a very Idle Experiment indeed,[90] which I cannot forgive since it retards all the Works, in which there is not a moments time to lose, it must therefore be remedied as soon as possible, without taking it out of the hands of those to whom it has been Entrusted, and as

General Lyman has been so good as to promise, that he would oversee it, I am Confident he will do everything that is possible to Set her going again, till Mr Dice can come up, who I am told, is the best Millwright in the Country, wherefore I shall Order him when he Comes, to look at it and give his Advice.

As to Sending to New York for Cranks at this time, that might do if they were wanted next Summer, besides when I mentioned /^{it} first, You told me there were None to be had there that were good for any thing, & that they could be made much sooner and better at Tienderoga, I do not See therefore why they cannot be made there now; Colonel Schuyler tells me a Wooden One would do very well, or One made out of an Anchor; I must therefore desire that You will be so good as to See it done out of hand, or otherwise all our Work will be at a Stand, which must not be, & I dare say You will Use all Your Endeavors to prevent it, and I make no doubt with Success.

WO/34/64 fol. 216

114
Major-General Jeffery Amherst to Brigadier-General Thomas Gage

Camp of Crown Point
[Copy in Secretary's hand]   21 September 1759

I can't but say that it is with some concern that I have received your Letter of the 11th Instant wherein I find you have determined not to take post at La Galette; it is now indeed too late in the Season, or will be before this can reach You to make any Alterations, and I must give over the thoughts of that very advantageous Post La Galette that might have been taken without a possibility of the Enemys obstructing it; the situation of their Army being such that they have been in an absolute inability of sending any Succours that way.

I am in hopes that so soon as You took your Resolution not to proceed to La Galette, you will have immediately detached as many men to Fort Stanwix as are necessary for compleatly finishing the Works there, and that You will have thought of cutting a road on the South side of Lake Oneyda, from Oswego to Fort Stanwix, as well as continuing the Road from Fort Herkheimers to Fort Stanwix, when that Communication is once made which will be Cover'd by the Mohawk River the Lake, and all the Posts, nothing can hinder a supply of Provisions being sent at any time in the Winter if should be Wanted (which I dont intend shall be the case this Winter) or of reinforcements marching to the relief of any of the Posts . . .

As the time of Service for some of the Provincial Troops does not extend beyond the first of November, I have applied to their respective Governors to continue the Troops for the Month of November, in case the service should require it, and I dont doubt but my request will be agreed to both for the New York and Newhampshire Troops . . .

WO/34/46A fols 182–3

WLC/AP/4

115
Brigadier-General Robert Monckton to Major-General Jeffery Amherst

Quebec
25 September 1759
[Holograph]   [Received 15 November 1759]

I have the Pleasure to acquaint you that our Army came to Action with the Enemy on the 13ᵗʰ Insᵗ near Quebec above the Town – in which we gain'd a Compleat Victory – Genˡ Wolfe fell – and I received a Wound which oblig'd me to quit the Field just as the Enemy began to Break – In consequence of this /ᵛⁱᶜᵗᵒʳʸ – The Town Surrender'd by Capitulation to Brigadier Townshend on the 18ᵗʰ – To him I must beg leave to refer you for the Particulars – Both of the Action, and Capitulation which he sends by this Conveyance.

The Town has suffer'd extremely from our Shot & Shells & it will be very troublesome the clearing of it – We are now preparing all the Habitable part of it for the Reception of the Garrison – And I purpose making some small addition to the Works, a Report of which I Inclose you –

From the Strength of our Army – (which you will see by the Inclos'd Return) I dont think that there is a Man more than ought to stay here – But as the Gen¹ promised that the two Nova Scotia Companys Should return there, I shall send them Back; and as the other four Companys of Rangers are so Expensive – & of so little use, I purpose sending them back to New England – reserving such of them as are Carpenters – If I should find myself enabled to send any others away, it shall be the Louisburg Grenadiers . . .

As the Sum of Money brought up the River by the Paymaster is only Sufficient to Pay the Troops to the 24ᵗʰ August last, with some Contingent Expenses – And as further supply will be absolutely Necessary – The Inhabitants of the Country, their well supplying the Garrison with Provisions [during] the Winter, in a great measure depending thereon – I thought proper to apply to the Aᵈˡ for a Ship of War, to be immediately Dispatch'd to New York – He has accordingly granted the Hunter Sloop for this Service with Orders to Return with the Money, if it is practicable to get up the River Sᵗ Lawrence . . .

I am well enough at Present to take upon me the Command of the Army, but as the Ball went in at my Breast & through my Lungs, Mʳ Adair is of opinion that I ought to Winter in a more Moderate Climate than this – I therefore purpose returning to New York.

Brigadier Townshend having acquainted me that he has your leave to go to England, takes his Passage with the Aᵈˡ so that Brigadier Murray will remain Commandant – and Col. Burton his Second . . .

I shall endeavour to get every thing regulated here, & put on a good footing before I depart.

The Season being so late, & the Town wanting so much repair for the Reception of the Garrison – It will be impossible for me to carry on any further Operations, higher up the River.

WO/34/43 fols 34–6

116
Colonel George Williamson to Major-General Jeffery Amherst

Quebec

circa 25 September 1759

[Holograph] [Received *circa* 15 November 1759

4th Of last June we Sail'd out of Louisbourg harbour with only 8240 men, Artillery people included, not mentioning the Marines, and our first anchoring was at the Island of Bic the 18th.

The 27th of June we anchor'd at midway up Orleans Island Channel and that evening we had a terrible Storm of Wind, hail thunder and lightening, some people were drowned, above 100 Boats stove, and as many anchors and Cables lost, several Ships were drove ashore on Orleans Island. Such was our distress that had the Tempest lasted an hour longer I verily believe our Campaign would have ended there; however it turned Calm and business went on with such dilligence that the 6th of July, Batterys were begun for Five large Mortars & 6 thirty two Pounders, and the 12th began to send our Shot & Shells into the Town of Quebec across the River St Lawrence at the intersected distance from ¾ of a mile, to a mile & a quarter.

The 16th of July another Battery was raised for three 13 Inch Sea Mortars (and one ten inch Sea Mortar was brought ashore also) as the Bombships did not come near enough to the Town to make them usefull, they were soon brought to play with extraordinary Success on the Town: soon after another Battery of Six 24 Pounders was rais'd and play'd a Ricochet fire through the whole town.[91] During the whole fireing from first to last 535 houses were burn'd down, among which is the whole Eastern part of the lower town (save 6 or 8 houses) which makes a very dismal appearance. Ricochet shot have done infinite damage to the houses which escaped the fire, many of them are in a tottering condition, & more which cannot be repaired, that in all likelyhood will tumble down this Winter.

We had entire possession of the Isle of Orleans, and had a strong Post below Montmorency river, as long as the General thought it necessary we were also strongly Posted at point Levi & Orleans point.

The Enemy were above double our number, by their own confession besides their Indians, and were intrenched, had breast works, fleches, Redoubts, Shore & floating batterys of 50 Cannon, besides Mortars all the way from the falls of Montmorency river to St Charles River, w[h]ere there were two men of Warr hulks (with Guns mounted & amunition) and a Boom across the mouth of it.

We found 180 pieces of Cannon besides Mortars mounted with proper ammunition on every Battery in the upper and lower towns of Quebec. The Enemy kept also a dilligent look out up St Lawrence river, from thence to hinder any communication with General Amherst, and had intercepted two Officers & four Indians coming from him to us.

With all these circumstances we were harrassing them daily & Masters of a great part of their country along shore, burn'd upwards of fourteen hundred of their farm houses for the people paying no regard to General Wolfe's salutary manifesto;[92] this has also hurt the Enemy greatly, & will take a long time, half a century to recover. Prisoners & Deserters told us that Messrs Vaudreuille and Montcalme did not hit it, that the People of the Country murmur'd and were discontented on account of their harvest which being neglected and rainy, windy weather following at the time we allow'd them to get it in, is rendered scarcely worth the labour. Their hay was lost long before, and really they will have a terrible time of it. Their latest allowance as they reported was three pound of bread & two of pork for four days, & had send to Montrealle to cut down new corn before it was ripe to furnish that allowance, and had we hindred the 14 Provision Ships from getting up some days before us, the Enemy from all reports and appearances could not have kept the field so long as they did.

Likewise the arbitrary proceedings of the Governor & principal Officers, added to the sharp look out of his Indians kept the Peasantry militia from Stealing home to their farms and familys.

The last day of July we attempted to land on the Beauport side with our Grenadiers but were unsuccessful, we also made two fruitless attempts to take Post some miles above Quebec & did them some damage. The Enemy were very watchfull there, and our strength could not admit of large detachments. At length General Wolfe having one more card to play at a place they least expected & which he communicated with all secrecy but two days before; the light field Artillery & their people were sent up to favour the intention, and the 13th of September at 4 in the morning we made another effort with about 5000 men and took Post with all expedition at the back of the Town within two small miles of Point Diamond.

We got two Six pounders to fire against the Enemy very soon, Six more & two Royal Howitzers came up two by two, & fell into Service occasionally, whilst the Enemy were makeing hast to attack before our Artillery should be got up, as they dreaded our quick fireing, but they were mistaken for we got so many into battery and fired so briskly, seconded by the small arms from the Regiments, who behaved with the greatest intrepidity, order & regularity, with such a chearfullness that foretold victory on our side, that we fairly beat them in the open field; drove them before us part into Quebec, the rest ran precipitately cross St Charles river, over a bridge of Boats and some through the water.

We remained that night on the field of Battle & had it not been reported that Monsr Boucanville with 5000 men were coming in our rear, which induced Brigadier [Townshend] to stop the pursuit (for before this General Wolfe was carried off Mortally wounded)[93] in all likelyhood we should have followed the Enemy pellmell into Quebec before they could Shut the gates & taken possession of it at once without any capitulation.

Mr Boucanville who had partly appear'd; on our success retreated. General Montcalme had three Wounds from our Six pounder grape of which he died next day, & with a little improvement one of our 13 Inch Shell holes serv'd him for a grave in the Hotel Dieu church yard; his second and a Brigadier were kill'd in the field, I have not learn'd the exact number of inferior Officers to them & men kill'd & Wounded, but in general it is say'd by the French they amount to 1400 & many say 2000.

Our good General Wolfe had three Wounds, but had the satisfaction before his death to see his own Plan so well executed, as to know we had beat the Enemy totally. He then said, I thank God, and now I shall die contented; I am told they were his last words.

We began to prepare for attacking the Garrison in form, and got up for that purpose 12 heavy twenty four pounders, 6 heavy twelve pounders, some large mortars & the four 8 Inch Howitzers to play on the Town, and when we had been employ'd three days, the 17th of Septem^r they thought propper to Parly, and the next day Capitulated, when the English colours were planted on the Grand Barbet Battery . . .

U1350/O/33/4

117
John Calcraft to Major-General Jeffery Amherst

[London]
28 September 1759

[Holograph]   [Received 13 February 1760]

I did in my last Letter wish you Joy of Niagarra &c^a, and now I am to Congratulate You on your being Governor of Virginia which I do most heartily and send Your Patent by the Bearer, which You shou'd have proclaimed at Williamsburgh in the usual form as soon as may be.

There is a small quantity of Plate given from the Ward robe on Your coming to this Government, the Warrant for which I have apply'd for, and will get the Plate out which I presume You wou'd have Sent to Mrs Amherst.

Inclos'd I have the honour to Send Your Commission as Major-General.[94]

You shall have a Separate letter about the Income of Your Government, & in It be inform'd what passes at an Interview I am to have to day with Your Lt Governors Brother . . .[95]

You cannot Imagine what Favour you are in with all Your Countrymen, who really do Justice to Your Zeal & Activity and Attribute the Speedy Conquest of America to Your Wise Conduct and Indefatigable diligence in their Service.

I Recollect what You wrote to me about an American Government, which makes me take the Liberty of Saying, That of Virginia will not Require Your Staying in America One moment longer than other /^Business^ Requires your Continuance there, So will be in a small degree a pecuniary Reward for Your Services without the Inconvenience which You apprehended woud be Attendants to a Governor there.

WO/34/99 fols 45–6

118
Brigadier-General Thomas Gage to Major-General Jeffery Amherst

Camp of Oswego
2 October 1759

[Holograph]   [Received 18 October 1759]

I received your Favor of the 21st Sep^t^ yesterday, am sorry my letter of the 11th gave you the Concern you mention & can assure you it did /^not^ give you more in Reading, than it did me in writing: But I am most thoroughly satisfyed, had I attempted erecting a second Post, I should neither have made one or the other tenable, or victualed either. This is the Second Fort I have been present at the Building, & can't say I have found Forts so easily compleated, That of Fort Edward began Three years ago, was not finished as you now see it till last Nov^r^, which is much smaller than what we are Building here. If your Plan of Operations was not to concern yourself with Forts, but push on all sides for the whole Country, I was certainly in a Condition to make vigorous Efforts on this side towards it; If your Plan is to secure what you have gained, by building a respectable Fort here, with Posts of Communication with the Inhabited Country, This I hope to be able to effect: But if your Plan is to do both, it's not in my Power to execute. I may execute either, but if I attempt both, I shall do neither.

The sending men to compleat F[ort] Stanwix I have often thought of, but the Numbers I furnish to the Batteaux Service has prevented my sending the Assistance I intended for that necessary work: I have been obliged to man Eighty Boats betwixt this & Fort Stanwix; 250 Yorkers & the N. Hampshire Company from N°. 4 employed in the same Service on the Mohawk River. And without this large Assistance to the Batteaux service, the necessary supplys could not be forwarded. These men are also daily falling sick & fresh Hands demanded, which considering their service, being every day up to their middles in water, does not Surprize me, & as the Season Advances, few men can stand it. This I have long foreseen, and on that Acc^t have taken every opportunity to press the forwarding of all things with the greatest Dispatch, before the cold weather should set in. The Road I gave also thought of; Capt Herkimer is at this work betwixt F. Stanwix & his Father's House, & I hope will compleat that Road, of which I have received very good acc^ts, & that it is made in a very good Direction. I have another Party cutting from hence to the Tree Rivers, and a Party of Indians with some other men, examining the Country & marking a Road from the Tree Rivers (or Seneca River) to the Post on the West End of Oneyda Lake . . .

I have already mentioned to you that the Troops could not continue here longer than October, you may possibly continue longer at Crown Point, Lakes will not be froze, & you will have the Conveniency of Carriages from Fort George. But the small Rivers betwixt this & Schenectady shut up early, & no Carriages to assist the Troops.

WO/34/46A fols 51–2

119
Major-General Jeffery Amherst to Lieutenant Stephens

Camp of Crown Point
[Copy in Secretary's hand]   4 October 1759

Herewith You will receive a Letter from me to Mr Bellows at N° 4 with which You will Immediately proceed thither, and on Your arrival there Deliver the same to the said Mr Bellows, Who is thereby Directed to furnish You Provisions sufficient to victual Major Rogers and his party consisting of 170 men from Wells

River to N° 4, by which Major Rogers proposes to Return, and with the said Provisions, and with a Competent number of men, which Mr Bellows is likewise ordered to furnish You with, to be aiding and Assisting In Conveying them to Wells River, You will proceed thither, and there Remain with the Said party, so long as You shall think there is any probability, of Major Rogers returning that way; at the Expiration of Which, You will Return with said provisions & party to No. 4 . . .⁹⁶

WO/34/81 fol. 52

120
Brigadier George Townshend to Major-General Jeffery Amherst

Quebec
7 October 1759

[Holograph]   [Received 11 December 1759]

I take this opportunity of sending you my best respects by Colonel Howe who I hear will most probably see you soon. I am afraid the advanced Season will not admit of the Troops having that happiness of Seeing you, notwithstanding reports see[k] to flatter us with your possession soon of Montreal. As Mr Monckton has no Commands for me, nor do I hear of any probability of being comanded any where, You will I dare say not repent the leave you gave me to return to England the Campaign finished on this Side. If Genl Monckton had any service in view for me I told him I was ready to stay. As a meer ~~Bystander I can be~~ /Resident at Quebec I can be of no use, & as such I embark with ye Admiral for England where I shall be proud of any Commands you may have for me. My inclination both to wait on you & to see our Colonies would have brought me to Boston, if the Season would have admitted of it.

I heartily wish you all success no less upon the Publick than your own account.

Before I take my Leave, I must beg one favour of you; which is, ~~that~~ Should any Idle & malicious Reports reach your Ears concerning any Negative The Brigadiers gave to Poor Mr

Wolfe's carrying the Operations above ye Town; or to his making the Descent at Foulon which has proved so successful; that you will not believe any such thing: my brother Brigadiers as well as myself are thank God prepared with materials sufficient to prove ye Contrary; but as it [is] /^right not to be the desire of any, unnecessarily to bring into discussion matters which may either put them, or tend to state their Conduct or opinion in an opposite Light to those who are gone; We Should be very glad that this justification were unnecessary: but if renderd ye contrary, I must then beg leave from you & to be told by you, that it is incumbent upon me together with them to set myself right in your opinion.

I pretend to no merit in this Campaign, but speaking honestly my Sentiments to my Superior Officer, and giving my opinion when calld upon, and that of Executing his Orders to the best of my ability when I received them.

If we receive as little justice in your army as I'm told we have met with from some in this, Brigadier Monckton has the Papers which will explain our Conduct ready to lay before you, tho' It is a Subject we both wish that no more may be said upon.[97]

WO/34/46B fols 217–18

121
Major-General Jeffery Amherst to Brigadier-General John Stanwix

Camp at Crown Point

[Copy in Secretary's hand]   9 October 1759

I am to Acknowledge the Receipt of Your favor of the 17th Ultimo from Pittsburgh, where I find You have begun the Fort, and that when it is finished, it is Judged, will be, agreable to Mr Pitt's Words, of Sufficient Strength and every way Adequate to the great Importance of its several Objects; So that I have only to Wish, You may meet with less difficulties than You seem to Apprehend, and that the Season will so far favor You as to Enable You to finish it before the Winter Setts in.

I have already said so much concerning the absolute necessity there is for Your relieving the Garrison of Niagara, that nothing remains for me to add on that Subject, Except that I trust You will have done every thing in Your power to See that Service Executed . . .

Tomorrow I send our Brig, Sloop, and Radeaus &ca, down the Lake to Endeavor to take or destroy the Enemies Vessells, and I myself, with what Troops can be Spared, accompany them to See what may be further attempted.

WO/34/45 fol. 235

122

Orders for the Troops passing Lake Champlain [98]

Camp of Crown Point

[Holograph draft]   10 October 1759

The advanced Guard is to consist of Gages light Infantry, with the flat bottomed English boat on their right & the other boat with the three pounder on their Left, their whole boats drawing up abreast covering the Heads of the Columns & the comanding officer will keep a party allways near the west Shore while the Troops advance to make discoveries of boats or any thing left by the Enemy on or near the Shore.

The troops to row in four Columns, the right & first Column to consist of the light Infantry of the Reg^{ts} & Grenadiers, the second Column of the Brigade of the Royal, the third Column of all the boats with the Artillery Stores, Tools Commissarys &ca, the fourth and left Column to consist of the Second Brigade, the rear Guard is composed of all the Rangers & Indians who are to draw up abreast covering the rear of the Columns; I & the comanding officer will keep a Party allways near the East shore for the same purpose as Gages on the west.

The first & second Columns will march & embark by the left, the front Rank in the boats on the right the Rear Rank in the boats on the left, the comanding officer of Corps on the left in a whale boat to lead their Corps. The fourth Column will march & embark

123

by the right, the front Rank in the boats on the left and rear Rank in the boats on the right, the comanding Officers of Corps in a whale boat on the Right of the Batt[ns], the Columns to row allways two boats abreast and the boats to follow very close, the Brig & Sloop will cruise and try to cut off the Enemy's Vessels from the Enemy's Posts on the other side of the Lake and will not wait for the Army, which the Artillery in boats will cover.

The Artillery commanded by Major Ord will form the Ligonier Radeau in the Center a Hautwitzer on the right & one on the left of the Radeau, a twelve pounder in Front of the Column on the Right & one in Front of the Column on the Left, and a twelve pounder in the Center of the rear of the whole following the Rangers.

Signals to be made on board the Ligonier at the main mast, a Small Union Flag for Adjutants to come for orders . . .

The Column of Artillery is allways to draw up between the first and second brigade and when the Troops land, /[the whale boats &] Batteaus of each Corps are to be closed in a single range along the shore. The Radeau & boats with Guns will be posted on the right left & rear to cover the Batteaus when the Army is landed great attention must be given to closing in and forming to either shore on the Signal that no Accidents may happen on Storms arising, but nothing is to be done in a hurry to create confusion. When the Troops land every comanding Officer of a Corps will immediately advance Front Platoons or a Picket. Every Corps is to Secure its own Ground, firing in the night is absolutely forbid. The Enemy if any should appear is to be received with fixed Bayonets & the same orders to be observed as were given on passing Lake George. The first Column is to be commanded by Col Haviland, the second by Colonel Forster, and the fourth by Col Grant.

WO/34/81 fols 66–7

123
Brigadier-General John Stanwix to Major-General Jeffery Amherst

Pittsburgh
10 October 1759
[Holograph]   [Received 9 November 1759]

Since my last letter to you of a few days ago, arrived here from Niagara Captain Lee & Lt Kennedy wth 14 men with a letter from Col. Farquire & Lt Kellet came here two days after him from the Same place with another letter from Col. Farquire the first of the 18th the other of the 22^d of Sepr. a Copy of both which with their information thereto Annex. You will find in Colonel Farquires letter of the 22^d that he says it is impossible for him to supply Batteaus for the relief of Niagara at Presquisle, and it is far more so for me to do it from hence, and as I have troubled you so very often with such long letters upon this (to me) unhappy subject, have called the Principle Officers here together to meet me and give their opinions upon it which I hereto enclose[99] & truly had it been possible for me to execute this piece of Service & I had not done it I know of no Censure that I should not have deserved, & as I would always do every thing in my power to justify my conduct to you could think of no methods so likely to do as this . . .

WO/34/45 fol. 106

124
Governor William Lyttelton to Major-General Jeffery Amherst

Charles Town
16 October 1759
[Secretary's hand, signed by Lyttelton]   [Received 1 December 1759]

. . . On the 30th of last month I received the Dispatch from Lieutenant Coylmore at Fort Prince George in the Lower Cherokee Nation, of which I inclose you a Copy & other Letters confirming the Intelligences contained therein [of Cherokee hostilities], Whereupon I orderd the Regulars & provincials in this Town Amounting to one hundred & fifty men, to hold themselves in readiness to March & directed the Colonels of three Regiments of Militia on the Frontiers to Collect their Corps. I likewise dispatchd Expresses to the Governors of North Carolina & Virginia & to Brigadier General Stanwix, and summoned the General Assembly to meet on the 4th. On the 5th I laid before them the several advices I had received from the Cherokee Country & at the same Time ask'd a Supply from them to enable me to relieve the Forts there & Secure the interior Tranquillity of the Province acquainting them that I wou'd go myself upon that Service. They proceeded to the Consideration of a Supply accordingly, but a Spirit of excessive Parsimony & some factious Humours that unhappily prevaild among them influenced all their Resolutions. The Council was unanimously of Opinion that a Declaration of War should be issued against the Cherokees, and the Assembly as unanimously Address'd me to defer it; I consented to do so, but express'd my expectations that they wou'd enable me by a Speedy grant of the Supply I had askd, to pursue vigorous measures which they themselves acknowledged they were fully convinced were necessary. Soon afterwards they sent me their Resolutions concerning a Supply, which finding exceedingly short of what the Service really requires, I made a Speech wherein I declared my Sense of the Scantiness & insufficiency thereof, but added that I shou'd nevertheless persevere in the intended Measures . . .

WO/34/35 fols 127–8

125
Major-General Jeffery Amherst to Field Marshal Viscount John Ligonier

[Holograph copy]

Camp of Crown Point
22 October 1759

I am yesterday return'd from a Cruise I set out on, on the 11th Instant so soon as I could get two vessells built to Attack the

Enemys with, which has so far Succeeded that I forced them to sink two which I believe we shall get up again, and to run one aground which has now Joyned H. M.'s Ships and they are in quest of a Schooner which I hope we shall take, so that the Enemy will have only remaining a Vessel which is not rigged, but is put across the Channel at the Isle Aux Noix, as a floating Battery, & whether or not Captain Loring may Succeed in taking the Schooner, the Kings Ships have now the full Command of the Lake.

I set out on a very late day for Operations in this part of the World, but I was resolved to try to demolish their Craft and thought I should Succeed the better by taking a detachment of Regulars with me, leaving the provincials to continue the works carrying on at this place, and if I could have had the Vessells ready some time sooner, I certainly had Executed a plan which I did not entirely give over when I set out, which was to have posted myself as near as I could to the Isle aux Noix, made a Shew of attacking it and to have march^d away the half of my detachment to Montreal to have surprised the place, but this was only feasible while the Enemys force was at Quebec, and I was very glad to give it over when I found it not practicable to proceed down the Lake and that at the same time I had an Account of the Surrender of Quebec, which is an infinitely more important Event.

I did myself the Honor to write to your Lordship last Winter, that guns were very much wanted for the Forts, & the want is now encreased by the New posts which are taken for which I have been obliged to apply to the Lieut. Govr of New York, who has lent twelve 18 pounders & Eight 12 pounders . . .

I have wrote to Mr Pitt a full account of every thing that has passed here since I dispatched Capt. Prescott to England,[100] and I should send Your Lordship plans of the Forts here if the Engineers or draftsman had had time to have Copied them . . .

The Lake is a most Noble thing, all the plans of it are very incorrect; there a[re] numbers of Islands not laid down in any draft I have seen, and very luckily both shores are indented with many bays, or the batteaus I went out with would not have returned. An Officer of Capt Lorings would have it that the sea was as bad as in the bay of Biscay.

I have not yet settled the Winter Quarters for the Troops here as I intend they shall compleat the works here as much as the season will permit.

I have had no Account the whole Campaign from the River St Lawrence but by the return of an Ensign of Rangers I sent to Major Gen¹ Wolfe & in bringing back dispatches to me he was taken by a pirate and threw all his dispatches into the Sea.

The Enemy must now Center everything at Montreal which place is so far from being defensible that I should not be surprised if an Offer was made to Capitulate rather than run a risk of Starving, or be Subject to a certainty of losing the whole when the Season will permit Military Operations to be carried on.

U1350/O/35/13

126
Major-General Jeffery Amherst to Lieutenant Alexander Grant

Camp at Crown Point
[Copy in Secretary's hand]   26 October 1759

That no Endeavours may be wanting to Recover the two Sloops lately sunk by the Enemy down Lake Champlain, together with their Guns Stores Tackle and Apparell, You are to morrow, Wind & Weather permitting, to proceed with His Majesty's Sloops the Boscawen and the Amherst, together with the two Small Raddeaus, to the Bay where the said two french sloops are sunk, and there with the Assistance of the party of men that shall be sent along with You and the Implements and Utensils necessary for that purpose, which Cap. Loring has Undertaken to provide You with, use Your best Endeavours to weigh said two sloops and to save every part of their Stores Guns & rigging, that may have been left in them; And when You have Succeeded therein You are then to Cause said Sloops to be so far repaired as to be able to bring them to this Bay; Whither You will Return with them and the Sloops and Raddeaus under Your Command.[101]

WO/34/81 fol. 88

127
Major-General Jeffery Amherst to Major Hawk

Camp at Crown Point

[Copy in Secretary's hand]   26 October 1759

Whereas nothing Contributes more to the Wealth & prosperity of a
Country, than free and open Communications to and from it on all
Sides, and that by our present possession of Tienderoga and Crown
Point, a Direct road from thence into New England by N°.4 must
prove of the greatest advantage to the Inhabitants and Settlers of the
latter, particularly those of the Provinces of the Massachusetts Bay
and Newhampshire, I have accordingly, for the mutual benefit of the
whole, as well as that of the Garrisons of Crown Point &
Tienderoga Caused a Road to be Marked & Cutt from hence to N°.
4;[102] And in order that the same may become known to, and
frequented by the people of New England, as well as to Save their
Troops a long and tedious march, I have resolved to send these last
home by this new road; and that they may meet with less fatigue
and Difficulties than are Common to new Roads in an Uncultivated
Country, I propose to have the same entirely Cleared, Streightned
and Widened; And as I am convinced that no one is more equal to
the task than Yourself and that from Your love for Your Country,
and Zeal for the Common Cause, You will Exert Yourself to the
utmost, to Carry this good Design into Execution in the best
manner possible, I hereby Repose that trust and Confidence in You.

You will accordingly take upon You the Command of the party
Appointed for that purpose by last night's orders, and with them
proceed to the Entrance of the said New Road from hence, Which
You will Carry on in the most direct Line possible to N°. 4,
Clearing the same all the way You go, and Widening it in every
part to at least Twenty feet, and wherever it may be necessary to
lay any Bridges across, You will make them Sufficiently Strong to
bear Carriages.

You will also at every fifteen miles Distance Cause Log'd fences
to be put up for harbouring and keeping together the Cattle that
will be drove thro' that road for the use of the Troops . . .

WO/34/81 fol. 89

128
Major-General Jeffery Amherst to Lieutenant-Colonel
William Eyre

Crown Point

[Copy in Secretary's hand]   31 October 1759

Whereas I find that the relief of Niagara, cannot as I Intended take place this Season, and that the present Garrison consists in part of the 44th Regiment, to which You are now appointed Lieut. Colonel, It therefore becomes Indispensably necessary that You should Repair thither without loss of time.

You will Accordingly Set out for Oswego, and upon Your arrival there, Communicate these Your Instructions to Brig^r Genl Gage, and Receive from him what further Directions, he shall for the good of the Service, think proper to Give You, with which, You will immediately Depart for Niagara, where being arrived, You will Examine into the State of the Works and Cause the Same to be Compleated and put into the best state of Defence possible, observing to follow the plan laid down, and making no Alterations without first Informing me thereof and obtaining my Approbation of the Same.

You will also, either thro' the Indians or others, as You shall find opportunitys, endeavor to learn and if possible find out an Easy Communication by which provisions might be sent from Niagara to Pittsburgh, which would be of the utmost advantage to the Service in General by removing the great difficulties we now labor under in Transporting Provisions by Land from Philadelphia thither, and a very great saving to the Publick, of the Cost of that Transportation which is Immense; You Cannot therefore Exert Yourself too much in any Endeavours to find out and form such a Communication.

Herewith You will Receive a Copy of my Letter to Your predecessor, bearing date the 11th of last month,[103] by which You will see my opinion fully in relation to the Work, as also with regard to the Indians, whom You may now Expect to have about You in Numbers and as their Consumption of provisions is beyond all Bounds, You must furnish them with a Reasonable

Quantity of Ammunition, that they may provide themselves as much as possible, and if You find it necessary making up the deficiency out of the King's stores, upon Condition that they behave well.

The better to keep them in awe, and to get any Service out of them, let Your Discourse /$^{\text{to them}}$ at first outset be that they shall be protected so long as they behave well and rewarded whenever they are of any Service; but that if on the Contrary, You find them Guilty of any misdemeanor or that they turn troublesome, that then they shall not only be sent about their business but likewise be punished . . .

WO/34/81 fol. 110

129
Lieutenant-Colonel Israel Putnam to Major-General Jeffery Amherst

Camp on the Point
1 November 1759
[Holograph]   [Received 1 November 1759]

I would acquaint your Excelency that this morning we had a mutany among the Soldrys of Ruggles and Willards rigements when ordered for worke they Paraded as usual but when ordered to march they threw down thar axes and took up thare arms and fixed bayonets and had thare Packs ready to sling at which I orderd the Coneticut and Rod islands to stand to thare armes and told the men if they Pirsisted in it I would order all my Pepel to fiar upon them and told them if they Pirsisted in it wold kill as many as i could. But upon thare threwing down thare arms and Prommising refirmation forgave them on thare good behavyour for the future; all but John Fits Patrick, Hazikiah Egerton of Col^o Willards regament and John Hooper, Ephrem Wheler, Artemus Manor of Col^o Rugeles rigement which I Have sent with a Proper guard to do with as Your Exelences wisdom shall think fit . . .

WO/34/78 fol. 119

130
Major-General Jeffery Amherst to Lieutenant-Colonel Israel Putnam

[Copy in Secretary's hand]

Camp at Crown Point
1 November 1759

The men You have Sent me, in which You have done extremely right, have since all repented & beg'd for forgiveness, on a promise that they would return to their Duty, and set an Example to all the Others that are upon the Works with You; On these Conditions I have pardon'd them, and I accordingly send them You back.[104]

WO/34/81 fol. 112

131
Governor Brigadier-General James Murray to Major-General Jeffery Amherst

[Holograph]

Quebec
1 November 1759
[Received 11 January 1760]

It gives me pleasure that it is now my duty to take every opportunity of writing to you. This is sent by Col° Gridley, who has left with me thirty of his carpenters. I have business for many more but those I have sent, were not willing to stay, & would have done little good had I kept them against their will, & their wages, including their provisions, are exorbitant. I flatter myself we shall make a shift without them. Tho' labor is very dear, and artificers very scarce; all the french inhabitants are obliged to leave the town, wood, lodging, and provisions are necessary articles in life, and there are none of them to spare after the troops are provided.

Since Mr Monckton left us (for all that pass'd before I must refer you to him) a spanish Ship came down the river . . . The Capt of this Ship agrees with other intelligence I have had, that the [French] King's frigates with the some of the merchant men are determin'd to winter in the river betwixt Batiscan, and Trois Riviers; I believe it, because I think it right for them to do so, as it is the only means they have left to dispute the command of the river with us next campaign; the dispute even in this case must be very trifling, ~~at all events~~, but if I can build twelve floating batteries after the french model, which in the course of the winter, I am persuaded I shall be able to do, their ships will not retard our progress a day. The few despicable troops they have left are in a miserable condition, destitute of necessaries, and ill provided with provisions, and I believe ammunition does not abound. The Canadians under their Subjection are plunder'd, and oppress'd by them, hate & dispise them; in short unless an armament from Europe arrives before our fleet gets up in the Spring every parish of Canada must submit ~~in th~~ before the month of July next. ~~for no~~ The little succours, or reinforcements they may be able to smugle by landing near the mouth of the river cannot avail them; the decrease is too far gone for such weak remedies to have any effect, & it will be difficult /$^{\text{if not impossible}}$ even to administer these, I think myself master enough of the country to prevent them.

Every body will inform you how powerful & how flourishing this Colony ~~might have been~~ was, and how formidable it might be under any other government, than that of Mr Vaudriell, un bon politique, it should be perhaps destroy'd, but there may be, too, reasons why it should remain as it is, a guarantee for the good behaviour of its neighbouring Colonys. It is not with me to judge, I know it is in your power now to decide the fate of Canada. Untill I have the honor to receive your orders I shall follow ~~my~~ the natural disposition of my heart, which dictates Clemency. This conduct can do no hurt, because the effects of it may be undone in one week, it may have a permanent advantage; the Canadians have been taught to look upon us as Barbarians, whose only view was their destruction; hence the obstinate resistance they have made and the eagerness they shew'd to take up arms against us; They begin now to be astonish'd with our conduct, will soon be convinced that there is not deceit in it, and hardly here after so easily be persuaded to take up arms against a nation they must admire, & who will always have it in their power to burn and destroy. Sufficient examples they have had this summer of the horrors of war; they were not treated tenderly before we had the

good fortune to take Quebec; they will remember that no doubt
and it may be supposed they will not forget any instances of
Clemency, & generosity that may be shewn them, since they have
been entirely in our power. I am sure of having intelligence
convey'd to you by the way of fort Halifax from time to time, after
the snow falls, and in return I may expect the honor of your
commands. I shall in the mean time endeavour all in my power to
cherish the troops, that they may be able to act with vigor in the
Spring, when I hope you will lead them yourself; and take this
route to Montreal, if you have not already got there by the other.
We have reason to think that at least you are very near it, and it has
been by earnest wishes that you may succeed in all you attempt.
Small craft, & a formidable artillery on floating batteries will make
every thing easy this way. Our wants as to provisions, cloaths,
money and ammunition, you know; and we doubt not of having
everything from you, we can wish, as early as possible. We have
little cash much labor no prospect of fresh provisions, a great
scarcity of fuel, and ill housed. But every body is chearfull &
happy in having Quebec as it is for a quarter; all those who did not
like it, are thank god gone to places they like better.
P.S. If Mr Levi does not keep at a very respectable distance, he
may repent it, I am busy at present securing my provisions etc. I
shall be at leasure by and by, to look at him; I will let slip no
opportunity to keep up the dread of our arms.

WO/34/4 fols 12–13

132
Major-General Jeffery Amherst to Major Robert Rogers

Camp of Crown Point,

[Copy in Secretary's hand]   8 November 1759

Captain Ogden delivered me Yesterday Your letter of the 1st
Instant, for which I am not only to thank You, but to assure You of
the satisfaction I had in reading it, as every step you inform me
You had taken has been very well Judged and Deserves my full
approbation.[105]

THE CAMPAIGN OF 1759

I am sorry Lieut. Stephens Judged so ill, in Coming away with the provisions from the place where I sent him to wait for You; An Indian came in last night said he had left some of Your party at Otter River, I sent for them, they are come this afternoon, being four Indians, two Rangers the German woman, and three other Prisoners, they quitted four of the party some days since and thought they had arrived here, I am in hopes all the rest will come in very safe, I think there is no Danger but they will, as You quitted them not till having march'd Eight days in a Body, the only risk after that would be meeting party's a hunting.

WO/34/81 fol. 140

133
Major-General Jeffery Amherst to Colonel James Montresor

[Copy in Secretary's hand]   Camp at Crown Point
                                          12 November 1759

. . . With regard to the Lieut. and his fellow Deserters, whom Lieut. Campbell met on the road, they belong to Willards, and have been taken up by Lieut. M'kean at Stillwater, who has Informed me thereof; the Lieut. particularly is unpardonable, and were it Earlier in the Campaign, I should not fail to make an Example of him, but it is now too late; and the only method to be followed with him, and his party now, is to get rid of them in the easiest & cheapest way, letting them go home by Nº.4 as the Regiment will be marched before they can be Sent here; You will therefore take any arms, Cartridge Boxes, or ammunition they may have, belonging to the Crown from them, and let the Scoundrels find their way home as they can, with that Infamous fellow at their head, who calls himself an officer; You will give them three days provisions to each, that they may not Starve and You will write to the different posts, that the Commanding officers may be advertised, of Your Sending them away & may not permit them to go into any of the posts.

I also see, by Your first Letter, that notwithstanding all that has been done, at Your post to prevent this Infamous practice, yet You have lately had ten of the Newhampshire, and two of Ruggles's gone off; The most effectual way of preventing it among the provincials was, I thought to keep the Labourers in arrears, & those that went off to forfeit the whole, as I Directed that no one for them, on any account whatsoever Should receive any part of it, and upon these Conditions, I do not care how many do go off now, as it is a saving to the Publick of which it has already greatly benefited here and at Tienderoga . . .

WO/34/81 fol. 153

134
Major-General Jeffery Amherst to Lieutenant Governor James De Lancey

[Copy in Secretary's hand]

Camp of Crown Point
13 November 1759

. . . Major Rogers is returned with a part of his Detachment to N° 4. he acquaints me that on the 22ᵈ day after his departure from Crown Point, he Arrived near the Village of Sᵗ Francis, reconnoitred it, Attacked it next morning before Sunrise on the Right, left, and Centre; The Indians, who the Night before were Assembled at a Wedding and of Course all Drunk, were all Asleep and Surprised, by Seven the Affair was over, he had killed about 200, and burnt all the Houses, as some tryed to Escape by getting to the Water, and to their Canoes, they were killed and some Children suffered by their attempting to Carry them off; he took twenty Women and Children, Fifteen of which he let go, and brought off five; and retook five English Prisoners. Captain Ogden was slightly wounded, and six men Dᵗᵒ and One Stockbridge Indian killed, – Several of his Detachment are come in loaded with more Indian Riches than I thought any of their Towns would have Contained, but by Capt Ogden's Account, the Houses were very good, and so large that several hid themselves in their Houses till the flames forced them to discover they were there, and many too late to be Saved. After ten days March towards No 4, when the detachment was Separated in small

Bodys, One was Attacked (I suppose by a Hunting Party) and Seven Men were taken Prisoners, two Escaped the same Night & Joyn'd Mr Rogers. These are all the particulars I have yet had; I don't doubt but the party will all Come in safe, Except the five Men . . .[106]

WO/34/30 fol. 93

135
Major-General Jeffery Amherst to Colonel John Bradstreet
Camp of Crown Point
[Copy in Secretary's hand] 16 November 1759

I Yesterday received the favor of Your Letter of the 12th Instant, with one Enclosed of the 10th to You, in which it appears by what Lt Grant Acquaints You, that the Farmers in general are averse to furnishing the Troops for the four pences. I Imagine the same Repugnancy would appear on the like demand to any Set of Farmers in every part of the Country, who will thereby hope to rid themselves of the Troops, a Burden in their fancy only, but were they really so, I can only Lessen it as far as the Protection of this Country, and their properties will permit it; It is the Service that requires such a Number of Men near to Albany, there they must be Quarter'd; and if the People of the Country will not provide the Men for the four pences (which I /am yet in hopes they will do) they must give them firing, and the Contractor must deliver provisions.

WO/34/56 fol. 81

136
John Appy to James Napier
Camp at Crown Point
[Holograph copy] 19 November 1759

In answer to Your Letter of the 15th Instant I am commanded by the General to Signify to You his pleasure, that immediately upon

137

receipt hereof You do Set out for and repair to New York, in order to prepare the hospital and make provision for the Sick and wounded, that are coming from the River Sr Lawrence, and as from the number of Transports they are reported to be coming in, they must Exceed 150, which is all that His Majesty's Hospital at New York is capable to Contain, You will therefore immediately after Your arrival in that City, repair to the Barracks and fix on such a part thereof, as You Shall find will be sufficient to receive the remainder of the Sick and Wounded, which you will accordingly Cause to be fitted up for an hospital and see the same provided with every thing necessary for that purpose.

With regard to the Invalids, the List of which was Enclosed in Your's, the General will have such of them as are absolutely unfitt, for any further Service, sent to New York by the first Sloops he Shall send down the River with Troops, and Such as are with the army, will be ordered to Albany to Accompany the others to New York, that all the Invalids who are Entitled to Chelsea, may be Sent to England in one of these hospital Ships, that are arrived at New York.

WO/34/64 fol. 76

137
Major-General Jeffery Amherst to Colonel James Montresor

[Copy in Secretary's hand]

Camp at Crown Point
23 November 1759

As I shall have finished here tomorrow, I Intend to move with the Army the day after, I must therefore desire that You will have Every thing prepared and ready for moving the Baggage, that Nothing may retard us on our march, for the Season is Advanced, and already so Severe that I am not without some Apprehensions we may be froze up, if We do not make dispatch.

WO/34/81 fol. 180

138
Major-General Jeffery Amherst to Colonel William Haviland

Camp of Crown Point

[Copy in Secretary's hand]   24 November 1759

As I have Ordered the Troops to March from hence tomorrow, Except those Intended for the Garrison of this Place, I shall leave the Command of this Post to You, the Importance of which, I am Confident, is so Evident to You, that I need not describe the great Consequence it is of towards the general good of this Country, and the protection of His Majesty's Dominions . . .

I have added two Companies of a hundred Each, Rangers, to the Inniskilling Reg^t as a Garrison for this Place, as I Judge they will be of Use to You, in keeping out necessary Scouts; and though I am far from thinking it likely that the Enemy should Offer to make any Attempts on this Place, I shall nevertheless give Orders, that in Case of any unforeseen or sudden motions of the Enemy, You may Judge necessary to have a Reinforcement, that half of the Garrison of Tienderoga shall be ready to Joyn You at Your Order, and if You should yet want a further Reinforcement, the Other half to follow the first, so soon as Troops are moved up from Fort George, for which I shall leave the necessary Orders.

I have ordered a Detachment of the Independent Companys Equal to a Company, to Garrison N° 4, and I shall Order Captain Ogilvie to send Reports to You as often as an opportunity may offer; the Communication from that to Crown Point may be kept open by Partys meeting halfway, which You will Order as You think right; and if You have more Rangers than You find You want, I would have You send an Officer and Twenty-five to Remain at N° 4, under the Command of Captain Ogilvie, for which I have already Ordered a proper Supply of Provisions in Case they should be Sent . . .

WO/34/52 fol. 10

139
John Calcraft to Major-General Jeffery Amherst

London

7 December 1759

[Holograph]   [Received 13 February 1760]

By the last Packet I had the honour to receive your letter of the 22^d
October, and was heartily Rejoic'd to hear of Your being Got safe
back to Crown Point after regaining the Mastership of Lake
Champlain, For I own I was not Sanguine enough to think it
possible for You to do more; I am glad to add Your Proceedings have
met with the Approbation of those who direct them, as also that
they are universally applauded – Your letters arriv'd the Saturday,
and on Monday Mr Pitt took an opportunity of acquainting the
House of Commons with their Contents & Giving You in the
properest manner that Commendation Justly due to Your Zeal &
Ability, in which the whole House Seemed to Join . . .[107]

WO/34/99 fol. 53

140
Major-General Jeffery Amherst to Governor Thomas Pownall

New York

[Copy in Secretary's hand]   13 December 1759

. . . I come now Sir to make You the Same requisition I did last
Year upon my entring on the General Command; for altho' I have
not at present no more than I had then any particular Orders,
relative to the Operations of the ensuing Campaign Yet I am
certain it must be of Infinite Service to the Publick Cause, that the
Province of the Massachusetts Bay, Should keep up during the
Winter the same number of Officers and men that its Assembly
voted for the Operations of this last Campaign, by which, as I have
often before observed, they will not only Procure a Saving to the
province, but those Troops will be ready upon all Occasions and
Whenever the Service may Require, the advantages of Which are

140

too obvious, not to make me flatter myself, that altho' this Essential & necessary measure, did not take place last Year, it will this, and I must beg You will be pleased to recommend the same in the Strongest manner to the Assembly. But if before this reaches You, the Massachusetts Troops Should already be disbanded, or that the above mention'd measure Should contrary to my Expectations, not take place, in that case I must further Recommend it to You, to take the earliest opportunity of Acquaint[ing] the Assembly that I Imagine the like Number of Troops will be wanted for the Operations of the ensuing Campaign, as have been furnished by the Several Provinces and Colonies for the Services of the last and that I trust the Province of the Massachusetts bay will make the earliest provision for those of their Province, that they may be ready at the first Call which will be sooner the next than this Year on Account of the greater distance they have to go to our present Frontiers.

And I would at the same time Recommend it to their most Serious Consideration, that in the provision they Shall so make, they will not limit the time of Service to any fixed period but as the Colonies of Connecticut and Rhode Island have very wisely done, Stipulate the Same either during the War or at least during the Campaign the length or Shortness of Which cannot be Ascertained as it depends Wholly on Circumstances . . .

WO/34/36 fols 173–4

141
Major-General Jeffery Amherst to Governor William Lyttelton

New York
[Copy in Secretary's hand]   21 December 1759

As Capt Stott Commanding His Majesty's Ship the Scarborough, Informs me, that he proposes to Sail for his Station on Sunday next, I seize that Opportunity of Acknowledging the receipt of Your two favors of the 16th and twenty third October . . . and of Conveying to You my best wishes for the Successful Issue of Your

Expedition, either by those Barbarians having given You the proper Satisfaction before You got to their Nests, or if You have been obliged to go on so far, that they may have felt the Weight of His Majesty's Arms, than which nothing, will Contribute more towards the Security of the Inhabitants and their Settlements, for when once these dastardly Scoundrels, know the Strength of the Province, and that its Troops are not afraid of them, they will be as meek as Lambs, and very glad to Accept any terms You will be pleased to prescribe to them, and I cannot therefore but think this Expedition of the utmost good Consequence to the Province; So soon as I heard of it I was not without Some thoughts, that You might perhaps have occasion for Some of His Majesty's Regular Forces, and I have accordingly brought two Regim^{ts} with me, that I may be ready to reinforce You in case You should require it; at the same time I much rather You had no Call for them, because as I observed before, if the Indians find that the province alone is able to resent and punish their Outrages they will Stand in greater awe of them, and be Cautious how they Offend for the future.[108]

From the little Experience I have of Indians, I find that the only way to deal with them is to reward or punish them according to their Deserts; this maxim I have laid down to myself I let them know it, and I keep to my Resolution: Agreeable to which, I have during this Campaign been Compelled to Cause two notorious Murderers to be Executed; altho' the Mohawks Claimed them, and that Some people apprehended if they were not given up, it would be Attended with bad Consequences; they were nevertheless Executed, and not the least Evil has resulted from it, on the contrary I Imagine much good . . .

WO/34/36 fol. 47

142

Section II
The Campaign of 1760:
the Conquest Completed

142
Major-General Jeffery Amherst to Field Marshal Viscount
John Ligonier

New York
[Copy in Secretary's hand]   9 January 1760

Since I did myself the Honor of Writing to Your Lordship by Captain Abercrombie,[1] Nothing material has happened here.

The Fowey Man of War, with the English Transports under Convoy, being ready to Sail, I sent all the Wounded and Discharged Men that are recommended to Chelsea, and I have taken Care that Every Man has been properly Discharged and Cleared, and have given Orders to Ensign Thorne to deliver them to their respective Agents in London.

Lt Colonel Robertson has been with me as Deputy Quarter Master General, on the Louisbourg Expedition, and this last Campaign, his Merits as an Officer, and his Activity, prudence, & punctuality in the Department he has Acted in, deserves all I can say for him; and if Your Lordship may Chuse to know any particulars in regard to Either of the Campaigns, or the Situation of the Affairs in this Country, he will give You very Clear Information, though he will Appear to be an Absent Man, until he has the honour of being known to Your Lordship.

I am glad to have had an Opportunity of granting a Majority to Captain Oswald, as Your Lordship mentioned him to me . . .[2]

U1350/O/35/14

143
Governor Thomas Pownall to Major-General Jeffery Amherst

Boston
22 Jan 1760
[Holograph]   [Receipt not dated]

By ye Copy of my Speech which I sent You, You will have seen that I recommended to the Genl Court the Considering the Services of the 2500 Men of My Province Troops continued beyond the time of their Enlistment at Cape Breton & N Scotia & then to proceed to measures of Providing for the ensuing Campaign. Upon this Plan The Assembly have voted Provision of 4£ Lawfull money p^r Man as a Reward to ye Men who have continued in the Service, and 9£ Lawfull Money p^r man to Every One of these who shall Enlist again for another Campaign. And further, exclusive of these, have voted ye same Bounty of 9£ Lawful Money p^r Man to 5000 more. I have infinite pleasure in being able to acquaint You of this Beginning.

WO/34/26 fol. 5

144
Governor Brigadier-General James Murray to Major-General Jeffery Amherst

[Quebec]
25 January 1760
[Holograph]   [Received 3 March 1760]

I send to you Lieu^t Montresor, that you may know how well we are here; We had some difficulties but they are removed, and we wish for nothing more than the Visit Mon^r de Levis has threatened to pay us; If he really intends it, I suppose he will think proper to put it off till the Spring: I am told he may then bring all the force they have in Canada against us, as it will be impossible to advance upon them by way of Crown point till July: the Isle aux Noix they esteem impregnable, and the approaches to Montreal by any other way impracticable – till the Sun has had his influence.

At present their regular Regiments are in cantonments in the Government of Montreal; Piquets from them, and twelve hundred of the troupes de Colonie, are at Jaques Quartur [Cartier] and its environs ten leagues from this, they have made a fort there, have some Cannon and are dayly bringing more. When I have got a sufficient number of Snow Shoes, there may be a possibility of surprising it; if I attempt it, I will be sure of my blow, it is a post of no consequence, and will be entirely out of the Question in the Operations of next campaign. If we are Masters of the River St Lawrence our passage to Montreal is open . . . My boats are in a very bad condition, but I flatter myself I shall be able to fit out as many as will contain 1800 men; I have only five floating batteries of one gun each, they shall be in order, but further I cannot promise, for this reason chiefly I send Montresor that you may be able to provide the craft necessary for this River [during] the insuing campaign.

Monʳ Vaudreuil has kept four frigates in Canada, they winter in the river Sorel, and as I am informed, are to be placed advantageously in the Spring to obstruct our passage to Montreal.

Everybody will inform you that last summer we never could call ourselves masters of the river Sᵗ Lawrence, in which our frigates have little command of the shore, besides their progress in it is very uncertain. Flat bottom'd vessels with oars are the things, a sufficient number of them will make all very easy.

Montresor will tell you of the villany of our English merchants, and of the methods I have taken to prevent the Effects of it. He will inform you too of the sobriety and good Behaviour of the troops, who will wait chearfully till cash arrives from You.

I have taken an oath of fidelity from every man of the lower Canada as far up as the parishes beyond my posts, and their arms are lodged with us; they have hitherto behaved well, and as they have reason to be pleas'd with us, I am satisfy'd they are glad of the change, and that their country men above will not take up Arms, nor desert their habitations next Summer as they did the last.

I need not tell you my Dear Sir! How glad I shall be to see you here that I may make the Campaign under your command.

I hope Lord Colvil will take care to be in the Basin of Quebec before the Enemy, nothing can hurt us but a french Squadron geting the Start of him. In case of this event I shall take my precautions, and as soon as the weather will admit, encamp, and fortify on the heights of Abraham, where I flatter myself I can defy them, as long as my provisions /^{will} hold out. This measure will prevent me perhaps from making the necessary provision of Gabions facines etc to facilitate, & quicken our Operations above, but you may depend upon all imaginable diligence on my part.

WO/34/4 fols 16–18

145
Brigadier-General John Stanwix to Major-General Jeffery Amherst

Fort Pittsburgh
26 January 1760

[Holograph]   [Received 11 February 1760]

. . . in our Treaty here with Various Nations of Indians they all agree to give up their Prisoners many have been given up and they are dayly giving up more and Capt Croghan the Depp^y Indian Agent under Sir William Johnson assures me that he has no doubt but the whole will be delivered up in the Spring, a few days ago L^t McDonald of Colo Montgomerys Hyland Regim^t was brought up here and delivered wth a Serg^t of that Regim^t, both from near Detroit & assure me that more of that Regim^t are on their way to this place to be delivered up, L^t McDonald & the Serg^t are gone down to Hudsons River to joyn their Corps & the rest shall be sent as soon as they arrive here, but what surprizes me most is that a great many of our prisoners absolutely refuse to leave the Indians and a good many gone back to them after being very formerly being delivered up here.[3]

WO/34/45 fols 125–6

146
Governor William Lyttelton to Major-General Jeffery Amherst

Charles Town
2 February 1760
[Secretary's hand, signed by Lyttelton]   [Received 28 February 1760]

Having received the Letter of which I inclose to you a Copy,[4] and other concurrent advices from the Cherokee Nation by which it appears that since the Treaty of Peace concluded with those Indians at Fort Prince George on the 26th day of December last, they have renewed their Hostilities and Slain a very considerable number of his Majesty's Subjects trading in their Towns; and having strong grounds to apprehend that they will very Speedily make Incursions in this and the Neighbouring Provinces: I have thought it necessary, with the advice of His Majestys Council to acquaint your Excellency thereof, & to apply to You for such a Body of Troops, as you shall judge sufficient to protect this Colony & Secure Fort Prince George & Fort Loudoun.

The General Assembly is Summoned to meet on the 4 Instant, & I shall with their Concurrence take the best measures I can for His Majesty's Service in the present Conjuncture, but without a Speedy Assistance from you Sir, I fear it will not be possible to preserve the interior Tranquillity of the Province, or prevent the two Forts above mention'd from falling into the Hands of the Indians; and I beg leave to remark, that if it shall be found necessary for the Troops you send to march into the Cherokee Country in order to relieve these Garrisons, or to subdue the Indians, those Troops should not (as I humbly conceive) consist of less than fifteen hundred or two thousand men, as it is a very Mountainous Region in which are many very narrow & difficult Passes & the Cherokees are computed to be two thousand Gunmen . . .

WO/34/35 fol. 148

147
Colonel James Bradstreet to Major-General Jeffery Amherst

Albany

4 February 1760

[Holograph]   [Received 9 February 1760]

. . . I beg leave to remind your Excellency that the preparations for the operations for the last campaign this way You judg'd necessary should begin the 15ᵗʰ Instant and that it will require near the same time this year to provide properly . . .

WO/34/57 fol. 102

148
Lord William Barrington to Major-General Jeffery Amherst (private)

Cavendish Square

8 February 1760

[Clerk's hand, signed by Barrington]   [Receipt not dated]

I transmit to you herewith a Memorial, and a letter recommending it, from the Duke of Argyll, which I do, because for every reason public and private, I wish to obey and to forward his Grace's Commands. You, Sir, are particularly oblig'd to him, For all the Highland Corps who have so eminently distinguish'd themselves in America, are, (Lord John Murray's 1ˢᵗ Battalion excepted), the effect of my Lord Duke's ability & inclination to serve the Public.

How far another Lieutenant Colonel may be necessary to Lord John Murray's Regᵗ I am no Judge, nor do I recommend it; but I do most strongly recommend Capᵗ McNeil to your favour and protection whenever a proper opportunity shall offer for his preferment.[5]

U1350/O/37/7

149
Major-General Jeffery Amherst to Governor Francis Bernard

New York

[Copy in Secretary's hand]   9 February 1760

Yesterday I was favored with Your Letter of the 5th Instant, accompanying the Vindication of the Mayor of Elizabeth Town, supported by sundry Affidavits, which I return, in order that the affair may take its due Course of Law and the Corporal, if proved Guilty, meet with the punishment due to his Crime, which is still greater, as it is against my express and repeated orders, which have ever been against fraudulent practices in the Recruiting Service: at the Same time I must beg leave to Observe, that even by those very Affidavits its appears, the man Asserted to have been illegally or not at all Enlisted was not only rescued, but the party abused and ill treated, which the Rescuers had no right to do, nor am I surprised, that on such an occasion, the Soldiers returned the Compliment; to prevent the like for the future I beg that You will signify to the People of your Government, that if any of them Should have cause to Complain, of having been thus illegally Enlisted, they do not resist the party, but lodge their Complaint either with You or the nearest magistrate, and upon due proof, I will not only do them justice, but punish the Delinquents . . .[6]

WO/34/31 fol. 175

150
Major-General Jeffery Amherst to Colonel John Bradstreet

New York

[Copy in Secretary's hand]   10 February 1760

. . . I am Still of opinion that the Preparations for the Operations of the ensuing Campaign, ought to begin early tho' from our present Circumstance it is not necessary they Should be begun quite so Soon as last Year, and I only Wait His Majesty's

Commands which I expect daily, to give Directions accordingly; meanwhile I shall begin by ordering all the materials & Stores for the Vessells on the Lakes as they will be wanted more or less at all Events; Indeed I have already wrote to Cap[t] Loring, to procure Sundries which M[r] Thornton said would be wanted for Lake Ontario.

WO/34/56 fol. 94

151
Major-General Jeffery Amherst to Captain Joshua Loring

New York

[Copy in Secretary's hand]   15 February 1760

Your Letter of the 21st Ultimo, did not Come to my hands till within these four days;[7] and I seize the Opportunity of an express going to Boston, not only to Acknowledge the receipt of it, but to Acquaint you that the Packett being come in, and finding it necessary to begin the preparations for the Operations of the Ensuing Campaign, You will upon receipt hereof Compleat and Purchase the Navall Stores wanted for the Vessells on Lake Ontario of which I transmitted You a List in mine of the 3[d] Instant,[8] to which You will add What You think may be further wanted there as likewise every thing necessary to Equip & Compleat the Vessells for Lake Champlain, and to have the Whole ready and there by the latter end of March. You will also Send me a Return of the Number of Seamen that will be requisite to man all the Vessells on both Lakes, Which it will be most likely to get in Connecticutt, from Which Colony I shall make a requisition of them, & doubt not but they will readily grant the same, against the above mentioned term. So that You have no time to lose in sending me said Return.

WO/34/65 fol. 130

152
Major-General Jeffery Amherst to Colonel John Bradstreet
New York
[Copy in Secretary's hand]   16 February 1760

I am glad to hear that you go on with transporting the Provisions to the westward & northward as well as can be expected or indeed desired, which are the words of Your Letter so that I am very well Satisfied.

I am now to Inform You, that the Packett has brought me Letters from M[r] Secretary Pitt, directing me to make all necessary preparations for pushing the War with the utmost Vigour as early in the Year as the Season will permit and thereby Compleat the great work so Successfully begun of rendring His Majesty entire Master of Canada.[9]

In Consequence of these Directions we must lose no time in making preparation for the Construction of What number of Additional boats will be wanted for Lakes Ontario & Champlain, Which You will make a Calculation of and Acquaint me with, that orders may be given to Set about them in due time, wherefore You will Inform me when You think the sawmills will be able to begin working, the time it will take up to saw the plank for the additional number of Boats You shall think necessary, the hands it will require to prepare and Compleat the Whole; having a due regard that the Boats now intended to be built are to be every way fit and proper for the use of the above mentioned two Lakes, and at least as strong as the french Boats that we met with and took there and in Short every thing else that shall occurr to You upon this Subject for the good of His Majesty's Service.

In my orders to Cap[t] Loring for the purchase of the naval stores &ca for all the Vessells, I have Directed him to have them ready and at the respective places by the end of March; and I have also ordered him to make me a Return of the number of Seamen that will be wanted to Navigate the Vessells on both Lakes, that I might Demand them against the said Period from the Colony of Connecticutt.

WO/34/56 fol. 95

153
Captain Frank Legge to Major-General Jeffery Amherst

18 February 1760
Boston

[Holograph]   [Received 24 February 1760]

I have the honour to acquaint your Excellency that I arrived here
with my recruiting party this first Instant I have Listed three fine
Recruits two of them for one Year and the other for three But as
this Province are now raising Men for the Ensuing Campaign and
give great incouragement I dispair of geting many more besides
the magistrates do not seem inclined to give me the least aid or
assistance.

I Listed a man the other day who came Voluntarily to my
Lodgings to inlist I sent him before the Justice Danna of this
Town in order have him sworn and Attested which the Justice
refused because the man had not been Listed Twenty four hours. I
have since found out that the Justices reason for not swearing the
man was to give some People of the Town who are imployed to
List for the Provincials an opportunity to intice the man away
from me which they did and Listed him for the Provincials first
making him return the advance money I gave him and paying
Twenty Shillings besides . . .

WO45/82 fol. 44

154
Colonel John Bradstreet to Major-General Jeffery Amherst

Albany
18 February 1760

[Holograph]   [Receipt not dated]

Agreeable to your Excellency's directions I enclose you what I
think absolutely necessary for the transportation between Albany
& Ticonderoga – all of which Boats are to built none being left
here last year; the Carriages to be repair'd and about 500 oxen to
be added to the number we have; and Boards are to be had /here

now, with workmen sufficient to compleat them by the middle of April. – What Boats are left at Ticonderoga I know not but if none are lost and they properly repair'd & seald with an addition of 150 New ones with what is at Fort George will be sufficient and for the repairing, Building & Colking these Boats it will take 100 good Carpenters & Colkers at least 2 Months.

For the Service to the Westward all is wanted of the Boat kind except a few and in my Opinion, if an army goes that way, 400 Battoes should be built at Schenectady and of the same Size & Sort as those they had last year for without the troops take with them three months provisions at Setting off they will be of little use – and People for the building them may be had at Schenectady & down the Country but a small distance.

Whale boats, none left to the westward of any consequence and I believe but few good to the Northward as the most of them I am told ly in the Ice; if your Excellency would please to have any built, if you will let me know the number I will prepare the Timber and let you know the number of Builders, but the Ceeder Boards must be sent from York on the breaking up of the River.

Your Excellency saw last year the great want of Teamsters, Waggons & Battoe Men and the necessity of getting them with the Consent of the several Provinces and many you are sensible will be wanted.

WO/34/57 fol. 105

155
Major-General Jeffery Amherst to Governor Thomas Pownall[10]

New York

[Copy in Secretary's hand]   21 February 1760

With his Majesty's Commands for the Reduction of all Canada, received last Night, I likewise had the Copy of Mr Secretary Pitt's Circular letter to the Northern and Southern Governors of the 7th January last,[11] the Original of which goes Enclosed, and whereby You will See, that His Majesty having nothing so much at heart, as to Improve the great and Important Advantages gained the last Campaign in North America, and not doubting that all His Faithfull and Brave Subjects there, will Continue most Chearfully to Co-operate with, and Second to the utmost the large Expence and Extraordinary Succours Supplied by the Kingdom of Great Britain, for their preservation and future Security, by Compleating the Reduction of all Canada; And that His Majesty not Judging it Expedient to Limit the Zeal and Ardor of any of His Provinces, by making a Repartition of the Force to be raised by each respectively for this most Important Service, He (Mr Secretary Pitt) was Commanded to Signify to You the King's pleasure, that You do forthwith Use Your utmost Endeavors and Influence with the Council and Assembly of Your Province, to Induce them to Raise with all possible dispatch within Your Government, at least, as large a Body of Men as they did for the last Campaign, and even as many more as the Number of its Inhabitants may Allow, and forming the Same into Regiments, as far as shall be found Convenient, that You do direct them to hold themselves in readiness as Early as may be to March to the Rendezvous at Albany, or such other Place as His Majesty's Commander in Chief in America, shall Appoint, in order to proceed from thence, in Conjunction with a Body of the King's British Forces, and under the Supreme Command of His Majesty's said Commander in Chief in America, so as to be in a Situation to begin the Operations of the Campaign by the First of May, if possible, or as soon after as shall be any way practicable, by an Irruption into Canada, in order to Reduce Montreal, and all other Posts belonging to the French in those parts, and further to Annoy the Enemy in such manner as His Majesty's Commander in Chief shall . . . Judge to be practicable.

As the King's Directions, on the foregoing Subject, are so fully stated in the above Abstract, I have only to Request that You would Exert Your utmost Endeavors to incite and Encourage Your Assembly to the full and due Execution of the King's Commands, in a Matter so Essential to the future Welfare and prosperity of the Several Provinces, and the Success of the Ensuing, decisive, and (it is greatly hoped) last Campaign in North America; which desireable Ends cannot be better Attained than by Commencing the Operations as Early as shall be practicable; and that Nothing may be left undone that it is possible for me to Attempt in the Execution of His Majesty's Commands, I must be Urgent with you to Quicken and Expedite the Levies of your Province, so that they may be Assembled at the Rendezvous at Albany, by the tenth of April next, at furthest; as the distances from that Place to the Frontiers are now so much greater than the preceding Year, and consequently require a much Earlier Junction with His Majesty's Troops than it did then . . .

WO/34/36 fols 177–8

156
Major-General Jeffery Amherst to Brigadier-General Thomas Gage

[Copy in Secretary's hand]

New York
22 February 1760

I write to Col° Bradstreet and leave it Open for Your perusal, I Shall prepare every thing for an active and I hope a last Campaign here, as fast as I can, in which I must Desire Your Assistance, and that You will inform me of any thing You think necessary, for the Routes I have ordered Col° Bradstreet to make preparations for.

A New Contract is come over at four pence three farthings, Col. Delancey has Shewn it me, but I have not a Word from the Lords of the Treasury about it, it commences the 25th of March, two Colebrooks, Nesbitt & Franks, they will Continue to Employ all Mr Kilby's People, So I hope it will not be attended with any difficulties that a Change of Contractors is apt to produce.

WO/34/46A fol. 211

WLC/AP/5

157
Major-General Jeffery Amherst to Colonel John Bradstreet

New York

[Copy in Secretary's hand]   22 February 1760

Yesterday by Express, I had Your two Letters of the 18th & 19th Instant, with a Calculation of what Number of Boats, Carriages &ca. that are wanted, for the Transportation of the Provisions &ca. for an army of 16,000 men, from Albany to Tienderoga, which I think rather high; however before I proceed on the Subject matter of Your Letters, I am to observe to You, that in the preparations we are now going upon, due attention must be had to the Department of the Mohawk River, & the same provisions & necessaries of every kind procured for the like Number of men in that Communication, as may be Employed in that of Crown Point, in order that, if at any time hereafter, the Circumstances Should Induce me to march, an equal Force each way, I may not be disappointed in any of its necessary supplies, but be able to proceed without any Obstacles, thro the want of Carriages & Conveniencies of all kinds, and then If I should encrease the Force either way the preparations may be easily made for the Augmentation of Numbers . . .

If as You say, for the Service to the Westward, all is wanted of the Boat kind except a few, they must be set about as soon as possible, but instead of building them at Schenectady, it is my opinion they should mostly be built at Oswego where they may be made much stronger, than at Schenectady where, by reason of the Carrying Places they must be afterwards hawl'd over, they must be made so much slighter and of course, much more liable to receive Damage, & become useless at the time they may be most wanted; the Same reason induces me, to have those for Lake Champlain built at Tienderoga, especially as the Boats I have left at Fort George, with proper and timely repairs will answer every end for that Lake; this must not hinder if they Should be wanted, the building of what few Boats, may be requisite for the Communication from Albany to Fort Edward and a proper number must also be built at Schenectady, to be afterwards fixed at the Several Posts on the Mohawk River for the Constant and continual transportation of provisions which I do not think there is any occasion for the Troops to take with them, three months at their Setting off.

You will accordingly prepare the Timber & every thing else /^{necessary} for all these and Send them as soon as possible to the Mills at Tienderoga & Oswego, that they may be set a going so Soon as the Weather will permit . . .

The very difficulties we Encountered last Year, in getting Teamsters, Waggoners, and Batteau men, the few we obtained at last, the great expence they Occasioned, the little use we had of them when done, added to the Complaints of the Several Provinces, who alledge that it prevents their Compleating their Levies, have determined me to make use of the Provincial Troops for all the above purposes, and I am confident the Service will in every respect be gainers by it . . .

WO/34/56 fols 96–7

158
Major-General Jeffery Amherst to Sir William Johnson
New York
[Copy in Secretary's hand]   23 February 1760

Having received His Majesty's Commands for the operations of the Ensuing Campaign, and being determined not to leave any difficulty undone, that can Ensure its being the last and decisive one in this Country, I am to beg of You immediately upon receipt hereof, to use all Your influence with the Several tribes and Nations of Indians in Amity with us, and to bring as many into the field as You can possibly prevail on, to Join His Majesty's arms in so Salutary a Work; and that You will have them ready as early as possible to act in conjunction with His troops, in Such Enterprizes and Attempts as I shall find most conducive to the good of the Publick Cause, and which I shall hereafter apprise You of. Meanwhile no time should be lost, in providing the necessary presents and what else may be requisite to Attach those Indians the more heartily & firmly to us for which I rely on Your usual Zeal, and doubt not but I shall soon receive a very satisfactory answer from You.

I must also Recommend it to You to exert Yourself to the utmost in bringing over to His Majesty's Interests all such or as many as possible, of the Enemy Indians as still remain attached to them, the advantages of which are too obvious, to need add anything further on that subject.

WO/34/38 fol. 97[12]

159
Major-General Jeffery Amherst to Colonel Archibald Montgomery

[Copy in Secretary's hand]

New York
24 February 1760

I have last Night received some Dispatches from Gov[r] Lyttelton, acquainting me that the Indians have Renewed their Hostilities, and Slain a very considerable number of His Majesty's Subjects, and as the Governor by the advice of His Majesty's Council, Applys to me for a Body of Troops to protect the Colony, I have determined to Send the following Corps under Your Command, for which I have this day given orders, that a moments time may not be lost in Assembling and Embarking the Corps. The Royal[13] is to furnish a Battalion of four Compleat Companies to be commanded by Major Hamilton, the Royal gives three Captains to four Companies. Your Regim[t14] is to furnish a Battalion of four Compleat Companies, to be commanded by Major Grant. The Royal and Yours give each a Company of light Infantry to be commanded by the Eldest Captain of the two Companys. The Royal & Yours give a Company of Grenadiers Each, to be Commanded in the like Manner by the Eldest Captain of the two Companys. With these four Corps, I am not in the least Doubt, but You will Effectually Protect the Colony and punish the Indians for this infamous breach of the Peace, they had so lately made, in such manner, that his Majesty's Subjects May hereafter

Enjoy their Possessions, without any dread of those barbarous and inhumane Savages.

WO/34/48 fol. 1

160
Major-General Jeffery Amherst to Governor William Lyttelton

New York
[Copy in Secretary's hand]   26 February 1760

On the 23^d in the Evening, I was favored with Your Letter of the 9th instant, accompanying a Duplicate of that of the 2^d (the original of which is not yet come to my hands) whereby I see, with great concern, that, that perfidious race of Savages, with whom You had so lately renewed alliance and friendship, have again dared to break the faith of Treaties, which from the wise precaution You had taken of obtaining Hostages from them, I must own, I had flattered myself would not have happened, nor can I help thinking they would, had all the Hostages been secured in the metropolis, & some of them not left on the Frontiers – however it remains for us now to Chastise their Insolence and endeavor to reduce them so low, that they may never more be able to be guilty of the like again, which I am hopeful we may Effect with the Detachment I have ordered to Your Assistance, consisting of a Body of 1300 men from two different regim^{ts} to be commanded by Col° Montgomery, who has my Instructions to be prepared for Embarking with them, so soon as the Shipping requisite for that purpose can be obtained, but I am sorry to say, that altho' immediately upon receipt of Your Letter, I sent the D.Q.M.G. to hire the necessary tonnage of Vessells, I have not as Yet been able to procure so much as one, the Merchants of this Town, who upon this Emergent occasion, & in duty to their King and Country, ought to have Exerted themselves to the utmost, having on the contrary, thrown all the obstacles in my way they possibly could, Whereupon I have applied to the Governor, who has promised me an impress warrant from Whence it is suspected little good will derive; Should that prove the Case, I shall take a method, which tho' disagreeable to me, I cannot avoid, and directly demand an Embargo to be laid on all the Shipping in this Port . . .

As the Detachment ordered upon this Service is every way sufficient to march against & overcome any Indians I flatter myself, that business will soon be over; and I am the more Sanguine in these my hopes, because as I have received the King's Commands to pursue the War in these parts with the utmost Vigour, and that I must expect to Encounter the main Strength of the Enemy at Montreal I shall have great occasion for that body of Troops, which are the Majority of two of my best Regiments, with which I am to pursue those Operations; I must therefore beg of You and I shall firmly expect it, that so soon as Your troubles cease they, or whatever number of them can be spared, may be immediately sent back to me, without any regard to the frights of the people, who will perhaps, even after all is Quelled, be desirous of having them Continue in the Country for no other reason, than because their fears are not subsided . . .

Before I conclude, I must beg leave to observe, that it has been represented to me, that during the Command of Col° Bouquet in South Carolina, His Majesty's Troops suffered considerably thro' the want of Quarters, which were Inhumanely and long refused them; I hope neither this, or any other aid, that this Corps of Troops may want, during their Stay in that Country will be refused them. – Indeed it must not. Men that go to defend, & protect the Lives & properties of the Subject, deserve a more gratefull Return and I please myself with the thoughts, that they will meet with all the Encouragements, this Service Entitles them to . . .

WO/34/36 fols 50–1

161
Major-General Jeffery Amherst to Oliver De Lancey
New York
[Copy in Secretary's hand]   27 February 1760

As You have laid before me the Copy of a Contract enter'd into, by and between the Right Honble The Lords Commissioners of His

Majesty's Treasury, on the part and behalf of the King of the one part, & Sr James Colebroke, Bar^t, Arnold Nesbitt, George Colebrooke, and Moses Franks of London merch^{ts}, of the other part, bearing date the 20th day of December 1759; by which it is Covenanted and agreed, that the said Sr James Colebrooke, Arnold Nesbitt, Geo: Colebrooke and Moses Franks, are from and after the 25th of March ensuing to Victuall H^s M$^{'s}$ Forces, in the several Places & Parts of N^o America, wherever they may happen to be in Garrison Stationed or Employed, agreable to the terms and on the Conditions set forth in the said Contract.

And as You have at the same time signified to me, that the above named Contractors, had appointed You to be one of their Agents, for the due performance of said Contract, & had sent You orders in Consequence thereof.

I am therefore to lose no time in Signifying to You, that I do expect, You will forthwith, make the Necessary Provisions for the due Execution of the said Contract and orders, observing to begin by that for the Garrison of Quebec, in order that the Same may be duly supplied, as early as the navigation of the River St Lawrence will permit, for which purpose, it will be necessary, that You do directly Commission at Philadelphia or Wheresoever You shall think fitt, the Quantity of Flower we have already in Conversation fixed upon, and observing that the one Eighth part of the same be in bread.

Next to this Important Service, You will also make Provision for the army, that is to assemble at Albany, which is to Consist of the same number of men as last Year, and that You take care You have for their use the Allotted Quantity of every species of Provisions agreeable to said Contract.

The army that is to serve to the southward,[15] is to Consist also of the like number of men it did last Year; You will therefore take care to see that supplied in the same manner.

And as I see by the said Contract, that Your Principals have Covenanted and agreed to furnish the Troops with fresh Provisions, whenever and for so long a time, as the Commander in Chief shall think fitt: I have no time to lose in reminding You, that as the Consumption of fresh Provision will be great, You cannot too early enough, Engage a large number of Live Cattle, as the same will be wanted & must be issued as last Year to the three different armies at Quebec, Albany, and to the southward, the particular numbers for each of which said places, as well as the method of Conveyance to them, I shall hereafter Inform You of.

The fresh Hostilities Committed by the Cherokee Indians having obliged me to make a Detachment from H^s. M^s army of 1300 men to be sent to South Carolina, in order to punish this Breach of faith, which Mr Kilby is to Victuall from hence, until the Expiration of his Contract, wherefore I must also give You this early notice, of providing for their subsistence after that term and during their stay in that Country, but also the Transportation of so large a Quantity of salt provision in almost, I am told, an Impracticable Country, would be attended not only with great difficulties, but great risk and Expence, all which it is necessary to avoid; I propose that upon their departure from that metropolis, they should drive live cattle with them, and only load themselves with Bread . . .

WO/34/66 fol. 68

162
Colonel John Bradstreet to Major-General Jeffery Amherst
Albany
27 February 1760
[Holograph]   [Received 5 March 1760]

I am this day honor'd with Your Excellencys letter of the 22^d inst and shall do all in my power to procure all the battoe Builders & other People for that Service to go to Oswego immediately, but am persuaded it will not be possible to get the necessary numbers to build the Boats there in time nither at Schenectady nor here and consequently a number must be had at York, of which I shall inform you as soon as I know the number I can raise which will be in two or three days. – If I understand your Excellency upon this Subject, you would have a sufficient number of Battoes built as is necessary to Transport about ten thousand men with provisions, Baggage &^{ca} from Oswego, if so it must exceed six hundred supposing the Chief part of the Army to go eighteen Men in a Boat which I conceive to be full enough supposing them to be built as large as the French Boats that way which is two feet longer than ours only: The Building of that number of Boats is a considerable work any where much more so at Oswego, where Sheds must be erected to build them in to be able to work at all times; no Carriages to draw out the Timber nor a possibility of Subsisting Oxen or Horses there so Early in the Year as is necessary together with the difficulty of getting a Sufficient number of workmen willing to go there as it will take no less than two hundred good men to compleat them 65 working Days exclusive of those necessary to draw the stuff out of the woods, work the mill and no possibility of getting the workmen with their tools &^{ca} there till the beginning of April, if so soon.– As your Excellency has desir'd me to mention whatever might occur to me upon these Subjects I flatter myself you will not be displeas'd at having these difficulties laid before you and that I still humbly continue to assure your excellency it will answer the Publick Service infinitely better to Build them at Schenectady as there will be a certainty of no disappointment . . .

WO/34/57 fols 108–9

163
Frederick Post to Richard Peters

Bethlehem
11 March 1760
[Copy signed by Peters]   [Received 29 March 1760]

Foreasmuch as this present undertaking of my going to the great Council of the different Nations of Indians, goes very near to my Heart . . . that Peace may be made with the numerous and dangerous Indian Nations; which by all probability is the wisest Step which Men in Power at this Juncture can take and wish for. Therefore it is fallen in my Mind that it wou'd be good and necessary if your Honour wou'd be pleased to let General Amherst know of my going to this Council, for I think it would be of great Consequence both to the Province and to the Indians, if I had a Word to bring them from the Chief Commander of all his Majesty's Forces here, for I am sure they will ask me very closely to tell them the real Truth of the intention of our great Warrior Chief in regard to them, who is sent from the King to this Country to act in his Name. For the Indians will much listen to what hope of advantage a Messenger will give them from the Chief Rulers. I know one of their principal Points in their Council will be, how to secure the limits between them and the white People, so that they may live by themselves a due distance from us, to Secure their hunting Ground, for they are more afraid of losing their hunting Grounds than their Lives, and they are very much prepossessed and Suspicious that that is our Scheme to incroach upon them, and Spoil their hunting, and to bring them to Misery and Slavery, and they like the Jews think we are free born and no Slaves, and will therefore rather die than submit to Work. I for my part doubt not at all but that the Indians will grant a Tract of Land for a Trading place, in a proper manner bought of them, and that the white people dont hunt on Land which is not bought of them, and in so doing, one can avoid all Quarrils with them, else it wou'd not be safe for anyone to live upon their Land. Otherwise for my part I can never see through how a Peace can be Settled with the Indians. To root them out, or to subdue them, I think it is impossible for this time, for there is not one who rightly knows their Country and their lurking holes and their several Nations and strength . . .[16]

WO/34/33 fol. 47

164
Captain Joshua Loring to Major-General Jeffery Amherst

Boston
13 March 1760

[Holograph]   [Receipt not dated]

I received your Excellency's Letter of the 6th Instant, this Day and shall do every Thing in my Power to procure Seamen, but am sorry to say there is but little Prospect of succeeding, as the greatest /[part] of the Navigation belonging to this Place is now at Sea, and the few seamen that is here ask such Exorbitant Wages that I shall be almost afraid to engage them, but shall send to Newbury to Morrow to see what can be got there.[17]

I expect to have all the Vessels ready for the Artillery by the 17th Inst[t] and all the Carpenters sent off to Albany by the 20th when I shall set out immediately for York . . .

WO/34/65 fol. 12

165
Colonel John Bradstreet to Major-General Jeffery Amherst

Albany
25 March 1760

[Holograph]   [Receipt not dated]

I beg leave to acquaint your Excellency that the number of Persons preparing to go to the westward in order to Trade with the Indians is so considerable and the Wages they give for Battoe Men being double the Sum the Crown ever gave they will induce & carry off every good Battoe Man upon the Mohawk River which is evidently to the great prejudice of his Majestys Service as it can be by their Assistance alone that the Publick Service can be forwarded that way untill the Provincials are here & ready which perhaps will not be in some time; . . . I hope your Excellency will effectually put a stop to it untill the Publick is first serv'd.

WO/34/57 fol. 124

166
Lieutenant-Governor James Hamilton to Major-General Jeffery Amherst

Philadelphia
26 March 1760
[Holograph]   [Received 29 March 1760]

The dilatory proceedings of the Assembly here since their Vote of 2700 men for the Service of the ensuing campaign, has given me a great deal of concern.

It was not less than ten days after passing the Vote, before they Sent up the Bill for my concurrence; Altho' as it is only a transcript of that passed by Mr Denny the last year, it might very well have been dispatched in four or five.

Immediately after presenting it they adjourn'd themselves, according to a privilege claimed by the House for Nine days without consulting me thereupon. And upon their first coming together again, they applied for my consent to a further adjournment of 13 or 14 days, which I absolutely refused, so that I had not before yesterday an opportunity of giving them my sentiments upon their Bill. And altho I find it big with injustice and mischief both to the property of the proprietors, and to the just rights of Government and framed as I verily think, with no other view than that I should reject it, in order to give occasion of drawing down the censure of the Government at home upon their Proprietors, with whom they are contending.[18] Yet in this I shall disappoint them, being in my own mind determined, however reluctantly, rather to submit to this most /^{odious} kind of extortion, and to make a sacrifice of the proprietors interest by giving my assent to the Bill, than that the Service should at this important Crisis, be defeated of the considerable Aid thereby granted to his Majesty.

Upon the whole matter, Your Excellency may be assured, that Delay is the principal point sought after, and that they will endeavour to postpone the passing of their Bill, untill they shall hear from their Agent in England, which may every day be expected, whether a peace is likely to be concluded.[19] in which

Case, there is little doubt, but they will curtail very considerably the Aids granted to the King by the Bill now under consideration. But at all adventures, the assistance expected from this Province cannot but be thrown greatly behind hand by means of this slow proceedure of the Assembly . . .

WO/34/33 fol. 35

167
Governor Thomas Pownall to Major-General Jeffery Amherst

Boston
30 March 1760
[Holograph]   [Received 5 April 1760]

. . . The Levies are not so forward as I shou'd wish oweing to the great Numbers who have served their turn in this Warr lyeing by to hire themselves out at exorbitant wages to such whose turn they suppose must now come to be impress'd but wou'd not go. The Court by all means willing to avoid an Impress have lengthen'd out the time for enlisting to ye 15th of April & I have adjourn'd the Court to ye 16th as I have his Majesty's Orders to have an Interview with Mr Bernard before I sail for England.[20]

I ordered Brigd^r Ruggles to form into Battalions such levies as he has ready[.] He acquaints me he is ready to march off to Worcester for forming immediately two Battalions, so that as soon as I have your intentions on that head I will give him orders to begin to move & shou'd hope ye rest might be ready as these march off.

The enclosed copy of a Vote of the Court, respecting such Men at ye Eastward as shall not reenlist to serve again, is very much ye general sense of the People, & an intimation of your intentions to comply with their desire wou'd give great & general content. I should imagine it will be necessary to send thither some number of Recruits to compleat those Detachments & the Vessels that carry such down might bring the others up here . . .[21]

WO/34/26 fol. 15

168
Major-General Jeffery Amherst to Governor Thomas Pownall

New York

[Copy in Secretary's hand]   6 April 1760

. . . I am no less Concerned to find, that Your Levies are not so forward as You Should wish; the reasons You give for it are obvious; so long as people whose Lot it is & are nominated to Serve, are permitted to purchase an Exemption, & to send others in their Stead, it must Occasion great backwardness in the Levies; and it were therefore to be wished that this Custom was abolished; but I rely on Your usual Zeal, & I am convinced that nothing will be wanting on Your Side, to obtain the hastening of the Levies . . .

There is nothing in my power, that I would not do to oblige the People of the Massachusetts Bay, but at the same time I cannot help saying, that the Vote of the Court Enclosed in Yours, distresses me greatly; as I know not how readily to Comply with it; first I had always understood that those of Your People, who during the last Campaign Served to the Eastward, had in Consideration of the Bounty granted them by the Assembly, all re-enlisted again;[22] next I know not what Numbers of these Troops will decline re-enlisting, which I ought to know, because they must be replaced out of these new Levies; and last of all, before this necessary Information can be obtained & the men sent to Relieve those that Decline continuing in Nova Scotia & Louisbourg, can get to those respective places, half the campaign will be Elapsed, and a number of these Mens Service be no ways of the use they are intended for; I should therefore be glad, they were all prevailed on to stay where they are; I must Conclude they will do so; this is certainly the last Campaign in this Country, & most likely will be but a Short one, and by their continuing to the end, they will acquire an Additional Honor and good repute.

From what precedes, You will see, that I am hopefull none of Your New Levies will be sent to the Eastward; and as all the others are to Assemble at the rendezvous of Albany, I need add nothing further on that Subject . . .

WO/34/27 fols 191–2

169
Colonel John Bradstreet to Major-General Jeffery Amherst

Albany
15 April 1760
[Holograph]   [Receipt not dated]

I beg leave to acquaint your Excellency that by the first of May
near all the Battoes & Carriages, except from Lake George to
Crown Point, will be built & repair'd for both Services and that it
will be necessary to discharge many workmen to avoid any
unnecessary expense and that I have not one Shilling to do it with;
wherefore I hope I may be supply'd in time.

I shall be glad to receive your Commands as to the time You
would have me collect & have all things ready here for the pushing
the provisions &^{ca} forward for I find nothing of any Consequence
in the Transportation will be done till the arrival of Troops.

The Communication is open to Oswego and to Crown Point
near it . . .

WO/34/57 fol. 131

170
Extract of Instructions to Brigadier-General Governor Murray

New York
[Holograph journal entry]   15 April 1760

I am now to acquaint you I have received His Majesty's
Commands for concerting the properest Measures for pushing on
the Operations of this Campaign with the utmost Vigour, & as
Montreal is evidently the great & Essential Object, to compleat the
Glory of His Majestys Arms in N^o. America, that I should proceed
to the vigorous attack of that place, & exert my utmost Efforts to
reduce it as well as the other Posts, belonging to the French in
those Parts, & Mr Secretary Pitt having signified to me that I
should not fail to send to the officer commanding at Quebec
timely information of my Operations, as well as such Direction for

his Conduct, as I should judge most Expedient for His Majesty's Service,[23] I come now to give you my determination thereon. As the Enemy must now center their whole Force for the defence of Montreal, the Avenues to which they will certainly try to guard, & to keep us at as great a distance as they can, that they may subsist, for this they must divide their Troops, & the more we can oblige them to do so, the weaker they will be in every part. I therefore intend to advance on them on three places, from Quebec up the River S[t] Lawrence, from Crown Point by the Isle au Noix, from Oswego down the River S[t] Lawrence. The first will depend entirely on you, by pressing on the Enemy with all the Troops you can spare from the Garrison of Quebec, which place cannot require any great force for its defence & Security, when you have a Fleet in the River, your Troops advanced between Quebec & the Enemy & that the Attacks are at the same time carrying on by Lakes Champlayn & Ontario. You will therefore make such disposition of the Troops under your Comand as you shall judge most expedient for pressing & annoying the Enemy on your side, by distressing them and taking any opportunities that may offer of attacking them, by forcing them back, by advancing your Corps (the Troops that can be spared from the Garrison) as near as possible to Montreal, & you will try to open a Comunication with the Troops /[that] I intend shall advance by the Isle au Noix, & down the River S[t] Lawrence from Lake Ontario, that in case the Enemy by finding themselves forced to give up their Out Posts should draw back the whole to their Center, & there attempt to make a last Stand, we may be able to press so close on them on every side, that we may joyn, if necessary, for the entire reduction of the Enemy & to compleat the Glory of H.M's Arms in N[o]. America; in which I have not the least doubt, as I am sure, you will on your part use your utmost Endeavours, & you may depend on it, I shall attack & press on them by the other Avenues, & that I shall pursue with all the might I can to the sole Object, the Reduction of the Remains of all Canada. At the same time that I do most earnestly desire you will exert yourself in this great & Essential Service, I must not omit recommending that a due attention be given to the Safety of Quebec, & that if You take the Field with the Troops you can spare for that Service, which from your Zeal & Experience I must wish to have immediately under your comand, yet a proper officer should be left with the Comand of the Troops at Quebec and a sufficient Garrison to be secure against any attempt the Enemy can make by land, this you will be best able to fix on the Spot, & I leave it for you to direct, as you will judge most conducive to the Success of the Campaign & the good of H^s. M^s. Service. Your floating Batteries will be excellent things against the few Ships they have remaining, which they can never put across the River in such manner, but you may force them away with your floating Batteries or by making Batteries on the Shore. I am confident I need not mention to you that a proper care in hindring the Canadians as much as you possibly can from joyning the French must tend greatly to dispirit them & make our Conquests easy. Nothing remains for me to say, but that I am making all the dispatch I can for assembling the Army.

U1350, O/14 (Personal Journal), p. 72

171
Governor Thomas Pownall to Major-General Jeffery Amherst

[Holograph]

Boston
25 April 1760
[Receipt not dated]

This day I receiv'd ye Enclosed Message – It does so fully explain its own purpose that as to the merits of the matter I can add nothing to it[24] – as to ye Prudential [sic] I woud wish to add that I do verily believe that the Success of the remaining Part of the Levies will intirely depend upon it. For if the Men perceive that difficulties arise about their being reliev'd when their time of Service expires no Bounty no Encouragement will induce them to enlist – And the House have alway been so tender on this head that this very apprehension has ever been, whenever this Case has arisen, an effectual Barr to their Voting for an Impress – They have on ye present occasion /^{waved} an impress & lengthen'd out ye time

171

for enlisting to the 20th of May – From a Return made me to day by Brigd^r Ruggles I see we have rais'd three thousand & almost three hundred, besides officers; & being able to enlist /^{more} will greatly depend on the Mens seeing that Measures are taken to releive & bring back those of ye last levies who at the Expiration of their Term of Service have not chose to reenlist again. From Louisbourg I hear by a Vessel arrived last night that out of 509 there, between three & four hundred have already enlisted, And when the Men's apprehensions of being detain'd are removed I cannot but entertain great hopes that ye most will reenlist there, & in the other posts also. But this will intirely depend upon ye measures taken to relieve & transport back those who do not so reenlist.

WO/34/26 fol. 26

172
General Amherst's Address to the Several Tribes and Nations of Indians

Fort George, New York

[Copy in Secretary's hand]   27 April 1760

Brethren Kings, Captains, and Warriors of the many Nations

Take notice of what I am going to say in the Name of the Chief Commander of all His Majesty's Forces on this Continent.

Brethren: I let you know that our Great King has sent Me into this Country to lead & command all his Warriors, and that he has given me a Sword to protect & defend his Subjects, & to act against his Enemies.

Brethren: As I have Nothing more at heart, than the Good & Welfare of the whole Community, I do assure all the Indian Nations that his Majesty has not sent Me to deprive any of you of your Lands and Property; on the Contrary, so long as you adhere to his Interest & by your Behavior give proofs of the Sincerity of your Attachment to His Royal Person, & Cause, I will defend and maintain you, in your just Rights, and give you all the Aid and Assistance you may stand in Need of, to repress the Dangers you may be liable to, from the Enemy, thro your Attachment to Us.

This I firmly mean to adhere too, so long as you behave like good & faithful Allies – But on the other Hand, if any of you should comit any Act of Hostility, or do any Injury to any of his Majesty's Subjects, You are sensible I must resent it, & retaliate upon Them, and you know that I have the Might so to do ten fold, for every Breach of Treaty, or Outrage you could be guilty of. And if any of his Majesty's Subjects under my Comand shoud kill or injure any of our Indian Brethren, they shall upon due Proof thereof receive equal Punishment. As a Proof of the Truth & Sincerity of what I have said I give you this.[25]

Brethren Kings Captains & Warriors: I mean not to take any of your Lands. But as the Necessity of his Majesty's Service obliges Me, to take Post & build Forts in some Parts of your Country, to protect our Trade with you, and prevent the Enemy from taking Possession of your Lands, and hurting both You and Us, as you are sensible that if we do not build Forts the French will. In that Case I assure you that no Part whatever of your Lands joining the said Forts, shall be taken from You, nor any of our People be permitted to hunt or settle upon Them. But they shall remain your absolute Property, and I will even promise You some Presents as a Consideration for the Land where such Forts & trading Houses are or may be built upon; and as it is expensive and inconvenient for Us to carry Provisions for our Warriors, from our Settlements to those Forts and also to supply our Brethren the Indians when they come to see Us, if you will lay out a Space of Ground adjoining every Fort to raise Corn: In that Case fix yourselves the Limits of that Part of your Lands so appropriated to Us, and you will receive such a Consideration for it as will be agreed between You and Us to your Satisfaction – As a Proof of the Truth & Sincerity of what I have said, I give you this.

Brethren Kings, Captains and Warriors of the Several Indian Nations – Those who will join his Majesty's Arms, & be aiding and assisting in subduing the comon Enemy, shall be well rewarded; and those that may not chuse to act in Conjunction with the Forces shall be equally protected, provided they do not join in any Act of Hostility with the Enemy, or carry Them Intelligence which might prove prejudicial to the public Good – Upon these Terms you shall find Me your fast Friend – But on a breach of Them you would force Me to treat you as our Enemies, the Consequences of which would be fatal to you, & very disagreeable to the King my Master – I say this out of the tender Regard I have for the Lives and Welfare of our Brethren the Indians, and I chuse you shoud know what you have to trust to, since I intend to be as good as my Word.

Given under my Hand & Seal of Arms at Head Quarters at Fort George in the City of New York.

WO/34/38 fols 101–2[26]

173
Major-General Jeffery Amherst to Brigadier-General Robert Monckton

New York

[Copy in Secretary's hand]　　　　　　　　　　29 April 1760

As Major-General Stanwix has received leave from England to return to Europe, it is absolutely necessary, that an Officer of Rank and Experience, Should Command His Majesty's Forces, in Conjunction with the Forces, directed to be raised in the Southern Provinces, as by M[r] Secretary Pitt's Letter of the 7th Jan[ry] in Consequence of which I have Applied to the Several Governors, and I herewith Enclose to You, Copies of Letters relative thereto, as far as is necessary for Your Information: And as Major-General Stanwix will (so soon as he has settled the Accounts of the last Campaign) repair to New York, to proceed to England You will please to set out for Philadelphia, as soon as You conveniently can, Where You will Inform Yourself from the Said Major-General, of any thing You Judge requisite for You to know, in regard to the State of the Several Posts on the Communication to Pittsburgh, the supply of Provisions & the Condition of the Country, where Major-General Stanwix has commanded, and when he leaves Philadelphia or gives up the Command to You, You will take on You the Command of the Troops before mentioned and make such Dispositions as You Shall Judge will best answer for executing the following Services.

1st to relieve the Garrison of Niagara, as soon as You possibly can, with 400 men, that the present Garrison may Join the Army to be employed in the Reduction of Montreal & Canada, this being the principal object of the Campaign.

2dly to secure a Communication between Pittsburgh and Niagara, by establishing Posts at Venango, Le Bouf and Presqu' Isle, or at such places, as You on the Spot, shall Judge best situated for shortening and ensuring a safe & uninterrupted Communication. And as it is not in the Power of the Enemy, to Send any Corps of Regular Troops to Attack these Posts, so long as Niagara is ours, I think this Communication may be Effectually protected, by building blockhouses at each Post, than which no better defence can be made against Indians, they will be easily erected, cost very little money, and what Should Chiefly be Considered, as we have now so many posts to Garrison, they may be well defended by a small number of men and a Retrenchment may be made to Enclose any part of the Ground round them as far as it may be thought necessary for Securing any Convoys on their march along the Communication, under cover of the Blockhouses, I therefore Enclose You Plans of such, as I Judge may best answer these purposes.

3dly to Compleat as much as possible without delaying the other Services, the Works of Pittsburgh according to the Plan it is built on.

I am very Sensible that the Number of Troops that can be Collected in Your Department, may not be Sufficient to Carry on all these Services, at the Same time, with so much dispatch as I could wish, and the delay of the Pensylvanians in raising their Quota, with the present Call for part of the Virginians on their own Frontiers,[27] must greatly retard the operations You have to Carry on, the length of road You have to get up Provisions, must occasion delays, Yet I am Sure these are appearances of difficultys that You will get over, and that You will do Your Utmost in Exerting Yourself to push forwards as much as possible the above Services.

The Garrison You send to Niagara will find Provisions there, and I am hopefull that when the Communication between

Pittsburgh & Niagara is once settled, Pittsburgh will be supplied with Provisions with more ease and less Cost from Niagara, than by that long and expensive road on the other side . . .

It may be necessary to keep the Indians in a proper Subjection, that You declare You take Posts at the Several Places, to Carry on an Expedition against Fort Detroit; that You do not Intend to disturb any of the Indians, in their Settlements; that their Women and Children may remain in their Houses and Shall not be molested, but that You will take the Fort from the French, and Secure a quiet possession to the Indians in all their habitations. This will make the Indians look at home, & hinder them from giving You any Disturbance in forming Your Posts, and tho' the attack of Fort Detroit cannot well immediately take place without interfering with other more Essential Services, I nevertheless intend to Execute it during the course of the Campaign . . .

WO/34/43 fols 136–7

174
Brigadier-General Governor James Murray to Major-General Jeffery Amherst[28]

Quebec
30 April 1760

[Copy in Secretary's hand]   [Received 19 May 1760]

The Intelligence I had the honor to Communicate to You, by Lieut. Montresor, of the Enemy's Designs, proves true.

The 17th of this Month I was Informed that they had Every thing in readiness to fall down the River with Eight Frigates, the Moment it was Cleared of Ice, and it did not break up here sooner than the 23d. Consequently as the Country was Covered with Snow, and the Earth was Impenetrable, it was impossible for me to Attempt Intrenching Myself on the Heights of Abraham, which I formerly told You was my Plan of Defence; before the 25th and even then, it will no doubt appear by the Journal of the Chief Engineer, it was hardly possible to drive the first Piquets, the Thaw having reached no farther than Nine Inches from the Surface.

As the River was Clear above, and I had reason to think the Enemy would take the first opportunity, of making themselves Masters of the Embouchure of the River Caprouge, the most convenient Place for Disembarking their Artillery & Stores, and for Securing their Retreat, I took possession of that Post the 18th with the Light Infantry Commanded by Major Dalling, which obliged them to Land their Army twenty miles higher up, and to Risk a Battle without Artillery, after a march of Thirty miles. At Three o'Clock in the morning of the 27th Instant, I knew they had marched from the Point au Tremble, with an Intention to take post at St Foix, and so Cut off our Communication with Major Dalling, and the Post I had established at Lorette; I instantly with Amherst's Reg^t, the Grenadiers & Picquets of the Army Commanded by Col Burton march'd & took post so advantageously, as to frustrate their Scheme, and to withdraw all my Posts with the Loss of two Men only.

They had began to form from the Defile they were obliged to pass, but thought proper to return on Reconnoitring our position, and receiving some Shot from the two Field Pieces I had with me.

About Four that afternoon, I marched back to Town, without the loss of a Man, tho' the Enemys Irregulars did every thing in their power to harrass my Rear.

As the Place is not Fortified, and Commanded every where towards the Land, my Garrison which was now melted down to Three Thousand Fighting Men, by the most Inveterate Scurvy, were daily mouldering away, and it was now Impossible for me to Fortify the Heights of Abraham, tho' Fascines and every Requisite material had been provided long ago, I could not hesitate a moment about giving the Enemy Battle; as every one knows the Place is not tenable against an Army in possession of the Heights – I therefore this Night gave the Necessary Orders, and by Seven o'Clock next morning I marched with all the Force I could Muster, & formed the Little Army on the Heights in the following Order; Amherst's, Anstruthers, the 2^d Batt^n of Royal Americans, & Webbs, Composed the Right Brigade, Commanded by Colonel Burton, Kennedy's, Lascelles's, Highlanders, & Braggs, the Left Brigade Commanded by Colonel Fraser; Otways, and the third

Battalion of the Royal Americans were formed as a Corps de Reserve.

Major Dalling's Corps of Light Infantry Covered the Right Flank, and Capt. Hazzen's Company of Rangers, with a Hundred Volunteers under the Command of Capt Donald McDonald, a Brave & Experienced Officer, Covered the left.

The Battalions had Each two Field Pieces – While the Line was forming I reconnoitred the Enemy, and perceived they had began to throw up some Redoubts, tho' the greatest part of their Army was on the March. – I thought this was a lucky moment, and marched with the utmost Order, to Attack them before they had formed. We immediately beat them from the Works they had begun, and Major Dalling, who cannot be too much Commended, forced their Corps of Grenadiers from a House they had Occupied to Cover their Left; Here he and several of his Officers were Wounded; his men however pursued the Fugitives to their Second Line, which soon Chequed our Light Infantry, who dispersed along the Front of our Right Wing, & prevented Colonel Burton from taking the Advantage of the first Impression they had made on the Enemies left Flank – They had immediately Orders to Clear the Front, and Regain the Right Flank, but in Attempting this, they were Charged, thrown into Confusion, Retired to the Rear, and could never again be brought up during the Action. I no sooner perceived this Disorder, than I sent Major Morris, who Commanded Otways Regim^t in the Second Line, to Wheel to the Right, and Support our Right Flank; this soon recovered Every thing there; but the left, a little after began to Retire, tho' they had Early made themselves Masters of two Redoubts; I ordered Kennedy's Regiment, and the third Battalion, to Sustain them, but they were too late; the disorder of the Left soon Communicated to the Right, and the Whole Retired under the Musquetry of our Blockhouses, abandoning their Canon to the Enemy.

As We have been Unfortunate, I am Sensible I may be universally blamed at home, but I Appeal to Every Officer in the Field, if any thing was wanting in the Disposition, or my Endeavors to Animate the Men, during the Whole Affair. The Superiority these Troops had Acquired over the Enemy ever since the last Campaign, together with the fine Field Train we were furnished with, might have tempted me to an Action, Supposing I had not been thoroughly Convinced of the Necessity of it.

We Lost in the Battle about one third of our Army, and I have certain Intelligence the Enemy had not less than Ten Thousand men in the Field – They have already Compleated their first Parallel, but I am in hopes We shall not be Reduced to Extremities, 'till the Arrival of the Fleet, which We Expect daily: In that Event, I shall Retreat with what I can to the Island of Orleans, and wait the Arrival of Reinforcements, unless I can do better; had We been Masters of the River, in which it is Evident Ships may safely Winter, they never would have made the Attempt.

I must do the Justice to Colonel Burton in particular, and to the Officers in General, that they have done Everything that could be Expected of them . . .

CO5/58 fols 192–4[29]

175
Major-General Jeffery Amherst to Governor Thomas Pownall[30]

Albany

[Copy in Secretary's hand]   11 May 1760

I arrived here on the 8th Instant, and none of the Provincial Forces being Yet arrived, altho' the Season is so far advanced, and so proper to begin the Operations of the Campaign; I cannot deferr renewing to You, my most pressing Instances, that if, upon receipt hereof, all the Troops of Your Province, are not in motion & on their way hither (for I will not doubt but most of them are) that You will immediately without loss of time Cause them to begin their march, and to proceed hither without Delay, as every moment that detains them from this, is a great backwardness to the Genl Service, which at this present time, merits and requires to be improved to the utmost.

WO/34/36 fol. 183

176
Major-General Jeffery Amherst to Brigadier-General Robert Monckton

Albany

[Copy in Secretary's hand]   18 May 1760

Major Tulleken Arrived here on the 16th by whom I had the pleasure of receiving Your Letter of the 8th Instant, with a Copy of a Treaty of Peace Concluded with some Indians at Pittsburgh, which I think they will keep, and I hope it will Ensure Safety to the whole Communication to Your Posts, as these People must now See they can have no Assistance but from Us, have every reason to believe they will have all the good Usage from Us that they may Merit, and cannot doubt but We have the means in our hands of Chastising them, if they deceive Us. – M. Tulliken mentioned to me a thought of Mr Croghans, to Employ these Indians against the Cherokees, but I can't Say I Approve of Mr Croghan's Scheme, the distance is too great, it will be attended with a great Expence to fit them out, and they would return with the Scalp of an Old Woman or an Infant; they would do no more, Except some Regular Officers were sent with them, and that I think had better not be done; this is what I Judge of that matter, but You on the Spot will be better able to decide . . .

WO/34/43 fol. 138

177
Major-General Jeffery Amherst to Brigadier-General Governor Edward Whitmore

Albany

[Copy in Secretary's hand]   18 May 1760

. . . I have strange Accounts of the Behavior of the Provincials in the Bay of Fundy, several of which have deserted their Posts, and I fear some of the Places will be almost entirely Abandoned: It is lucky that the Enemy is not in a Situation of taking any Advantage of this unwarrantable Conduct of the Massachusett Troops, who I was in hopes would have been Cured of their home Sickness for some little time, from the Measures their Government took of rewarding them for their Services, and the Money that was sent them to Induce their Re inlisting . . .

The small Number of Troops at present in Nova Scotia will not Suffice for Govr Lawrence to Garrison all the Places; I therefore should be glad, in Case You can Spare the 40th Reg^t Late Hopson's, that You would send them immediately to Hallifax; I know the Work You must have in destroying & Razing the Works, which I wish for many Reasons to have soon finished,[31] and the more hands You have, the Quicker it will be done, yet I can't help desiring that in Case You can do without the Corps I have mentioned, You will without waiting for any further Orders from me, send them by the first Vessells to Hallifax . . .

I have as yet but a very small Appearance of Provincials with me, there being only Twelve Companies of the Massachusetts, and one Sloop with Rhode Islanders Arrived: The Notions of Peace, and hopes of Saving the Bounty & Levy Money has prevailed in every Province; This retards, but I don't think will be of any bad Consequence, as I hope we shall have time Enough to Execute every thing that is yet to be done in this part of the World, & indeed I do not doubt but We shall do it.

WO/34/17 fol. 196

178
Major-General Jeffery Amherst to Governor Brigadier-General James Murray

Albany

[Holograph rough draft]   19 May 1760

This day I am favor'd with Your dispatch of the 30th Ultimo, containing the Accompt of the unfortunate Check you met with on the 28th of said Month, which fills me with real concern, but will I hope be retrieved, and for that purpose I have immediately sent Major Christie the d.Q.M.G. to Boston, to take up a necessary ~~quantity~~ number of Transport Vessells to repair to

181

Louisburg to take on board Whitmores & late Barringtons Regiments, which is all the reinforcement I have it in my power to send You, which ~~together~~ with the force You have still remaining, I am Confident You will do every thing that shall occurr to You for the good of the Service, whilst I, on this side, shall pursue the plan of Operations I transmitted You by Lieut Montresor, in which I am So unalterably fixed, and ~~altho~~ You may be assured that wherever I can make any Impression, no Attempts or Efforts shall be wanting on my part to Accomplish the same.

[Additional paragraph in margin] My Orders to Major Christie are so pressing and Accompanied with such strong recommendations to Governor Pownall & all those concerned in procuring & fitting such Vessells, that I cannot doubt but they will meet an immediate & punctual Execution; and Convey this Intended reinforcement to You, with all possible dispatch.[32]

. . . The loss of Your Cannon is much to be regretted as they ~~may prove~~ must greatly strengthen the hands of the Enemy; I likewise Sincerely Lament the loss of so many brave Officers and Men, to whose Memory You do so much Justice.

WO/34/3 fol. 2

179
Major-General Jeffery Amherst to Brigadier-General Governor Edward Whitmore

Albany

[Copy in Secretary's hand]   19 May 1760

The Accounts I have this day received by Express, to which I reckon You will be no Stranger, by the time this reaches You, obliges me to send Governor Murray an immediate Reinforcement; accordingly I now dispatch Major Christie the D.Q.M.G. to Boston to take up Two Thousand Ton of Transport Vessells, to repair without loss of time to Your Port, where upon their arrival, I must Desire, You will with all possible dispatch, Cause Your entire Regim[t] and that [of] late M.G. Barrington's, to be embarked on board the same, and directly after, order them to proceed to Quebec to Join Governor Murray; if any of His Majesty's Ships of War should happen to be in Your Port, at the time of this reaching Your hands, You will Desire the Commanding Officer thereof, to order them a Convoy; but if there should not, they must then depart without, as not a moment that can be prevented must be delayed in their proceeding to their Destination.

Tho' I am Confident You may have occasion for this body of men, in the Execution of the orders, I transmitted You lately from His Majesty, yet as the present service the 22^d & 40th reg^{ts} are now destined for is so Essential as absolutely to require their Assistance, I cannot possibly leave them with You; but at the same time, that the other Service may not be too much retarded, I write to Govr Pownall that Three Hundred of the five hundred men, which he very Judiciously & instantly ordered to be raised upon receipt of the Intelligence from Quebec, for the relief of the Garrison in Nova Scotia, are to be embarked on board the Transports above mentioned, and to be forwarded to You in them, without delay, or waiting to arm them; as You should provide them with Arms on their arrival. This is indeed but a small number of hands, considering the Works You have to do, but I am certain, You will make the most of them; & Effect as much with them and Warburton's Regiment, as any one can do . . .

WO/34/17 fol. 197

180
Major-General Jeffery Amherst to Viscount William Barrington (private)

Albany

[Copy in Secretary's hand]   19 May 1760

Since my arrival at this Place, Captain Mackneill delivered to me Your Lordship's Letter of the 8th February, Enclosing a Letter from the Duke of Argyll to Your Lordship, with Captain Mackneill's Memorial.

The strong Reasons Your Lordship is pleased to give me for obeying the Duke of Argyll's Commands, cannot fail of having

AMHERST AND THE CONQUEST OF CANADA

their due Weight with me, whenever the Service will permit me to promote Captain Mackneill.

I enclose the Duke of Argyll's Letter, which Your Lordship transmitted to me.

U1350/O/38/17

181
Brigadier-General Governor James Murray to Major-General Sir Jeffery Amherst

Quebec
19 May 1760
[Holograph]   [Received 20 June]

I have the honor to acquaint you that Mr de Levis last night rais'd the Seige of Quebec, after three weeks open Trenches. He left behind him his camp standing, all his Baggage, Stores, Ammunition, thirty four pieces of Cannon, four of which are Brass 12 pounders, Six mortars, four petards, a large provision of Scaling ladders, & intrenching tools beyond number; some of the field train we lost the day of the action, we have again recovered. What the Kings troops have done during this Siege, I dare not relate if I had time, is so romantick, & our loss considering has been very inconsiderable. I had intended a Strong sortie this morning, and for that purpose had the reg^{ts} of Amherst, Bragg, Lascells, Anstruther, & Frazer with ye Granadiers & light Infantry under arms, but was inform'd by Lieut McKelpin, who I had sent out to make a small sally below le regle,[33] that the trenches were abandoned. I instantly push'd out at the head of these Corps, not doubting, but I must penetrate their rear, and have ample revenge for ye 28th of Ap^l; but I was disapointed, their rear had cross'd the River Carouge before I could come up with them; however we took several prisoners, Straglers and much baggage, which otherwise would have escaped . . .

This enterprize has cost the Enemy upwards of 3,000 men by their own confession. They are now at their old Asilum of Jaques Quartier and for want of every necessary, must soon /$^{I\ imagine}$

184

surrender at discretion. We are very low, the Scurvy makes terrible havock. For Gods sake send us up molasses, and seeds which may produce vegetables. Whoever winters here again must be better provided with beding, & warm cloaths than we were; our medicines are entirely expended, at present we get a very Scanty supply from Lord Colvills Squadron which arrived this day. But Cap[r] Swanton in the Vanguard with two frigates came into the Bason from England, the night of the 17th, and next day destroy'd & dispersed the Enemys Squadron. I have not words to express the alacrity, & bravery of Swanton, Dean, & Schomberg, the honor they have acquired on this occasion should render their names immortal.[34] Our Louisboug friend Mon[r] Voucklin who commanded the french Squadron is taken prisoner, and his Ship distroyd. But poor Dean after all was over ~~lost his~~ struck upon a rock, and I fear his Ship will be lost . . .

We have received the 20,000 pounds sent in the Hunter it is a poor Sum for a Garrison which has had no pay since the 24th August . . .[35]

This instant Lieut Montresor is arrived, and has delivered to me your Letter of the 15th of April. The orders in it shall be obey'd to the best of my abilities. M[r] Montresor tells me you would not credit the accounts, I sent you of the Enemys designs upon Quebec, but you find they are not so prudent as you imagined. I flatter myself the cheque they have met with here, will make every thing very easy afterwards. I do declare to you upon my Salvation that they had an army of 15,000 men before Quebec, ten of which consisting of eight Batt[ns] of regulars, 2 of the Troops de Colonie, and the Monrealists were actually engaged in the battle of the 28th of April. The other five thousand were the Canadians of the lower Canada, who join'd them after the Battle. The Regulars are still at Jaque Quartier with a few Canadians, who serve in those corps, & make in all about five thousand men. They have little powder left, and I am confident they have as little provision, deserters come in dayly. If you make haste, for the Honor of their Colours, they may give you battle, but if you do not, for want of something to eat, they will surrender to me, for I have destroy'd all the Magazines they had prepared for the Siege of Quebec. You may depend on my pressing them; I have but five hundred men, it shall never be said with justice that any thing has been wanting in me. But if I know the country, & I believe I have a tolerable idea of it, I must beat their army, before I can open your passage /by the Isle au Noix. The Enemy are wiser than to divide their force, & be assured they have only 2 hundred of the Troop de Colonie, and four hundred Canadians at that post. When they know of your motions, I dont know what they may do. I shall watch theirs, and take every advantage of them in my power; I make no difficulties, the Enemy have supply'd us with boats or battoes, but God almighty has reduced the large body of troops which were left at Quebec to an inconsiderable number, and had not the Enemy's fleet in the river been destroy'd, I apprehend without proper craft, I could not have been master of it – it is not in a river, as it was in the harbour of Louisbourg; batteries a Shore ~~may make~~ must certainly destroy Ships, where they can not get out of their reach, but Ships in a river like that of St Lawrence, can shift out of reach of your battery, ye moment it opens, so the Summer at this rate here might have been spent in erecting battery after battery; If the Enemy gives you battle, which I cannot think they will do, it will be at Trois Riviers. They have fortified that post, and I am well informed they mean there to capitulate; they still talk confidently of the impracticability of forcing the Isle au Noix weakly garrisoned as it is till the month of July, but I look on that to be chimerical, and that the last effort they meant to make was the Enterprize against Quebec . . .The moment I can, which will be soon, I will move up the River, and leave Col^o Burton to command at Quebec.

P.S. As I am entirely of your oppinion, that Quebec is now in no danger, and Burton whose assistance I shall always Egarly grasp at, is very desirous of sharing the laurels, we must reap in reducing the Enemy, insists upon accompanying me, I shall leave Col^o Frazer to command at Quebec.

WO/34/4 fols 19–23

182
Major-General Jeffery Amherst to Messers Oliver
De Lancey and John Watts

Albany

[Copy in Secretary's hand]   23 May 1760

As Colonel Bradstreet from his Department of Deputy Q^r Mr Genl, and from the knowledge his Experience must have given him, of the requisite Quantities of Provisions it is necessary to have here, in order to supply the army properly and prevent thro' the want thereof, His Majesty's orders for penetrating into the heart of the Enemy's Country, from being punctually attempted and Executed; I thought him the properest person I could Consult thereupon, I have Accordingly Demanded of him, what Quantity of Provisions would be necessary, to enable me to put his Majesty's Instructions into Execution, and his answer is, that there must be had here immediately Three months provisions Compleat for Twenty five Thousand mouths, from the 1st of June; and that four months more, for the like number of mouths must follow directly, as it is supposed that Quantity will be wanted and expended by the time the armies quit the field; so that the provisions necessary for the Troops in the Winter Garrisons, will be over and above what is required for the before mentioned seven months, and must be provided accordingly.

Altho' I dare trust that the supplies already here, and those You may have ordered up, would in the end be equal to the Consumption; yet I must observe, if the whole Quantity specified by Colonel Bradstreet is not here immediately, it will not be in my power to feed the Army, but from hand to mouth, which will by no means answer; wherefore it is absolutely requisite, that the three first months should be here, in order for the army to take it with them; I must accordingly insist, that You will, immediately, cost what it will, Cause said three months provisions Compleat for Twenty-five Thousand men from 1st June, to be laid in here for the Troops to take with them, and that You do at the same time directly provide for the other four months over and above what shall be wanted for the Troops, in the Winter Garrisons . . .

WO/34/66 fol. 75

187

183
Major Gabriel Christie to Major-General Jeffery Amherst

Boston
25 May 1760
[Holograph]   [Received 28 May 1760]

Agreeable to your Excellencys order I left Albany on the 20th and arrived here the 23^d; I immediately waited on Govr Pownall deliver'd the letters to him as well as the other dispatches for Halifax Louisburgh and Quebec to Mr Hancock took his receipt for the same which were put on board some vessells in the harbor ready to sail when the wind will permit . . .

I should have been glad to have inform'd your Excellency of my success in obtaining of Transport vessells – I have Spent now two days in fruitless meetings and arguments [with the merchants]. Also represented matters as they stood from time to time to Governor Pownall all which Consisting likewise with the knowledge of Mr Hancock & Jervis who were present and saw what steps I took . . .

The Governor has advised in answer to my remonstrances Steps unprecedented and what I would of my Self by no means have fallen in with was it not the urgent necessity of the Service and the difficulty I am or may be under if I reject the advice of the Governor of the Province in an affair of Such importance when deprived of applying to your Excellency (without a manifest loss of time) for orders – in short Sir them rascals must, it seems have what ever they please to demand viz fifteen p^r Cent Sterling premium upon their respective Sums as bills of Imprest from time to time in the usual way – a monstrous usery and advance.³⁶ This was the Conclusion of last night, to day, they hoisted in and added to the former proposal four months Certain Employment which it seems must likewise be given them; for the reasons before mention'd I have been obliged to acquiesce with all this: but to save Appearances and my acting on a Contrary footing at N. York, it is done through the means of Mr Hancocks security to them fellows upon my giving him a Counter Security to

188

indemnify him, in which Case the Charter partys, bills of Imprest etc are all to run in the usual style and price . . .

WO/34/26 fols 55–6

184
Major-General Jeffery Amherst: Orders to Major Robert Rogers

Albany

[Holograph copy]   25 May 1760

You are to take under Your Command a party of three hundred men composed of two hundred and Seventy five Rangers with their proper Officers, and a Subaltern, two Sergeants and twenty five men of the light Infantry of Regiments, with which detachment You will proceed down the Lake under Convoy of the Brig; where you will fix on the safest and best place for laying up your boats (which I imagine one of the Islands will best answer) while You are executing the following Services. You will with the 250 Men land on the West side in such manner that you may get to St John's (without the Enemy at the Isle au Noix having any Intelligence of it) where you will try to surprize the Fort and to destroy the Vessels, boats, provisions, or whatever may be there for the use of the Troops at the Isle au Noix. You will then March to Fort Chamblé where You will do the same, and You will destroy every Magazine You can find in that part so as to distress the Enemy as much as you can, this will soon be known at the Isle au Noix and You must take care not to be cut off in your retreat, for which reason when you have done all that you think practicable on the Western side, I Judge your best and safest retreat will be to cross the River and to March back by the East Side of the Isle au Noix. When you have landed on the West side you will send such Officer with the fifty Rangers as You think will best Answer their intended Service, which is to March to Wigwam Martiniques[37] to destroy what he may find there and on the East of the River, and afterwards to Join you or to retreat in such manner as you'll direct him. You'll take such provision as You judge necessary with You, and fix with Capt Grant, who shall have orders to remain for your return, the places where he may look out for You when you come back. You'll take your Men as light with You as possible, and give them all the necessary cautions for their conduct and their Obedience to their Officers, no firing without Order, no unnecessary Alarms, no retreating without an Order, they are to stick by one another and nothing can hurt them, let every Man whose firelock will carry it have a Bayonet. You are not to suffer the [friendly] Indians to destroy Women or Children. No plunder to be taken to load Your Men, who shall be rewarded at their return as they deserve.

WO/34/84 fol. 204

185
Major-General Jeffery Amherst: Orders to Major Alexander Campbell[38]

[Copy in Secretary's hand]

Albany
29 May 1760

You will, agreeable to the Orders of this day, Early to morrow morning, set out for and proceed on Your March to Schenectady, where You will Receive from Col° Bradstreet, or the Person Acting under him there, a Certain Number of Batteaus loaded with Provisions, on board of Each of which, You will put Ten or Twelve Men, and Load the Batteaus with such a Quantity of Provision, as Col° Bradstreet, or his Deputy, shall think right to put in them; and then proceed with the Whole to the Little Falls, where You will Land, Encamping Your men in the Center of the Carrying place; and taking under Your Guard the Batteaus & Provisions, in order to get the provisions across the Carrying place, & to See it forwarded to Fort Stanwix, in the most Expeditious manner; and during Your Stay in that Camp, You will Observe to keep two Small Guards, one at the hither, and the Other at the further End of the Same; and You will also Cause the Road to be repaired, and to keep the same Constantly in good Order . . .

WO/34/84 fol. 227

186
Major-General Jeffery Amherst to Colonel John Thomas

Albany

[Copy in Secretary's hand]   1 June 1760

You will pursuant to my Verbal orders of this day early tomorrow morning, with the whole of the Massachusetts Forces at present here (except Lt Col° Ingersol whom You will leave for the care of such of the said Forces, as are still to come in,) apply to Colonel Bradstreet the D.Q.M.G or the person acting under him, for the number of Batteaus he shall think it requisite to send with You, which Batteaus You will Cause to be Loaded & manned, with such Quantities of Provisions & by so many of Your people, in each as he shall direct, and when the same are so Loaded, You will proceed to Halfmoon, where, if such should be the Direction of the said Colonel Bradstreet or his Deputy, You will take such further Batteaus and Provisions as they shall direct; and with the whole, from thence proceed to Fort Edward, Observing at the rifts to lighten Your Batteaus, as there may be Occasion, and at the Carrying places to Land and take the provisions across.

Upon Your arrival at Fort Edward, You will deliver said provisions & Batteaus to Major Reid, or Officer Commanding & receive from him what Carriages may be necessary for the Transportation of Your Camp Equipage to Fort George.

Such of Your men as have their arms, shall receive here six rounds of Ammunition, and altho' there is no reason to Apprehend, any parties of the Enemy, on the road between Fort Edward & Crown Point; except that 'tis not impossible one single Indian might be lurking for a Scalp, You will nevertheless in Your march to Fort George post half of Your armed men in the front, and the other half in the rear.

At Fort George the Commanding Officer, will furnish You with Batteaus & take You and Your Whole Detachment across the Lake, at the north end of which, You will Land Your men, deliver the Batteaus into the care of the Person appointed to have the Charge of them, and then proceed to Tienderoga where the Officer Commanding, upon Your producing him this part of Your

Instructions, will Cause such part of Your Detachment as are without arms to be Compleatly armed and such men as have not Powder horns, and to receive Cartridge boxes.

This done You will leave Lt Col^o Miller, with Three hundred men of Your Detachment, with Commissioned and non Commissioned Officers in proportion at Tienderoga, there to follow the orders and Directions, he may receive from Col^o Forster or Officer Commanding; and with his party to be aiding and Assisting in Carrying on every branch of the service that may be required of him.

You will then, with the remainder of Your Detachment Embark on board the Batteaus, that shall be allotted You for that purpose, and with all the dispatch possible continue Your route to Crown Point, where You will put Yourself & men under the Command of Colonel Haviland & follow and obey such orders & Directions as You shall receive from him . . .

WO/34/84 fol. 246

187
Captain Anthony Wheelock to Major-General Jeffery Amherst

Worcester
8 June 1760

[Holograph]   [Received 11 June 1760]

I imagine Lieutenant Governor Hutchinson has informed Your Excellency that in order to compleat the Forces from this Province, the Assembly has voted a larger Bounty & prolonged the Time of Establishment: what Effect this may have is uncertain; but in Case the Numbers should fall short, I presume to acquaint Your Excellency with what occurs to me in Respect to the People of this Country.

The apprehension of military Discipline, the Fatigues of the Service, & also the Danger, are strong Objections with the Common People against enlisting, notwithstanding the Great Premium now given – cou'd they be taken on the Footing of

192

Smiths, Carpenters etc I believe many wou'd come in. I imagine the Bounty Money now offerred, & the Province Pay together wou'd make up their Wages as Workmen (in the pay of the Province) at two Shillings or half a Crown per Day from the latter End of this Month to the first of November.

The Assembly here being chose annually, the members in general are afraid of disobliging the Inhabitants by voting an Impress; & at the same Time wou'd willingly appear Zealous for the publick service; from hence they are very liberal in their Bounties & wou'd be glad their Numbers were compleated by Volunteers: But the Common people by the Experience of former Years are cunning enough to keep off enlisting at first, & by that means (if they enlist at all) get greater Premiums & do less Duty by deferring their Enlisting to the last.

By all accounts Lt Governor Hutchinson is a very worthy man, is at present in high Esteem with the people & wou'd (to preserve his popularity) be glad to avoid an Impress; from hence I conclude that if Your Excellency approves of taking the Deficiency of the Massachusetts Troops in <u>workmen</u>, the Lt Governor wou'd be very glad of it (even at an additional Expense) to preserve the Credit of the province, which must suffer considerably at Home, if they fail in that Article; upon which most have valued Themselves[.] I believe by these Means, the Numbers may be completed. What induces me to think so the more, is that one of the Provincial Officers enlisted many Carpenters in the <u>Month of May</u> for Captain Butterfields Company, by telling them that they shou'd be employed as Artificers & receive Pay as such, tho' the Officer did very ill to promise what he was not entitled to do, yet from his Success, I judge that many wou'd engage on the Footing of Workmen who have no notion of it as Soldiers . . .

WO/34/98 fol. 56

188
Major-General Jeffery Amherst to Brigadier-General Robert Monckton

Albany
[Copy in Secretary's hand]   11 June 1760

I Just now receive Some Indian Intelligence which I believe may be likely true, vizt. that the French are returned from Quebec, where they were repulsed with a great loss of Men Cannon &ca, and that two of our men of War & a Frigate took four of their Ships loaded with Provisions and two loaded with Ammunition. Soon after, Eight of our men of War arrived there and they raised the Siege, these must be of the twenty ships sailed from Rochefort and probably they have some up the River, much about at the same time with our men of War.

Major Rogers has had a little Affair on the sixth, within Eight Miles of Isle au Noix, he Landed with 200 men, the Enemy Attacked him with about 300, he beat them, and pursued them about half a mile, and took three Indian Scalps – Says he must have killed about fifty, but they took off the dead & wounded, all except the three above mentioned.

WO/34/43 fol. 142

189
Major-General Jeffery Amherst to Colonel William Haviland

Albany
[Copy in Secretary's hand]   12 June 1760

Most of the Provincial Troops of the Several Governments are Arrived, Except those of Connecticut, which I hope will be up soon, and that I shall be able to proceed forward.

I am therefore now to Communicate to You my Intentions of giving You the Command of the Troops that are to Assemble at Crown Point, to Advance on & Attack the Enemy from that Side, and to Acquaint You of my Resolves on the Operations of this Campaign, as far as may be necessary for Your Conduct.

You will therefore take on You the Command of all the Troops, Ordered to Rendezvous at Crown Point, as likewise of the Troops at and in the Garrisons of Tienderoga and Fort George, some of which are hereafter to Join You, and as far as necessary, You will send to the Commanding Officers at those Posts any Orders for the Defence of those Places, and the Security of the Communication.

Montreal is now undoubtedly the Sole Object to Compleat the Glory of His Majesty's Arms in these Parts, the Reduction of all Canada depending entirely on the Fall of that Place; The Enemy must of Course Center their Whole Force for the Defence of it, and will be Obliged to Guard the Avenues to keep Us at as great a distance as they can. I therefore Intend to Advance on them by their three Avenues; Namely, from Quebec up the River St Lawrence; from Lake Ontario down the River St Lawrence; and from Crown Point by the Isle au Noix; that I may force them to divide their Troops, which will Weaken them in every Part, and that I may press on them as nearly as may be, by those Routes at the same time.

The Attack on the Isle au Noix will be Your Care, for which I have allotted You such a Corps of Troops, with such a Proportion of Artillery, and such a Number of Batteaus, as I am hopefull will Render that Conquest Easy. – When You proceed down the Lake for the Attack of the Above Place, for which You will be prepared, I would have you Encamp Your Troops, Either on the Eastern or Western Shore, as You on the Spot will Judge best for the Security of Your Camp, the Attack of the Post with Your Artillery, and that You may at the same time, try to Cutt off the Enemy's Communication by St John's & Chamblé, which, if that can be Effected, is the Easiest method of Reducing the Isle au Noix, as thereby it must inevitably fall. – You will not begin to play any Artillery against the Place, 'till You are so prepared, as that You may be almost Certain of Subduing it by Your Fire, as any Failure on our Side may greatly Encourage the Enemy, and we should lose time instead of gaining it . . .

As it must be some time before the Troops Allotted to Serve under Your Command can possibly be Assembled, as likewise

195

those that are to Assemble at Oswego, that both may Advance at the same time, I would have You make all the Use You can of the Intermediate Space in finishing the Works at Crown Point, Rebuilding the Barracks at Tienderoga, and Compleating the Works at Fort George . . .

Although the Isle au Noix cannot be Attacked 'till You proceed down the Lake in full force, and that it appears to be best not to Attempt it 'till nearly the same time, that I shall have advanced from Oswego, of which I shall give You Notice, Yet I would have You make all Your Preparations directly, for being able to proceed to the Isle au Noix, that in Case it should be necessary, from Circumstances that may happen, to Attack the Enemy there before the Attack by Lake Ontario can take place, You may be ready for it.

You will at present take all the Advantages You can of the Command We have, from a Superiority of Vessells on the Lake, by which You may keep the Enemy in a Continual Alarm, and distress them much with very little Risk, and this You will do by sending any such Partys as You shall Judge proper, without waiting for further Orders from me . . .

WO/34/52 fols 48–50

190
Major Robert Rogers to Major-General Jeffery Amherst,
On board the *Duke of Cumberland*[39]
Lake Champlain
21 June 1760

[Secretary's hand, signed by Rogers]   [Received 25 June 1760]

Lieut M'Cormick having Joind me with the Indians, I Gave him the Command of the Light Infantry and with two Hundred Twenty men, Officers Included, Landed the 10ᵗʰ about midnight on the west Shore opposite the Isle Au N[oix] from thence marched as fast as Possible to Sᵗ Johns, and came to the Road that Leads from it to Mountreal. About the Evening of the Fifteenth at 11 °Clock this night I Marched with an Intent to

Surprize the Fort To within four hundred Yards of the Place, where I halted to Reconoitre it which I Did and found that they had more men there than I Expected, the Number of Centrys within the Fort, was Seventeen and so well Fixed that I thought it was not Possible for me to take the fort by Surprize, I left it at two °Clock and marched Down the River to St Etherese, at 8 °Clock in the Morning I Reconoiterd this Place, and found that the Enemy had at it a Picquetted fort Defencible Against Small Arms, I Observed two large Store Houses in the Inside of it, and that the Enemy was Carting Hay into the Fort, I waited for an Opportunity when the Cart had Just Entered the Gateway, Run Forward and got into the Fort before they Cou'd Clear the way for Shutting the Gate, I had at this time Sent Different parties to the several Houses about Fifteen in Number, which was near the Fort, and were all Surprizd at the Same Instant of Time and without Firing a Single Gun, I took in the Fort and the Different houses Seventy Eight Prisoners woman and Children Included. I Examined the Prisoners and found I could not proceed to Chambelie, with any Prospect of Success, therefore I Concluded my best way was to Burn the Fort /^{at St Therese} and Village, which I Did, together with a Considerable Magazine of Hay and Some Provisions, with Every Batteau and Canoe Except Eight Batteaus which I kept to Cross the River that were Afterwards Cut to Pieces, I Carefully Killd their Cattle and Horses, and Destroy'd their Waggons and Every other thing I thought wou'd be of Service to the Enemy; when this was Done I sent back fifty one Woman and Children and gave them a Pass to go to Mountreal Directed to the Officers of the Different Detachments under my Command . . .

I got to the Vessells last Evening with all my Party in good health, and brought with me Twenty four french Men and Two French Boys . . .

WO/34/51 fol. 55

197

191
Major-General Jeffery Amherst to Field Marshal Viscount John Ligonier

Schenectady

[Holograph copy] 21 June 1760

On the 1st of June I had the honour of receiving you Lordship's letter dated in April which brought a confirmation of what had been some time here reported, of the packet boat being taken; wherein Lt Col West went Passenger, but as I seldom keep duplicates of the letters I write to your Lordship, the one I did myself the honour to write to you then is annihilated.

This morning at three o' clock two Lieutenants of Lascelles's Reg^t,⁴⁰ vizt. Goddard, & Sheriffe arrived here by Crown point, from Montreal, & brought me a confirmation of news which I had before received only by Indian intelligence, of the French having on the 18th May raised the siege, leaving all the cannon they had taken with them behind them, which the Garrison of Quebec instantly took possession of, & made several prisoners.

By what I can find from these gentlemen, who have been prisoners at Montreal, the enemy gave over the Siege, as soon as they saw our Ships appear, their losses on the 28th April were great, & when I think of their present situation & ours, I can't help flattering myself that the Conquest of all Canada is certain, though I doubt not Monsr de Vaudreuil will assemble the whole for a last effort, for which I will be prepared.

I send your Lordship a list of the Prisoners I have received, & that are arrived at Crown point, from whence I shall send them to New York, that I may exchange an equal number for them & send our Prisoners to joyn their respective Reg^{ts} at Quebec.

The persuasions the people were in on this continent of an approaching peace, has greatly hindered the levying of their quotas, & much retarded the march of such as they have raised to the rendezvous of the army, the first I have tried to remedy by applying to the several Governors in the strongest manner I could to compleat their troops, & the second by pushing forward the troops to our out posts as fast as they arrived at their rendezvous at

Albany, yet I shall be late, but I think I shall have time enough, & I hope numbers sufficient to compleat the work of this campaign.

U1350/O/35/20

192
Captain Joshua Loring to Major-General Jeffery Amherst

Niagara
26 June 1760
[Holograph]   [Receipt not dated]

I take this opportunity to acquaint Your Excellency, that I am in hopes to be able to Launch the Snow by the 5th of Next Month, And to be at Oswego by the 15th if the Seamen Arrive to carry her up, there is not one to be had Here. This Vessell would have been ready Much Sooner, could they have had any assistance from the Garrison – I should be much Oblig'd to your Excellency, if the few Sawyers I have not got from the 44th Regiment, might Be left here as long as they can possibly be Spared, as it will forward the building of the Sloops very much – I wrote Your Excellency from Oswego, for Some Provincial Carpenters, which I hope will be here Soon, as I have all the Gun Carriages to make for the Snow and Sloops – Your Excellency may depend Upon my doing every thing in my power to forward the Service & hope not to Exceed the time Mentioned of being at Oswego.

WO/34/65 fol. 18

193
Colonel William Haviland to Major-General Jeffery Amherst

Crown Point
5 July 1760
[Holograph]   [Received 14 July 1760]

Our Boats are repairing I think but slowly. The Brigg is at Tienderoga and Capt Grant writes me there is not any one

Material there to refitt her, Such as Iron, Pitch, Tarr, Oakam &c, so that there has been a neglect some where, I have wrote to Col° Bradstreet to send those things up though I don't know that it is in his department.

Brig^r Ruggles Arrived yesterday and he is now busy in Regimenting the Massachusetts, so that I hope I will be soon able to know the Numbers that are here, which I never could know by their Confused Returns, he tells me he believes they are not much above twelve Hundred, and that he expects another Battalion in about a fortnight. As the Numbers of Provinc^{ls} are so small I hope I shall have some days notice before I am to move down the Lake, that I may call in the New hampshire Regiment, and get the Remainder of our boats from Tienderoga, where they are much safer (till wanted) than they can be here . . .

WO/34/51 fols 65–6

194
Captain Joshua Loring to Major-General Jeffery Amherst
Niagara
6 July 1760
[Holograph]   [Receipt not dated]

I must beg leave to acquaint your Excellency that as the two Snows will be Compleatly fitted for Service in five or Six Days, Should be glad to know in what manner I am To proceed with them, if it is agreeable to Your Excellency, should be very glad to go and look For the Enemy, by the last accounts they were Cruseing in the mouth of the River, and off Cataraque, if we could get below them in the Night, I think we might stand a good Chance To prevent there geting down the River again, I shall want about Eighty Seamen to Compleat There Compliments, and a few Soldiers for Marriners [marines], we have the Frame of one of the Sloops a good part of the plank Saw'd, hope to had [have] her ready by the first of August, no Canvas or Twine yet arrived which are the things Most Wanted. I intend Sailing for Oswego Thursday.

WO/34/65 fol. 19

195
Major-General Jeffery Amherst to Captain Joshua Loring

Oswego

[Copy in Secretary's hand]   9 July 1760

I have immediately on my arrival here ordered One Hundred Seamen for You, which are to proceed directly under the care of Lt Phipps to Niagara, who likewise takes with him Some Canvas, twine, Guns & ammunition that it is imagined You may want.

You will have heard the French Ships were off this place the 6th past, they are not returned to the River St Lawrence, if You can get between them and the River it would be a Sure Victory for You and will be of great Consequence to the Operations of the Campaign, this is Such an opportunity, as may not happen again, and I therefore cannot recommend it to You too Strongly too Seize this Occasion of taking those Vessells.

WO/34/65 fol. 143

196
Major-General Jeffery Amherst to Major Hubert Munster

Oswego

[Copy in Secretary's hand]   12 July 1760

I have ordered a Detachment of Four Captains, Eight Subalterns, and two Hundred men to Assemble immediately at the Water side near the Batteaus with their arms, Ammunition, Blancketts, without Tents. You will take the said Detachment under Your Command, and apply to Mr Schuyler for ten good batteaus . . .

You will try to amuse the French Vessells and make them Stay on this Side the Lake, from the appearances of Your going to Niagara, and the hopes they may have of Cutting You off from thence; and whenever they pursue You, You will of course make to the Land, Secure Your Batteaus, and post Yourself so that they can do You no hurt, making all the Shew You can of Your

Intentions of going to Niagara, whenever You can push forward; and You will Use Your best Endeavors to divert these Vessells in this manner, that ours may have time to come from Niagara, to cutt them off from their Port.

When You have Executed this Service, or that the Enemy's Vessells may not be tempted to try to take the Batteaus under Your Command and that You find You cannot be of any further Service to this intended Scheme You will then return with Your Detachment to this place.

WO/34/85 fol. 4

197
Major-General Jeffery Amherst to Captain Samuel Willyamos

Oswego

[Copy in Secretary's hand]   20 July 1760

You will take the Detachment of three Subalterns, Seven Sergeants, and One hundred & Thirty Four men under Your Command, the Above Detachment being Ordered this Night, and to parade tomorrow at four o'Clock at the Navy Yard . . .

So soon as the Detachment is ready, You will proceed along the East Coast, and make what Expedition You can, consistantly with a due Care of Your Men, to <u>La Grande Isle</u>, or <u>Les Isles aux Iroquois</u>,[41] where You will take the properest Post You can for Your own Security, the safety of Your Batteaus, and Care of Your Provisions, which You will do by throwing up any such Work, for the defence of Your Post, as You shall Judge necessary, and putting Your Provisions under such Cover, that they may Come to no damage; and You will at the same time, try to fix Your Post in such manner, that the Soldier who is gone to Captain Loring may not fail of finding You.

For Your full Information of my Intentions, I Enclose You an Extract of my Letter to Captain Loring, by which You will Guide Yourself; You will take what Opportunitys You can of Reconnoitring the Position of the Islands, the Depth of the Bays, and Entrance of any Rivers into the Lake, and if You should find any Other Place, than the <u>Isle aux Iroquois</u>, that may better Answer the Intention for which You are Detached, You will post Yourself accordingly, taking Care, at the same time, that Captain Loring may know where You are Posted, and that You may be Sure of Supplying him with Provisions, in case he should want any.

When Captain Loring has taken the Enemys Vessels, You then may Return to this Place, or if from any Unforeseen Event, the Vessels should Escape him, and he should Return, You will then Come back, Your Stay there must depend on the Motions of Our Vessels, in which You will Guide Yourself to the best of Your Judgement . . .

WO/34/85 fol. 11

198
Captain Joshua Loring to Major-General Jeffery Amherst

Off Grand Island
23 July 1760
[Holograph]   [Received 24 July 1760]

I am extremely sorry that I am obliged to acquaint your Excellency, that the Enemy notwithstanding my utmost Endeavours to intercept them, have escaped me, I proceeded immediately to the North Shore when I left Oswego, where I remained till the Boats returned, which I sent in search of the French Vessells. They returned on Monday and reported that they had been all round the Island /called Les Isles Galeaua[42] [?] and the two small Islands to the Northward of them which by all the Information I could get were the places where the French Vessells used to lay, and from thence to Grand Island, where they could look into Cataraqui[43] Harbour, and they were very certain the Enemy's Vessells could not be there. I then determined to sail immediately for Cataraqui and to send the Boats out again as I thought He might have passed in the Night, I accordingly

203

sailed that afternoon and the next morning was off Les I^s Couis, but the Wind coming to the Eastward, I could not fetch in to the Northward of those Islands, so stood on till 9 o'Clock when I was up with the Northward most of Les Isles au Galeaua [?] and in a few minutes afterwards the Enemy hove in sight, bearing down upon us with all the sail they could set; I then had not the least doubt but that they would have engaged us, but they soon convinced us that they had no such Intentions, for when they had got within about two or three Miles of us, they hauled their Wind and made all the sail from us they could. I immediately gave Chace, and while the Breeze continued came up with them fast, but it soon fell calm, when they made use of their Oars and Boats and rowed off as fast as they could, We did the same after them, sometimes we gained upon them, and sometimes they upon us. In this manner we continued to chace till 10 o Clock at Night, when we were got in among the Islands near to Cataraqui. The Weather then came on so thick and Foggy, that we could not see the Land, tho' we were very near to some of the Islands, which obliged us to come to an Anchor, I immediately sent off three Whale Boats to observe their motions, they were then about 3 miles from us. The Boats returned at 12 this Day, and Capt Thody who I sent with this party, informs me that He went a few miles below Cataraqui, and into the Harbour in the morning, but saw nothing of the Vessells, He thinks, He heard them pass by in the Night, so that I doubt not in the least they are got to Lagulet.[44] No person can be more uneasy than I am at this Disappointment, especially after having been so near them, I thought several times Nothing could have prevented my getting alongside, but having no Wind worth mentioning and they rowing lighter than we did has Occasioned their Escape . . . I am now at an anchor off Grand Island, about 10 Miles from Cataraqui Harbour, and in as thick a Fogg as we generally have on the Banks of Newfound Land. I must remain here till the Weather clears up, when I shall proceed to the Island where Capt Williamson[45] is and there await for further Orders . . .

WO/34/65 fols 22–3

199
Major-General Jeffery Amherst to Colonel William Haviland

Camp at Oswego

[Copy in Secretary's hand]   29 July 1760

I am to own the receipt of Your Letter of the 21ˢᵗ Instant and to Express to You the pleasure I have, in learning that Your Works go on much better than they had done of late, and that Your Preparations for going down the Lake were pretty forward; I am sure, as this Comes from Yourself it must be so . . .

Agreeable to my Instructions I am now to Inform You of my Intentions Soon to proceed against the Enemy; the Army being Assembled all to the Garrison of Niagara, & Troops I sent from hence to Presqu'Isle which I expect daily, as I have had intelligence the Relief from Pittsburgh is arrived at Niagara; The 46ᵗʰ, Montgomery's & Schuyler's are on the Road and will I hope be here ere long, but whether they are or not, I propose to be gone from hence by the 10ᵗʰ of next month at farthest, perhaps sooner, but You may rely on the former, and therefore I would have You proceed down the Lake on that day or as nearly as You can do it.

I shall proceed down the River, to wherever the Enemy may be, and endeavor to dislodge them from the Isles Royal & Galot,⁴⁶ or give them Battle if I should find them on my way, Whatever my Operations or the Success of them may be, I shall Acquaint You therewith by Letters, when I think necessary, which I shall send to You across the Country, and You will do the Like to me, directing Your Messengers to follow the Path that Capᵗ Tuite did last Year from Lake Champlain to La Galette, which any two or three men may do without fearing to be Intercepted, when the Army from hence is advanced beyond Oswegatchie.

WO/34/52 fol. 74

200
Sheriff Jacob Van Schaick to Major-General Jeffery Amherst

Albany
1 August 1760
[Holograph]   [Receipt not dated]

I am very sorry Lt Coventry has given /^{you} an idea of the arrest of Capt Brown so Inconsistent[47] – the Case is this, if any Subject thinks a person in the Kings imploy hurts his property he Issues the Kings writ against /^{him} to answer the Complaint – to which the person gives bail to answer that is all, and if Mr Coventry had thought Capt Browns attendance on the service of the least Consequence, I would have taken Lt Coventrys word for Capt Browns appearance and he would not give it, and he refused it therefore he must know best – this is matter of fact, tho he has so egregiously represented the Case to your Excellency. The morning after Capt Brown was committed he found bail and was released which he Could have done the moment he was arrested if he pleased, but would not, and still his Majesty's service requires his attendance.

It is hard your Excellency that the whole burden should fall on me, I am obliged by my oath of office to Execute the process sent to me if I can and the arrest when made is at my Risque . . .[48]

WO/34/82 fol. 305

201
Major-General Jeffery Amherst to Brigadier-General Robert Monckton

Camp at Oswego
[Copy in Secretary's hand]   2 August 1760

Major Gladwin, with the late Garrison of Niagara, Arrived here on the 31st . . .

As I find that You can answer Supplying Your Garrison far Cheaper Your way, than by the way of Niagara (Which I am extremely glad to hear) I shall drop all thoughts of Supplying from thence, Which was only intended by way of Savings . . .

I am glad to hear Your Indians are in so good a humour; ours here are likewise very quiet, and I can't Say but what they are much more so than I Expected; they are upwards of 1300, it is true that there are more than 600 Women & Children among them; but these are for the most part going home; the sooner the better for tho' they are all of them satisfied with the soldier's Ration (for I allow them no more) the Consumption of Such a Number of useless mouths is Considerable; and I must recommend it to You, to allow Yours no more than I do those here; as likewise to be Watchfull, whom of them You make Presents to; observing to distinguish as nearly as You can between friends and foes . . .

I propose to set out from hence by the tenth at farthest. The New Jersey Troops & Murrays' Reg^t being the only ones now that are to Joyn me, & I expect them immediately and I Flatter myself, I Shall soon be able to Send You some Accounts of Our Success in our way to Montreal.

WO/34/43 fols 145–6

202
Major-General Jeffery Amherst to Colonel Frederick Haldimand

Camp at Oswego
[Copy in Secretary's hand]   6 August 1760

You will, agreeable to my verbal orders of this Evening, with the Detachment I have ordered under Your Command, early tomorrow morning proceed down the Lake, and take the Safest route You can to the Grande Isle, on the Point of which You will Encamp Your Detachment, or on such part thereof, or any Island near it as You Judge the properest for the Security of Your Post, and to help Capt Loring with the Ships under his Command, whom, agreable to his Instructions of which you have Enclosed a Copy, You will see is to be Assisted with Such parties, as he may want for Sounding the Passage for the Vessells, and You will also

Cause the River to be Reconoitred, as far as You can in Safety, and if in the Course of this research You find the Isle Cochoia, a more advantageous Situation than the Grand Isle You will remove Your Camp thither, from whence You will watch the Motions of the Enemy; as it is not unlikely they may send out Small parties, to obtain Intelligence of our motions, You will therefore Cause a good look out to be Constantly observed, and try to Cutt off all such parties.

There are on board one of the Snows, two Six Pounders with an officer and ten men of the Artillery which are at Your disposal, whenever You shall have occasion, & please to Call for them.

An Engineer will likewise attend You with Tools that may be of Use to You.

Capt Wlyamoz is likewise to accompany You in order to be assisting in Shewing You the best and Safest passage, and in Exploring the River, immediately after which You will send him or Lieut Ratzen, back to me, as it will be of great Service in Conducting the Army to You, which I propose shall be in three or four days hence.

The Indians that sett out this morning for Swegatchie, have been warned, that if they returned to the Army, they were at a proper distance to hoist a red flag, and that they should be received as friends; that if they did not return, & were hereafter found in Arms, they should be looked on as Enemies & treated as Such; You will Conform thereto; and all those that shall come to remain with You as Friends, You will treat Civilly, & all others as Enemies, and You will not permit any that may come to You to return to the Enemy, unless You should see some reasons for so doing.

In case any thing Extraordinary should happen which You Judge necessary to Inform me of, You will of Course Dispatch a Whaleboat to me, and if any Flag of Truce should be sent from the Enemy, You will demand the Dispatches, and send them to me giving a receipt for them, & sending the flag of Truce back, or if an answer is required, You will keep the Flag of Truce at a proper distance from Your Post with a Guard, untill You shall receive my answers thereto.

WO/34/9 fol. 173

203
Major-General Jeffery Amherst to Captain Joshua Loring
Camp at Oswego
[Copy in Secretary's hand]   9 August 1760

As You informed me, that You could not, agreeable to my verbal orders of this day, weigh Anchor this Evening, You will observe to do so to morrow at break of day, or so Soon as You possibly can, and immediately with His Majesty's two Snows, the Onondaga & Mohawk, under Your Command proceed to Frontenac, as if there is a Chance left for the Enemy's Vessells venturing out, if may be on the report of the Swegatchie Indians, that went from hence this day, and who Could not know of this Your so Sudden Departure, but will Suppose You here, and may be tempted to get out for Intelligence, of the Motions of this Army; You will therefore make it Your business to attack, take, Sink, Burn, or destroy them, if You should be so lucky to meet with them.

As You know the Route to Frontenac, You will proceed directly to that place, and I shall order Colonel Haldimand, with the Detachment under his Command to take a safe route for the Batteaus, and to take Post at the <u>Grand Isle</u>, from which place he will Assist You, in giving You Such partys, as You may want for sounding the Passages for the Vessells to pass, & Col⁰ Haldimand will post himself on the <u>Isle Cochoia</u> if he should on reconoitring of it, find it a more Advantageous Post than the Grande Isle; You will therefore in Concert with Colonel Haldimand Use Your best Endeavors for Exploring the safest Navigation for the Vessells, that when the Army Arrives the whole may proceed down the River to Swegatchie without loss of time.[49]

WO/34/65 fol. 149

204
Colonel William Haviland to Major-General Amherst
Crown Point
10 August 1760
[Holograph]   [Receipt not dated]

I was this day favoured with your Duplicates of the 29th Ult, and
refer you to my answer by Lieu^t Small of the 8th Instant. I was in
hopes of getting away this day, but could not for reasons not worth
troubling you at this time; but Orders are out for Embarking
tomorrow morning and I may say with Certainty that I shall sail
tomorrow.

This day five hundred of the Massachusetts arrived, I am in
hopes of taking them with me, if they can be ready; but I shall not
wait for them.
[PS] Though I wrote the above Yesterday I thought it best to
detain the Express till this morning, to Inform you the Certain
time of our Embarking, which will be in two hours. The wind is
fair, so that I don't see any thing that can detain us. 11th Augt a
Quarter after six in the morning.

WO/34/51 fol. 89

205
Major-General Jeffery Amherst to Colonel John Bradstreet
[St Lawrence River]
[Copy in Secretary's hand]   15 August 1760

I Write this from an Island some few Miles down the River St
Lawrence, whither the Army has got this day, after having
[buffeted] me with some high Winds & heavy Rains, upon the
Whole, however, We have got on pretty well, and lost but a few
Batteaus and I intend to proceed tomorrow,[50] I shall depend on
You for Provisions, and You will give strict Orders to Your People
within the Communication, to forward it up, as fast as possible, to
Oswego: If You find any remissness in them, and that Your health
will permit, which I am willing to hope, You will Attend to it

210

Yourself, If not I desire that You will not make Yourself Uneasy, but give Your Orders to those Under You, on whose diligence You can rely; I would not neither have You be under any anxiety, if You are not able to follow me, as I make no doubt, that with the Orders You will give, for forwarding the provisions to the Army, we shall be properly Supplied, which is indeed a more Essential Service to the Army than your presence here could be. Once more, therefore, avoid all Anxiety of Mind, and You will recover so much the sooner, which I most sincerely Wish.

WO/34/56 fol. 123

206
Major-General Jeffery Amherst to Colonel Nathan Whiting
Camp of Swegatchie
[Copy in Secretary's hand]   18 August 1760

You will take on You the Command of the Corps I shall leave here for the present, consisting of Your own Regiment, Wooster's, Fitch's, & a part of the New York Troops with Artillery and Stores, which You will Encamp on the River side near the Fort, in the most Convenient manner for Protecting the Batteaus of Artillery and Provisions, and for Guarding and making a proper Hospital, and, what I must particularly Recommend to You, the Repairs and making of Ovens, and the Establishing a Brewerie to supply the Army with Spruce beer; I have ordered four Pieces of Artillery to be Landed near the Fort, that it may not be possible for the Enemy while I am Investing the Island to run out their boats with Artillery to hurt Your Batteaus.

WO/34/85 fol. 45

207
Major-General Jeffery Amherst: Orders to Colonel Bartholomew Le Roux

Camp before Isle Royalle

[Copy in Secretary's hand]   19 August 1760

Colonel Le Roux, with the three Regiments of New York Troops, all the Batteaus Loaded with Artillery, and Artillery Stores, and all other Batteaus which are manned by those Regiments (excepting Such as have been ordered to remain with the Hospital) are to leave Swegatchi this Evening when it begins to grow Duskish, & are to proceed along the North Shore down the River as the Officer of Artillery, who is sent to Guide him will Shew him the Route. The boats to go Singly but they are to follow pretty Close & not leave too large Intervals, they'll Join the Artillery at an Island a little below Isle Royalle.

WO/34/85 fol. 46

208
Major-General Jeffery Amherst to Captain Joshua Loring

Camp before Isle Royalle

[Copy in Secretary's hand]   22 August 1760

I have received Your Letter by Lieutenant Sinclair; my Intentions were and are, that the two Snows should approach towards the Fort, putting themselves in a Line with the Williamson,[51] when the Batterys begin to fire, as the Batterys will at the farthest begin to fire to morrow morning early; You may make this alteration in Your Station, when You will, in the night or early in the morning.

I shall see what Effect our Batterys will have, and I shall hope in a very short time after their firing to desire You to take the Vessells close on the Fort, to make use of Your marksmen to drive the Enemy from their Batterys, that I may push in Batteaus safely with Troops to Assault the Place.

WO/34/65 fol. 151

209
Major-General Jeffery Amherst to Colonel Frederick Haldimand

Headquarters, Camp before Fort Levis
[Copy in Secretary's hand]   23 August 1760

Orders to Colonel Haldimand Commanding the Brigade on the South Shore
The vessells are immediately to warp in Close to the Fort, and keep the Garrison from the Batteries by their Small Arms; The Batteries during this time will throw all the Shot they can into the Fort.

Two Captains, four Subalterns, Eight Sergeants and one hundred and fifty men of the Light Infantry of [the] Regiments, & the same number of Gage's, under the Command of Major Gladwin, with their arms and ammunition only, to receive twenty five Batteaus from Montgomery's Regiment, which are to be Loaded with a Thousand Fascines, at the Islands at the Tail of the Trenches, and they are then to Assemble at the Island upon the Right.

The Grenadiers of the Army under the Command of Lt Colonel Massy, are to Embark in twenty five Batteaus, and are to Storm the Fort; The Officers & Sergeants only will take their Arms; The Grenadiers will Land in their Shirts, Caps on, & Broad Swords flung over their Shoulders.

Six men of the Light Infantry of Regiments & Gage's to Secure each Batteau of the Grenadiers when they Land, and Major Gladwin will with his small arms keep the Enemy from the Batteries, in case the Platoons from the ships, & the men in the round tops should not Effectually do it.[52]

An Engineer to attend Lt Colonel Massey, & a Batteau with Tools in case they should be wanted; Lt Colonel Massey will fill the Ditch, Assault the Place, & take possession of it as fast as possible. If the Enemy beats a Parley, or Calls out for Quarter they are to be Prisoners at Discretion, and on no other Terms.

WO/34/9 fol. 182

210
Major-General Jeffery Amherst to Field Marshal Viscount John Ligonier

Camp at Fort William Augustus

[Copy in Secretary's hand]   26 August 1760

I Set out with the Army from Oswego on the 10th Instant, the first moment I could get the Troops to their Destination at that place, after Rowing & Sailing Eight days successively on the Lake, and in this River, I passed, in the last day, our Vessells, that I had dispatched on the 7th to get into the Entrance of the River St Lawrence, by the time the Army could Arrive there, as it would have been difficult for the Army to have proceeded down the River against two of the Enemys Vessells; I however received Advice, that One of the Enemys Vessels had run aground and was disabled, and not to lose time in Waiting for the Passage of our Vessels into the River, I proceeded with the Army on the 17th Intending to Attack the Enemys Vessells with the Row Galleys I had build at Oswego, four of them mounting 12 p^{rs}: and a Fifth an 8 Inch Howitzer. On the 17th Col. Williamson with the Row Galleys Attacked the Vessel & took her very handsomely; She had ten 12 p^{rs} very good Guns, the Army took possession of La Galette, or what is generally called Swegatchie,[53] which was Abandoned by Every thing but stragling Indians: On the 18th I Invested Monsieur de Levy's Impregnable Island; the 23^d I had all my Batterys ready, and the whole Artillery began to play at once: Monsieur Pouchot, the Commandant very wisely drew in all his Guns; that did not last long, as our two Ships had now Joined, they with the Prize fell down near the Fort, and I intended to Assault the Place, but Every thing not being as I Wished I did not Attempt it; our Batterys have Continued Firing till Yesterday in the Afternoon that [when] the Commandant beat a Parley, and Wrote me a Letter, which has produced a Capitulation whereby the Garrison are Prisoners of War; there were about 300 in the place, of which the Officer of Artillery & Ten Men were killed, One officer & 40 Wounded; the Remainder I am sending to New York; I have been very lucky in my passage, for tho' I have lost

214

several Batteaus, I have had only one man Drowned, and during the Siege, Including the taking of the Vessel on the 17th I have had 21 men killed & 23 wounded; Considering all things the Number is not great . . .[54]

This Post I think, most effectually Commands the entire possession of Lake Ontario; the Rapides begin half a mile below it, but round the Fort the Vessels may lay all Winter, the Enemy has been so good to leave us two, One that is not finished, and the Other then run aground, which may be easily repaired, so that if necessary His Majesty has a Fleet now of Five large Vessels and an Armed Sloop on Lake Ontario, and the Enemy cannot now get a Batteau on the Lake. The Inhabitants on the Mohawk River may now till their Ground without being in continual dread of the Indians murdering them in the Fields, and may Sleep in quiet at Night without any Risk of being Scalped in their Beds. I shall make all the Expedition I can to proceed down the River; I hope by about this time Colonel Haviland will be Master of the Isle au Noix, as Governor Murray will undoubtedly be Advancing towards Montreal, for that is certainly the Easiest Route, when I think Monsr de Vaudreuil will have so much to do that it will not be possible for him to Save any part of Canada. Monsieur Pouchot who commanded in the Fort, is the same Officer who Commanded at Niagara, and was Exchanged in the beginning of the Winter.

U1350/O/35/22

211
Major-General Jeffery Amherst to Governor Brigadier-General James Murray

Camp of Montreal

[Copy in Secretary's hand]   8 Sept 1760

I have Just now received the Articles of Capitulation[55] signed by the Marquis de Vaudreuil, I am Copying them to sign and Send to him, and at the same time I shall take possession of the Town with the Grenadiers and Light Infantry, who march for that purpose under the Command of Colonel Haldimand.[56] I am taking all the precautions I can that not the least Disorder may be Committed, and I shall not Suffer any One to go in or out of the Town except by a written order from me or Col° Haldimand who will take care to Post a Guard at the Port leading from Your Camp, with orders for any officer who may be sent from You shall be Admitted. I Shall be glad to see You, bring Your Camp where You think best, the Vessells You have will Serve to take away the French Troops, which My Lord Colville will forward to France, the Articles are long that I cannot tell You the Whole; they lay down their Arms, and are not to Serve during the War. I Dispatch Capt Malone with this, Major Barré Shall go through the Town to You, when I send the Capitulation in and take possession. Major Rogers is arrived at Longueil,[57] Col° Haviland on his March there.

WO/34/3 fol. 11

212
Major-General Jeffery Amherst to Field Marshal Viscount John Ligonier

[Copy in Secretary's hand]

Camp of Montreal
8 September 1760

Major Barré who will have the honour of delivering this to Your Lordship, will give you a very Clear and faithfull account of the March of the Army from Albany to this Place, which is this day Added to the King's Dominions. I shall try to make the best use I can of the remainder of the Campaign in Employing the Troops to such purposes, as shall Secure the future possession of this Country to His Majesty. I could not retaliate on the Enemy by permitting any Inhumanitys to be Committed on the Peasants, when I entered the Inhabited Country but I was resolved the [French] Corps should be disgraced for having Carried on a Cruel and barbarous War while they had the Appearance of Superiority.

U1350/O/35/23

213

Major-General Jeffery Amherst to the Governors on the Continent from Cape Breton to Georgia

Camp of Montreal
[Copy in Secretary's hand]   9 September 1760

In mine of the 26th Ultimo I acquainted You with the progress of the Army after their Departure from Oswego, and with the Success of His Majesty's Arms, against Fort Levis, now Fort William Augustus, where I remained no longer, than was requisite to make Such preparations, as I judged Essentially necessary for the passage of the Army down the River, which took me up till the 30th.

In the morning of the following day, I sat [sic] out and proceeded from Station to Station, to our present Ground, where we arrived on the 6th in the Evening; after having in the passage, Sustained a loss of Eighty Eight men drowned; twenty nine Batteaus of Regiments; Seventeen of Artillery, with some Artillery and Stores, Seventeen Whaleboats and One Row Galley Staved, Occasioned by the Violence of the Current, and the rapids being full of broken Waves.

The Inhabitants of the Settlements I passed thro', in my way hither, having Abandoned their Houses, and run into the Woods, I sent after them, Some were taken, and Others came in of their own Accord; I had them disarmed, and Caused the Oath of Allegiance to be tendered to them, which they readily took; and I Accordingly put them in quiet possession of their habitations, with which treatment they Seemed no less Surprised than happy.

The troops being formed, and the Light Artillery brought up: the Army lay on their arms the Night of 6th.

On the 7th in the morning two officers came to an Advanced Post, with a Letter from the Marquis de Vaudreuil, referring me to what one of them, Colonel Bougainville, had to say. The Conversation ended with a Cessation of Arms, till twelve o'Clock, When the proposals were brought in; Soon after I returned them with the terms I was willing to grant; which both the Mrs de Vaudreuil and Monsr de Levis, the French General, were very

217

Strenuous to have Softened; this occasioned Sundry Letters to pass between Us during the day as well as the Night (when the Army again lay on their Arms) but as I would not on any Account, deviate in the least from my Original Conditions, and Insisted on an immediate and Catagorical Answer, Mo^r de Vaudreuil, Soon after day break, notified to me that he had determined to Accept of them, and two setts of them were Accordingly Signed by him and me, and Exchanged Yesterday, when Colonel Haldimand with the Grenadiers, and Light Infantry of the Army, took possession of one of the Gates of the Town,[58] & is this day to proceed in fullfilling the Articles of the Capitulation; by which the French Troops are all to lay down their Arms; are not to Serve during the Continuance of the present War; and are to be Sent back to Old France, as are also the Governors and principal officers of the Legislature of the Whole Country, which I have now the Satisfaction to Inform you, is entirely Yielded to the Dominion of His Majesty, on which Interesting & happy Event I most Sincerely Congratulate You.

Governor Murray with the Troops from Quebec landed below the Town on Sunday last, & Colonel Haviland with his Corps (that took possession of the Isle Au Noix, abandoned by the Enemy on the 28th) arrived Yesterday at the South Shore, opposite to my Camp.

WO/34/36 fols 187–8[59]

214
Major-General Jeffery Amherst: Orders to Colonel Nathan Whiting

Camp of Montreal

[Copy in Secretary's hand]   10 September 1760

You will put Yourself & Regiment, under the Command of Colonel Lyman, who has my orders to Embark all the Connecticutt Forces, early to morrow morning, and immediately thereafter to proceed with them to Fort William Augustus, and from thence to Fort Ontario, where on his arrival, he is directed to

Detach You, and Your regiment to Fort Stanwix, whither You will accordingly proceed to, with all possible Diligence, and upon Your arrival there, You will acquaint Capt Marsh, Whom I have left as Commandant in the Fort, with these orders, and that You are to Encamp Your Regiment, & give all the help You can in forwarding the works of said Fort, which are to be Compleated according to the intended plan and to be carried on under the direction of Capt Lieut. Williams[60] the Engineer, to whom You will give all the Assistance You possibly can for that purpose, & You will continue at Fort Stanwix, with the Troops under Your Command, for the aforesaid services, untill You receive my orders for quitting the same . . .

WO/34/85 fol. 86

215
Major-General Jeffery Amherst to Colonel John Bradstreet

Camp of Montreal,

[Copy in Secretary's hand]   11 September 1760

I am to own the Receipt of Your three Several Letters of the 23^d, 27th & 31st Ultimo, by which I find You were getting plenty of Provisions to Oswego; and altho' thro' the entire Reduction of all Canada, which Capitulated on the 8th, I shall now Victual this Town and Quebec, by the way of Crown Point, or up the River St Lawrence, Yet I am not Sorry at a Quantity of Provisions being in the Communication of, and at Oswego; Since I have already ordered away all the Provincials; those of Colonel Haviland's Corps march'd back Yesterday towards Crown Point; the others Sett out this morning and are to be stationed as follows; Schuyler's at Fort William Augustus; Lyman's, Worcester's, & Fitch's, at Oswego; & Whiting's at Fort Stanwix: All these Troops during the remainder of the Campaign, are to be Employed in Compleating the Several Forts above mentioned: in the Winter, their Garrisons will be but Small; at Fort Wm Augustus I propose to leave 300 men, and at the others in proportion; This last mentioned Garrison, & those of Niagara & Presqu'Isle, I intend Shall be Supplied from Oswego;

219

and as I said before, those of Montreal, Trois Rivieres, & Quebec, by way of Crown Point or by sea up the River St Lawrence; agreable to which You will now alter Your Dispositions, and make such Arrangements as You shall see best.

WO/34/56 fol. 125

216
Major-General Jeffery Amherst to Brigadier-General Robert Monckton

Camp of Montreal

[Copy in Secretary's hand]   12 September 1760

I enclose You a Copy of my Circular Letter to the Several Governors, on the Capitulation I have made with the Marquis de Vaudreuil, by which You will See all Canada is added to the King's Dominions, the great distance of the Out posts, makes it impossible for Monsieur Le Marquis de Vaudreuil, to send officers to those Posts, without their losing the opportunity of going to France, with the Troops which are Soon to Embark; and as his Orders will be Sufficient to Call in those Garrisons, I send them to You for that purpose, and You will please to direct the French Troops to be Escorted the Shortest way to the Coast that they may be Sent to France, agreable to the Capitulation. Monsieur Vaudreuil says, the Number of Troops in these Posts are triffling, in Some not above two or three men; however it is right we should take and keep possession, and that all the Militia & Inhabitants should give up their Arms, and take the oath of Allegiance; I send You Some Articles of the Capitulation, as many as necessary for You to know for the Execution of this Service, the whole of it is so long, it would take up too much time to Copy now, as I am full of business, I will send it You hereafter. – The Reduction of all Canada, must give a free and undisturbed Communication to all your Posts, which now will not want the Numbers to defend them, that have as Yet been requisite; You will therefore please to Establish such posts on our new acquisition, as you shall Judge proper, for keeping possession, peace and Quiet.

I send Major Rogers with this, with two Companies of Rangers, that I think may be of Service in taking this new Acquisition, & Exploring the Country, You will make Such Use of him, and his Command as You please, in disarming the Inhabitants, tendering the oaths, & getting all the Intelligence You may require, but You will fix the Posts of the Regular Troops, and Send back Major Rogers, with the two Companys to Oswego, that they may come down to Albany there to be broke, as they are much too expensive, to be kept on Foot, when I think, we can have no Use of them . . . I shall write to You again, so soon as I have fixed what will become of myself, in all probability I shall leave B^r General Gage here, and I shall go (after I have worked out the End of the Campaign, with the Provincials in Compleating the Forts) to New York to be à portée of the King's Orders.

[P.S.] What the remains of the Troops will be, after I have settled every thing here, I know not, but if I have a sufficiency for the Mississippi, I should be glad to take possession of it. – this may give you Employ.

WO/34/43 fol. 149

217
Major-General Jeffery Amherst: Orders to Major Robert Rogers

[Copy in Secretary's hand]

Camp of Montreal
12 September 1760

You will upon receipt hereof with Capt. Waite's and Capt. Hazzen's Companys of Rangers under Your Command, proceed, in whaleboats from hence to Fort William Augustus; taking along with You, one Joseph Poupas, alias la Fleur, an Inhabitant of the Detroit, and Lieut. Brehme Assistant Engineer.

From Fort William Augustus, You will Continue Your Voyage, by the North Shore, to Niagara, where You will Land Your Whaleboats, and transport them across the Carrying place into Lake Erie; applying to Major Walters, or Officer Commanding at Niagara for any Assistance You may want, on that, or any Other

Occasion: requesting of him, at the same time, to deliver up to You Mons[r] Gamelin, who was made Prisoner at the reduction of said Fort, and has Continued there ever Since, in order to Conduct him, with the above mentioned Poupas, to their Habitation at the Detroit; where upon taking the Oath of Allegiance to His Most Sacred Majesty, whose Subjects they are become by the Capitulation of the 8th Instant, they shall be protected in the peaceable and quiet possession of their properties, and so long as they behave as becometh good & faithful Subjects, Shall partake of all the other privileges & immunities granted unto them by the Said Capitulation.

With these & the Detachment under Your Command You will proceed in Your Whaleboats across Lake Erie to Prequ'isle, where upon Your arrival, You will make known the orders I have given to the Officer Commanding at that post, and You will leave said Whaleboats and Party, taking only a small Detachment of Your Party, and marching by Land to join Brig[r] Gen[l] Monckton, wherever he may be.

Upon Your arrival with him, You will deliver into his hands the Dispatches You shall herewith receive for him; and follow & obey Such Orders, and Directions, as he shall give You, for the relief of the Garrisons of the French posts at Detroit, Michilimakinack, or any Others in that District; for gathering in the Arms of the Inhabitants there; and for administering unto them, the Oath of Allegiance, already mentioned; when You will likewise administer or see the same administered to the before named Gamelin & Poupas: and when this is done, and that You have reconnoitred and Explored the Country as much as You can without losing time, Unnecessarily, You are to bring away the French Troops & arms, to such place as You shall be directed by Brig[r] Monckton.

And when the whole of this Service is Compleated You will march back Your Detachment to Presqu'Isle or Niagara, according to the Orders You receive from Brig[r] Monckton, where You will Embark the whole, and in like manner as before You will transport Your whaleboats, across the Carrying place into Lake Ontario, which You will pass, & Land at Fort Ontario, where You will deliver over Your whaleboats into the Care of the Commanding

Officer, marching Your Detachm^t by Land to Albany or wherever I may be, to receive what further orders I may have to give You.[61]

WO/34/85 fol. 94

218
Captain Thomas Moncrieffe to Major-General Jeffery Amherst

Les Cedres
13 September 1760
[Holograph]   [Received 14 September 1760]

I send Sergeant Balang of the 55th Reg^t with one hundred and twelve Firelocks I have sollicited from the Inhabitants Round about me And I enclose your Excellency a Roll of those who have Signed the Submission. Numbers from each Village declare to me that they Surrendered their Arms on the Isle Perrot Others that the Indians took them from them. Your Excellency is the Best Judge of the truth of this. I have a few More to Come in, that I know of, and I have Sent off an Officer in Captain Ogdens to Look in to each house, And Pick up any Arms they may have. After I had sent them a Summons, there Seemd to be a sort of Empressment, Who shoud be First. There are Some of them still Dispersed, Who Drop in by twos and threes, As they have Escaped from the Indians or are Returnd from Looking after their Effects . . .

WO/34/83 fol. 43

219
Major-General Jeffery Amherst to Governor Brigadier-General James Murray

Camp of Montreal
[Copy in Secretary's hand]   14 September 1760

Several Complaints having been made to me of the Sailors who belong to His Majesty's Ships of War, who in Conjunction with those of the Transports, have Landed, plundered, & robbed the Inhabitants, Committed all sorts of Disorders, and have stolen Several of the Arms, particularly Yesterday in the afternoon, a party that was coming from Detroit by my orders, which party was to have, according to the articles of Capitulation given up their Arms; were beset by some sailors below the Town, plundered of all they had, & their Arms taken away.

That I may thoroughly put a stop to any further Outrages, and that this Country which is now become a part of the King's Dominion, as much as any other Colony in America, may enjoy all the benefits of His Majesty's Government, and Protection equally with the rest, I do desire, You will please to order proper Officers and Guards on board of the Several Transports, Who are to apply to the Masters Commanding the Same for their Aid, and Assistance in Searching for Arms, or necessarys which have been taken from, the poor people, that the Arms may be delivered to Colonel Williamson Commanding the Royal Artillery for His Majesty's Service, and the necessarys to be delivered to the Owners.

You will likewise please to give Orders to the Several Lieutenants of His Majesty's Ships of War that they do in like manner Search amongst their men, and that any Arms or necessarys, which may appear to have been stolen, are to be given in immediately as directed above. That I may put an entire stop to any further Disorders I am determined the Provost Martial, who has orders to go his Rounds, and take up Straglers, Shall have an officer to Attend him, and whoever is found in the fact of plundering the Inhabitants Shall be hung immediately; You will please to give Notice of this, that the men may not be permitted to come on Shore, or that they may behave better when they are there.

WO/34/3 fol. 13

220
Major-General Jeffery Amherst: Orders to Captain Stirling *et al.*

Camp of Montreal
[Holograph draft]   15 September 1760

Whereas by the Capitulation of the 8th Ins^t all Canada makes part of H.M.'s dominions, & the Inhabitants thereof, are become /The Kings Subjects; It is therefore requisite, not only to tender the Oath of Allegiance to these New Subjects, but also to disarm them; Wherefore You will upon receipt hereof, immediately set out /for & proceed ~~from~~ to the several Villages & parishes set forth in the within List, being the district allotted to You for the aforesaid Service: which you will Execute & perform in the following manner.

You will Convey yourself, with the party order'd to attend you upon this occasion, to the first of the Villages sett down in the aforesaid List; and on your arrival there, you will summon the Captain or Commanding Officer of the Militia in the same, to attend You; & when there, you will demand his Commission; a List of the Officers & men of the Militia under his Command & of the number of Arms they are possessed of; Likewise a List of the names of the Inhabitants of said Village or parish.

When you are informed of all this; You will then Order the said Officer of Militia to Collect all the Militia as well as the Inhab^t of the Male kind /within his district & Assemble them on the most Convenient Spot of Ground within the district, where they are to bring in, & deliver over to You, every Arms, without Exception, they are possessed of; after which You will tender & administer unto them the Oath of Allegiance herewith: You will then return to the said Officer Commanding the Militia, & the Officers under him a firelock to each, in order to be the better able to keep good order & discipline in his Village; and You will at the same time inform him, that I shall send him a Commission in the room of that you bring away as also others for his Inferior Officers, ~~which~~ /whose present Commissions you are likewise to bring away with You.

225

When you have thus Executed the aforesaid Services, at this first Village; You will then continue Your route to the next, and so on /from the one to the other until the last, sett down in the List; at every one of which you will perform and Execute the aforesaid Instructions: And when the whole is finished, You will return to head Quarters where you will deliver the Arms you shall in the progress of your Circuit, have Collected into the Care of the Commanding Officer of the Artillery; and the Lists of the names of the Militia & Inhabitants of the respective Villages & parishes, with the Commissions You will deliver to me.

WO/34/85 fol. 103

221
Major-General Jeffery Amherst to Colonel Ralph Burton

[Copy in Secretary's hand]

Camp of Montreal
16 September 1760

Canada by the late Capitulation, being annexed to His Majesty's American Dominions; and the Government of the Trois Rivieres, within the same, being Vacant, I have the Satisfaction to Inform You, that I have made Choice of You to fill that Post; and I do Accordingly, hereby appoint You Governor for His Majesty, in and over the said Government of Trois Rivieres, Untill the King's Pleasure shall be known.

You will therefore, with that part of His Majesty's 48th Regiment of Foot, which is Encamped here (the remainder being already ordered thither) immediately sett out for, and proceed to Trois Rivieres aforesaid, and upon Your Arrival there, take possession of the Same, and all its Dependencies, in the King's name; and accordingly take upon You the Administration of the whole: Governing the Same untill the King's Pleasure shall be known, according to the Military Laws, if You Should find it necessary; but I should Chuse that the Inhabitants, whenever any Differences arise between them, were Suffered to settle them among themselves, agreable to their own Laws and Customs, this

226

toleration nevertheless not to Extend beyond what Shall appear consistent with Safety & Prudence.

To Enable You the better to fullfill the terms of the Capitulation, and that the Inhabitants may Enjoy the Privileges & Immunities they are entitled to, from them, so long as they behave like good and Faithfull Subjects, I Enclose You a Copy of those Articles, which You will Cause to be Scrupulously and Strictly observed.

I likewise transmit to You Copies of all Such Inventories and Lists of the Artillery, Arms, Ammunition, Stores etc, found in the French King's Magazines at the Trois Rivieres, which You will also take possession of, for the use of the King, and Cause to be lodged and stowed, under the Care of the Proper Officers, that no part thereof may be Embezzled; nor even Expended without Your particular orders; and as there may be many things at the Trois Rivieres, and the Posts depending thereon, that have not been reported to me, You will Cause Inventories to be taken of the whole, & transmitt the Same to me, that I may be fully informed of the State of that Government. You will likewise, for the King, take possession of the Iron Foundry of St Maurice . . .

Your Garrison is to Consist of the 48th Regim^t under Your Command, and a Detachment of the Royal Artillery Consisting of one officer, and Twenty three men, which You will post within Your government, in the best & most eligible manner for the defence of the Same, & for keeping up Peace and Quiet throughout the Whole, and so as to be ever ready to act in Concert, in case of any sudden, and unsuspected attack, with Brig^r General Gage (whom I leave in the Command of the Troops at Montreal, and within its department) and Governor Murray at Quebec, who have likewise Directions to reinforce You in case of Necessity; You will therefore Correspond, and Co-operate with those two Gentlemen, giving them such Informations as You shall receive from time to time, & which You think it may be necessary they should be acquainted with . . .

Immediately after Your taking possession of Your Government, You will Dispatch officers to gather in the Arms of the Inhabitants, and to tender them the Oath of Allegiance; to render this business the easier, I transmit You a list of the Villages and

Parishes within the Government of the Trois Rivieres; a Copy of my Instructions to the officers that have been Employed in that Service, within this Government; and the form of the Oath of Allegiance, as it is to be tendered & administered to them.

And as when the Inhabitants have Complied with those orders, and have taken the aforementioned Oath, they are as much His Majesty's Subjects as any of Us, and are therefore entitled to the Same protection. I would have You recommend it particularly to the Troops, to live in good harmony & Brotherhood with them; and to avoid all Differences Whatsoever.

That You may the better Enforce these orders, and keep a due Subordination among the Troops, I enclose You a Warrant for holding General Courts Martial, and approving the Sentences, altho they should Extend to Death, but that for Desertion only.

WO/34/7 fols 206–7

222
Major-General Jeffery Amherst to Lieutenant-Colonel John Darby

[Copy in Secretary's hand]

Camp at Montreal
17 September 1760

. . . Only two, of upwards of Seven hundred Indians we had at Oswego, having followed us hither, and the remainder having Shamefully Deserted,[62] I am determined to make the necessary Distinction, that ought between good and bad; and I have therefore Sent to Sir William Johnson for an Exact List of those that have remained attached to Us till the Last, whom I intend to Decorate with Some distinguishing Mark, with which You shall be Acquainted, that all such who shall wear the Same, may be admitted with friendship and Civility at all His Majesty's Forts & posts; and those, who were not Decorated therewith, be refused all Admittance whatsoever, as persons on whom no Dependence is to be had . . .

WO/34/85 fols 110–11

223
Major-General Jeffery Amherst to Captain Anthony Wheelock

Camp at Montreal
[Copy in Secretary's hand]   17 Sept 1760

I take the opportunity of Lieut. Brown, who Sets out to morrow morning for New York, & proposes to make great Dispatch, to inform You that by the last Article of the Capitulation, which I granted to Canada on the 8th Instant, it is Stipulated that the Officers as well as the men of the Militia of this Country Prisoners of War in our Colonies, Should be sent back to their Settlements; agreeable thereto, You will, upon receipt hereof, Sunder out not only all those under that Denomination, but likewise all the Inhabitants of Canada (except Such as belong to the Regular Troops, or Troupes de Colonie, who are to be sent to Old France) and that You Cause them to be Embarked in one or more Sloops if necessary, bound to Albany, Consigned to Colo Bradstreet or his Assistant, with a Letter acquainting him that it is my Orders, he does upon their arrival furnish them with what provisions may be necessary, and forward them by an Officer to Crown Point from whence they shall be sent on to this place and with regard to Provisions for their passage to Albany, You will apply to Messrs Delancey & Watts the Contractors Agents at New York, who will supply You with the Quantity necessary for that purpose. – With regard to the Regulars and Troupes de Colonie You shall receive further Directions. Several of the Canadians here are desirous to go to New York & the other Provinces to get a lively hood so that if amongst those that are Prisoners, some may Chuse to stay & work they may be permitted.

WO/34/98 fol. 174

229

224
Captain Thomas Moncrieffe to Major-General Jeffery Amherst

Les Cedres
18 September 1760
[Holograph]   [Receipt not dated]

Mr Prevost waits on your Excellency with a Roll of the Inhabitants who have Taken the oaths of Allegiance. Some few are out of the Way, as Soon as they Return, they are to be Sent to Me. I had that part of your letter, Relating to their not Returning all their arms Translated. And after Reading it to them Delivered it to them to Chew upon. I should be Glad to know how the Eclesiasticks are to be Managed. If they are to take this oath of allegiance or if they are to have a Particular form administered to them. I send down five English Prisoners that have been Returnd from the Indians and a Man of the Forty Sixth, Who is not Very Clear how he Came here. All the Provincials at Length are Past. The First Division Strippd the Country Pretty well, However what was Left did not Escape the Second. My Detachment has been Distributed for two Leagues Round to Protect them; but in Vain. As I informd your Excellency by Mr Watson that my Provisions were just out. Till a Supply shoud Arrive, I put the Detachment on half allowance, As I coud not think of Quitting this Post without Some order.

WO/34/83 fol. 70

225
Major-General Jeffery Amherst to Reverend Dr Hughes

Camp at Montreal
[Copy in Secretary's hand]   20 September 1760

The bad Choice that has been made of Persons to Officiate for the Chaplains of the Army, which has made it necessary to Discharge one lately for imbibing Seditious principles into the Soldiery, & the other Your Deputy having seldom appeared during the

Campaign, added to the few Chaplains that have come out to
Attend their Duty: renders it of absolute necessity, in order to
Convince His Majesty's new acquired Subjects, that their
Brethren have a sense of the Duty they owe to God; that all those
who are appointed to have the Care of their Souls should attend to
Discharge that trust; and the Regim^t. to which You belong being
to winter in these parts, I can not longer admit of Your absence
from the Same; You will therefore immediately upon the receipt
hereof, Set out for, and with all possible Diligence, repair to this
place, in order to remain with them & duly to Discharge the
Office, You have taken upon You by Your Acceptance of the
Commission You Enjoy . . .[63]

WO/34/85 fol. 123

226
Major-General Jeffery Amherst to Colonel Ralph Burton

Montreal
[Copy in Secretary's hand]   23 September 1760

Since my Instructions to You of the 16th Instant by which You are
recommended, in cases of Necessity, and untill the King's pleasure
shall be know, to Guide Yourself in the Governing the People over
which You preside, by the Military Law, and as much as is
consistent with safety and prudence, to let those people Settle
their Differences among themselves and agreable to their own
Laws and Customs.

Since that I have made a little Alteration which I am of Opinion
will Answer, and I have accordingly Instructed Govr Gage to
follow it, untill the King shall be pleased to Order any Other
Form; and You will in like manner Observe the Same within Your
Government, untill His Majesty shall otherwise direct. It is as
follows:

That with respect to Thefts & Murder, it is absolutely necessary
the Military Law should take place: but with regard to differences
between the Inhabitants, I would, as I Observed before, have them
Settled among themselves, and by their own Laws; for which

purpose You will Authorize the Several Captains of the Militia, to preside over the different Parishes & Districts to which they belong; and to terminate all Such Differences. And when it shall so happen that any of these Captains cannot Settle the same; then the Parties must Apply to the Officer Commanding His Majesty's Troops within the said District, to whom You will give such Limited Power as You Judge proper for his Examining and pronouncing thereon, according to the best of his Judgement; but if the Affair Should prove so Intricate, as to make him decline the Decision, the Same is then to be brought before You, that Either thro' Yourself, or with the Advice of Councill (Consisting of as many Captains as You shall think proper, which You will Assemble for that purpose as often as You shall see Occasion) You may finally Determine thereupon.

This is the Plan laid down to Govr Gage with this difference only, that his Councill is to Consist of Field Officers: and, that same Form may take place throughout the whole Country, I propose leaving the same Instructions with Govr Murray.

With my former Instructions, You likewise received a Copy of my Orders to the Officers Employed in Administring the Oath of Allegiance, & in Collecting the Arms; by which, You will have seen, that they were also to Ask for the Commissions under which the Militia Officers Acted, & that I should grant them Others in their Stead: this likewise has met with some Alteration: as I think it better that the Field Officers and Captains of Militia should Act by the Authority of the Governors immediately Presiding over them, and I have therefore Authorized Govr Gage to Grant them within his Government, agreable to the Form I have given him thereof, of which You herewith have a Copy, that You may in like manner grant them within Your Government, Observing to keep in Place those that Acted under the French King, & that have delivered up their Commissions . . .

I also Send You my Proclamation to the People of the Country,[64] which I need not Enlarge upon, as it is very full of itself; It has been published, and Affixed in this Town, and is to be so in Every parish and District of the Government, for which purpose I Send You One Copy of it, that You may likewise Cause it to be published and Affixed throughout Your Government, Observing to fill up the Blank left for the day upon which they are to bring in their Arms, which will Vary according to the Distances, and cannot therefore be fixed but by You.

WO/34/7 fols 217–18

227
Major-General Jeffery Amherst to Governor Brigadier-General James Murray

Montreal

[Copy in Secretary's hand]   23 September 1760

Altho' it is next to Impossible that any thing can, in the Course of this Ensuing Winter, be attempted against His Majesty's Acquisitions in Canada, Yet to leave nothing to Chance; I have for the Defence and Protection of the Same, made the following Disposition of the Troops; viz'; Under Your Command & within Your Government of Quebec; the following Batt^{ns}, Amherst's; Townshend's; Otway's; Kennedy's; Lascelles's; Anstruther's; Murray's; Lawrence's; & Fraser's; with a Detachment from the Royal Regiment of Artillery of two Companys under the Command of a Major.

Under the Command of Colonel Burton within the Government of the Trois Rivieres, Webb's Regiment, and a Detachment from the Artillery of one Subaltern and twenty three men of the above two Company's.

And under the Command of Brig^r General Gage within the Government of Montreal, Barrington's; two Battalions of the Royal Highlanders, Abercromby's, Thos Murray's; fourth Battalion Royal Americans; and Gage's; with a Detachment of a Field Officer, a Captain, four Lieut^s and Seventy One Sergeants, Corporals, and men of the Royal Regiment of Artillery.

All which Undoubtedly are more than sufficient to frustrate any Attempts that the Enemy can be supposed able to Undertake: I nevertheless have Directed both Brig^r Gage and Colonel Burton, to support You in case of necessity; as You will, in like manner them, if occasion Should require it; Wherefore and the better to thwart any Designs the Enemy might form, it will be necessary, that You all three Correspond, and Co-operate together; and reciprocally give each other all the Information & Intelligence You may receive, to enable one another the better to Carry on His Majesty's Service, and Your respective Commands. This I have particularly recommended to them, and I must do the same to You.

And as You have Informed me, that You had not hitherto received any Instructions from His Majesty for the Administration of Your Government and that I cannot approve of the French Form, that has been proposed to me, nor Yet leave the Country entirely without; I have formed a Plan by which to Govern them (untill His Majesty's Pleasure thereupon be known) which appears to me most Just and Equitable, and I have accordingly directed that it Should take place, both in this and in the Government of Trois Rivieres; and as the Whole Country Should be on the same footing, and under one and the same Regulations: I must also recommend it to You to follow the same form, untill You receive Your Instructions from the King, or untill His Majesty's pleasure hereupon Shall be known . . .[65]

WO/34/3 fols 25–6

228
Captain Anthony Wheelock to Major-General Jeffery Amherst

New York
25 September 1760
[Holograph]   [Received 11 October 1760]

By your Excellency's Letter of the 9th Instant I apprehend all the Prisoners are to be sent to Europe, except such whose Cases are particular.[66] – On this Occasion 'tis very likely /some desertion will ensue especially among those who have Wives & Children in Canada: It has already began among the Regulars, three of whom have absented themselves from the Prison and it is likely the

Canadians will be more tempted to it, as they are better acquainted with the Country & have stronger Motives to induce them to continue in it.

When it comes to be known that they are to go to Europe, (in order to be exchanged) I foresee that several of the Canadians will offer to pay the Provision & Ransom money rather than leave their Families – ~~and~~ I should be glad of your Excellency's Directions in that Particular.

The Number of Prisoners, (besides those who I hear have taken the Oaths,) appears by /^{my} Books to be 555 of which 233 are Regulars 147 of the Marine & 175 of the Militia – How many /^{are} gone away in Flags of Truce, or have otherways deserted, I cannot ascertain till they are ordered to be collected; but it is likely that upon a Muster they may not exceed 500 – This is exclusive of the Prisoners taken this Year by Your Excellency, who are not yet arrived from Albany but are Expected every Tide . . .

WO/34/98 fols 77–8

229
Lieutenant-Governor William Bull to Major-General Jeffery Amherst

Charles Town
19 October 1760
[Duplicate in Secretary's hand, signed by Bull]   [Received 26
November 1760]

. . . Soon after Colonel Montgomery departed, I received an account of the Surrender of Fort Loudoun, reduced to the last three days provisions, on a Capitulation, agreed on the 8th of August, The Articles whereof were; the Fort and Military Stores to be faithfully delivered to the Savages, and the Garrison to be permitted to march with the Honors of War safe to Fort Prince George; Peace and Trade to be restored. The Letters from the Commander Captain Demere acquaints me; that the Savages were desirous of Peace, and that nothing but that Disposition could have saved the Garrison, praying that nothing might be

235

undertaken here, that might endanger the Garrison on their March. This was received the 20th day of August by Express. The day on which an Act was passed here, for raising a Regiment of Eleven hundred men, to carry the war with Vigour, into the Cherokee Country, as the only means to procure an Honorable and lasting Peace.

Upon this Intelligence, I was advised the 22d of August, to send messages to the Indians, to signify my Readiness to accept their Overtures, and that they might come safely down to treat; and I forbore to issue the Commissions for raising the Regiment. But about fourteen Days afterwards, I received accounts, that the Indians had fallen upon the Garrison at Day break, about Sixteen miles from Fort Loudoun, and killed Captain Demere of the Independants; Lieutenant Adamson of the Provincials; Ensign Bogges of the Independants; and Ensign Wintle of the Provincials (Captain Stuart of the Provincials was protected, and delivered to the little Carpenter). They killed twenty five privates and three women. This was said by them to be done in Revenge for their warriors confined at Keowee, and killed there last February. The remainder of the Garrison was distributed among the Over Hill Towns. On the 27th of August they in a Grand Council determined to make the English Prisoners assist in transporting over the Mountains, some of the Cannon, and a Cohorn to Besiege and Batter Fort Prince George, where Governor Lyttelton last December carried and left Six Thousand Weight of Powder, Ball in proportion, and a large Quantity of Guns and Woolens suitable for Indians, which he shewed to them after his Treaty, as Goods intended for them. These Goods, they say, they will take by Force, and if they make Peace they expect them to be delivered up as their own property.

In these Circumstance of danger and doubt, which I have had the Honor to lay before You, it will appear how much we stand in need of your Excellencys powerful assistance . . .

WO/34/35 fols 174–8

230
Captain Robert Prescott to Major-General Jeffery Amherst

London
21 October 1760

[Holograph]   [Receipt not dated]

On delivering your dispatches to Mr Pitt the 6th Inst^t, I was agreably surprised to find Major Barré had arriv'd the day before with the News of the Conquest of Canada,[67] believe me 'twas with the utmost pleasure I heard it, and I most sincerely congratulate you on your Success.

I last Sunday paid my Respects to Mrs Amherst, who is perfectly well, Captn Amherst[68] is in Gloucestershire . . .

On finding you had finished the Campaign with the Reduction of all Canada, I thought the opportunity of being with Mr Pitt was not to be lost of hinting your desire to be recalled, he told me your Presence in America was now absolutely necessary, and would be so 'till a Peace was concluded, was lavish in his Encomiums, and still hoped if the War continued to have an opportunity of employing you; In obedience to your directions I wait his Comands.

WO/34/83 fol. 130

231
Field Marshal Viscount John Ligonier to Major-General Jeffery Amherst

London
21 October 1760

[Secretary's hand, signed by Ligonier]   [Received 31 December 1760]

I take the earliest opportunity of congratulating You most sincerely on your late extraordinary and glorious Success, which has made the Publick in general and your Friends in particular exceeding happy.

When you have finish'd the business which must necessarily arise from such a Conquest made, I hope We shall have the pleasure to see You once more in England where no one will be more happy to receive you than myself.

I think it proper to acquaint You that Major Barry since his arrival here, has strongly solicited the Rank of Lt Colonel as he has acted in the Capacity of Deputy Qua^r Mas^r Genl under Mr Wolfe at the Siege of Quebec. The Commission He had for this Department advances Him from Lieut: to the Rank of Captain in the Army, and to that of Major in N^o America only. From Hence I confess I do not see what pretensions he can have to the Rank he ask's, especially when I reflect that it is in the last Year only that he got the rank of Captain; but if what he ask's, is what you shall think proper to request for Him, it is possible his Majesty may show Him this very distinguish'd mark of his favour: However this Affair is not intirely determin'd.[69]

U1350/O/35/25

232
Major Isaac Barré to Major-General Jeffery Amherst

London
22 October 1760
[Holograph]   [Received 2 January 1761]

After a very fine passage of 21 days & a few hours, I arrived in London the 5th Instant at day break. The news was received with greater joy than I expected, which was owing to Germany's not producing any Minden or other action of Eclat to blast our American Laurels. I was presented to the King, Prince &^{c}, & being the freshest post boy was asked many questions, & treated with so much attention, that I was vain enough to think myself a man of some consequence.

After Mr Pitt had got all the Information he desired, I met him at Court, where he assured me of his immediate protection, Telling me that he thought it due to a man of so much merit, A man whom he knew to be much esteem'd by ye late Mr Wolfe, And one whom he now saw highly honour'd by Mr Amherst, whose services to his Country were so glorious & important. I was however desired by him, first to apply in the proper channels of Office; I obey'd, & found Ld Barrington (who by a disagreement with Wolfe was originally my enemy,) now by your recommendation, the more determined to prevent my promotion. Lord Ligonier at first said I ought to have the rank, He soon changed his mind, & join'd the War Office.

When I had the honour of receiving your dispatches I expected to find London in peace, at least could not suspect that I was to have a winter's campaign: However, so it was to be, & such were the forces on each side . . . My Enemys reproach'd me with being a young Captain – If I had merit, the reproach on that head was surely theirs. I took the Commission of D.A.G on lower terms – Was that to preclude me from higher honours if my General thought I deserved them? Lord Colvill spoke highly in praise of Captain Deane, while Mr Amherst dispatches Maj. Barré without the least mark of applause. – G^l Amherst never publishes Panegyriecks on his officers, but recommends them to the Ministers at War. This last objection & answer hurt me much; When the attention of the publick was high, what was said of the two messengers seem'd to place me in an indifferent or cold situation, much to my disadvantage. Even Mr Pitt said that if you desired that I should have preferment, you ought to have recommended me to his protection in your public letter.

I am often reproach'd by the merit of the Officers serving in Germany: An American war is unfashionable with such people, & therefore it required firmness to oppose them. I told my Lord Ligonier, (who seem'd excessively moved with the sufferings of some Minden Heroe)[70] that I believed it was not known in England, but I could affirm it as a truth, that we really bled when we were wounded in N. America. Any Seam or Scar got in that Country is call'd a mark of honour, when the same in a poor American is /^{either unnoticed or} supposed to be got by inoculation . . .

Sunday last, I waited on Mrs Amherst, who is a little impatient. Really, Sir, your living in that house argues great foresight; You have too much virtue to continue any time in an exalted Station amidst the present depravity, & therefore content yourself with a mansion which would suit the old Roman Dictator much better than a modern Conqueror of an Empire . . .

WO/34/83 fols 134–5

233
Major Isaac Barré to Major-General Jeffery Amherst

London
29 October 1760
[Holograph]   [Received 31 December 1760]

[Barré had had a second interview with Mr Pitt about being promoted to Lieutenant Colonel]

. . . The rest of his conversation was on the public business, the whole of it I am bound in Duty to inform you of.

He seem'd to over rate the N°. of troops in N. America, yet he said it was not clearly his opinion that a sufficient body could be spared from a vast conquer'd country to carry on ulterior operations; Yet some people differ'd from him. The Mississippi, says he, is a difficult step; The Season for carrying on Land operations there, is attended with such Storms in Navigation, that the Seamen will probably object to such a Plan. The Mobile is rather the easiest of the two, is not in any posture of Defence, & might be subdued by a small Corps; The Object is not very considerable, yet it may affect the neighbouring Indians, & besides *cela arrondit nos Colonies*, (an Expression somewhat like *le Droit de Bienseance* of Louis the 14th).

He ask'd whether you would go upon any Expedition of this kind, hinting it could be done by an inferior Officer, I told him I did not know, but could affirm so far, that I was sure you thought no Corps of Troops inferior to your Command provided you expected to be useful to your Country.

Martinico he mention'd, & thought it could be taken by carrying on the war there in a new method; That is, not to attack their principal Fortress, but land elsewhere, & try by ravaging the rich Settlements, to force the natural discontent of the inhabitants, to work out a Capitulation to save their immense property. – I told

240

him that my Idea of that Country was, that it was mountainous, & of course furnish'd abundance of good Posts, which might be maintain'd by very few /regular troops, to whom the common danger would certainly unite for a time, the People of the country. His answer was, that he had certain Intelligence that the Inhabitants were discontented, would certainly tremble for their riches & of course betray their country.

His schemes of the above sort must be put in execution early, And indeed he desired me to stay for his further dispatches,[71] Adding that I could serve my Country by Staying with him . . .

WO/34/83 fols 156–7

234
Frederick Post to Major-General Jeffery Amherst

Bethlehem
30 October 1760
[Holograph]   [Received 13 November 1760]

I hope Your Excelency has rec'd from our Governor a full information of my late Journey, as also my reason for not sending & Delivering the message to the Indians, indeed I doubted their Doing it faithfully & as Your Excellency had entrusted me with it, I prepared the Belts & send them & the message, to General Monckton; all suited for the Purpose. Next Sir I rejoice & heartily thank the Lord Jehovah for the happy Success with which he has crowned your Excellency in Overcoming the common Enemy in Canada, and bringing them to a Reasonable Subjection under the Crown of England. May the Lord God continue to do so with you & stretch out his hand in Battle before you that fear & trembling may come on the Enemy, so that they may fly before you, and may his Angells be about your Encampment, wherever You move, till you accomplish the happy effect of a General Peace. – Although I am no military Person, nor chosen for that Part, yet my Spirit & Prayer to the Lord God has been with you; And I count myself as one of the least of his majesties Subjects, yet thank God he gave me that Resolution, not to think my life & health too Precious to venture them unto the hazard & fatigue of going among the Indians, in order to Reconcile them to the King & Country's Interest. I am also tolerably recovered of the fall I got on my journey toward New York, this Spring. – And as I believe that the intention of the Crown of England, through this Conquest, is to open a Door for the Servants of our Lord Jesus Christ, to Declare & Proclaim to the Poor heathen & others Salvation & Redemption, through his Incarnation, Bloody Suffering & Death on the Cross, for us poor mankind. I hope also to have my share & Part in that Glorious message of the Lord, whose Servant I am, & in to whose harvest I am ready to enter, & hope at least to see the Indians Civilized & reconciled to the Christian Religion & British Interest by the privilege & Power of hearing the Gospell & that will be to me a Great Reward.

But one thing Particular I would begg leave to lay before your Excellency: that Should the Indians any time or place be calld to a Publick meeting or treaty, it will (with submission) be for the Publick good & blessing, as well as the British honour, that it be insisted on that the Indians Deliver up all our People who are Captives among them, as I am informed by Indians that the Senecas has many Captives in their Back Towns, where they will suffer no person willingly to Pass, for fear of Discovering it. It is my humble oppinion it Should be Solemnly, requested, & insisted, of the whole five nations to Deliver up all the Captives they have belonging to us, and their Doing it or not will have its proper influence, & Example, for other Nations, to act accordingly.

And indeed, to me, it appears a Scandal to Christianity, to Permit or Suffer our flesh & Blood to be made & used as heathen by the Indians for they have already forc'd many, to marry with them; Although they first stole them away from us, & I doubt not But the Indians will readily Answer, they are not willing to come from amongst us, But Give me leave to add, it may very justly, be insisted & demanded of them, to bring every living Person Down, to such meeting or treaty & then /^{the} white People, may speak free & without fear, for themselves. & those who refus'd to bring down their Captives to be Declared as Enemies, & then every thing woud appear in its true light. For should it be said it may secure them best in our interest, in letting them keep & marry those Captive women, I answer its no otherwise than making the poor women slaves to such Indians, & giving them a liberty to mock & Ridicule at our holy Christian Religion . . .

WO/34/83 fols 158–9

235
Memorial of Johan Herehiemer to Major-General Jeffery Amherst

Albany
2 November 1760
[Holograph]   [Receipt not dated]

That your Memorialist, begs leave to Congratulate your Excellency on Your Safe return to this City, after Reducing **All Canada** to his Majesty's Subjection; for which he Sincerely wishes that your Excellency may receive Rewards Adequate to the Service done. And also to return your Excellency his Hearty thanks, that he is (by your Excellency's Order) again in Possession of his House (late Fort Hereheimer). – And also begs leave to remind your Excellency of your Promise to see him Justice done for the great Devastation done, on his House and Farm; Capt. Gates Having Cutt down an Orchard of upwards one hundred bearing Apple Trees, and a Young Orchard of about as many more beside Burning the Barn and other Outhouses, and all the Fences: So that the Damage he hath Sustain'd is insupportable; All the Hire that he hath Receiv'd for the House is not sufficient to Repair that, to the State it was in when taken from him: And as his Confidence in your Excellency's known goodness in the Administration of Justice & Relieving the Distress'd (tho' your Excellency had not Promised to See him Justice done) Emboldens him to Commit the Same to your Excellency's **Wise** Consideration . . .

WO/34/83 fol. 164

243

236
Major-General Jeffery Amherst to Brigadier-General
Robert Monckton

Albany

[Copy in Secretary's hand] 3 November 1760

. . . I join in opinion with You, that wherever the Navigation will admit of it, a Vessell is every way preferable to Batteaus; and I am very Glad, You Ordered Colonel Bouquet to build one; so soon as I knew Your Intentions, which was thro' Major Walters sometime ago, I ordered the latter to furnish Colonel Bouquet, with all the Naval Stores he might require, and what the Magazine of Niagara was deficient in to have recourse to those of Oswego, where I likewise send Directions to furnish Whatever they Could.

A small Blockhouse Such as You mention at Le Boeuf, is full sufficient there indeed Since the Capitulation, by which Detroit is to be in our possession, all our Posts within that Communication may be small, & the Numbers in each very few . . .[72]

There is no Guarding against the Treachery of the Indians; so long as they have any Connections with the French, we may Expect that they will Scalp, or Carry off any Single man or Small party, that will Expose themselves to their Villainy: but I am apt to think that so soon as we are in possession of the Detroit, Your Communication will be entirely free and safe; as then they will have no body at whose Door to lay their Guilt, and must Expect the punishment due to their Crimes, which upon Conviction they must meet with; and by Such treatment only will it be possible to Deterr them from Evil, and keep them within due Bounds.

Thus You see, Sir, we perfectly agree in our way of thinking concerning these Savages, who doubtless cannot be trusted; indeed there need not [be] a more Glaring proof of it, than that Inhuman breach of the Capitulation of Fort Loudoun, of which I have not received any Accounts from Authority, till that You have now transmitted me in the Extract of Colonel Bird's Letter;[73] and tho' I saw it in the Publick Papers, I was willing to hope it was without foundation: more particularly so, as I had Conceived no

244

Idea, that one of the King's Forts, could yield to a parcell of Miscreants, without Artillery, or Apparatus capable to Reduce it, if properly defended . . .[74]

I see with pleasure that Major Rogers had Joined You, and that You had Sent him on with Capt Campbell; the party You sent with them is full sufficient to Carry my Instructions into Execution . . .

Under the present Circumstances of Affairs, if the Season will not allow of Garrisoning the Posts of Michillimackinack, St Joseph, and others, I shall be under no Anxiety for them, as that of the Detroit will sufficiently answer every purpose . . .

WO/34/43 fols 151–3[75]

237
Major-General Jeffery Amherst to John Calcraft

Albany

[Holograph copy]   6 November 1760

. . . The time for elections coming on makes me think it not impossible, that from the success of His Majesty's Troops in this part of the world some Freeholders & Burgesses may be induced to chuse the Commander as their Representation.[76] If such an intention should appear I must beg you will decline it for me in the beginning with my acknowledgements, & thanks for the honour designed me, for which I am as much obliged to them as though I accepted it, I am likely providing against what will not happen, but my precaution would not surprise you, if you knew how much I should dislike it, & no Person, Place or manner by which the offer may be made can alter my determination on that affair . . .[77]

WO/34/99 fol. 150

238
Major-General Jeffery Amherst to Lieutenant Spearing

Albany

[Copy in Secretary's hand]   7 November 1760

Your letter of the 2^d Instant was delivered to me Yesterday; the request it Contains for leave to go to England, is what I should not willingly Grant, as I think it not right for Officers to be Absent from their Corps, or the Duties of them: besides I have already some time since wrote to Capt. Gates, that he was to Compleat his Company, and that he should Inform me which of his Officers, he intended to Send on that Service, I must therefore wait his Answer, if it Should not fall to Your Lot, and that it is absolutely necessary You should go to England (and unless it is, I dare say You would not Desire it) as I would not willingly Refuse You, I shall Grant You leave to go.

WO/34/85 fol. 200

239
Memorial of Hans Feeling to Major-General Jeffery Amherst

Schenectady

20 November 1760

[Secretarial hand, signed by the memorialist]   [Receipt not dated]

That your Memorialist's Waggon was on the sixth day of august in the year of our Lord one thousand seven hundred and fifty eight pressed in his majesty's service by Mr Hendrick Fry Junr and ordered up to Fort Stanwix there to transport his Majesty's Stores over the Carrying place – That after the said waggon had been employed in the Service aforesaid Eleven days was discharged by Coll. Bradstreet. But immediately repressed at the said place to forward the works of Fort Stanwix, where the said Waggon continued for Twenty nine days Longer when Christophur Young your Memorialists Driver of the said waggon was taken sick so as to render him unfit for Service – Whereupon one Mr Williams Ingineer at that place, discharged the said Driver, but retained the

246

said Waggon (which said discharge your Memorialist is ready to produce to your Excellency if required) tho before the Driver obtained the said Discharge both his horses were stole by the native Indians, yet he has had the Luck to get one of his horses again the following year – That your Memorialist afterwards applied to the said Hendrick Fry in order to be paid for the Service aforesaid, who told him he must make his Application to the General. That your Memorialist Later in the Fall of the same year went up to Fort Stanwix to endeavour to get his waggon again from the Commanding Officer but was confined for Twenty four hours for his request, and threatened to be confined again if he did not immediately depart from the said place – That your Memorialist's Driver received for the Service aforesaid the sum of five pounds ten shillings new York Currency which is not near the full amount for the Service aforesaid according to the Customary Rate paid by his Majesty . . .

WO/34/83 fol. 206

<h2 style="text-align:center">240</h2>

Mayor, Aldermen and Commonalty of the ancient City of New York: Address to Major-General Jeffery Amherst

New York

[Copy in Secretarial hand]   [27] November 1760

To the united Suffrages of the British world in favour of your Excellencys Distinguished Merit, The Mayor Aldermen and Commonalty of the city of New York beg Leave to add their most grateful Tribute of Thanks for the invaluable Services wrought by Your Superior wisdom, and valour in annexing the extensive Country of Canada to his Majesty's Dominions in America. An acquisition so inestimable in itself, so pregnant with the most important consequences, cannot fail to Shine with a Supreme Lustre, amidst the most Luminous Events, and Give to its author a rank Exalted in the train of British worthies. Minutely to describe the Innumerable advantages resulting from so Signal a Conquest would be a vain attempt: <u>Let Millions yet unborn mark</u>

the distinguished Blessings as they rise, and While they reap the happy fruits of your martial virtues they will not Cease to Bless the name of Amherst.

Yet that we ourselves may not seem insensible of our Happiness, permit us, Sir, to turn our Eyes to the wide extended frontiers of our many fair Colonies, over which his Sacred majesty has So long Swayed his Gracious Sceptre. How Strangely altered is the amazing Scene. There the Savage native & more Savage Canadian was lately wont to Seize the defenceless and in-offending peasant doomed with his tender wife & helpless children to the most excruciating Deaths, or a more Dreadful Captivity. Hence an universal Horror Seized the Borderers: To this Succeeded a General Dereliction, and the numerous Settlements abandoned to the Relentless fury of an insatiate foe, were soon Reduced to dismal and undistinguished Ruin. Husbandry felt the fatal Effects of such a waste of Country, and this City famous for its extensive Commerce beheld and wept the Diminution of its Staple. Thus besides the keenest Sympathy for our Suffering fellow Subjects we have acted our own sad parts in the affecting Tragedy.

But Canada is no more. The peasant may return in Security to his fields, Husbandry will soon revive, the face of Nature Smile with the Blessings of peace and this flourishing City rejoice in the plenty of its markets. This surprizing Change we attribute with the most humble gratitude to the paternal Care of our most Gracious Sovereign in appointing Your Excellency to Conduct his Victorious armies in America . . .

U1350/O/34/5

241
Major-General Jeffery Amherst: Answer to the Address of the Mayor, Aldermen, and Commonalty of New York City

New York

[Holograph draft]   27 November 1760

I return you my most sincere thanks for the address you have been pleased to make to me. It gives me very particular Pleasure that the Success of his Majesty's Arms in the Reduction of Canada has contributed so much to the Happyness of the People on this Continent, and it is my most hearty wish that this City may reap all the advantages /^{it} can desire from this Conquest, and that it may prosper & and Flourish to the latest time.

WO/34/85 fol. 216

242
Colonel John Bradstreet to Major-General Jeffery Amherst
Albany
7 December 1760
[Holograph]   [Received 13 December 1760]

I beg leave to inform your Excellency that by an Act of the Assembly of this Province all Persons employ'd to impress Carriages are made Lyable for the payment of the Hire & damages done during the time of their being in the Publick Service and that the Persons, in General, who were found proper to carry into execution this part of his Majestys Service were Poor[78] and that in so extensive a work as this has been[,] many disputes have happen'd between the Inhabitants & me for their neglect of Duty, pretended loss of Carriages & Horses with their constant endeavour to draw from the Publick more money than they were intitled to, and tho I have always endeavour'd to do them the strictest justice, & that they have seemingly been contented at Settling their Accounts still I find there are some, nay, I fear there are many whoes insatable Avarice & thirst for Oppression prompted by those whose Existence depend on discord & injustice seem determined to make a Sacrifice of many of those poor people; many of them have been Arrested & given Bael; more expect it and One is actually in Gaol & has been for some time who is an Expence to the Publick as he was in his Majestys Service when taken & put there and I am persuaded your Excellency will think it but just he remain so while in the hands of oppression & ingraditude for having done his Duty. – Your Excellency is Sensible neither gratitude to the King; the

249

Benevolence of their Mother Country nor regard to their own safety could induce the Principal part of the Inhabitants upon Hutsons & the Mohawk River to give the necessary Assistance which was absolutely wanted & could not be dispens'd with and which they had in their power to give to enable his Majestys Troops to penetrate into Canada and that what Carriages & other things was had from them was obtained chiefly against their consent; what have not those poor People to apprehend from those who have acted such an ungrateful & unnatural part, that pay no regard to their being sav'd from a Cruel & Barbrous Enemy and being Sett down with their Families in Ease, Plenty & Security and indulge themselves with being spur'd on by a Nest of Harpies whoes rapacious Claws extended wait with impatience to lay hold of them. – As these People have acted under me and to my certain knowledge have only done their duty; my honor & Conscience with my Duty to his Majesty, the Publick & you, Sir, Command me to lay this their unhappy fate before you for protection.

WO/34/57 fol. 167

243
Major-General Jeffery Amherst to Lieutenant-Colonel James Grant

New York

[Copy in Secretary's hand]   15 December 1760

The Correction the Cherokees had received from Colonel Montgomery and the Troops I had put Under his Command for that purpose had made me hope, that those Savages, sensible of the weight of His Majesty's Arms and Displeasure, would of Course have Renounced their Erroneous Connections, and have Sued for that peace, under which only, in the present Circumstances of their perfidious Allies, they can Enjoy that tranquility and plenty, which it is so much their true Interest to Sollicit and Render themselves deserving of: Nevertheless soon after Colonel Montgomery quitted Charles Town, on his Return to this place, they repeated their Hostilities against Fort Loudoun, and notwithstanding the most Solemn Engagements to protect the Garrison and to Conduct them in safety to Fort Prince George, they, on their march Inhumanely butchered the Commanding Officer with Several Others, dragging the remainder into Captivity: and all this whilst these Barbarians, were actually Sueing for peace, & that measures were Concerting by the Legislature of the Province to agree thereto.

These Repeated Enormous outrages (of which, however, I had no Certain Intelligence, till the middle of last month) calling aloud for the most Exemplary Vengeance I immediately Resolved to Send such a Force to South Carolina as would at the same time not only be sufficient to Chastise the Cherokees, for this new breach of Faith, but also to reduce them to the absolute necessity of sueing for Pardon, and Effectually to put it out of their power of Interrupting the Peace, which it may hereafter be thought Expedient to grant them.

And as from Your Zeal for His Majesty, as well as Your Experience, and the great share you have had in the operations Carried on by Colonel Montgomery, against these perfidious Savages, I am Confident You will Exert Yourself, to Your utmost, effectually to bring about the above desired purposes; I have therefore thought proper to Entrust You with the Command of the Body of Troops destined for that Service, which are to Consist of:

Two Battalions of the Independent Companys lately arrived from England each Composed of Four Hundred and Forty Men Officers Included; The Light Infantry of Monckton's & Whitemore's Regiments, with another Company from each of the said Corps all Compleat, some Mohawk & Stockbridge Indians Attached to Capt Kennedy Commanding Monckton's hat [sic] Company; and the four Companys of the Royal already in Carolina at present under the Command of Major Hamilton . . .

WO/34/48 fols 39–45

244
Jacob Van Schaick to Major-General Jeffery Amherst

Albany
20 December 1760
[Holograph]   [Receipt not dated]

Last Week I arrested Lieut. Coventry upon a Supreme Court writ, he rushed into his Room, and Seized a pistol, and swore if I came a step nearer he would blow my brains out, and abused me Grossly with his tongue – and kept me off from further prosecuting the arrest. – I am obliged by my oath and office to serve the Kings writs in this County, my life and fortune are in danger from the resistance I meet with from the Gentlemen of the Army. I am compelled to desire your Excellencys favour to put a stop to these proceedings, and that Lieut. Coventry may be obliged to give bail to the action as the Law requires.[79]
P.S. the day after he was arrested he sent me Six Soldiers and two days after three more with their wives and Children, It is with pain I can live in my house, I beg redress from your Excellency.

WO/34/83 fol. 266

Epilogue
Amherst's Subsequent Career,
1761–97

The war for Amherst did not end with the fall of Montreal but continued for another two full years. During this time, as Commander-in-Chief on the North American mainland, he was responsible for organising or supporting various expeditions to the Caribbean, notably those against Martinique in 1761 and Havana in 1762. Even with the signing of peace at the end of 1762 Amherst still had to remain in America to implement the new peacetime military establishment and it was while doing this that a serious war with the Indians broke out, traditionally known as Pontiac's Rebellion. As a result his homecoming was not quite the triumph it originally promised to be. Other disappointments followed. By 1768 the ministry wanted a resident governor in Virginia who was on hand to bring that unruly colony to order. Since Amherst was still unwilling to live in America, he was effectively dismissed in favour of Lord Botetourt. His response was to resign all his positions in the army and the rift was only partially healed by his appointment as Governor of Guernsey in 1770 and the restoration of his regimental honours. However as the disputes with America deepened, Amherst was drawn back into military affairs, though he twice refused the command there, for reasons that are not entirely clear. But after the disaster at Saratoga and threat of invasion in England, he accepted Ligonier's old position as Commander-in-Chief in Britain with a seat in the Cabinet. But he had little effect on American policy, where he wanted to end the rebellion by means of a naval blockade. The defeat of Cornwallis at Yorktown and dismissal of the North ministry should have been the end of Amherst's public career, but in 1793, on the outbreak of the French Revolution, though now seventy-six years of age, he was again appointed Commander-in-Chief in Great Britain. He held the position for just two years, being finally succeeded by the Duke of York. However, in recognition of his many services he was subsequently promoted field marshal in July 1796, but died the following year on 3 August 1797.

The slightly equivocal nature of Amherst's legacy was reflected in his obituary in the *Gentleman's Magazine*. This began with the obligatory patriotic assertion that 'the name of Sir Jeffery Amherst was as much dreaded by the enemies of Great Britain as it was revered by his countrymen . . . No ostentation of heroism marked any of his actions; the whole of his conduct evinced the firm simplicity of a brave mind, animated by the consciousness of what was due to himself and to his country.' The comment 'what was due to himself', however, led the writer also to note: 'it has been said that he was induced, by the sweets of office, to retain his situation longer than his strength permitted the active execution of its duties' and that 'he occasionally employed the patronage of his situation in promoting his friends'. Nevertheless, at a time when military heroes were few, the magazine concluded: 'The laurels he reaped will for ever flourish round his tomb.'[1]

Appendix
British Regiments or Battalions
serving in North America, 1758–60

1st or Royal Regiment (St Clair), 2nd Battalion
15th Amherst
17th Forbes
22nd Whitemore
27th Blakeney (Enniskillen)
28th Bragg
35th Otway
40th Barrington
42nd Royal Highland Regiment (Lord John Murray), 1st Battalion
42nd Royal Highland Regiment, 2nd Battalion
43rd Kennedy
44th Abercromby
45th Warburton
46th Thomas Murray
47th Lascelles
48th Webb
55th Prideaux (Oughton)
58th Anstruther
60th Royal American Regiment, 1st battalion (Stanwix)
60th Royal American Regiment, 2nd Battalion (Prevost)
60th Royal American Regiment, 3rd Battalion (Lawrence)
60th Royal American Regiment, 4th Battalion (Monckton/Murray)
77th Montgomery
78th Fraser
80th Light Infantry (Gage)

Four New York independent companies
Three South Carolina independent companies

Biographical Notes

Position after the name and date of birth indicates the rank held on first mention in the text.

Abercrombie, James (1732–75), Captain of the 42nd Foot Regiment. Lieutenant 1st Foot 1744; and Captain 42nd Foot 1756. Appointed ADC to Amherst in May 1759. Promoted Major of the 78th Regiment in 1760 and sent to the Marquis de Vaudreuil with the articles of capitulation that September. Went on half pay when his unit was disbanded in 1763, returning to active service in 1770 as Lieutenant-Colonel of 22nd Regiment. Killed at Bunker Hill.

Abercromby, James (1706–81), Major-General and Commander-in-Chief in North America from December 1757 to September 1758. Ensign 1717, Captain of the 1st Foot 1736, and Colonel 1746. Came to America in 1756 and commanded the land offensive against Canada in 1758 but recalled after his setback at Ticonderoga. Promoted Lieutenant-General in 1759 and made Governor of Stirling Castle in 1772.

Adair, John (?–1799), Surgeon. Served with the Port L'Orient expedition in 1746, before coming to America with Braddock in 1754. Appointed Director of the Hospital with Monckton for the expedition to Martinique in 1761. Retired on half pay 1766.

Amherst, John (1718–78), Captain of the *Captain* 64-gun warship and younger brother of Jeffery Amherst. Served with Boscawen in North America 1755, with Byng in the Mediterranean 1756, before returning to North America in 1757 and 1758. At Belleisle in 1761 and Gibraltar 1762. Promoted Rear Admiral in 1765 and Commander-in-Chief at Plymouth in 1776.

Amherst, William (1732–81), Captain of the First Foot Guards and brother of Jeffery Amherst. Ensign First Foot Guards 1753, Captain 1757. Appointed Deputy Adjutant-General with the rank of Lieutenant-Colonel in America only for the 1759 campaign, serving in the same capacity in 1760 as a full Lieutenant-Colonel. He commanded the expedition to recapture St John's Newfoundland in September 1762 and was made Governor of Newfoundland as reward. Promoted Colonel in 1766, Major-General in 1777, and Lieutenant-General in 1779.

Appy, John (?–1761), Secretary to Amherst and Judge Advocate General. Previously secretary to James Abercromby. Died 14 October 1761.

Apthorp, Charles Ward (dates unknown), New York banker, agent for the English specie contractors, John Thomlinson and John Hanbury.

Atkin, Edmund (?–1761), Agent and Superintendent of Indians Affairs for the Southern Department. According to his wife, the Crown owed him £2,000 at the time of his death in October 1761 for carrying on the service.

Babcock, Henry (1736–1800), Colonel of the Rhode Island Regiment. First appointed Captain of a company in Colonel Christopher Harris's Regiment in 1755. Later retired to Stonington in Connecticut.

Barré, Isaac (1726–1802), Lieutenant in the 32nd Foot and Adjutant-General to Wolfe's Quebec expedition in 1759 with the rank of Captain in America only. Born in Dublin of Huguenot family, he first secured an Ensigncy in the 32nd Regiment in 1747 and then Lieutenancy in 1755. Served with Amherst in 1760, taking news of the fall of Montreal to London, for which he was eventually promoted Lieutenant-Colonel of the 106th Regiment in January 1761. He then went into Parliament, but spent most of his parliamentary career in opposition, with only short spells in office.

Barrington, William Wildman, Viscount (1717–93), Secretary at War. MP for Berwick-upon-Tweed 1740–54, Lord Commissioner of the Admiralty 1746–54; MP for Plymouth 1754–78, Secretary at War 1755–61, Chancellor of the Exchequer 1761–2, Treasurer of the Navy 1762–5 and Secretary at War 1765–78.

Barrow, Thomas (dates unknown), Deputy Paymaster General. Came to America with Braddock in 1755. Appointed commissioner for settling the accounts for the 1758 campaign in Pennsylvania. Later paymaster at Quebec until 1772 when he succeeded James Mortier as Paymaster.

Bastide, John Henry (c. 1700–70), Colonel of Engineers. Ensign in the 11th Foot 1711, Lieutenant 1718, Engineer in charge at Guernsey 1726–39, Chief Engineer at Annapolis Royal 1740, Engineer in Ordinary 1744. Bastide was present at Louisbourg in 1745 and later made Chief Engineer at Minorca 1754–6. He was commissioned Lieutenant-Colonel in 1757, on the recognition of the Engineers as a branch of the military. Made Chief Engineer in 1758 with Amherst at Louisbourg, where he remained until the dismantling of that fortress. Promoted Major-General in 1761 and Lieutenant-General in 1770.

Beckwith, John (dates unknown), Major of the 44th Regiment. Ensign in the 8th Foot 1742, serving in Flanders and Scotland during the 1745 campaign. Promoted Captain of the 44th Foot in 1748 and Major in 1758. He came to America in 1755, being present at the Monongahela in 1755, Ticonderoga in 1758 and Niagara in 1759, after the fall of which he was temporarily appointed commander. Breveted Lieutenant-Colonel in June 1762.

Bougainville, Louis Antoine de (1729–1811), French Colonel. Commanded a corps above Quebec during the 1759 campaign. After the war he entered the French naval service and became a distinguished explorer, discovering the New Hebrides and New Caledonia Islands. Served with Admiral de Grasse during the War of American Independence.

Bouquet, Henry (1719–65), Lieutenant-Colonel of the first battalion of the Royal American Regiment. A Swiss soldier of fortune, he achieved the rank of

Lieutenant-Colonel in the Dutch service during the War of the Austrian Succession. Bouquet came to America in 1756 as a Lieutenant-Colonel of the 60th Regiment, serving first in South Carolina and then with Forbes in the 1758 campaign to capture Fort Duquesne. Breveted full Colonel in June 1762, he led the relief force to Pittsburgh in 1763, fighting a notable tactical battle with the Native Americans at Bushy Run. Later he commanded one of the armies sent westwards to pacify the Indians in 1764. Appointed Brigadier-General and commander of the southern American district in 1765, he died shortly after his arrival in Pensacola.

Bourlamaque, Francois Charles de (1716–64), Senior French officer. Second Lieutenant 1740, Lieutenant 1742, Captain 1745, and Colonel in 1756, when he accompanied Montcalm with his regiment to Canada. Present at the siege and capture of Oswego 1756; Fort William Henry 1757; and the defence of Ticonderoga 1758. He commanded the force which opposed Amherst's advance in 1759 and led the advance guard of Levis's army at Quebec in 1760. Returned to France on the surrender of Montreal. Promoted Major-General and Governor of Guadeloupe in 1763.

Braddock, Edward (1695–1755), Major-General and Commander-in-Chief in North America 1755. Ensign in the Coldstream Guards 1710, Lieutenant 1716, Captain 1736, Major 1743, Lieutenant-Colonel 1745, Colonel of the 14th Foot 1753 and Major-General in March 1754. Appointed commander of the 1755 expedition against Fort Duquesne, during which he was mortally wounded.

Bradstreet, John (1714–74), Lieutenant-Colonel and Deputy Quartermaster General. Born in Nova Scotia, he began his military career in 1735 as a volunteer and then Ensign of the 40th Foot. Present at the siege of Louisbourg in 1745, he served as Adjutant to Governor William Shirley during the ill-fated attack on Niagara in 1755 with the rank of Captain in the 51st Foot 1755. An Aide-de-Camp to Lord Loudoun, he secured a Captain's commission in the 2nd Battalion of Royal Americans in 1757. Subsequently appointed Deputy Quartermaster General by Abercromby with the rank of Lieutenant-Colonel, a position he held for the remainder of the war, until promoted full Colonel in 1762. He later commanded one of the armies sent to suppress the Native Americans led by Pontiac. Promoted Major-General in 1772.

Brehm, Dietrich (dates unknown), Lieutenant of the 60th Foot and acting Assistant Engineer. Lieutenant in the Royal American Regiment 1756. Placed in charge of the works at Ticonderoga after its capture in 1759. Accompanied Major Henry Gladwin to Detroit in 1761 and was present during its siege by Pontiac. Promoted Captain in 1774 and Major in 1785.

Brown, John (dates unknown), Captain in the Royal American Regiment and in charge of 'his Majesty's Teams at Schenectady'. Lieutenant in 1756, being promoted Captain in 1760. He later served at Niagara.

Browning, William (dates unknown), Major of the 46th Foot Regiment. Captain 1747, and Major in 1757. He was made commanding officer at Fort Stanwix in 1759 with responsibility for protecting the communication to Oswego.

Promoted Lieutenant-Colonel in 1761. Temporarily in command at Niagara during the war with the Indians.

Bull, William (1710–91), Lieutenant-Governor of South Carolina. A member of a wealthy planter family, Bull trained as a doctor, but followed his father into public life, serving as Lieutenant-Governor and acting Governor five times from 1759–75.

Burton, Ralph (?–1768), Lieutenant-Colonel of the 48th Foot Regiment. Obscure origins but had become a Lieutenant-Colonel by 1754 when he came with Braddock to America. Served with Amherst at Louisbourg in 1758, and with Wolfe at Quebec in 1759. Helped Murray with the defence of Quebec in 1760 before being appointed Governor of Trois Rivières on the fall of Montreal. Promoted full Colonel in December 1760 of the 95th Foot, he served on the expedition to Havana in 1762 before returning to Trois Rivières. He subsequently succeeded Gage as Governor of Montreal but was recalled to England in 1766 following disagreements with Murray over the role of the army in Canada.

Calcraft, John (1726–72), Regimental Agent for the 15th Foot, Amherst's Regiment. Enjoyed close ties with the War Office and other government departments through the patronage of Henry Fox, which gave him access to various ministers. He also held several other agencies. Amherst granted him powers of attorney before his departure for America in 1758 so that he could deal with regimental business during his absence. Served as MP for Calne 1766–8, and Rochester 1768-72.

Campbell, Alexander (dates unknown), Major of the 77th Foot Regiment. Captain of the 1st Foot 1753 before securing a Major's commission in 1757. He commanded the Regiment while Colonel Montgomery was fighting the Cherokee. Promoted Lieutenant-Colonel in March 1761, later Colonel and Deputy Governor at Fort George (Inverness) 1771.

Campbell, Donald (?–1763), Captain of the 1st Battalion Royal Americans. Born in Scotland of obscure origins, he secured a Lieutenancy in the 1st Battalion of the Royal Americans in 1756, and Captaincy in 1759. Accompanied Rogers on his expedition to Detroit in September 1760. Killed by the Indians besieging Detroit in June 1763.

Christie, Gabriel (1722–99), Major and Deputy Quartermaster General. Captain of the 48th Foot 1754. He came to America with his Regiment in 1755. Appointed Assistant DQMG under Bradstreet for the 1759 campaign, then DQMG with Gage for the western offensive. Breveted Lieutenant-Colonel in June 1762 of the second battalion Royal American Regiment. He remained in Canada until 1777, when he was promoted Colonel of the 60th. After the War of Independence Christie settled once more in Canada to become a landowner, but continued to rise in seniority, being promoted Major-General in 1781 and General in 1798.

Colden, Cadwallader (1688–1776), President of the New York Provincial Council and acting Lieutenant-Governor from August 1760. Born in Ireland of Scots ancestry, he studied medicine in London before coming to Philadelphia in 1710. Made Surveyor General of New York in 1720 and a member of the council in 1721. Author of numerous botanical, philosophical and historical works, most notably his *History of the Five Nations* (1727). He remained a staunch supporter of the imperial authority until his death at the outbreak of the Revolution.

Colebrooke, Sir James (1722–61), merchant and MP for Gatton. A member of the partnership which took over responsibility for supplying the army with provisions in March 1760.

Colville, Lord Alexander (1717–70), commander of the naval squadron wintering at Halifax. Served in the West Indies and Mediterranean during the 1739–48 war, being posted for the first time in North America with the *Northumberland* in 1753. He accompanied Boscawen in 1755 to America and acted as commodore at Halifax on the return of Admiral Holburne to England in 1757. He led the relief squadron to rescue of Quebec in May 1760. Promoted Rear Admiral in 1762, he resumed command of the North American station in 1763 until 1766 when he returned to England.

Coventry, George (dates unknown), Lieutenant of the 55th Foot and Assistant Deputy Quartermaster General. Commissioned an Ensign in 1755 and Lieutenant in 1758. He was Promoted Captain of a New York independent company in September 1761 but resigned from the service in April 1763 for private reasons.

Croghan, George (?–1782), Deputy Agent for Indian Affairs in the northern department. Born in Dublin, Croghan came to Philadelphia in 1741, where he engaged in the Indian trade, becoming proficient in the Delaware language. He accompanied Braddock as an interpreter in 1755 and in 1756 he was appointed Deputy Agent to Sir William Johnson. In 1763 he requested permission to retire following losses incurred during his service with the department, but was sent later in 1765 to the Illinois country to receive the surrender of Pontiac and other Indian leaders.

Dalling, John (dates unknown), Major of the 28th Foot Regiment. Captain 4th Foot 1753, then Major 28th Foot in 1757, before serving at Quebec in 1759 and the subsequent defence of that city. Promoted Lieutenant-Colonel of the 43rd Foot in 1760, transferring to the 36th Foot in 1767. Appointed Colonel of the 3rd Battalion of the Royal American Regiment in 1776. Made a Major-General in 1777.

Danks, Benonie (c. 1720–76), Captain of a Ranger company in Nova Scotia, which he raised after the reduction of Beausejour in 1755. Served with Major Scott at Quebec and was wounded. Also at Havana with Major Goreham. Retired at the end of the war, to become a member of the Nova Scotia Assembly in 1765.

Darby, John (dates unknown), Lieutenant-Colonel of the 17th Foot Regiment. Captain of 17th Foot 1748, Major in 1756, and Lieutenant-Colonel in 1759. He commanded briefly at Albany in the summer of 1761. Made a Colonel in 1772.

D'Arcy, Peter (dates unknown), Captain of the 47th Regiment and Aide-de-Camp to Amherst. Given his Captaincy in 1758. He returned to England in October 1762, after selling his commission.

Deane, Joseph (dates unknown), Captain of the *Lowestoff* 24-gun frigate, one of three vessels to relieve Quebec in May 1760. Commodore at Halifax from 1766.

De Lancey, James (1703–60), Lieutenant-Governor of New York. Member of a wealthy Huguenot family, he trained as a lawyer in England before holding various legal positions in New York, including that of Chief Justice in 1733. Promoted Lieutenant-Governor in 1753, which position he held till his death on 30 July 1760.

De Lancey, Oliver (1718–85), Colonel and senior officer of the New York forces. Member of one of the wealthiest New York families, De Lancey prospered in commerce, before turning his attention to the raising of men for the war effort. He commanded the New York Regiments at Ticonderoga in 1758. However early in 1760 he decided to join his brother-in-law, John Watts, as one of the New York agents for the supply of provisions to the British army in America. From 1760 he was a member of the Provincial Council and raised various loyalist units for the Crown during the Revolution. He died in exile.

Denny, William (dates unknown), Lieutenant-Governor of Pennsylvania. A former army Captain, he arrived to take up his appointment in 1756, returning to England in 1759, having helped negotiate the various peace treaties with the western Indians at Easton.

Du Quesne, Marquis de (*c.* 1700–78), Governor of New France, 1752–5. Served many years with the French navy before going to New France. Established the important post at the Forks of the Ohio which bore his name until its capture by Brigadier John Forbes in November 1758.

Durell, Philip (1707–66), Rear Admiral. Joined the navy as an ordinary seaman in 1721. Promoted able-seaman in 1724, Lieutenant in 1731, and Captain in 1743. Present at siege of Louisbourg in 1745 and the second battle of Finisterre in 1747. Raised to Rear Admiral of the Blue in 1758. He commanded the squadron left at Halifax in the winter of 1758 and was blamed subsequently for being too slow in the spring of 1759 to prevent succours reaching Quebec. Appointed Port Admiral at Plymouth in 1761 and Commander-in-Chief in North America in 1766 but died shortly after arriving.

Eyre, William (?–1765), Lieutenant-Colonel of the 44th Foot. Began his career as a Practitioner Engineer in 1744, serving at Bergen-op-Zoom in the Netherlands in 1747. He subsequently acquired a commission as a Captain in the 44th Foot in 1747 and accompanied his Regiment to America early in 1755. He was immediately seconded to assist Sir William Johnson in his advance on Lake George as acting Quartermaster and Engineer, for which he was subsequently promoted Major in January 1756. Advanced Lieutenant-Colonel in 1758, he was appointed acting Engineer at Ticonderoga in 1759 before being sent to Niagara to succeed William Farquhar. He accompanied Amherst in the advance on Montreal in 1760, returning to Niagara that autumn. He drowned on his way home to England in 1765.

Farquhar, William (?–1759), Lieutenant-Colonel of the 44th Foot. Previously Major of the 15th Foot 1754. He was promoted Lieutenant-Colonel in 1759, and was sent to command at Niagara after its capture, where he died on 11 October 1759.

Fauquier, Francis (c. 1704–68), Lieutenant-Governor of Virginia. Member of an English banking family, Fauquier was a director of the South Sea Company before going to Virginia early in 1758. A relatively popular Governor, he survived despite the later tribulations of the Stamp Act controversy and died while still in office at Williamsburg.

Fitch, Thomas (c. 1700–74), Governor of Connecticut. A member of a prominent family from the town of Norwalk, Fitch graduated from Yale intending to be a lawyer, but in 1726 he was elected to the Connecticut Assembly. He was first chosen Deputy Governor of Connecticut in 1750 and then Governor from 1754 until 1766, when he failed to secure re-election following the Stamp Act controversy, a measure which he reluctantly had to uphold.

Forbes, John (1710–59), Brigadier-General and commander of the southern area. Joined the army as a cornet in the 2nd Dragoons (the Scots Greys) in 1735, being promoted Lieutenant in 1742, Captain in 1745, Major in 1745, and Lieutenant-Colonel in 1750. He was appointed Colonel of the 17th Foot in 1757, the year he came to America and made commander of the expedition against Fort Duquesne in 1758, with the rank of Brigadier. He died on his return to Philadelphia in March 1759.

Franks, Moses (dates unknown), Philadelphia merchant and partner of Sir James Colebroke from 1760 for the supply of provisions to the army. Franks spent much of his time in London, leaving his brother David to handle the American end of the contract.

Fraser, Simon (1726–82), Lieutenant-Colonel of the 78th Highland Regiment. While still a student at St Andrews, he was summoned by his father to lead the Fraser clan for the Pretender in 1745. Though convicted of treason, he was pardoned. After practising as an advocate, he was commissioned in 1757 to raise a battalion of his kinsmen for service in America. He served first at the siege of Louisbourg in 1758, next with Wolfe at Quebec, and then with Murray during his advance on Montreal in 1760. Breveted full Colonel in 1762, he served as a Brigadier-General with the forces sent to Portugal that year. Thereafter he concentrated on his political career as MP for the County of Inverness. Promoted Major-General in 1771.

Gage, Thomas (1719–87), Brigadier-General. First commissioned a Lieutenant of the 48th Foot in 1741, Captain of the 62nd Foot in 1743, Major of the 55th Foot in 1748, and Lieutenant-Colonel of the 44th Foot in 1751, accompanying his Regiment to America in 1755 with General Braddock. He was promoted Colonel on the formation of a Regiment of Light Infantry (the 80th) in 1758.

One of a small number of officers to marry an American. Major-General 1761. Gage succeeded Amherst as Commander-in-Chief in America in 1763, a position he held until 1772 when he returned to England. On the outbreak of the American Revolution, he returned as Commander-in-Chief with the rank of Lieutenant-General, but was recalled following the setback at Bunker Hill. Made a full General in 1782.

Gamelin, Laurence (dates unknown), Captain of the Detroit militia. Gamelin was probably a member of the Montreal family of that name, who were important traders. He acted as an interpreter and go-between during Pontiac's War.

Garth, George (dates unknown), Engineer Extraordinary. Appointed Sub-Engineer with the rank of Lieutenant in 1757 and Engineer Extraordinary with the rank of Captain early in the 1759 campaign.

Gates, Horatio (c. 1728–1806), Captain of a New York independent company. He began his military career as an Aide-de-camp to Colonel Edward Cornwallis at Halifax in 1750 and accompanied Braddock on the expedition against Fort Duquesne in 1755. Later a staff officer with Monckton, he accompanied Monckton to Martinique, being promoted Major in 1762. Gates retired from the army in 1769, emigrating to Virginia in 1772, before joining the patriot cause as Adjutant-General in 1775. He was promoted Major-General in 1776 and commanded the army that defeated General Burgoyne at Saratoga in 1777. However, his military career suffered a near-fatal setback in the battle of Camden in 1780. At the end of the war he retired to his estate in Virginia, but disliking the institution of slavery, he removed to New York.

Gist, Christopher (1706–59), surveyor and frontier explorer. Born in Maryland of obscure parents, Gist served as agent for the Ohio company, before acting as guide for General Braddock in the advance on Fort Duquesne. In 1756 he went to South Carolina to help enlist the services of the Cherokee where he died of smallpox.

Gladwin, Henry (1729–91), Captain in Gage's 80th Light Infantry. Secured his first commission as a Lieutenant in the 48th Foot in 1753, subsequently accompanying his regiment to America with Braddock in 1755. Secured a Captain's commission on the formation of the 80th Light Infantry, being promoted Major in December 1760 and commander of Fort William Augustus. He was sent to command at Detroit in July 1762 and was there on the outbreak of Pontiac's War in May 1763. He successfully held the place throughout the siege, the only post west of Niagara to do so. He requested permission to return to England in 1764 and saw no further active military service. He was made a Colonel in 1777, and Major-General in 1782.

Goddard, Henry (dates unknown), Lieutenant of the 47th Foot Regiment. An Ensign in 1750, he obtained his lieutenancy in 1755, and was promoted Captain in 1761.

Goreham (or Gorham), Joseph (1725–90), Provincial Ranger Captain. Massachusetts born, he joined a Ranger company as a Lieutenant in 1744, serving at Annapolis Royal, before succeeding his brother as Captain that same year. His unit continued in service after the 1739–48 war to defend the frontiers of Nova Scotia. He joined Loudoun in 1757 and then Amherst at Louisbourg in 1758, who described him as 'a very good ranging officer . . . his company is the best of any I have seen'. The following year his company was placed under the command of Major Scott as part of Wolfe's force for Quebec. These services secured him a regular commission in 1761 as Major of that corps. In 1762 he saw service at Havana. Much of the next decade was spent seeking preferment and staving off financial problems. With the coming of the Revolution he raised a provincial corps to help defend Nova Scotia, for which he was subsequently promoted Colonel in 1782 and Major-General in 1790, the only Ranger officer to attain that rank.

Grant, Alexander (1734–1813), Lieutenant in Montgomery's 77th Highland Foot. Grant began his career in 1755 as a midshipman in the navy, before securing an ensign's commission in 1757 in the 77th Foot. His naval expertise led Amherst to place him in charge of the *Boscawen* sloop on Lake Champlain in October 1759. At the end of the war he was put in charge of the naval yard at Niagara and similarly from 1771 at Detroit. During the American Revolution he did much to retain British control of the lakes. Thereafter he held several administrative positions, being on the Executive Council for Upper Canada.

Grant, Francis (dates unknown), Lieutenant-Colonel of the 42nd Regiment. Major 1745, appointed Lieutenant-Colonel in 1755, and breveted Colonel in February 1762. He became Colonel of the 63rd Foot in 1768, a Major-General in 1770 and Lieutenant-General in 1777.

Grant, James (1720–1806), Major of the 77th Foot. Commissioned Lieutenant in the 1st Foot (Royal Scots) in 1741, Captain 1744, then Major of the 77th Foot in 1757. He commanded the advance guard of Forbes army in 1758. Promoted Lieutenant-Colonel of the 40th Foot Regiment in July 1760, he served under Montgomery in the first expedition against the Cherokee in early 1760 before leading the second expedition against the same nation the following year. Elected MP for Wick Burghs in 1773, he served as a Brigadier in America from 1775 to 1778, before accepting the Governorship of St Lucia in 1778. Promoted Lieutenant-General in 1782; and full General in 1796.

Gray, Robert (dates unknown), Lieutenant in the 55th Foot. Promoted Captain in August 1759. Later served at Oswego in 1761 and the siege of Detroit in 1763. Promoted Major in 1772.

Green, William (1725–1811), Captain-Lieutenant and Engineer in Ordinary. He began his career as a Cadet Gunner in 1737, being promoted Practitioner Engineer in 1743, Sub-Engineer in 1747, Chief Engineer for Newfoundland in 1755 and Engineer in Ordinary in 1758. He was present at Louisbourg that year, serving with Wolfe in 1759 and Murray in 1760. Appointed Chief Engineer at Gibraltar in 1770, Colonel in 1777, and Major-General in 1781, he played a crucial role in the siege of that fortress from 1779–83. He was created a baronet in 1786, Lieutenant-General in 1793, and full General in 1798.

Gridley, Richard (*c.* 1711–96), Colonel of the New Hampshire Regiment. Born in Boston, he studied British military engineering while apprenticed as a merchant, which helped him achieve the rank of Lieutenant-Colonel in the 1745 expedition to Cape Breton Island as commander of the provincial artillery. He showed particular talent organising a force of carpenters, both at Louisbourg in 1758 and Quebec in 1759. Gridley returned to civilian life after 1760 but played a key part in fortifying Bunker Hill in 1775 and assisting the siege of Boston, and is often considered the father of the United States Army Corps of Engineers.

Haldimand, Frederick (1718–91), Lieutenant-Colonel of the 4th Battalion of the Royal American Regiment. Swiss born, he saw early military service in the Dutch service, attaining the rank of Lieutenant-Colonel. In 1756 he was appointed one of the German-speaking officers to help recruit the Royal American Regiment. He served with Abercromby in 1758, being wounded at Ticonderoga. During Prideaux's attack on Niagara in 1759, he was left in charge at Oswego with orders to build a strong fort. In 1760 he commanded the advance guard for Amherst down the St Lawrence. Made full Colonel in June 1762, he was appointed commanding officer of the Floridas in 1767, being promoted Major-General in 1772, and Governor of Canada from 1778 to 1786.

Hale, John (dates unknown), Lieutenant-Colonel of 47th Foot Regiment. A Captain in 1752, promoted Major in 1755 and Lieutenant-Colonel in 1758, he served with Amherst on the 1759 campaign but returned to England at the end of that year to raised a Corps of Light Dragoons (the 18th). Made a Major-General in 1772 and Lieutenant-General in 1777.

Hamilton, Frederick (dates unknown), Major of the 2nd Battalion of the 1st Foot Regiment. A Captain of the 1st battalion in 1742, he became Major of the 2nd battalion in 1757 and Lieutenant-Colonel in 1761. He served with Montgomery and Grant against the Cherokee in 1760 and 1761.

Hamilton, James (*c.* 1710–83), Lieutenant-Governor of Pennsylvania. Son of a distinguished Pennsylvania lawyer, he trained similarly for that career, becoming a member of the Assembly in 1734, Mayor of Philadelphia in 1745, and Lieutenant-Governor from 1748 to 1754 and 1759 to 1763. He was imprisoned briefly during the Revolution, even though acknowledging the new order.

Haviland, William (1718–84), Lieutenant-Colonel of the 27th Foot (Enniskillen Regiment). Began his career as an Ensign with the 43rd Foot in 1739, before becoming Captain in the 27th Foot in 1742, Major in 1750, and Lieutenant-Colonel in 1752. He came to America in 1757 and was present at the attack on Ticonderoga with Abercromby in 1758. He led Amherst's advance guard in the 1759 offensive against Ticonderoga, before enjoying his own command the following year. Promoted Colonel of the 3rd Battalion of the Royal American Regiment in December 1760, he accompanied Robert Monckton on the expedition to Martinique as one of his Brigadiers, serving in a similar capacity at Havana the following year, after which he was promoted Major-General.

Made a Lieutenant-General in 1772, Haviland returned to active service during the American Revolution, first as a member of Amherst's staff, then as commander of the western district. He was promoted full General in 1783.

Hazen, Moses (1733–1803), Captain of Rangers. Served at Crown Point in 1757, at Louisbourg in 1758, at Quebec in 1759, and with Murray in 1760. Accompanied Rogers to take possession of Detroit, before securing a lieutenancy in 44th Regiment in 1761. He settled in Quebec at the end of the war but later joined the revolutionary forces, assisting the invasion of Canada, for which he raised various locally recruited forces. Promoted Brigadier-General in the continental army in 1781.

Howe, William (1729–1814), Lieutenant-Colonel of the 58th Foot Regiment. Began his career as a cornet of horse in the Duke of Cumberland's light dragoons in 1746, promoted Lieutenant in 1747, Captain in the 20th Foot in 1750, Major in the 58th Foot in 1756, and Lieutenant-Colonel in 1759. Present at the siege of Louisbourg in 1758, he served with Wolfe at Quebec, where he commanded the light infantry, and remained with Murray during the subsequent siege and advance on Montreal. At Belleisle in 1761, he was breveted Colonel in 1762 before becoming Colonel of the 46th Regiment in 1764, and Major-General in 1772. He succeeded Gage as Commander in Chief at the start of the War of American Independence with the rank of Lieutenant-General, but resigned after the disappointing outcome of the 1777 campaign. Made full General in 1793.

Hughes, Philip (dates unknown), Chaplain to the 44th Foot Regiment, to which he had been appointed in 1752.

Hutchinson, Thomas (1711–80), Lieutenant-Governor of Massachusetts. A member of a wealthy Boston merchant family, he graduated from Harvard in 1727 for a career in commerce. He entered the House of Representatives in 1737, being elected speaker from 1747 to 1749, before becoming a Judge of the Common Pleas in 1752 and Lieutenant-Governor in 1758. Always a strong advocate of the royal prerogative, he later played a key role in the events leading to the Revolution in Massachusetts. Ordered to London in 1774, he died in exile.

Jacobs, Cheeksonkaun (dates unknown), Captain of a company of Stockbridge Indians. He served from 1757 to 1760 in the several campaigns against the French and their Indian allies.

Johnson, John (?–1759), Colonel of the New Jersey Regiment. First appointed to the command of the New Jersey forces in 1758, he served at Ticonderoga that year, but was subsequently killed during the siege of Niagara in 1759.

Johnson, Sir William (c. 1715–74), Colonel of the New York provincial forces and Superintendent of the Northern Indian Department. Johnson came to America in 1738 and settled on the Mohawk river, becoming a successful landowner, trader, Indian agent and justice of the peace. He was appointed Colonel of the militia in 1748. At the start of the Seven Years' War he commanded the expedition against Crown Point, defeating the French under

Baron Dieskau near Lake George in 1755, for which he was knighted. The following year he was appointed Superintendent for the northern Indian Nations, with responsibility for mobilising Indian support, which he did successfully in 1759 for the expedition to Niagara and 1760 for the advance on Montreal. After the war Johnson played a key role in imperial policy regarding Indian affairs until his death.

Kennedy, Quinton (dates unknown), Captain of the 80th Light Infantry Regiment. Commissioned an Ensign in the 44th Foot 1748, a Lieutenant in 1755. He was employed for a time by Johnson in the Indian department before securing a Lieutenancy in Gage's Light Infantry in December 1757. He was captured while attempting to carry dispatches for Amherst to Wolfe in August 1759. Served later in the West Indies on the expedition to Martinique.

Kilby, Christopher (dates unknown), Contractor for the supply of provisions to the army. In partnership with William Baker, MP for Plympton Erle. Kilby was an American by birth and handled that end of the business.

Lawrence, Charles (c. 1709–60), Brigadier-General and Colonel of the 3rd Battalion of the 60th Regiment. Commissioned an Ensign in the 11th Foot in 1727, Lieutenant in 1741, Captain in 1742, and Major in 1747, the year he came to America to serve at Louisbourg. He was promoted Lieutenant-Colonel in 1750 of the 40th Foot, becoming Acting Governor of Nova Scotia in 1753 and Governor in 1756. He commanded a brigade at Louisbourg in 1758, thereafter returning to be Governor of Nova Scotia, where he died in October 1760.

Leake, Robert (dates unknown), Commissary of Stores and Provisions. He entered the Commissary in 1730 and came to America with Braddock. In a memorial to Amherst dated 16 November 1763, he asserted that although he had been in the service thirty-four years, he had been unable to save anything to sustain his family, for whom he craved a few thousand acres.

Legge, Francis (c. 1719–83), Captain of the 46th Foot Regiment. Ensign in the 35th Foot in 1741, Lieutenant in 1754, Captain of the 46th Foot in 1756, and Major in 1767. Appointed Lieutenant-Colonel of the 55th Foot and Governor of Nova Scotia in 1773.

Le Roux, Bartholomew (dates unknown), Colonel of the first New York Provincial Battalion. First appointed Lieutenant-Colonel of the second battalion in 1758, being wounded at Ticonderoga. He served on the 1759 expedition against Niagara before being promoted Colonel of the first battalion for the 1760 campaign with Amherst.

Levis, François (1719–87), French General and second in command to Montcalm. Entered military service in 1735, spending much of his early career in Germany. He came to Canada in 1756 and commanded the advance guard at Fort William Henry in 1757. He helped with the defence of Ticonderoga in 1758 and was subsequently promoted Major-General. He helped thwart Wolfe at the falls of Montmorency in 1759, but was then sent by Montcalm to aid the defence of Montreal, following the loss of Niagara. On Montcalm's death he became Commander-in-Chief and succeeded in defeating Murray in the second battle on the Heights of Abraham, but could not save the colony. Levis later served in Germany. On the return of peace he served as Governor of Artois. Although he did not see active service again, he was created a Marshal of France in 1783 and a Duke in 1784.

Little Carpenter, Attakillakulla (*c.* 1700–*c.* 1778), Cherokee Chief. A consistent supporter of peace with the British after a visit to London in 1730, he led the delegation that finally signed a treaty in September 1761. He later joined the patriot cause during the Revolution, raising a Cherokee regiment of 500 in support.

Loring, Joshua (1716–81), naval officer. Born at Roxbury, Massachusetts, Loring began his naval career in privateering before obtaining a lieutenant's commission in 1745. On the outbreak of the Seven Years' War he was appointed an agent for transports in America but quickly extended his interests to the inland waters and was subsequently given the position of 'Commissary for building and Expediting the Vessels and Boats for the several Lakes', a position he held for the rest of the war. On the signing of peace he bought an estate in Roxbury, but fled to England on the outbreak of the Revolution.

Lottridge, John (?–1763), New York Ranger Captain. He began his career as a 2nd Lieutenant in an Albany militia company, but joined the Indian service in 1758 with responsibility for one of the Stockbridge companies. He was promoted Captain in 1758 after serving with Bradstreet in the expedition against Fort Frontenac. He accompanied the expedition to Niagara in 1759 and was with Amherst in 1760. He died while exploring Lake Champlain.

Lyman, Phineas (1715–74), Colonel and commanding officer of the Connecticut provincial forces. Studied law at Yale, becoming successively a militia Captain and member of the Provincial Assembly and Council. He was second-in-command to Johnson in the 1755 Lake George campaign, serving thereafter on the same front under various commanders. He was present in 1759 at Ticonderoga, where he was responsible for supervising the reconstruction of that fort with the rank of Major-General. He later accompanied Lord Albemarle in the capture of Havana. Spent the latter years of his life in various land ventures.

Lyttelton, William Henry (1724–1808), Governor of South Carolina. Matriculated from Oxford in 1742 and was called to the bar at Middle Temple in 1748, becoming MP for Bewdley from 1748 until 1754, when he was appointed colonial Governor. It was Lyttelton's ill-advised detention of the Cherokee peace chiefs which precipitated the attack on Fort Loudoun in 1760. He returned to England in 1760 to become Governor of Jamaica. Appointed to be ambassador to Portugal in 1771, he was raised to the peerage in 1776.

Mackneill, John (?–1762), Captain in the 42nd Foot. Commissioned Captain in 1752, he commanded the advanced guard of his Regiment at Ticonderoga in July 1758, losing 41 killed. He was promoted Major in 1761 but was killed at Havana.

Marsh, James (dates unknown), Captain in the 46th Foot. First commissioned Captain in 1757, later promoted Major in 1773, Lieutenant-Colonel of the 43rd regiment in 1776, and Colonel in 1782.

Massey, Eyre (1719–1804), Lieutenant-Colonel of 46th Regiment. Ensign in 27th Foot 1741, Captain 1747, and Major 1755. He came to America in 1757, being promoted Lieutenant-Colonel of the 46th in 1758. He served with Prideaux in 1759 and Amherst in 1760 and subsequently accompanied the expedition to Havana in 1762. After the war he served at New York, Quebec and in Ireland, being promoted Colonel in 1773 and Major-General in 1776, when he was made commander at Halifax. Promoted full General in 1796.

Mercer, Hugh (1725–77), Lieutenant-Colonel of the 3rd Pennsylvania Regiment. Born in Scotland, he studied medicine at Aberdeen and fought for the Pretender as a surgeon's mate, fleeing to America in 1747. He practised medicine on the frontier, before securing a commission in one of the Pennsylvania volunteer corps, rising to Colonel of the 3rd battalion in 1759. He was left in command of Pittsburgh by Brigadier John Forbes. In 1775 he received a commission in the continental army as Brigadier, being killed at the battle of Trenton while leading the advance guard.

Monckton, Robert (1726–82), Brigadier and Colonel Commandant of the 4th Battalion of the Royal American Regiment. Lieutenant in the 3rd Foot Guards 1741, Captain of the 34th Foot 1744, and Major 1747. Appointed Lieutenant-Colonel of the 47th Foot in 1751, when Monckton was posted to Nova Scotia with his Regiment. He commanded the force that captured the French fort of Beausejour in 1755, after which he was appointed Lieutenant-Governor of Nova Scotia and, in 1757, Colonel Commandant of the 4th Battalion of the Royal American Regiment. Monckton served as one of Wolfe's Brigadiers on the Quebec expedition, being rewarded with the Colonelcy of the 17th Regiment. He was promoted Major-General and Governor of New York in 1761, the same year that Amherst appointed him to command the expedition to Martinique. He returned to England in 1764, becoming Governor of Berwick in 1765, and Lieutenant-General in 1770. He played no part in the War of Independence other than as Governor of Portsmouth from 1778 till his death.

Moncrieffe, Thomas (dates unknown), Lieutenant of the 50th Foot. Lieutenant 1754, Aide-de-camp to Amherst during the 1759 campaign, he was promoted Captain of the 55th Regiment in 1760. As Major of brigade, he carried dispatches to Gladwin at Detroit during the siege by Pontiac in 1763. He secured a Captaincy of the 59th Foot in 1768.

Montcalm, Louis-Joseph, Marquis de (1712–59), commander of the French forces in Canada, 1756–9. Born of an old noble family, he began his military career as Ensign in the Regiment de Hainaut; becoming Captain in 1729, Colonel of the Auxerrois Regiment in 1743, Brigadier in 1747, and Major-General in 1756, on being appointed to the Canadian command. He led expeditions to capture Oswego in 1756, Fort William Henry in 1757, and successfully defended Ticonderoga in 1758. Killed in the battle on the Heights of Abraham in 1759.

Montgomery, Archibald (1726–96), Lieutenant-Colonel of the First Highland Regiment or 77th Foot. Major of the 36th Foot 1751, he was appointed to command the 77th Highlanders on their formation in 1757. He accompanied Forbes on his expedition against Fort Duquesne in 1758 and commanded the expedition against the Cherokee in 1760. Appointed Colonel of the 51st Foot in 1769, the same year he became the eleventh Earl of Eglinton. Promoted Major-General in 1772, Lieutenant-General in 1777, and full General in 1796.

Montresor, James (1702–76), Lieutenant-Colonel of Engineers. First appointed Artillery Matross at Minorca in 1727, then Practitioner Engineer at Gibraltar in 1731. Montresor first came to America as Chief Engineer with Braddock in 1755. He was given army rank of Major in 1757; and made a Lieutenant-Colonel in 1758. During the 1759 campaign he remained at Fort William Henry (Fort George) to secure the Army's line of communication when Amherst advanced on Ticonderoga. He returned to England in the spring of 1760. Chief Engineer at Chatham in 1769, and full Colonel in 1772.

Montresor, John (1736–99), Lieutenant of Engineers. Eldest son of Colonel James Montresor, whom he accompanied to America in early 1755. Promoted Practitioner Engineer in 1758, he served with Amherst at Louisbourg, Wolfe at Quebec (with the rank of Sub-Engineer), and Murray in the advance on Montreal. He was employed subsequently at Detroit during the Indian war. In 1765 he was advanced to Engineer Extraordinary and Captain Lieutenant. Later he served as Chief Engineer during the first half of the War of Independence, but returned to England in 1779 and retired from active service. He died in prison for debt.

Morris, Arthur (dates unknown), Lieutenant-Colonel of the 17th Foot. Major 1751, then Lieutenant-Colonel in 1756, but either died or left the service early in 1761.

Mortier, Abraham (?–1772), Deputy Paymaster General in North America.

Munster, Herbert (dates unknown), Major of the 4th Battalion Royal American Regiment. Captain 1755, promoted Major 1758. Breveted Lieutenant-Colonel in June 1762, but placed on half pay in 1763.

Murray, Alexander (c. 1715–62), Major of the 45th Foot. Ensign in the 17th Foot 1739, Lieutenant in the 6th Foot 1740, Captain in the 45th Foot 1742, and stationed at Louisbourg from 1746 to 1748. Promoted Major in 1755 and breveted Lieutenant-Colonel in America only for the 1759 Quebec campaign. Made Lieutenant-Colonel of the 55th Regiment in 1760.

Murray, James (1722–94), Brigadier and Lieutenant-Colonel of the 15th Foot. Second Lieutenant of Marines 1740, Captain in the 15th Foot 1741, Major 1750, and Lieutenant-Colonel 1751. Murray came to America with his Regiment in 1758, serving first with Amherst at Louisbourg and then with Wolfe at Quebec. Made Governor of Quebec on the capture of that city, he succeeded Monckton in November 1759 as Colonel Commandant of the 4th

Battalion Royal American Regiment. He was defeated on 22 April 1760 in the second battle on the Heights of Abraham, but successfully defended the city until the arrival of the British fleet. He then led the advance up the St Lawrence River on Montreal in co-operation with Amherst and Haviland. He remained thereafter as Governor of Quebec until his return to Britain in 1766. Promoted Major-General in 1772, and Governor of Minorca in 1778, he organised the defence of Fort St Philip on that island from August 1781 until February 1782. Made full General and Governor of Hull in 1783.

Napier, James (1701–99), Director of the Hospital and Chief Surgeon. Served as a surgeon in the Low Countries during the War of Austrian Succession, before coming to America with Braddock in 1755 as Director of the Hospital there. Appointed Inspector General of the regimental infirmaries from 1762 to 1766, and Superintendent of all hospitals in North America for the period 1777 to 1781. Knighted 1778.

Ogilvie, William (dates unknown), Captain in the third New York Regiment and Commanding officer at No. 4.

Ord, Thomas (dates unknown), Major of Artillery. Appointed Captain in 1746, Major and then Lieutenant-Colonel in 1759. Ord commanded the artillery with Amherst at Ticonderoga and Crown Point.

Pitt, William (1708–78), Secretary of State for the Southern Department. Cornet of Horse 1731, MP for Old Sarum 1735–47, Paymaster General of the Forces 1746, MP for Seaford 1747–54, MP for Aldborough 1754–6, and Bath 1757–66. Secretary of State for the Southern Department, including responsibility for North America, from October 1756 to April 1757 and from June 1757 until October 1761, when he resigned over the issue of war with Spain. He was raised to the peerage in 1766 as Lord Chatham and promoted Lord Privy Seal and head of the ministry, but retired from office in October 1768 because of ill health. Made only intermittent appearances in public thereafter.

Post, Christian Frederick (1710–85), Moravian missionary. Arrived in America in 1742, working first with the Mohicans, Iroquois and then Delaware Indians, his second wife being of the latter nation. Post played a key role in the peace process that culminated in the Treaty of Easton in 1758. After further missionary work among the Ohio Indians, he went to Nicaragua to work with the Mosquito Indians.

Pouchot, Pierre (1712–69), French military engineer. Appointed Second Lieutenant of the de Bearn Regiment in 1734, and Captain in 1744. Pouchot came to America with his regiment in 1755, being appointed commander at Niagara in 1756, and Fort Levis in 1760. Killed in Corsica.

Pownall, Thomas (1722–1805), Governor of Massachusetts. Member of an old Cheshire family, Pownall came to America in 1753 as Secretary to the Governor of New York. Appointed Lieutenant-Governor of New Jersey in 1755, he also acted as secretary to Lord Loudoun on his arrival in 1756 before receiving the appointment at Boston the following year. Pownall later wrote extensively about the relationship between Britain and America. Elected MP for Tregony in 1767, and Minehead from 1774 to 1780.

Prescott, Robert (1726–1815), Captain in the 15th Foot. Ensign in the 15th Foot 1745, Lieutenant 1748, and Captain 1755. Appointed Aide-de-Camp to Amherst in May 1759. Promoted Major in the 95th Foot in 1761 and Lieutenant-Colonel of the 72nd Foot in 1762. Saw extensive service during the American War of Independence. Promoted Colonel in 1777, Major-General in 1781, and Lieutenant-General in 1793. He commanded the expedition to capture Martinique in 1794 and became full General in 1798. Governor of Canada from 1796 to 1799.

Prevost, Augustine (?–1786), Major of the 2nd Battalion Royal American Regiment. Joined his corps as Major in 1756, and promoted Lieutenant-Colonel in March 1761, full Colonel in 1775 and Major-General in 1779.

Prideaux, John (1718–59), Brigadier and Colonel of the 55th Foot. Ensign in the 3rd Foot Guards 1739; Adjutant 1743, Captain in 1747. Appointed Colonel of the 55th Regiment in 1758, following the death of Lord Howe. Described by Ligonier as 'a very active diligent officer' on his dispatch to America early in 1759. Appointed to command the expedition to Niagara in May 1759, where he was killed on 19 July. Buried in the chapel at the fort.

Putnam, Israel (1718–90), Lieutenant-Colonel of the Connecticut forces. Born in Danvers, Massachusetts, but moved to Connecticut as a young man. Appointed Lieutenant in 1755, then Captain of a Ranger company under Robert Rogers. Promoted Major in 1758, then Lieutenant-Colonel with the Connecticut forces in 1759. He served at Havana in 1762 and accompanied Bradstreet on his 1764 expedition through the Great Lakes. Appointed Major-General in 1775 by Continental Congress, he commanded one of the divisions besieging Boston at the start of the American Revolution, playing a leading role at the battle of Bunker Hill.

Robertson, James (c. 1720–88), Lieutenant-Colonel and Deputy Quartermaster General. Began his military career as a private and then sergeant on the Cartagena expedition which enabled him to get an Ensign's commission in 1740. Promoted Captain in the 30th Foot in 1749. He came to America in 1756 as a Major in the 60th Foot, serving as Deputy Quartermaster General on the Louisbourg expedition in 1758 with the rank of Lieutenant-Colonel. He was similarly employed in 1759 for the advance on Crown Point. Amherst thought so highly of him that he refused to allow him to join Stanwix's forces in Pennsylvania. He succeeded James Murray as Lieutenant-Colonel of Amherst's own regiment, the 15th Foot, in 1760. At the conclusion of the war he was appointed commander of the detachment sent to take possession of the Floridas, Mobile and New Orleans. He commanded a brigade during the early years of the American War of Independence, enjoying the rank of Major-General from 1777. Made Governor of New York in 1779 and a Lieutenant-General in 1782.

Rogers, Robert (1731–95), Major of Rangers. Born in 1731 in Methuen, Massachusetts, he was appointed Captain of a New Hampshire company and served with Sir William Johnson during the 1755 Crown Point campaign. He received his first Ranger company from William Shirely in 1755, being breveted Major of Rangers by James Abercromby in 1758. He was described by Gage as 'a true Ranger, not much addicted to regularity', though 'a good man in his way'. Attached to Haviland's force for the 1760 campaign, he was subsequently sent to Detroit to receive its surrender following the capitulation of Canada. With the disbanding of the Rangers he was reduced to Captain of an independent company, serving first in South Carolina against the Cherokee, and then at Detroit against Pontiac. Appointed commandant at Fort Michilmackinac, he was subsequently disgraced for various breaches of discipline. During the War of American Independence he commanded a loyalist battalion. His last years were spent in poverty, debt and drunkenness.

Ross, Patrick (*c.* 1740–1804), Lieutenant of Engineers. Appointed Practitioner Engineer in 1758 for the expedition to Guadeloupe before coming to America as a Sub-Engineer in 1759. He returned to England in 1762 as an invalid, but was promoted Engineer Extraordinary and Captain Lieutenant in 1763. From 1770 he was Chief Engineer and Lieutenant-Colonel at Madras. He saw action in various campaigns there until returning to England in 1793, but returned to India in 1794. Promoted Major-General in 1797.

Ross, Robert (dates unknown), Major of the 48th Foot. Captain 1754, Major 1758 and Lieutenant-Colonel 1762.

Ruggles, Timothy (1711–95), Massachusetts Provincial Colonel. Born in Rochester, Massachusetts, he graduated from Harvard in 1732, practised the law and sat in the Assembly from 1739 to 1752. Made a Colonel of a Massachusetts regiment serving with Johnson in 1755, he was appointed Brigadier with Amherst in 1759, but left the service after the capture of Montreal, becoming a judge for Worcester County in 1762. Opposing the Revolution, he helped raise loyalist volunteers, which resulted in his banishment in 1778. He settled in Nova Scotia after the war.

St Clair, Sir John (dates unknown), Lieutenant-Colonel and Deputy Quartermaster General in the southern department. Promoted Major in 1754, he accompanied Braddock on the 1755 expedition to Fort Duquesne as DQMG. According to John Forbes he was apt to exceed his brief by interfering in matters not connected with his department. Nevertheless he was appointed Lieutenant-Colonel of the third battalion of the 60th Foot in 1756 and breveted full Colonel in June 1762, but returned to England in 1764.

Saunders, Charles (*c.* 1715–75), Rear Admiral. He began his career as a Midshipman in 1734, then First Lieutenant in 1739, serving on the *Centurion* during Anson's voyage round the world. Promoted Captain in 1744, he saw action at the second Battle of Finisterre in 1747. Elected MP for Plymouth in 1750, he was made a Rear Admiral of the Blue in 1756 before being appointed commander of Mediterranean squadron in 1757 and Vice Admiral of the Blue in 1759, when he was selected by Anson for the expedition to Quebec. He returned to the Mediterranean in 1760, being promoted Vice Admiral of the White in 1762. He served briefly as First Lord of the Admiralty in 1766 before being raised to Admiral of the Blue in 1770.

Schomberg, Alexander (1720–1804), Captain of the *Diana*, a 36-gun frigate, one of the three warships which relieved Quebec in May 1760. Lieutenant in 1747, he served under Saunders at Quebec in 1759. Present at the capture of Belleisle in 1761.

Schuyler, Peter (1710–62), New Jersey Provincial Colonel. Member of a prominent family, he commanded a New Jersey regiment in 1746 for the planned invasion of Canada and again in 1755. Captured at Oswego in 1756, he was exchanged in 1758 and served with Amherst in 1759 and 1760.

Scott, George (?–1767), Major of Light Infantry. Origins obscure but probably a New Englander by birth. Present at the capture of Louisbourg in 1745, receiving his first recorded regular commission as a Captain of the 40th Foot in Nova Scotia in 1751. He was appointed Lieutenant-Colonel of a Massachusetts battalion in 1755, but reverted to a regular commission as Major of Light Infantry for the Louisbourg campaign in 1758, and at Quebec in 1759. Given brevet rank of Lieutenant-Colonel for the expedition to Martinique in September 1761, he was made Governor of Grenada in 1762 and Dominica in 1766. He died in a duel.

Sherriffe, William (dates unknown), Lieutenant of the 47th Foot. Ensign 1751, Lieutenant 1755, promoted Captain in 1762, Lieutenant-Colonel in 1776, and Colonel in 1782.

Stanwix, John (*c.* 1690–1766), Brigadier and Colonel of the first battalion of the 60th Foot. Entered the army in 1706, rising to Captain, then Major of Marines in 1741. Promoted Lieutenant-Colonel in 1745, he was elected MP for Carlisle from 1746 to 1761. Appointed Colonel of 1st Battalion of the Royal American Regiment in 1756, he was made commander of the southern district (Pennsylvania and colonies to the south) in March 1759, and subsequently promoted Major-General that June and Lieutenant-General in 1761. He drowned on 29 October 1766, while crossing the Irish Sea.

Stirling, Thomas (1733–1808), Captain of the 1st Battalion of the 42nd Foot. Enlisted with the Scots Brigade in the Dutch service 1747–56, before securing a Captain's commission in the 42nd Foot in 1757, seeing action at Ticonderoga in 1758 and 1759, Montreal in 1760, and Havana in 1762. Promoted Major in 1770 and Lieutenant-Colonel in 1771, he served in North America from 1775 to 1780. Made a Major-General in 1782; Lieutenant-General in 1790; and full General in 1801.

Swanton, Robert (?–1765), Captain of the *Vanguard*, a 70-gun ship of the line. Acting Commodore, he led the relief of Quebec in May 1760. Towards the end of the war he served in the Caribbean and was promoted Rear Admiral in October 1762.

Thomas, John (1724–76), Colonel of a Massachusetts Regiment. Began his military career as a physician with the provincial forces. Served with the

Massachusetts forces in Nova Scotia during the 1759 campaign, and then with Amherst in 1760. Later achieved the rank of Major-General in the revolutionary forces before dying of smallpox during the retreat from Canada in October 1776.

Townshend, George (1724–1807), Colonel, later fourth Viscount and first Marquis. First commissioned in 1743, he was made a Captain of the 7th Dragoon Regiment in 1745 and Lieutenant-Colonel of the 1st Foot Guards in 1748, but retired in 1750 following differences with the Duke of Cumberland. Appointed Colonel in 1758 and Brigadier on the Quebec expedition in 1759, he was made Colonel of the 28th Regiment in November 1759 and a Major-General in 1761. He was appointed Lord Lieutenant of Ireland in 1767, becoming a General in 1782 and Field Marshal in 1796.

Townshend, Roger (?–1759), Lieutenant-Colonel and Deputy Adjutant-General. Younger brother of George Townshend. Captain of the 3rd Foot 1751, he was appointed Deputy Adjutant-General for the 1758 and 1759 land campaigns, but was killed during the investment of Ticonderoga on 25 July 1759.

Tullikens, John (dates unknown), Major in the 60th Foot. Appointed Captain in the 60th in 1755 and Major in 1757. Later acting Governor of Louisbourg in 1761 and Lieutenant-Colonel of the 45th Regiment in June 1762. Placed on half pay with the disbanding of the 94th Foot.

Vaudreuil, Pierre-François de Rigaud, Marquis de (1698–1778), Governor of New France. Born at Quebec of an old Canadian family, his father having been Governor-General before him. Vaudreuil was commissioned into the colonial regulars in 1711, made Captain in 1715, Major in 1725, and appointed Governor of Trois Rivières in 1733 and Louisiana from 1740. He returned to Canada in 1755 to take up his father's old position but found himself frequently at odds with the French military. He was subsequently tried in France for agreeing to Amherst's terms of surrender, but was cleared of all charges, and spent the last fourteen years of his life in quiet retirement.

Walters, William (dates unknown), Major in the 60th Foot. Captain in the 45th Regiment in 1747. He was present at the siege of Niagara in 1759 and later commanded there. Appointed Major of the 45th Regiment in June 1762.

Watson, Brook (1735–1807), merchant. Served as commissary to Monckton at Beausejour in 1755. Present at the siege of Louisbourg in 1758 and Montreal in 1760. Commissary General to the army in Canada from 1782. Elected MP for the City of London from 1784 to 1793. Appointed Commissary to the Duke of York 1793–95 and Commissary General in 1798. Made a baronet in 1803.

Watts, John (1715–89), New York merchant. Member of the partnership to supply provisions to the army from March 1760. Served on the Provincial Council from 1758 to 1776, when he forfeited all his estates for supporting the Crown.

West, George (dates unknown), Lieutenant-Colonel, 55th Foot? Promoted Captain in 1755, Major in 1758. Returned to England in November 1759 on receiving a commission in the First Foot Guards. Promoted full Colonel in 1766.

Wheelock, Anthony (dates unknown), Captain in the 27th Foot (Enniskillen Regiment). First received his Captain's commission in 1747. Employed in 1759 mustering the provincial soldiers of Massachusetts and New Hampshire. From the summer of 1760 Commissary for the prisoners-of-war at New York.

Whiting, Nathan (1717–71), Lieutenant-Colonel of a Connecticut regiment. Present at Louisbourg as a lieutenant with the provincial forces in 1745 and later given that rank with Sir William Pepperell's Regiment (the 51st Foot) in 1755, serving on the expedition against Crown Point under William Johnson. Promoted Major with the provincial forces in 1759, and Lieutenant-Colonel in 1760. On the ending of the war in Canada, he requested a commission with the regular army in December 1760, but seemingly without result.

Whitmore, Edward (c. 1694–1761), Brigadier-General and Governor of Louisbourg. Ensign in the 36th Foot 1710, Lieutenant 1723, Captain 1739, Major 1747, Lieutenant-Colonel 1747, and Colonel of the 22nd Foot in 1757, the year he came to America. Brigadier during the siege of Louisbourg in 1758 and then Governor. Drowned in December 1761 while sailing to Boston. Described by Amherst as 'a worthy good man'.

Willard, Abijah (1724–89), Colonel of a Massachusetts battalion. Born in Worcester County, Massachusetts, of a family with a long record of provincial military service. Served on the 1745 expedition to Louisbourg as a Captain of the 4th Massachusetts Regiment; enjoying the same rank at the siege of Beausejour in 1755. Promoted Colonel in 1756, Willard commanded a provincial battalion under Timothy Ruggles during the 1759 and 1760 northern land campaigns. Willard supported the Crown during the American Revolution, spending much of it as an assistant commissary, and subsequently resettled in New Brunswick, where he had lands.

Williamson, Adam (1736–98), Captain Lieutenant of Engineers and son of George Williamson. Cadet Gunner 1748 and Practitioner Engineer 1753, he accompanied Braddock to America in 1755. He was later promoted Engineer Extraordinary and Captain Lieutenant in 1758, being wounded at Quebec the following year. Appointed Captain of the 40th Foot in 1760, he served at Martinique in 1761 but was not promoted again until 1770 when he was made Major of the 16th Foot. Appointed Lieutenant-Colonel in 1775, he fought at Bunker Hill before returning to England in 1776. Made a Major-General and Lieutenant-Governor of Jamaica in 1791 and a Lieutenant-General in 1797.

Williamson, George (c. 1704–81), Colonel of Artillery. Commissioned Ensign of Artillery in 1722, Second Lieutenant in 1731, Captain in 1740, Major in 1747, and Lieutenant-Colonel in 1757, the year he came to America. He served successively with Amherst at Louisbourg and Wolfe at Quebec. Described in October 1762 by Amherst as a 'Brave & Good Officer', he was promoted Major-General that same year; but spent most of his remaining career at Woolwich, where he was promoted Lieutenant-General in 1772.

Willyamos, Samuel (dates unknown), Captain in the 60th Foot. He joined the 60th in 1757 with the rank of Captain.

Wolfe, James (1727–59), Major-General. Second Lieutenant of Marines 1741, Ensign in the 12th Foot 1742, Lieutenant 1743, Captain of the 4th Foot 1744, Major of the 20th Foot 1749, Lieutenant-Colonel 1750, and Quartermaster General on the Rochefort expedition in 1757. He was appointed Brigadier under Amherst at Louisbourg in 1758 and also made Colonel of 67th Foot. Breveted Major-General in 1759, he was given command of the expedition to Quebec where he was killed in the battle on the Heights of Abraham, which sealed the fate of the city.

Notes

Introduction

1 This is the version given in the *Dictionary of National Biography* and is also followed by John C. Long, *Lord Jeffery Amherst, A Soldier of the King* (New York 1933). The obituaries in the *Gentleman's Magazine & Historical Chronicle for 1797*, 800–2, and *The Times* for 5 August 1797 merely state that Amherst received his first commission in 1731 without specifying which regiment or anything else about him until he became an aide to Ligonier. It is possible that Amherst was attached as a cadet without a formal commission.

2 The traditional version is challenged by C.P. Stacey in the *Dictionary of Canadian Biography* (Toronto, 1979). Ligonier's recommendation of Amherst in 1740 is noted in Rex Whitworth, *Field Marshal Lord Ligonier, A Story of the British Army, 1702–1770* (Oxford, 1958), 46, and is based on a letter from Ligonier to Dorset, dated 8 July 1740, in the Public Record Office, London, SP/63/403.

3 For a fuller description of these events, see R. Middleton, *The Bells of Victory: The Pitt–Newcastle Administration and the Conduct of the Seven Years' War, 1757–1762* (Cambridge, 1985), 43–5.

4 *Ibid.*, 51–4.

5 He only sailed on 15 March 1758 because the Treasury insisted he accounted for his conduct of the Hessian Commissary first.

6 This view was supported by Sir Julian Corbett, *England in the Seven Years' War: A Study in Combined Strategy*, two vols (London, 1907), I, 322–8.

7 See Long, *Lord Jeffery Amherst*, 62, 67.

8 For a discussion of the tensions between the civil and military authorities during the war, see Alan Rogers, *Empire and Liberty: American Resistance to British Authority, 1755–1763* (Berkeley, CA, 1974).

9 For Bradstreet's early career and burning ambition, see William G. Godfrey, *Pursuit of Profit and Preferment in Colonial North America: John Bradstreet* (Waterloo, Ontario, 1982).

10 The bateau was a flat-bottomed craft, tapered towards each end, which was large enough to transport twenty men with provisions. It was widely used on North American rivers at this time.

11 See document 36 for Admiral Boscawen's comments on the exceptional treatment accorded to Wolfe.

12 For Loudoun's difficulties on this issue, see Stanley M. Pargellis, *Lord Loudoun in North America* (New Haven, CT, 1933), 187–210.

13 Attempts to impress in previous wars had been bitterly resisted, especially in Boston. See Douglas Edward Leach, *Roots of Conflict: British Armed Forces and Colonial Americans, 1677–1763* (Chapel Hill, NC, 1986), 134–62; Daniel A. Baugh, *Naval Administration in the Age of Walpole* (Princeton, NJ, 1965), 215–25; and J. Gwyn (ed.), *The Royal Navy and North America: The Warren Papers, 1736–1752*, Navy Records Society Publications, CXVIII (London, 1973), 261–2, 279–80.

14 The contract between Baker and Kilby with the Treasury was signed on 26 March 1756. A copy is in WO/34/69 fols 86–9.

15 For Forbes's letters to Amherst during this period, see A.P. James (ed.), *The Writings of General John Forbes Relating to his Service in North America* (Menasha, WI, 1938), 275, 283, 288–90.

16 Stockbridge was a town in western Massachusetts which had originally been established as a reservation for the remnants of the Mahican people, though other groups of refugees from neighbouring tribes had sought sanctuary there. See Bruce G. Trigger (ed.), *Handbook of North American Indians*, vol. XV, *The Northeast* (Washington, DC, 1978), 207–9.

17 The attack on Martinique was a failure, but the expedition under General Barrington did subsequently take Guadeloupe.

18 Pitt's letter is printed in Gertrude S. Kimball, *The Correspondence of William Pitt, when Secretary of State, with the Colonial Governors and Military and Naval Commissioners in America*, two vols (London, 1906), I, 432–42.

19 On 11 March 1759, in Philadelphia.

20 For an explanation of the internal politics of Pennsylvania at this time, see James H. Hutson, *Pennsylvania Politics, 1746–1770: The Movement for Royal Government and its Consequences* (Princeton, NJ, 1972).

21 For the details of Loudoun's visit, see Pargellis, *Loudoun*, 218–24.

22 A snow was a small sailing vessel, similar to a brig, but with a supplementary trysail mast.

23 Amherst to Whitmore, 29 May 1759, WO/34/17 fol. 179.

24 The contractors for the supply of specie from England were John Hanbury and John Thomlinson.

25 Paper money was disliked by British merchants who feared that they might be forced to accept payment in depreciated paper. For a discussion of this issue see Joseph A. Ernst, *Money and Politics in America, 1755–1775* (Chapel Hill, NC, 1973).

26 Montcalm had constructed these the previous year as a temporary protection for his army, which was too numerous to camp inside the fortress itself.

27 He was relatively restrained in his correspondence with Pitt too, writing just one letter after his arrival at Quebec, on 2 September 1759, printed in Kimball, *Correspondence of Pitt*, II, 149–58.

28 Amherst however made no mention of these problems a few days later when describing his naval armament to Admiral Saunders. See document 96.

29 St Francis was a missionary settlement near Montreal.

30 However Murray was certainly exaggerating the readiness of the inhabitants to accept British rule.

31 J. Clarence Webster, *The Journal of Jeffery Amherst, Recording the Military Career of General Amherst in America from 1758–1763* (Toronto, 1931), 197–8.

32 On 27 December 1759 Lyttelton wrote that he had successfully signed a peace treaty. See note 106 to this document, p. 336.

33 Printed in Kimball, *Correspondence of Pitt*, II, 216–19.

34 *Ibid.*, 237–42.

35 As an afterthought Loudoun had been given discretion in 1757 whether to attack Louisbourg before proceeding to Quebec, Pitt to Loudoun, 17 March 1757, Loudoun Papers, 3076, Huntington Library. See also Pargellis, *Loudoun*, 232.

36 Pitt had ordered the demolition of Louisbourg in a letter to Amherst on 9 February 1760, Kimball, *Correspondence of Pitt*, II, 250–2.

37 Amherst's intention of creating a diversion by the dispatch of Rogers is stated in his letter to Murray of 4 June 1760, WO/34/98 fol. 164.

38 Amherst to De Lancey, 28 July 1760, printed in C. Colden, *The Letters and Papers of Cadwallader Colden*, seven vols, New York Historical Society Publications, L–LVI (New York, 1917–23), V, 324.

39 Haviland was ready to set out just one day later, as he informed Amherst on 10 August, WO/34/51 fol. 89.

40 Webster, *Journal of Jeffery Amherst*, 227.

41 According to Amherst's Personal Journal, 1758–1762, U1350/O/14, the eight French battalions had 2,600 men and the two battalions of marines 1,168 men at the time of capitulation.

42 For the disagreements between Vaudreuil and his senior officers, see George F.G. Stanley, *New France: The Last Phase, 1744–1760* (London, 1968), 258.

43 Webster, *Journal of Jeffery Amherst*, 247.

44 For the constitutional position, see Sir William Blackstone, *Commentaries on the Laws of England* (Oxford, 1765), vol. I, 408–21.

45 Amherst's progress to Quebec and back can be followed in Webster, *Journal of Jeffery Amherst*, 255–62.

46 Under the Septennial Act, elections were due in the spring of 1761.

Section I The Campaign of 1759

1 Ligonier's secretary at this time was Richard Cox. He was also regimental agent for the 1ˢᵗ Foot Guards, of which Ligonier was colonel.

2 Usually referred to as the Royal Americans. The regiment was originally created in 1756 to attract recruits from the large German population of

Pennsylvania, for which an act of Parliament was passed allowing the commissioning of German-speaking officers. The regiment comprised four battalions, each under a colonel commandant, with an overall colonel-in-chief. Previous to Amherst the colonels-in-chief had been the Earl of Loudoun and General James Abercromby.

3 Lieutenant-Colonel William Amherst, Amherst's youngest brother. Amherst also had an elder brother, Sackville, an elder sister, Elizabeth, and a younger brother John, who was a captain in the Royal Navy. See John C. Long, *Lord Jeffery Amherst, A Soldier of the King* (New York, 1933), 9.

4 The original version of this letter arrived on 19 November 1758, along with Ligonier's letter of 15 September 1758. See U1350/O/20/7.

5 The original instructions under the royal sign manual are in the Kent Archives, U1350/O/20/8.

6 This letter can be found in Gertrude S. Kimball, *The Correspondence of William Pitt, when Secretary of State, with the Colonial Governors and Military and Naval Commissioners in America*, two vols (London, 1906), I, 354–5.

7 Forbes had been ordered to capture the strategic post of Fort du Quesne at the Forks of the Ohio River as part of the 1758 campaign. See document 7.

8 Cadaraqui was more commonly known as Fort Frontenac. Bradstreet successfully captured and burnt the place on 27 August 1758 before retreating back across Lake Ontario. See Abercromby's letter to Pitt, 25 November 1758, printed in Kimball, *Correspondence of Pitt*, I, 403–4.

9 A separate shorter letter was written to the Governors of Cape Breton, Nova Scotia, Newfoundland, North and South Carolina, and Georgia, WO/34/36 fol. 158.

10 This letter has been published in several compilations, notably in Charles F. Hoban (ed.), *Pennsylvania Archives*, 8th series, vol. VI, *Votes of the Assembly, 1756–1764* (Philadelphia, PA, 1935), 4911–12.

11 The same letter, slightly amended, was sent to Edmund Atkin, the superintendent for the southern Indian nations, WO/34/38 fol. 52.

12 This document is also printed in James Sullivan *et al.* (eds), *The Papers of Sir William Johnson*, fourteen vols (Albany, 1921–65), III, 12.

13 A similar response was received from all the colonies about keeping their men in pay over winter. See Albert C. Bates (ed.), *The Fitch Papers*, I, *1754–1758*, Connecticut Historical Society, Collections, vol. XVII (Hartford, CT, 1918), 366–7.

14 Forbes renamed his conquest Pittsburgh in honour of the Secretary of State.

15 This was an extraordinary oversight by Abercromby not telling Forbes what he should do with Fort du Quesne once he had captured it.

16 This was to be the first of many such references to the need for economy. For Amherst's early experience of military finance and accounting, see Long, *Lord Jeffery Amherst*, 36–40.

17 Field Marshal Viscount John Ligonier.

18 i.e. Major Alexander Murray.

19 Wolfe believed molasses would prove a valuable anti-scorbutic.

20 The authorship of this document is uncertain, but is almost certainly the work of Ligonier, in consultation with Pitt and Wolfe. It is also undated, but attached to the dispatches that Pitt sent on 29 December 1758. There is another copy in the Germain Papers, I, in the William L. Clements Library, Ann Arbor, Michigan. Germain at this time corresponded regularly with Ligonier, being commander of the British forces in Germany, and was privy to most of his thoughts concerning the war. For further information on the background to the planning of the expedition see Richard Middleton, *The Bells of Victory: The Pitt–Newcastle Ministry and the Conduct of the Seven Years' War, 1757–1762* (Cambridge, 1985), 98–107.

21 A copy of Wolfe's instructions can be found in Arthur G. Doughty and G.W. Parmalee (eds), *The Siege of Quebec and the Battle of the Plains of Abraham*, six vols (Quebec, 1901), VI, 87–90.

22 Burton was subsequently replaced by Colonel George Townshend, see Middleton, *Bells of Victory*, 103. The change was notified to Amherst by Lord Barrington on 1 January 1759, U1350/O/36/11.

23 Necessaries included items such as firewood and candles.

24 Amherst gave a similar answer to Governor Denny of Pennsylvania shortly afterwards when similar difficulties arose there, 13 January 1759, WO/34/32 fol. 35. For the earlier problems concerning quartering see Stanley M. Pargellis, *Lord Loudoun in North America* (New Haven, CT, 1933); and Alan Rogers, *Empire and Liberty: American Resistance to British Authority, 1755–1763* (Berkeley, CA, 1974).

25 Amherst sent an almost identical letter to Brigadier-General Governor Charles Lawrence at Halifax, WO/34/46B fol. 98.

26 See Amherst's letter to Ligonier of 18 January 1759, document 16, for the details.

27 The ministry originally planned to draft a large number of men from the regiments in England to recruit the units in North America. However in the autumn of 1758 it was decided to send the drafts as part of the expedition to take Martinique before joining the corps on the continent. See Pitt to Major-General Hopson, 13 November 1758, printed in Kimball, *Correspondence of Pitt*, I, 396.

28 Printed in A.P. James (ed.), *The Writings of General John Forbes Relating to his Service in North America* (Menasha, WI, 1938), 283.

29 This duly happened, as Governor Denny informed Amherst on 3 March 1759, WO/34/33 fol. 2. See document 37.

30 Because of disputes with the Proprietary government, the Maryland Assembly refused to make any further contribution for the remainder of the war. They were in part encouraged to do this since Maryland had few exposed frontier settlements and no western land claims. See Lawrence Henry Gipson, *The British Empire before the American Revolution*, vol. VII,

The Great War for the Empire: The Victorious Years, 1758–1760 (New York, 1949), 45–6, 143, 249, 296–7, 333. See also Aubrey C. Land, *Colonial Maryland: A History* (New York, 1981).

31 Units in the West Indies always suffered high mortality rates.

32 The Huron had long been allies of the French. Most had been scattered around the Great Lakes during the beaver wars with the Iroquois, but some had settled in a mission at Lorette near Quebec. See Bruce C. Trigger, *Natives and Newcomers: Canada's 'Heroic Age' Reconsidered* (Montreal, 1985), 259–71.

33 i.e. carrying Pitt's dispatches of 29 December 1758 to Amherst and the Colonial Governors. See Kimball, *Correspondence of Pitt*, I, 432–45.

34 The unit sent by Amherst was the 44th Foot regiment commanded by Lieutenant-Colonel Ralph Burton. See Amherst to Burton, 20 March 1759, WO/34/79 fol. 41.

35 This order to Loring concerning molasses was in response to Wolfe's request of 29 December 1758. See document 9.

36 L'Assomption was a fort on the Mississippi near modern-day Memphis and was founded in 1740 to assist the French in their war with the Chickasaw Indians. It had long been abandoned when Amherst wrote this letter. Fort Prudhomme was an even earlier structure built by La Salle during his exploration of the Mississippi in 1682. It was named after one of his captains.

37 i.e. 7,000 men.

38 Concerning a recent request of the Penobscot Indians for a peace treaty, WO/34/25 fol. 197.

39 This is the nearest that Amherst came to showing annoyance at the partiality given to Wolfe.

40 Regarding the refusal of the Pennsylvania Assembly to vote any supplies until the grievances of the inhabitants had been settled over the failure of the army to pay for its services during the 1758 campaign, WO/34/32 fol. 36. This letter of 7 March and Denny's earlier letter of 3 March first raising the subject have been published in Hoban, *Pennsylvania Archives*, VI, 4941–2.

41 However as John R. Cuneo, *Robert Rogers of the Rangers* (New York, 1959), 91–6, points out, Gage was scarcely the most disinterested commentator, given the need to justify the recent formation of his own regiment of Light Infantry.

42 The Assembly wanted to tax the proprietary estates of the Penn family. For the background to this dispute, see James H. Hutson, *Pennsylvania Politics, 1746–1770: The Movement for Royal Government and its Consequences* (Princeton, NJ, 1972), 58–61.

43 Pownall is referring here to the refusal of the Quaker inhabitants of Massachusetts to do military service, as conscientious objectors, though their numbers were very small and hardly worth mentioning.

44 Burton's regiment had previously been involved in some fracas with civilians while in winter quarters in Connecticut. See Fitch to Amherst, 25 January, 17 February, and 2 March 1759, WO/34/28 fols 23, 33 and 36. Amherst was inclined to blame the subsequent trouble in Boston on the availability of rum and was confident the inhabitants would be asking to quarter the men by the following winter, Amherst to Pownall, 18 April 1759, WO/34/27 fol. 144.

45 Regarding patronage matters, U1350/O/35/7.

46 This regiment had been quartered at Fort Stanwix on the Mohawk River.

47 Amherst to Pitt, 16 April 1759, printed in Kimball, *Correspondence of Pitt*, II, 88–90. Ligonier subsequently confessed that he did not always see Amherst's letters to Pitt and requested that in future he write more fully, 19 May 1759, U1350/O/35/11.

48 In the event Gage failed in his plea, as he reported to Amherst on 21 April 1759, WO/34/46A fol. 36.

49 i.e. for distribution to their respective platoons.

50 The dispensing of swords was not to apply to the Highlanders who were to keep their traditional claymores, see Amherst to Colonel Archibald Montgomery, 26 April 1759, WO/34/79 fol. 92. This sensible lightening of the troops' clothing followed a precedent set by Lord George Augustus Howe before his death at Ticonderoga in July 1758.

51 The actual date of this letter was 20 January 1759, in which Wolfe reiterated the need for provisions, pleading 'We shall want all the help, all the assistance you can spare', WO/34/46B fols 290–1.

52 i.e. Along the Mohawk River.

53 In the event Thomas Hutchinson, the Lieutenant-Governor of Massachusetts, managed to secure 300 pioneers as part of that colony's 1759 quota, see Amherst to Hutchinson, 30 May 1759, WO/34/27 fol. 154.

54 Hinted in Amherst's letter of 16 March 1759, see document 31. However, Amherst may have mentioned his design of attacking Niagara more fully to Stanwix when he visited Philadelphia in the second week of April 1759.

55 The Pennsylvania government, assisted by Forbes, had signed several Treaties with the Ohio Indian nations at Easton. See Francis Jennings, *Empire of Fortune: Crowns, Colonies, and Tribes in the Seven Years War in America* (New York, 1988), 274–80, 342–8, 396–403.

56 Lieutenant-Colonel Frederick Haldimand.

57 A reference to Johnson's letter to Amherst of 21 April 1759, printed in Sullivan, *Johnson Papers*, III, 27–30.

58 A snow was a two-masted sailing vessel, similar to a brig, with a mainmast, foremast and supplementary trysail.

59 Wolfe was rightly concerned that Durell should get on station as soon as possible, given his own slender resources. A number of French supply ships did get into the river, for which Durell was subsequently blamed by

historians, notably Sir Julian Corbett, *England in the Seven Years' War: A Study in Combined Strategy*, two vols (London, 1907), I, 407–14.

60 See Amherst to Johnson 19 May 1759, printed in Sullivan, *Johnson Papers*, III, 42.

61 The poor calibre of the rangers had been a complaint since the formation of the first companies in 1756, not least because of the difficulty recruiting genuine frontiersmen. One of Rogers's first companies had to enlist several Spanish seamen, Irish immigrants, and Royal Navy deserters, 'Notes on Mr Shirley's Letter of 13 September 1756', Loudoun Papers, box 41, Huntington Library, San Marino, Los Angeles, California.

62 i.e. The drafts from the West Indies.

63 Amherst had already confirmed the execution of two regulars, see Amherst to Lieutenant-Colonel John Hale, 27 April 1759, WO/34/79 fol. 94; and Amherst to Lieutenant-Colonel William Farquhar, 8 May 1759, WO/34/79 fol. 103.

64 The cause of this particular incident concerned the right of the King's messengers to use one of the Hudson river ferries above Albany. See Jacob Van Schaick to Amherst, 22 June 1759, WO/34/77 fol. 89.

65 Amherst had asked De Lancey to look after a couple of prisoners, and he had replied that he would accommodate as many as Amherst wished to send, De Lancey to Amherst, 18 June 1759, WO/34/29 fol. 39.

66 The New York Assembly agreed to the loan and issue of paper money on 28 June 1759, Resolves of the Assembly, WO/34/27 fol. 47.

67 Amherst renewed his entreaty on 17 July, reminding Kilby of the need to consider Wolfe's army at Quebec as well as the garrison at Louisbourg, WO/34/69 fol. 138.

68 Prideaux was killed on 19 July by a shell fragment from one of his own cannon. John Johnson was colonel of the New Jersey Regiment.

69 This letter has been published in John Knox, *An Historical Journal of the Campaigns in North America for the Years 1757, 1758, 1759, and 1760*, Arthur G. Doughty (ed.), three vols (Toronto, 1914–16, reprinted 1970), II, 182–5.

70 Colonel Roger Townshend, the Deputy Adjutant General and brother of Brigadier George Townshend.

71 A post on the Hudson River between Albany and Fort Edward.

72 See document 96 for further details of Amherst's naval armament.

73 This letter has been published in E.B. O'Callaghan (ed.), *New York Colonial Documents*, vol. VII, *Documents Relative to the Colonial History of the State of New York procured in Holland, England and France, 1756–1767* (Albany, 1856), 403.

74 The contract of Kilby and his partner, William Baker MP, allowed them to terminate the contract on six months' notice, which they were planning to do from March 1760. See Articles of Agreement, 26 March 1756, WO/34/69 fols 86–9. See also document 161.

75 Amherst agreed to Bradstreet's suggestion the following day, WO/34/58 fol. 33. See also document 87.

76 The Otter River had also been spoken of as a potential route to Lake Champlain bypassing Ticonderoga and Crown Point. For the outcome of this expedition, see document 95.

77 Bradstreet sent this with a covering letter to Amherst on the same day, WO/34/57 fol. 54.

78 The dispute arose over the pressing of a wagon for the army and the failure of the joint High Sheriff, Abraham Yates, to help prosecute an inhabitant who refused to hand over his wagon. Yates shared his position with Jacob Van Schaick. See the testimony of John Striker, Wagon Master, 20 August 1759, WO/34/57 fol. 45.

79 The guns had been forwarded to Crown Point instead of being left at Ticonderoga where the brig was being built.

80 i.e. Lake Champlain.

81 i.e. of 16 August 1759.

82 This may have been Joseph Hopkins who formed a volunteer ranger company in 1761 with rank of captain and served at Detroit during the Indian siege.

83 A Spanish port, normally spelt Monte Christi, on the north coast of the island of Santo Domingo, now the Dominican Republic.

84 Pownall had reported a rumour that Wolfe had suffered a setback at Quebec, which had indeed occurred, when Wolfe attempted to storm the cliffs near the Falls of Montmorency on 31 July 1759. See Pownall to Amherst, 3 September 1759, WO/34/25 fol. 292. For an account of Wolfe's campaign see George F.G. Stanley, *New France, The Last Phase, 1744–1760* (London, 1968), 215–41; and Gipson, *The British Empire before the American Revolution*, VII, 371–427.

85 Another reference to Wolfe's setback at the Falls of Montmorency.

86 Amherst was misinformed about the date of Wolfe's attack, which took place on 31 July 1759. Admiral Saunders had converted two transports (catts) to provide covering fire for the troops as they stormed the cliffs. See Saunders to Pitt, 5 September 1759, printed in Kimball, *Correspondence of Pitt*, II, 159–63.

87 Amherst's reasoning was that the French were behaving better because they feared they in turn might be prisoners themselves shortly.

88 According to Johnson, Gage discussed the matter again with his senior colleagues on 16 September 1759. Both Massey and Johnson believed a raid by 500 men could be successful, not least in securing the Swegatchie Indians in the British interest. Haldimand and Graham were much less optimistic. Gage then asked Johnson to consider the matter further but subsequently refused to talk to him about it, *Sir William Johnson's Private Diary at Niagara and Oswego, 1759*, printed in Knox, *Historical Journal*, III, 220–2.

89 Amherst found that he had to reverse this order two days later to keep the works going at both Ticonderoga and Crown Point. See Amherst to Major-General Lyman, 18 September 1759, WO/34/43 fol. 246.

90 i.e. To test how fast the crank could turn. See Amherst to Lyman, 21 September 1759, WO/34/43 fol. 246.

91 For a description of this type of artillery fire at Quebec, see Knox, *Historical Journal*, II, 430.

92 i.e. calling on the Canadians to desist in their support for Montcalm and the Indians in the French interest, printed in Beckles Willson, *The Life and Letters of James Wolfe* (London, 1909), 439–40.

93 Townshend had taken command following the death of Wolfe and wounding of Monckton.

94 Amherst had until now been breveted Major-General in America only.

95 William Fauquier (1708–88), who was a director of the South Sea Company.

96 The orders to Rogers have not been found, other than the version in Rogers' *Journals of Major Robert Rogers: Containing An Account of the several Excursions he made under the Generals who commanded upon the Continent of North America, during the Late War* (London, 1765), 144–5. In his journal Amherst wrote on 12 September: 'As Capt Kennedy's Journey was now over I ordered a detachment of 220 chosen men under the command of Major Rogers to go & destroy the St Francois Indian Settlements and the French Settlements on the South side of the River St Lawrence', J. Clarence Webster, *The Journal of Jeffery Amherst, Recording the Military Career of General Amherst in America from 1758 to 1763* (Toronto, 1931), 168. That Amherst intended something more than a simple attack on the St Francis Indians is indicated in his letter to Lieutenant-Governor De Lancey of 28 September 1759, in which he commented: 'Major Rogers is out, chiefly intended to hinder the Enemy from Sending anything towards La Galette, till our Fleet can make their Appearance,' WO/34/30 fol. 83.

97 This was the first indication to Amherst that there had been serious differences between Wolfe and his Brigadiers. See Willson, *Wolfe*, 447–94.

98 Knox, *Historical Journal*, I, 496–9, erroneously reproduces these orders as those for proceeding down Lake George on 20 July 1759.

99 The minutes of Stanwix's Council and the supporting testimony from Colonel Farquhar are in WO/34/45 fols 108–11.

100 See Kimball, *Correspondence of Pitt*, II, 186–202. Amherst's previous letter to Pitt, alluded to here, was that of 5 August 1759, printed in *ibid.*, 146–8.

101 Grant was successful in retrieving the two vessels and their guns, as Amherst reported to Whitemore on 16 November 1759, WO/34/17 fol. 183.

102 Amherst had ordered Rogers on 8 August 1759 to select 200 men to start marking out this road, WO/34/80 fol. 113.

103 Lieutenant-Colonel William Farquhar. See Amherst to Farquhar, 11 September 1759, WO/34/23, fols 11–12.

104 However, when Amherst heard that thirty-eight men had deserted from Fort George, he took the view that it would be a saving to the public, since they would not be entitled to their pay. See Amherst to Colonel James Montresor, 12 November 1759, WO/34/81 fol. 153.

105 There is a copy of Rogers' letter to Amherst in Rogers' *Journals*, 146–50, though Rogers dates it as has having been written on 5 November 1759. The *Journals* have recently been republished by Timothy J. Todish, ed., *The Annotated and Illustrated Journals of Major Robert Rogers* (Fleischmanns, New York, 2002). Rogers was so uncertain about the success of his expedition, which he had initially proposed, that he wrote a second letter to Amherst expressing his concern that he 'would be disappointed of that Footing in the Army which I have long endeavoured to merit,' meaning a permanent commission in one of the long established regular regiments, Rogers to Amherst, 12 December 1759, WO/34/78 fol. 182.

106 In giving this account of the St Francis raid, Amherst followed Rogers' own version in his letter to Amherst of 5 November 1759. See Rogers, *Journals*, 146–50.

107 There is a reference to Pitt's speech praising Amherst in Horace Walpole, *Memoirs of the Reign of King George II*, Lord Holland (ed.), three vols (London, 1846–7), III, 235.

108 Initially Amherst's hope that the province could deal with the situation itself seemed fulfilled when Lyttelton wrote on 27 December 1759 that, after marching into the back country, he had been able to sign a peace treaty with the Cherokee. This included the provision of twenty-four hostages for the fulfilment of the Cherokee pledge to surrender the same number of tribesmen accused of killing white settlers and traders, WO/34/35 fol. 136. A copy of the Treaty with the Cherokee is attached, WO/34/35 fols 138–9.

Section II The Campaign of 1760

1 i.e. Amherst's letter of 22 October 1759. See document 125.

2 Lord Barrington, the Secretary at War, had also interested himself in the case of Captain Oswald, not least because Oswald's brother was a Treasury Lord and political ally of the Duke of Newcastle. See Barrington to Amherst, 6 June 1759, U1350/O/36/38.

3 Amherst could only ascribe such 'very extraordinary' conduct 'no otherwise, than because they live an idle and unconstrained life', Amherst to Stanwix, 15 February 1760, WO/34/45 fol. 247. For a discussion of such instances, see James Axtell, 'The White Indians of Colonial America', *William and Mary Quarterly*, XXXII, 1975, 55–88.

4 i.e. from Lieutenant Coytmore at Fort Prince George, 23 January 1760, WO/34/35 fols 153–5.

5 As eldest captain, Mackneill was seeking the Lieutenant-Colonelcy of the second battalion, if such a position were to be created. The unit was

currently commanded by a major. There is a copy of Mackneill's memorial in U1350/O/37/7A.

6 An affidavit by the officer concerned in the incident, Ensign Faunce, can be found in WO/34/31 fol. 174.

7 Loring had reported the loss during a storm of the two small schooners at Oswego on 2 December 1759, WO/34/65 fol. 1.

8 See Amherst to Loring, 3 February 1760, WO/34/65 fol. 127. After the accident to the two schooners, the remaining vessels on Lake Ontario were two snows, the *Mohawk* and the *Johnson*, carrying eighteen and sixteen six-pounder guns respectively.

9 See Pitt to Amherst, 7 January 1760, printed in Gertrude S. Kimball, *The Correspondence of William Pitt, when Secretary of State, with the Colonial Governors and Military and Naval Commissioners in America*, two vols (London, 1906), II, 237–42.

10 A similar letter was sent to the Governors of New Hampshire, Rhode Island, Connecticut, New York and New Jersey.

11 Printed in Kimball, *Correspondence of Pitt*, II, 231–7.

12 This letter has also been published in James Sullivan *et al.* (eds), *The Papers of Sir William Johnson*, fourteen vols (Albany, 1921–65), III, 192–3.

13 i.e. First Foot Regiment.

14 The 77th Highland Regiment.

15 The southern command was defined as the provinces from Pennsylvania to the south, though the principal theatre of operations was western Pennsylvania and the Ohio.

16 Amherst agreed to Post's request (see document 172) though he had to be requested to tone down the first draft of his address. Rather unrepentantly he told Stanwix on the 23 April 1760: 'I can't say I am for softening any speeches to the Indians; I don't think it is the best method of dealing with them.' WO/34/45 fol. 255. Nevertheless the conference was a success, as Amherst informed Johnson, 16 May 1760, WO/34/38 fol. 104.

17 Amherst had proposed that Loring raise proper crews in Boston rather than rely on men recruited from the provincial land forces, 6 March 1760, WO/34/65 fol. 133.

18 For the political background to Pennsylvania at this time see James H. Hutson, *Pennsylvania Politics, 1746–1770: The Movement for Royal Government and its Consequences* (Princeton, NJ, 1972), 6–40.

19 Prussia had initiated moves for a peace congress at Augsburg the previous autumn. See Richard Middleton, *The Bells of Victory: The Pitt–Newcastle Ministry and the Conduct of the Seven Years' War, 1757–1762* (Cambridge, 1985), 135–6, 150.

20 Pownall was returning to England and was being replaced as governor by Francis Bernard.

21 A copy of the House Message and vote can be found in WO/34 fols 7 and 17. For the provincial attitude to military service, see F. W. Anderson,

A People's Army: Massachusetts Soldiers and Society in the Seven Years' War (Chapel Hill, NC, 1984).

22 See document 143.

23 Pitt to Amherst, 7 January 1760, printed in Kimball, *Correspondence of Pitt*, II, 242.

24 The gist of the Assembly's message was that those who had served continuously since the previous spring should be granted a discharge if they wished, since they could easily be replaced by men from the new levies, *Address of the Massachusetts House of Representatives*, 24 April 1760, WO/34/26 fols 29–30.

25 The document does not state what was to be presented at this point, but almost certainly it comprised a belt of wampum.

26 This document has been published before in *The Aspinwall Papers*, Massachusetts Historical Society, Collections, 4th series, IX (Boston, MA, 1871), 240–2.

27 i.e. to prevent incursions by the Cherokee.

28 This letter is similar to the one Murray subsequently wrote to Pitt on 25 May 1760, printed in Kimball, *Correspondence of Pitt*, II, 291–7.

29 Part of this letter is in Amherst's Personal Journal, U1350/O/14, pp. 75–6.

30 A similar letter was sent to the Governors of Rhode Island, Connecticut, New York, and New Jersey. See WO/34/36 fol. 183.

31 The ministry had decided to demolish the fortifications of Louisburg, a decision which Pitt communicated to Whitmore on 9 February 1760, printed in Kimball, *Correspondence of Pitt*, II, 252.

32 See Amherst to Christie, 19 May 1760, WO/34/59 fol. 150; and Amherst to Pownall, 19 May 1769, WO/34/27 fol. 200.

33 i.e. the regular fortifications of Quebec.

34 Joseph Dean and Alexander Schomberg were the commanders of the two accompanying frigates, the *Lowestoff* and *Diana*.

35 Murray's force had also received no clothing since the start of the previous campaign, as he complained in a further postscript to this letter, dated 23 May 1760. 'I fear the Vessell with the Cloathing of the Troops from Halifax is lost. Every thing from that place is arrived but her, should this be the case God have mercy upon Us.'

36 According to Pownall, in his letter to Amherst of 25 May 1760, the merchants wanted this premium to cover the discount on Navy Board bills, with which they were to be paid, WO/34/26 fol. 59.

37 An Indian village on the Yamaska River.

38 Campbell commanded the eight companies of the 77th Highland Regiment that had not accompanied Colonel Archibald Montgomery to South Carolina to fight the Cherokees.

39 This brig was one of the vessels built the previous year and carried eighteen six-pounder guns. For a list of the vessels on the various lakes at this time, see WO/34/65 fol. 109.

40 i.e. the 47th Foot.

41 Part of the group known as the Thousand Islands, around the entrance to the St Lawrence River.

42 Galloo Island, near the later settlement of Sackets Harbor.

43 Usually called Fort Frontenac, now Kingston.

44 i.e. La Galette.

45 i.e. Captain Samuel Willyamos.

46 Gallop Rapids, just below Isle Royale.

47 For details of the original incident, see Lieutenant Coventry to Bradstreet, 24 July 1760, WO/34/57 fol. 141.

48 Other letters concerning this incident, between Amherst, Jacob Van Schaick and Lieutenant-Governor James De Lancey, can be found in Cadwallader Colden, *The Letters and Papers of Cadwallader Colden*, New York Historical Society, LIV, Collections for 1921, vol. V, *1755–1760* (New York, 1923), 324–6.

49 Swegatchie was an Indian village opposite La Galette. See document 210.

50 For additional details of Amherst's progress after leaving Oswego, see J. Clarence Webster (ed.), *The Journal of Jeffery Amherst, Recording the Military Career of General Amherst in America from 1758 to 1763* (Toronto, 1931), 227–31.

51 This had originally been one of the French vessels, the *Outawa*, which had gone aground in the St Lawrence and been captured on 17 August by Colonel Williamson, with some artillery mounted on row galleys (see document 210). The two snows were the *Onondaga* and *Mohawk*, which Loring had fitted out at Niagara.

52 Round tops were circular platforms at the masthead, suitable for marksmen.

53 See note 49 above.

54 For a French account of the siege, see Pierre Pouchot, *Memoirs on the Late War in North America between France and England*, Michael Cardy (trans.), Brian Leigh Dunnigan (ed.) (Youngstown, New York, 1994), 300–15. Because he was the opposing commander during this part of Amherst's advance, Pouchot goes into the event in considerable detail.

55 There is an English translation in J. Knox, *An Historical Journal of the Campaigns in North America for the Years 1757, 1758, 1759 and 1760*, A.G. Doughty (ed.), three vols (Toronto, 1914), II, 566–89. A translation is also available in various other publications.

56 Amherst apologised to Murray later the same day, that he would have asked him to take over the port of Montreal with a detachment of his own army, but did not realise he was so close, Amherst to Murray, 8 September 1760, WO/34/3 fol. 12.

57 The village of Longueil was on the southern shore of the St Lawrence opposite Montreal. Rogers was with the vanguard of Haviland's army.

58 For further information about the chronological sequence of events at this point see Amherst's letter to Pitt, 8 September 1760, printed in Kimball,

Correspondence of Pitt, II, 329–33; and Webster, *Journal of Jeffery Amherst*, 245–7.

59 This document has been published in several printed collections. See Albert C. Bates (ed.), *The Fitch Papers*, Connecticut Historical Society, Collections, vols XVII–XVIII (Hartford, CT, 1918–20), II, 79–81; and Colden, *Letters and Papers*, 336–8.

60 The captain lieutenant was the senior lieutenant in a battalion or corps.

61 Rogers kept a journal of his expedition from 13 September to 28 November 1760, a copy of which he gave to Amherst, U1350/O/49. It was later published by Victor H. Paltsits in the *Bulletin of the New York Public Library*, XXXIII, April 1933.

62 The reason why the Indians deserted was because Amherst refused them any plunder or scalps on the taking of Fort Levis at Isle Royale, 25 August 1760. This at least is the reason given in a document prepared for Amherst in England, entitled 'Account of the whole American Campaign between 1758 and 1762', U1350/O/53/15. See also Amherst's entries in his diary for 25 August to 2 September 1760, in Webster, *Journal of Jeffery Amherst*, 239–43.

63 Amherst felt so strongly on the matter that he sent his thoughts to Lord Barrington to pass on to the Archbishop of Canterbury, 9 December 1760, U1350/O/38/26.

64 Not found.

65 For the gist of the remainder of this letter see above, Amherst to Burton, 23 September 1760, document 226.

66 This was in accordance with the articles of the surrender signed on 8 September 1760. For an English translation of the articles, see Knox, *Historical Journal*, II, 566–89.

67 Prescott had left Amherst on 26 August with dispatches for Pitt and Ligonier, following the capture of Fort Levis. Barré left Montreal on 8 September (see document 232). See also Amherst to Pitt, 26 August 1760 and Pitt to Amherst, 24 October 1760, printed in Kimball, *Correspondence of Pitt*, II, 324–9, 344–5.

68 A reference to Amherst's brother, John, who was a year younger and serving with the Royal Navy in command of the 64-gun *Captain*, which was about to be laid up.

69 Lord Barrington initially took the same view as Ligonier that such rapid promotion would be unfair to many older captains, Barrington to Amherst, 10 October 1760, U1350/O/37/31. However on 20 October Barrington changed his objection to the fact that Amherst had made no specific request, U1350/O/37/28. Amherst accordingly then wrote on 6 January 1761 supporting Barré's claim, U1350/O/38/30, though by the time this letter arrived Barré had secured the position of Lieutenant-Colonel of the 106th Regiment.

70 A reference to Lord George Sackville who had been disgraced after failing to implement the orders of Prince Ferdinand at the battle of Minden. See

Piers Mackesy, *The Coward of Minden: The Affair of Lord George Sackville* (London, 1979).

71 See Pitt to Amherst, 24 October 1760, printed in Kimball, *Correspondence of Pitt*, II, 344–7.

72 This tragically did not prove the case during Pontiac's War, when every post west of Niagara and Pittsburgh, other than Detroit, fell to the Indians or had to be evacuated. See Howard H. Peckham, *Pontiac and the Indian Uprising* (Princeton, 1947).

73 Colonel William Byrd, the commander of a regiment of Virginian volunteers.

74 Amherst was not aware at this point that the garrison had been starved into surrender (see document 229).

75 This letter has been published in *The Aspinwall Papers*, 346–8.

76 Under the terms of the Septennial Act the next general election was due by the spring of 1761.

77 Calcraft reported on 14 February 1761 that no such desire to nominate him had been indicated, WO/34/99 fol. 83.

78 Most were also civilians in the pay of the Commissariat.

79 For Amherst's response, see his letter to Jacob Van Schaick, 26 December 1760; and letter to acting Lieutenant-Governor of New York, Cadwallader Colden, 27 December 1760, printed in Colden, *Letters and Papers*, V, 388–90.

Epilogue

1 *The Gentleman's Magazine & Historical Chronicle for 1797*, LXVII, 800–2. However, by 1885, H.M. Stephens, in the *Dictionary of National Biography*, could write dismissively: 'Lord Amherst's great military services were all performed in the years 1758, 1759 and 1760 . . . Of his later life in office little need be said. He was by no means a good commander-in-chief, and allowed innumerable abuses to grow up in the army. He kept his command till almost in his dotage with a tenacity which cannot be too much censored.'

Bibliography

Manuscripts

WO/34 Amherst Papers, Public Record Office, London.
U1350/O Amherst Papers, Official Correspondence, Kent Archives, Maidstone.
CO/5 Colonial Office Records, Public Record Office, London.
WLC/AP Amherst Papers, William L. Clements Library, Ann Arbor, Michigan.

Printed sources containing Amherst documents for the period 1758–60

The Aspinwall Papers, Massachusetts Historical Society, Collections, 4th series, vol. IX (Boston, MA, 1871).

Bartlett, John Russell (ed.), *Records of the Colony of Rhode Island and Providence Plantation in New England*, vol. VI, *1757–1769* (Providence, RI, 1861).

Bates, Albert C. (ed.), *The Fitch Papers*, Connecticut Historical Society, Collections, vols XVII and XVIII (Hartford, CT, 1918–20).

Browne, William H. (ed.), *Archives of Maryland*, vol. IX, *Correspondence of Governor Horatio Sharpe*, II, *1757–1761* (Baltimore, MD, 1890).

Colden, Cadwallader, *The Colden Letter Books*, New York Historical Society, IX, Collections for 1876, vol. I, *1760–1765* (New York, 1877).

——, *The Letters and Papers of Cadwallader Colden*, New York Historical Society Publications, LIV, Collections for 1921, vol. V, *1755–1760* (New York, 1921–3).

Doughty, Arthur G., and Parmalee, G.W. (eds), *The Siege of Quebec and Battle of the Plains of Abraham*, six vols (Quebec, 1901).

Hazard, Samuel (ed.), *Pennsylvania Archives*, 1st series, vols III–IV, *1756–1776* (Philadelphia, PA, 1853).

Hoban, Charles F. (ed.), *Pennsylvania Archives*, 8th series, vol. VI, *Votes of the Assembly, 1756–1764* (Philadelphia, PA, 1935).

James, A.P. (ed.), *The Writings of General John Forbes Relating to his Service in North America* (Menasha, WI, 1938).

Kimball, Gertrude S., *The Correspondence of William Pitt, when Secretary of State, with the Colonial Governors and Military and Naval Commissioners in America*, two vols (London, 1906).

Knox, Captain John, *An Historical Journal of the Campaigns in North America for the Years 1757, 1758, 1759, and 1760*, Arthur G. Doughty (ed.), three vols (Toronto, 1914–16, reprinted 1970).

Mays, Edith (ed.), *Amherst Papers, 1756–1763: The Southern Sector: Dispatches from South Carolina, Virginia and His Majesty's Superintendent of Indian Affairs* (Bowie, MD, 1999).

O'Callaghan, E.B. (ed.), *New York Colonial Documents*, vol. VII, *Documents Relative to the Colonial History of the State of New York procured in Holland, England and France, 1756–1767* (Albany, NY, 1856).

Reed, George Edward (ed.), *Pennsylvania Archives*, 4th series, vols II–III, *Papers of the Governors* (Philadelphia, PA, 1900).

Reese, George (ed.), *The Official Papers of Francis Fauquier, Lieutenant Governor of Virginia, 1758–1768*, vol. I, *1758–1760* (Charlottesville, VA, 1980).

Rogers, Robert, *Journals of Major Robert Rogers: Containing An Account of the Several Excursions he made under the Generals who commanded upon the Continent of North America, during the Late War* (London, 1765).

Sullivan, James, *et al.* (eds), *The Papers of Sir William Johnson*, fourteen vols (Albany, NY, 1921–65).

Webster, J. Clarence (ed.), *The Journal of Jeffery Amherst, Recording the Military Career of General Amherst in America from 1758 to 1763* (Toronto, 1931).

Wendell, Lewis M., *et al.* (eds), *The Papers of Henry Bouquet*, five vols (Harrisburg, PA, 1951–94).

Willson, Beckles, *The Life and Letters of James Wolfe* (London, 1909).

Secondary sources

Alden, John R., *General Gage in America* (Baton Rouge, LA, 1948).

Anderson, F.W., 'Why Did Colonial New Englanders Make Bad Soldiers? Contractual Principles and Military Conduct During the Seven Years' War', *William and Mary Quarterly*, XXXVIII, 1981, 395–417.

——, 'A People's Army: Provincial Military Service in Massachusetts During the Seven Years' War', *William and Mary Quarterly*, XL, 1983, 499–527.

——, *A People's Army: Massachusetts Soldiers and Society in the Seven Years' War* (Chapel Hill, NC, 1984).

Anderson, Fred, *The Crucible of War: The Seven Years' War and the Fate of Empire in British North America, 1754–1766* (New York, 2000).

Auth, Stephen F., *The Ten Years' War: Indian–White Relations in Pennsylvania, 1755–1765* (New York, 1989).

Ayling, Stanley, *The Elder Pitt, Earl of Chatham* (London, 1976).

Barrington, S., *The Political Life of William Wildman, Viscount Barrington* (London, 1818).

Beattie, Daniel J., 'The Adaptation of the British Army to Wilderness Warfare, 1755–1763', in Ultee, Maarten (ed.), *Adapting to Conditions: War and Society in the Eighteenth Century* (Birmingham, AL, 1986).

Bowler, R. Arthur, *Logistics and the Failure of the British Army in America, 1775–1783* (Princeton, NJ, 1975).

Brumwell, Stephen, *Redcoats: The British Soldier and War in the Americas, 1755–1763* (Cambridge, 2002).

——, '"A service truly Critical": The British Army and Warfare with the North American Indians, 1754–1764', *War in History*, V, April 1998, 146–75.

Calloway, Colin G., *The Western Abenakis of Vermont, 1600–1800: War, Migration and the Survival of an Indian People* (Norman, OK, 1990).

Corbett, Sir Julian, *England in the Seven Years' War: A Study in Combined Strategy*, two vols (London, 1907).

Corkran, David H., *The Cherokee Frontier: Conflict and Survivval, 1740–1762* (Norman, OK, 1966).

Cuneo, John R., *Robert Rogers of the Rangers* (New York, 1959).

Dowd, Gregory Evans, *A Spirited Resistance: The North American Indian Struggle for Unity, 1745–1815* (Baltimore, MD, 1992).

Dunnigan, Brian Leigh, *Siege 1759: The Campaign against Niagara* (Youngstown, OH, 1986).

Eccles, W.J., *The Canadian Frontier, 1534–1760* (New York, 1969).

——, *The French in North America, 1500–1783* (East Lansing, MI, 1998).

Ferling, John E., *A Wilderness of Miseries: War and Warriors in Early America* (Westport, CT, 1980).

Flexner, James T., *Mohawk Baronet, Sir William Johnson of New York* (New York, 1959).

Fortescue, Sir John, *A History of the British Army*, thirteen vols (London, 1899–1930).

Fregault, Guy, *Canada: The War of the Conquest* (Toronto, 1969).

Gipson, Lawrence Henry, *The British Empire before the American Revolution*, vol. VII, *The Great War for the Empire: The Victorious Years, 1758–1760* (New York, 1949).

Godfrey, William G., *Pursuit of Profit and Preferment in Colonial North America: John Bradstreet* (Waterloo, Ontario, 1982).

Guy, Alan J., *Oeconomy and Discipline: Officership and Administration in the British Army, 1714–63* (Manchester, 1985).

Hamilton, Edward P., *The French Army in America* (Ottawa, 1967).

—— (ed.), *Adventures in the Wilderness: The American Journals of Louis Antoine de Bougainville, 1756–1760* (Norman, OK, 1964).

Hamilton, Milton, *Sir William Johnson: Colonial American, 1715–1763* (Port Washington, WI, 1976).

Houlding, John A., *Fit for Service: The Training of the British Army, 1715–1795* (Oxford, 1981).

Jacobs, Wilbur R., *Wilderness Politics and Indian Gifts: Anglo-French Rivalry Along the Ohio and Northwest Frontier, 1748–1763* (Stanford, CA, 1950).

Jennings, Francis, *Empire of Fortune: Crowns, Colonies and Tribes in the Seven Years War in America* (New York, 1988).

Labaree, Leonard Woods, *Royal Government in America: A Study of the British Colonial System Before 1783* (New Haven, CT, 1943).

Leach, Douglas Edward, *Arms for Empire: A Military History of the British Colonies in North America, 1607–1763* (New York, 1973).

——, *Roots of Conflict: British Armed Forces and Colonial Americans, 1677–1763* (Chapel Hill, NC, 1986).

Long, John C., *Lord Jeffery Amherst, A Soldier of the King* (New York, 1933).

McCardell, Lee, *Ill Starred General: Braddock of the Coldstream Guards* (Pittsburgh, PA, 1986).

McConnell, Michael N., *A Country in Between: The Upper Ohio Valley and its Peoples, 1724–1774* (Lincoln, NA, 1992).

McLeod, Peter D., *The Canadian Iroquois and the Seven Years' War* (Toronto, 1996).

Mackesy, Piers, *The Coward of Minden: The Affair of Lord George Sackville* (London, 1979).

Middleton, Richard, *The Bells of Victory: The Pitt–Newcastle Ministry and the Conduct of the Seven Years War, 1757–1762* (Cambridge, 1985).

Namier, Sir Lewis, and Brooke, John, *The History of Parliament: The House of Commons, 1754–1790*, three vols (London, 1964).

Nester, William R., *The First Global War: Britain, France, and the Fate of North America, 1756–1775* (New York, 2000).

Pargellis, Stanley M., *Lord Loudoun in North America* (New Haven, CT, 1933).

——, *Military Affairs in North America, 1748–1765: Selected Documents from the Cumberland Papers in Windsor Castle* (New York, 1936).

Parkman, Francis, *Montcalm and Wolfe: The Decline and Fall of the French Empire in North America*, two vols (London, 1884).

Peckham, Howard, *Pontiac and the Indian Uprising* (Princeton, NJ, 1947).

——, *The Colonial Wars, 1689–1762* (Chicago, IL, 1964).

Pouchot, Pierre, *Memoirs on the Late War in North America between France and England*, Michael Cardy (trans.), Brian Leigh Dunnigan (ed.) (Youngstown, NY, 1994).

Richter, Daniel K., and Merrell, James H. (eds), *Beyond the Covenant Chain: The Iroquois and Their Neighbours in Indian North America, 1600–1800* (Syracuse, NY, 1987).

Rogers, Alan, *Empire and Liberty: American Resistance to British Authority, 1755–1763* (Berkeley, CA, 1974).

Russell, Peter R., 'Redcoats in the Wilderness: British Officers and Irregular Warfare in Europe and America, 1740–1760,' *William and Mary Quarterly*, XXXV, 1978, 629–52.

Schutz, John A., *Thomas Pownall, British Defender of American Liberty* (New York, 1951).

Selesky, Harold E., *War and Society in Colonial Connecticut* (New Haven, CT, 1990).

Stanley, George F., *New France: The Last Phase, 1744–1760* (London, 1968).

Steele, Ian K., *Warpaths: Invasions of North America* (New York, 1994).

Todish, Timothy J. (ed.), *The Annotated and Illustrated Journals of Major Robert Rogers* (Fleischmanns, New York, 2002).

——, *America's First World War: The French and Indian War, 1754–1763* (Grand Rapids, MI, 1982).

Wainwright, Nicholas B., *George Croghan: Wilderness Diplomat* (Chapel Hill, NC, 1959).

Walpole, Horace, *Memoirs of the Reign of King George II*, Lord Holland (ed.), three vols (London, 1846–7).

White, Richard, *The Middle Ground: Indians, Empires and Republics in the Great Lakes Region, 1650–1815* (New York, 1991).

Whitworth, Rex, *Field Marshal Lord Ligonier: A Story of the British Army, 1702–1770* (Oxford, 1958).

Index

Figures in **bold** indicate correspondence to or from Amherst

52, 57, 58, 79, 91, 150, 151, 170, 196, 215, 222

L'Assomption (fort), 34, 283 (n. 36)

Lawrence, Brigadier-General Charles, 61, 181, 267

Leake, Robert, xxviii, xxix, **71–2**, 267

Legge, Captain Francis, xxxvii, **152**, 267

Le Roux, Colonel (Provincials) Bartholomew, **212**, 267

Levis, General François, xliv, xlv, 134, 144, 184, 217–18, 267–8

Light Infantry, xxi, xlv, 15, 16, 17, 48, 61, 70, 74, 77, 158, 177, 178, 184, 196, 213, 215, 218, 251

Ligonier, Sir John, xv, xvii, xviii, xx, xxi, xxv, xxxiv, xxxvii, xliv, xlv, xlviii, 1, 8–10, **16–17**, 27, **45–6**, **126–8**, **143**, **198–9**, **214–15**, **216**, **217–18**, **237–8**, 239, 278 (n. 1), 282 (n. 20), 283 (n. 47)

Little Carpenter, 229, 268

Loring, Captain Joshua, xxi, xxiv, 268
    Construction and manning of vessels, xxvii, xxxi, xxxviii, xxxix, xlii, **19–20**, 25–6, **32–3**, **59–60**, **84**, **96–7**, 98, 107, 108, **109–10**, **111–12**, 128, **150**, 151, **165**, **199**, **200**, **201**, 291 (n. 51)
    Command of lake naval armaments, xxxiv, xliii, xliv, 127, 202–3, **203–4**, 207, **209**, **212**

Lottridge, Captain (Rangers) John, 41, 268

Louisbourg, xviii, xix, xxi, xxiii, xxiv, xxvii, xxxvii, xli, 50, 115, 168, 182, 280 (n. 36), 290 (n. 31)

Lyman, Colonel (Provincials) Phineas, xxxi, **84–5**, 108, **110**, 112, 218, 268

Lyttelton, Governor William, xxxvi, xxxix, **125–6**, **141–2**, **147**, 158, 236, 268, 288 (n. 108)

MacDonald, Captain Donald, 178

Mackneill, Captain John, 148, 183–4, 268, 288–9 (n. 5)

Marsh, Captain James, 219, 269

Martinique, 27, 240–1

Maryland, 25, 282 (n. 30)

Massachusetts, xx, xxiii, xxxvii, 13, 14, 21, 30, 129
    Provincial troops, xxxv, xxxvii, 30, 34–5, 36–7, 43–4, 61–2, 64, 67, 140–1, 152, 154–5, 167, 168, 171–2, 180–1, 183, 191–2, 192–3, 200, 210, 290 (n. 24)

Massey, Lieutenant-Colonel Eyre, 213, 269

Mercer, Lt Colonel (Provincial) Hugh, 91, 99, 269

Michilimackinac, xlv, 222, 245

Militia, xxv, 34, 126
    French, 116, 220, 225–6, 229
    see also Provincial Forces

Miller, Lieutenant-Colonel (Provincials) Stephen, **107–8**, **108**, 110, 192

Mississippi, 16, 221, 240

Mobile, 16, 240

Mohawk Indians, 28, 41, 142, 251

Mohawk River, xxiv, xxvi, xxix, xxx, 11, 33, 63, 67, 71, 72, 73, 85, 91, 113, 156–7, 165, 215

Monckton, Brigadier-General Robert, xxxiv, xl, 11, **113–14**, 121, 122, 132, **174–6**, **180**, **194**, **206–7**, **220–1**, 222, **244–5**, 269

Moncrieffe, Lieutenant Thomas, xlvii, 77, 223, **230**, 269

Montcalm, Louis-Joseph, Marquis de, xxxii, 62, 99, 105, 116, 117, 269–70, 279 (n. 26)

Montgomery, Colonel Archibald, xxxix, xlviii, **68**, 70, **158–9**, 250, 270

Montmorency, 116
Montreal, xxvi, xxxviii, xliii, xliv, xlv,
xlvii, 9, 28, 62, 76, 79, 82, 121,
128, 144, 154, 169–70, 195, 215,
219, 220
Montresor, Lieutenant-Colonel
(Engineers) James, xxxv, 76,
135–6, 138, 270
Montresor, Lieutenant (Engineers)
John, 49, 144, 145, 176, 182, 185,
270
Morris, Lieutenant-Colonel Arthur,
47–8, 270
Morris, Major Roger, 178
Mortier, Abraham, 26, 29, 65–6, 67–8,
270
Munster, Major Hubert, **201–2**
Murray, Major Alexander, 9, 270
Murray, Brigadier-General James,
xxxv, xxxvii, xl, xli, xlii, xliv, xlvi,
xlvii, 11, 114, **132–4, 144–6,**
169–71, 176–9, 181–2, 183,
184–6, 215–16, 218, **223–4,** 227,
233–4, 270–1

Napier, James, 271
Navy *see* Royal Navy
Newfoundland, 62, 204
Newhampshire, 129
Provincial troops, 67, 70, 76, 95,
113, 120, 136, 200
New Jersey, 12
Provincial troops, 205, 207
Newspapers, 13–14, 104
New York, xvi, xix, xxv
Provincial troops, xxv, xxvi, xxviii,
xxxi, 5–6, 47, 57, 67, 103, 113,
120, 212
New York City, xxvi, xxxvi, xlviii, 138,
162, 188, 247–8
Niagara, xxiv, xxiv, xxvi, xxvii, xxviii,
xxix–xxx, xxxiv, xl, xlii, 34, 55,
86, 90, 91–2, 95, 99, 103, 104–5,
107, 123, 125, 129, 175, 176,

201–2, 205, 219, 221, 244, 284
(n. 54)
Attack against, 51–2, 53, 54–6,
57–9, 63–4, 77–8, 78–9, 81–2
Nova Scotia, xvi, xxiii, xxiv, xxxvii,
30, 61, 168, 181, 183
see also Halifax

Ogden, Captain (Provincials), 134, 136
Ogilvie, Captain (Provincials) William,
139, 271
Ohio Indians, 25, 92
Ohio River Valley, xvi, xvii, xxiv, 24,
91
Ord, Major (Artillery) Thomas, 17,
100, 107, 124, 271
Ordnance, Board of, 31
Oswald, Major Thomas, 143, 288
(n. 2)
Oswegatchie, xliii, xliv, xlvii, 208, 209,
214
Oswego, xvii, xxvi, xlii, xliii, 51, 52,
53, 56, 57, 58, 59, 73, 76, 77,
78–9, 82, 88, 89, 113, 156, 157,
169, 170, 196, 199, 203, 205, 210,
214, 219
Otter River, 88–9, 97, 135, 286 (n. 76)

Parliament (House of Commons),
xlviii, 140
Pennsylvania
Provincial troops 25, 175
Peters, Richard, 163–4
Philadelphia, xxiv, xxv, 33, 45, 130,
174
Pitt, William (later first Earl of
Chatham), xvii, xviii, xxii, xxiii,
xxxviii, xlviii, **2–3,** 10, 16, 33, 46,
61, 122, 127, 140, 153, 169, 174,
237, 240, 271
Post, Frederick, xl, 163–4, **241–3,**
271
Pouchot, Captain Pierre, 214, 215,
271, 291 (n. 54)

St Francis Indians, xxxiv, xxxvi, xlii,
105, 136–7, 280 (n. 29)
St Johns, xxxii, xli, xlii, 82, 90, 189,
195, 196–7
St Lawrence River, xviii, xx, xxiii,
xxiv, xlii, xliii, xliv, 8, 14, 16,
19–20, 26, 28, 30, 35, 51, 59,
89–90, 96, 115, 128, 145, 170,
176–7, 178, 186, 208, 217, 220
Saunders, Rear Admiral Charles, 62,
82, **98**, 273–4, 286 (n. 86)
Schenectady, xxxix, 57, 63, 88, 89,
106, 120, 153, 156, 162
Schomberg, Captain (Naval)
Alexander, 274
Schulyer, Colonel (Provincials) Peter,
112, 274
Scott, Major George, 29, 274
Seven Years' War, xvi
Sherriffe, Lieutenant William, 198,
274
Shirley, Governor William, 29, 93
Six (Five) Nations *see* Iroquois
South Carolina, xxxvi, xlviii, 125–6,
158–9, 162, 251, 288 (n. 108)
Spearing, Lieutenant, **246**
Stanwix, Brigadier-General John,
xxiv, xxvi, xxvii, xxx, xxxi, xxxiii,
xxxiv, xxxvii, xl, 11, 18, **33–4**, 39,
48, **51–2**, **54–6**, 58–9, **63–4**, 77,
78, **80–2**, 91–2, 99–100, 104, 105,
107, **122–3**, **125**, 126, **146**, 174,
274
Stephens, Lieutenant (Rangers),
120–1, 135
Stirling, Captain Thomas, **225–6**,
274
Stockbridge Indians, xxii, 22, 39–40,
251, 279 (n. 16)
Swanton, Captain (Naval) Robert,
185, 274–5
Swegatchie *see* Oswegatchie
Swegatchie Indians, 209, 286
(n. 88)

Thomas, Colonel (Provincials) John,
191–2, 275
Ticonderoga, xviii, xxiii, xxix, xxxi,
xxxv, xlii, 5, 28, 76, 80–1, 84–5,
86, 90–1, 92, 97, 103, 107–8, 111,
129, 139, 152–3, 156, 157, 191,
195, 196, 200
Townshend, Brigadier-General
George, xxxv, 113, 114, 117,
121–2, 275, 287 (n. 93)
Townshend, Lieutenant-Colonel
Roger, 81, 275
Transports, 30, 32, 35, 36, 182,
188–9
Treasury (British), 66, 155, 160–1, 278
(n. 5)
Trois Rivières, xlvi, 186, 220, 226–8,
231–4
Tullikens, Major John, 91, 99, 180,
275

Van Schaick, Sheriff Jacob, xlix, 69,
94, **206**, 252, 285 (n. 64), 286
(n. 78)
Vaudreuil, Pierre François, Marquis
de, xliv, xlv, 28, 116, 133, 145,
198, 215, 220, 275
Venango, xxvi, xxxii, 51, 55, 63, 77,
91–2, 99, 175
Virginia, 118–19, 175

Walters, Major William, 221, 244,
275
Watson, Brook, 230, 275
Watts, John, 275–6
West, Lieutenant-Colonel George,
198, 276
Wheelock, Captain Anthony, xliii,
xlvii, **60**, **192–3**, **229**, **234–5**, 276
Whiting, Colonel (Provincials)
Nathan, **211**, 218–19, 276
Whitmore, Brigadier-General
Edward, xxvii, xl, xli, **15–16**, 50,
61, **180–1**, **182–3**, 276

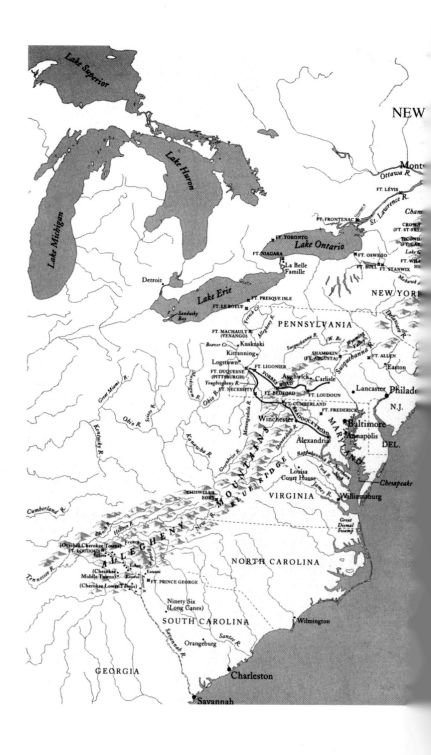